Muslim Civic Cultures
and Conflict Resolution

The Brookings Project on U.S. Policy towards the Islamic World is a major research and outreach initiative, housed under the auspices of the Saban Center for Middle East Policy at the Brookings Institution. It is designed to respond to some of the profound questions that the terrorist attacks of September 11th have raised for U.S. policy. In particular, it seeks to examine how the United States can reconcile its efforts to eliminate terrorism and reduce the appeal of extremist movements with its need to build more positive relations with Muslim states and communities. The Project seeks to serve as a convening body for ideas, people, and perspectives, and a catalyst for enhanced understanding, strategy development, and successful policy implementation.

As part of its work, the Project has launched a series of publications that aim to introduce new perspectives and policy thinking on current issues, focus on critical issues and regions, and attempt to lay the foundation for longer term policy success. The Brookings Series on U.S. Policy towards the Islamic World will explore, among other topics, how to fight militant radicalism with human development, the roots of anti-Americanism and political violence, what moderate Muslims can do to promote democracy, and the media's role in the Middle East. As with all publications, the judgments, conclusions, and recommendations presented in the studies are solely those of the authors and should not be attributed to the trustees, officers, or other staff members of the Brookings Institution.

Muslim Civic Cultures and Conflict Resolution

The Challenge of
Democratic Federalism in Nigeria

John N. Paden

BROOKINGS INSTITUTION PRESS
Washington, D.C.

Library of Congress Cataloging-in-Publication data
Paden, John N.
 Muslim civic cultures and conflict resolution : the challenge of demo-
cratic federalism in Nigeria / John N. Paden.
  p.   cm.
 Summary: "Examines how a diverse country with a significant Muslim
population is working to make the transition to a democratic society,
balancing rule-of-law concerns against rising communal tensions"
—Provided by publisher.
 Includes bibliographical references and index.
 ISBN-13: 978-0-8157-6817-3 (pbk. : alk. paper)
 ISBN-10: 0-8157-6817-6 (pbk. : alk. paper)
 1. Democratization—Nigeria. 2. Islam and politics—Nigeria. 3. Federal
government—Nigeria. 4. Conflict management—Nigeria.   I. Title.
JQ3090.P33 2005
320.9669—dc22   2005022911

9 8 7 6 5 4 3 2 1

Typeset in Minion

Composition by OSP, Inc.
Arlington, Virginia

Maps on pages 6–7, 14, and 51 by Meridian Mapping
Minneapolis, Minnesota

Printed by R. R. Donnelley
Harrisonburg, Virginia

Contents

Foreword   vii

Acknowledgments   ix

List of abbreviations   xi

Introduction   1

Part I. International and National Contexts

1   Nigeria in the World   13

2   The Emergence of Democratic Federalism in Nigeria   37

Part II. Nigerian Muslim Identities and Civic Cultures

3   Variations in Muslim Identities and Values   55

4   Emirate Civic Cultures   70

5   Nonstate Muslim Variations on Civic Culture   99

6   National Muslim Identities and Values   115

Part III. Challenges of Nigerian Democratic Federalism

7   Challenges of the Fourth Republic (1999–2005)   139

8   Challenges of the Shari'a Issue   157

9 The Shari'a Issue and Sociopolitical Conflict 171

10 Religious Tolerance and Conflict Resolution 183

Part IV. Conclusions: Muslim Civic Cultures and Conflict Resolution

11 Civic Cultures and Conflict Resolution 203

12 Nigeria in International Perspective 210

Appendixes

A. Selected Electoral Patterns: The First Three Republics 227

B. Selected Biographical Summaries 233

Notes 241

Index 285

Foreword

Transitions from military to civilian rule are amongst the most trying—and often turbulent—stages of governance. In large and diverse countries, local values are key factors in the success or failure of such a process. The cultural contours of political values can make or break the democratic experiment. Thus, understanding grassroots civic cultures, and how they can serve as the foundations of democratic federalism, requires great attention and study.

At the same time, the questions of whether and how Islam is compatible with democracy are not just an academic matter, but of crucial policy importance. However, while the focus of U.S. attention on the Muslim world has been on the cauldron of the Middle East, such questions may best be answered from the lived experiences of Muslim communities around the world.

Nigeria, set within the non-Arab Muslim communities of West Africa, is a critical case study to answering such questions. By far the most populous country in Africa, Nigeria has a population of about 138 million, of whom about half are Muslim and half Christian or traditional, making it a key fault line. At the same time, Nigeria is one of the most strategically important states in the world. It plays a regional power role in West Africa and is also the seventh largest producer of oil in the world. It has gone through a series of political traumas ranging from civil war and military rule, to struggling attempts at a U.S.-style presidential federal system. The Fourth Republic, which emerged in 1999 after fifteen years of military rule, is trying to balance states' rights with national priorities and rule of law concerns at a time when many communal tensions are coming to the surface. Conflict mediation, settlement, and resolution are top priorities in this context, and a precondition for stability and economic development.

As our guide to understanding these dynamics, we are lucky to benefit from John Paden's expertise. One of the world's leading experts on the region, his experiences in Nigeria extend from the First Republic to the current Fourth Republic. He has lived and taught in the major northern universities of Nigeria, has conducted research on the Sufi brotherhoods in Kano, and written a major biography of the first (and only) northern premier. He monitored the presidential elections in Kaduna (1999) and Kano (2003).

Professor Paden takes us inside the world of Nigerian religion and politics, with a focus on the ways Muslim civic cultures, ranging from the emirates of the far north to the more individualized patterns of the southwest, deal with matters of leadership and conflict resolution. The book provides a case study context for the current international concern with issues ranging from shari'a law and communal violence, to the war on terrorism. The book argues that the political necessity for cross-regional alliances in Nigeria serves as a counterbalance to more extreme forms of political movements. Other mechanisms of inter-ethnic or inter-faith links and interdependencies are also explored. If the Nigerian model of democratic federalism works, it negates the "clash of civilizations" predictions of both the academic variety and the less benign al Qaeda version.

More broadly, this book will be essential reading for anyone trying to understand the dynamics of Muslim civic cultures and conflict resolution. We are delighted that it is part of our new series at Brookings Institution Press on U.S. policy toward the Islamic world.

P. W. SINGER
Senior Fellow
Director, Project on U.S. Policy
towards the Islamic World
Brookings Institution

Acknowledgments

Many Nigerian scholars and colleagues from all points on the religious and political spectrum have assisted me over the years. My deepest appreciation goes to those who persevere despite the real challenges of shaping a just political reality that can accommodate diversity and pluralism and those who are often involved, in unsung ways, in trying to mediate the inevitable conflicts of nation building. I am particularly grateful to Ahmad Abubakar who has read this manuscript and added a depth of insight.

On the U.S. side, five colleagues have read the manuscript at various stages and provided very helpful comments and suggestions: Peter W. Singer, director, Project on U.S. Policy toward the Islamic World, Brookings Institution; Princeton Lyman, director of African Policy Studies, Council on Foreign Relations; Pauline Baker, president, Fund for Peace; Sulayman Nyang, professor and former director of African Studies, Howard University; and Howard Wolpe, director, Africa Program, Woodrow Wilson International Center for Scholars. My sincere thanks to all. I recognize there are many points of view on the issues raised in this book, and I take sole responsibility for the perspectives and selection of content.

I would also like to thank my colleagues at George Mason University, especially those in the Robinson Professor program, who encourage cross-disciplinary thinking "outside the box." My colleagues at the Institute for Conflict Analysis and Resolution (ICAR) continue to provide role models in the way they combine intellectual endeavor with hands-on efforts at conflict resolution.

Finally, I would like to thank my wife, Xiaohong Liu, who remains an inspiration. Having lived through the Cultural Revolution in China, she knows the challenges of moving from chaos to reforms in an increasingly interdependent world.

This book is dedicated to all who engage in conflict resolution efforts, without which it is hard to imagine a peaceful and prosperous world. I am especially grateful to those who serve as "gateways" between communities and provide the critical function of communication and mediation.

List of Abbreviations

AAPW	Academic Associates/PeaceWorks
ABU	Ahmadu Bello University
ACF	*Arewa* ("Northern") Consultative Forum
AD	Alliance for Democracy (Fourth Republic)
AG	Action Group (First Republic)
ANPP	All Nigeria People's Party (Fourth Republic)
APGA	All Progressive Grand Alliance (Fourth Republic)
APP	All People's Party (Fourth Republic)
BUK	Bayero University, Kano
CAN	Christian Association of Nigeria
CHOGM	Commonwealth Heads of Government Meeting
CNPP	Conference of Nigerian Political Parties (Fourth Republic)
CRK	Christian Religious Knowledge
CSA	Christian Students Association
ECOWAS	Economic Community of West African States
ECWA	Evangelical Church of West Africa
EU	European Union
FCT	Federal Capital Territory (Abuja)
FG	Federal government
FOMWAN	Federation of Muslim Women's Associations of Nigeria
GCFR	Grand Commander of the Federal Republic
GNIJ	Global Network for Islamic Justice
GNPP	Great Nigeria People's Party (Second Republic)
HRW	Human Rights Watch
IDB	Islamic Development Bank
IFMC	Inter-faith Mediation Center

INEC   Independent National Electoral Commission
(Fourth Republic)

IRK   Islamic Religious Knowledge

JIBWIS   Jama'atul Izalatul Bid'ah Wa'ikhamatul Sunnah (Society
against innovation and in favor of Sunnah)

JNI   Jama'atu Nasril Islam (Society for the Victory of Islam)

KSAS   Kano School for Arabic Studies

LGAs   Local government authorities

MSO   Muslim Sisters Organization

MSS   Muslim Students Society

MULAC   Muslim League for Accountability (Fourth Republic)

NACOMYO National Council of Muslim Youth Organisations of Nigeria

NAMLAS National Association of Muslim Law Students

NCNC   National Council of Nigeria and Cameroons (First Republic)

NCNW   National Council of Nigerian Women

NCP   National Conscience Party (Fourth Republic)

NCRA   National Council for Religious Affairs (under Babangida)

NPRD   National Political Reform Dialogue (Fourth Republic)

NEPU   Northern Elements Progressive Union (First Republic)

NDSC   National Defense and Security Council (under Babangida)

NGO   Nongovernmental organization

NIA   National Intelligence Agency (Fourth Republic)

NIREC   National Interfaith Religious Council (Fourth Republic)

NMC   Nigerian Muslim Council

NNA   Nigeria National Alliance (First Republic)

NPC   Northern People's Congress (First Republic)

NPN   National Party of Nigeria (Second Republic)

NPP   Nigerian People's Party (Second Republic)

NRC   National Republican Convention (Third Republic)

NSCIA   Nigerian Supreme Council for Islamic Affairs

NTA   Nigerian Television Authority

NUO   National Unity Organization (Abacha regime)

OPEC   Organization of Petroleum Exporting Countries

PDM   People's Democratic Movement (Third Republic)

PDP   People's Democratic Party (Fourth Republic)

PFN   Pentecostal Fellowship of Nigeria

PMSA   Professional Muslim Sisters Association

PRC   Provisional Ruling Council (Abacha regime)

PRP   People's Redemption Party (Second Republic)

PTF   Petroleum Trust Fund (Abacha regime)

SAP	Structural Adjustment Policy
SCSN	Supreme Council for Shari'a in Nigeria
SDP	Social Democratic Party (Third Republic)
SIM	Sudan Interior Mission
SSS	State Security Service
TBO	The Buhari Organization (Fourth Republic)
TMG	Transition Monitoring Group (Fourth Republic)
UMBC	United Middle Belt Congress (First Republic)
UPGA	United Progressive Grand Alliance (First Republic)
UPN	Unity Party of Nigeria (Second Republic)
USCIRF	U.S. Commission on International Religious Freedom
WIN	Women in Nigeria
WRAPA	Women's Rights Advancement and Protection Alternative
WTO	World Trade Organization

Introduction

A crisis of confidence is emerging in relations between the Western and Muslim worlds, especially in the aftermath of September 11, 2001. Heightening the tension is the war on terrorism, whether defined as preventing nonstate networks from attacking global infrastructure or warding off the challenge of so-called rogue states. To complicate matters, the Western and Muslim worlds themselves are divided on political and policy issues, while constituencies on all sides fail to recognize or understand the basic forces at play. Hence they tend to rely on symbols and slogans rather than informed thinking in addressing their differences. In democracies of the West, even national populations and political leaders differ in their perceptions of the nature of the threats looming on the world's horizon. Those leaders may well face a backlash at the polls if they fail to educate their populations about the realities of today's globalizing, interdependent world, which has clearly entered a new era in international relations.

Nowhere is the West's poor grasp of these matters more noticeable than in its approach to the non-Arab Muslim world, which since the end of the cold war has been mainly one of benign neglect. This has ranged from downsizing embassy, consular, and aid resources to curtailing forms of human engagement such as student and scholar exchanges or professional and business interactions. Policies that rest on such a base tend to be fraught with unintended consequences, concentrate only on the short term, and consist of either overactions or underreactions. If the war on terrorism is to be consequential, which is a concern of virtually all governments of the world, plus organizations ranging from the United Nations to the Organization of the Islamic Conference, a precondition for engagement is clearly some effort at

1

mutual understanding. Power politics of the might-makes-right variety are hardly sufficient to assess the root causes of mistrust and often produce negative reactions that hinder constructive engagement. Furthermore, images of forceful interaction that can now be transmitted globally with the aid of modern technology may abet a clash of civilizations (which is the stated goal of groups such as al Qaeda) rather than a dialogue, or more hopefully, cross-cultural cooperation focusing on our common human problems and challenges.

Even a dialogue approach that democratizes participation in policies of interaction, perhaps through a vast increase in nongovernmental organizations with specific agendas or through the spread of democratic electoral institutions, may complicate statesmanship, especially in determining how concepts such as women's rights or human rights might fit into U.S.-Muslim world relations. Another idea that must be entertained in a pluralistic world seeking to live in peace is that of multiple jurisprudential systems (or alternative dispute resolution systems), since the desire for justice is at the heart of many current grievances exploding into violent conflict.

Before any real dialogue can begin, Westerners must recognize that the Muslim world rests on a wide variety of cultural foundations and historical legacies and that many reforms (and reactions to reform) are well under way there. Also, they must remember that economic globalization creates new winners and losers (or in oil-producing countries, new classes of haves and have-nots). As the pace of change accelerates and uncertainty intensifies, many will turn to their spiritual foundations for guidance. Such fundamentalism, or going back to basics, is a worldwide phenomenon and a typical human response to uncertainty. It should not be an excuse for launching a new era of religious wars.

These complexities are well illustrated in Nigeria. Of its approximately 138 million people, about half (69 million) are Muslim and half Christian or traditional. This makes Nigeria tied with Turkey and Iran for having the sixth largest Muslim population in the world, after Indonesia, Pakistan, India, Bangladesh, and Egypt. Yet all its religions rest on a solid foundation of African cultural traditions. Hence religious identity may not have the same meaning in Nigeria as it does elsewhere, whether in Saudi Arabia or in Texas. Indeed, there are probably more commonalities among Nigerian ethnoreligious groups than differences. Part of the challenge for Nigerian scholars is to reclaim this African heritage without being overwhelmed by the forces of religious globalization or the extreme forms of secularism that emerged during the cold war.

Without doubt, Nigeria is central to global stability. If some form of dialogue among Nigerian groups or between the Western world and the Muslim world is not forthcoming, the prospect of violence and terrorism may well persist, and, in extreme cases, nations may fail. As a stark reminder of what can happen when political leadership or systems crumble, more than 2 million died in Nigeria's civil war of 1967–70. A failure in Nigeria today would have even more extreme consequences in view of its oil wealth and military technologies, which would be available to destabilize the whole of West Africa.

In 1999 Nigeria returned to civilian rule expecting that a "democratic dividend" would be improved conditions for all. But when expectations go up and realities go down, as Ted Gurr has long maintained, "men rebel."[1] Perhaps that is why Nigeria's several attempts at democratic federalism have failed. Tensions are again high in the current Fourth Republic iteration owing to the polarization of wealth, overt corruption, increase in poverty and crime, and some extreme forms of election fraud. Whether democratic federalism will turn out to be part of the problem or part of the solution remains to be seen. At a minimum, the Western world has an interest in strengthening the institutions of a multiparty democracy in which rule-of-law principles pertain, and in which state and local forms of federalism balance the considerable centralization inherited from the military periods.

The key to democratic federalism is the engagement of civil society, which must then strengthen its capacities for resolving conflicts to ensure that minor local issues do not blow up into system-threatening crises. To sacrifice these principles of democracy for the short-term gains of allies in the war on terrorism may create more problems down the line.[2]

While it is too early to assess Nigeria's Fourth Republic, an essential first step to this end is to understand the state's historical and cultural underpinnings. Since humans tend to see the world as a projection of themselves, it is fair to say that Westerners are more familiar with the Westernized, Christian, secular, southern parts of Nigeria than with the Muslim north. Some Nigerians believe such a north-south dichotomy exists and is so deep that it threatens the existence of the nation. At the same time, many of Nigeria's leaders have worked hard to build bridges of understanding and to mediate conflicts between the country's factions.

A caveat to mention at this point concerns the modes of analysis appropriate to the Nigerian context. Western social sciences (and indeed most Western governmental organizations) tend to distinguish between the economic, political, religious, social, and other dimensions of culture. In non-Western cultures, including those of Nigeria, these dimensions overlap.

Hence it makes no sense to debate whether events (such as the 2000 and 2004 riots in northern Nigeria) are political, religious, or socioeconomic in nature. The answer is all of the above. If anything, Westerners usually overemphasize the religious dimension (often in an alarmist manner) or undervalue it (secular analysts, for example, tend to assess almost everything through an economic lens).

For historical reasons, religion in Nigeria, whether Islam or Christianity, is largely based on ethnic tradition or location. Religious practices differ even within the same ethnolocational context, particularly between elites and the grassroots masses. To judge whether the country's civic society has the capacity to engage in conflict resolution behavior under a system of democratic federalism, it is important to recognize that by international standards the levels of religious commitment, belief, and practice in Nigeria are extremely high, in both the Muslim and Christian communities.[3] Hence secularism is mainly a minority perspective in a country that explicitly regards itself as multireligious. This intense multireligious nature makes Nigeria an important case study in the academic and policy domains.

This volume is for the general Western reader, including those interested in policy issues, who may be unfamiliar with the particulars of the Nigerian case. Its central tenet is that most current developments do not make sense unless viewed in their historical and cultural framework. Indeed, the unintended consequences of actions and policies that lack this broader perspective often undermine the best of intentions. Historical patterns and incidents are therefore summarized briefly throughout the book, with suggestions for further reading in the footnotes. Electoral patterns and selected biographies are provided in the appendixes.

My interpretations and assessments are based on four decades of research and teaching in Nigeria, as well as extensive travel throughout the federation. Over the years, I have been indebted to many Nigerian colleagues and scholars. The views expressed in this study, however, are my own. They are an attempt to contribute to the cross-cultural bridge building that has helped keep Nigeria together. Now, in a highly polarized world, the need for international bridges is more urgent than ever.

This study focuses on issues of conflict and conflict resolution in contexts where civic cultures interact with electoral politics. Some issues have acquired broader significance since the end of the cold war world and September 11. Western scholars and policymakers often emphasize the headline-grabbing instances of conflict in Nigeria, especially in the face of September 11 and the international war on terrorism. This volume provides context for a more balanced perspective, concentrating on the Nigerian Muslim community, especially in the northern emirate states and the southwestern Yoruba states, but with some attention to the Islam experience in the northeastern Borno area and the northern Middle Belt. The Muslim community in Nigeria has evolved over time both in its relations with other Muslims and with Christian communities.[4] During the democratic phases of the federation, Muslim civic culture bequeathed two major legacies on Nigeria: a state-based (northern emirate) system and a nonstate (for example, southwestern Yoruba) system.[5] Since the national elections of 1999 and 2003, political relationships between the Muslim emirate states in the north and the Yoruba cultural states in the southwest have become an urgent issue challenging the unity of the federation.

In examining these and other challenges, the book follows four main avenues of discussion. Part 1 provides background information on Nigeria's place in international affairs and its experience with federalism. Part 2 examines Nigerian Muslim identities and civic cultures, as reflected in the practices of sufi brotherhoods and anti-innovation legalists, emirate and Yoruba Muslim civic groups, and Muslim political and national identities. Part 3 highlights the challenges of Nigerian democratic federalism, notably those related to the emerging Fourth Republic and the shari'a issue (that is, debate about the application of Islamic law based on the Qur'an), plus others arising from the country's civic cultures and attempts at conflict resolution, including religious tolerance. In part 4, the discussion turns to Nigeria's approaches to conflict resolution, an evaluation of conflict models, key elements of Muslim civic cultures and conflict resolution, and their implications for Nigeria's relations with the international community.

Democratic federalism in Nigeria represents a critical experiment in the global quest for political frameworks that can achieve unity in the presence of diversity. Some issues of basic concern in such an experiment are how the component states and local governments are configured and what kinds of relations exist between different levels of federal, state, and local government.

Nigeria's civilian periods have been profoundly affected by the centralizing practices under military rule and its oil economy.[6] Nonetheless, the state has managed to cohere by recognizing its regional and geocultural zones and allowing power to be shared across such zones. As a result, political alliances across regions (and thus across ethnoreligious groups) have become a necessary condition for national unity (see map 1 showing the states of Nigeria). That is why Nigeria relies on both traditional cultural and more modern mechanisms to resolve conflicts. The Nigerian case is central to

Map 1. Nigeria and Its Thirty-Six States Today

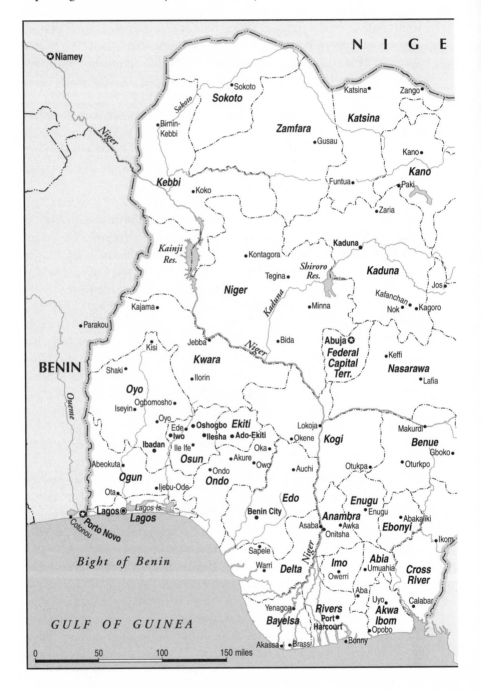

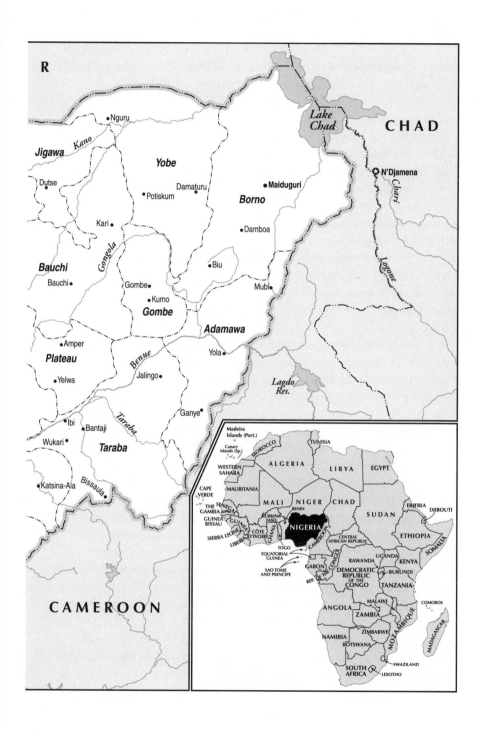

models of conflict and broader issues both in Africa and in U.S.-Muslim world relations.[7]

In particular, the case sheds light on two questions of great concern to the global community. First, when a nation of extreme ethnoreligious diversity shifts from military rule to democratic federalism, will indigenous civic cultures in predominantly Muslim areas reinforce or undermine efforts at conflict resolution? Second, what is an appropriate role, if any, for the international community in encouraging troubled zones to resolve their conflicts?

The discussion in Part 1 lays the groundwork for the analysis of these questions. Chapter 1 covers four main topics: Muslim Nigeria's role in the international community (especially on matters of dialogue with the Western world and with the Islamic world); Western public opinion and policy perspectives, as well as the challenges ahead; conflict theory and its links to civic culture, religion, and democratic federalism; and the relevance of the Nigerian case in evaluating conflict theories. Focusing on the emergence of democratic federalism in Nigeria, chapter 2 considers the implications of the legacy of north-south regionalism, the idea of geocultural zones, the challenges of political structure, and the country's Muslim civic cultures and their issues.

Nigeria's Muslim identities and civic cultures are examined more closely in the next four chapters, beginning in chapter 3 with the major categories of religious identity in the Nigerian Muslim community and their general value orientations, both of which will have bearing on the state's transition to a stable system of democratic federalism over the long term. Chapter 4 concentrates on the traditional civic culture of the emirate states of northern Nigeria, with an emphasis on its five value orientations: time and destiny, community, authority and decisionmaking, civic space (including scope of the state), and conflict resolution (including concepts of justice). Chapter 5 then turns to the Yoruba Muslim community, the Yoruba blend of Christians and traditionalists, civic values and capital city issue, and the emphasis on family values and religious tolerance. As chapter 6 demonstrates, Nigeria's national Muslim identities and values can also be divided along progressive, progressive-conservative, and military lines, or on the basis of their affiliation with women's organizations and national umbrella organizations. As is also pointed out, each category has a particular orientation to authority, community, change, and conflict resolution.

With the end of military rule and establishment of the Fourth Republic on May 29, 1999, Nigeria began yet another attempt at democratic federalism. The patterns of federal-state-local relations under the current three-tier structure are the subject of chapter 7, which explores emerging issues of Nigerian federalism, politics and federal character, states' rights and criminal law, and the aftermath of the 2003 elections, through 2005. Since the reintroduction of shari'a law, however, new tensions and conflicts have arisen both within the Muslim community and between the Muslim and Christian communities. Relations grew even tenser following the elections of 2003, especially when the results were contested. Contributing factors include the politics of shari'a in the north, the mediating influence of "federal character" appointments, processes of implementation, and patterns of implementation in the shari'a states, all discussed in chapter 8. Interestingly, several patterns of sociopolitical conflict are associated with the shari'a states, as noted in chapter 9. In chapter 10, the information gathered to this point is applied in the exploration of four broad issues: religious tolerance and conflict within the Muslim community, religious tolerance and conflict within the Christian community, tolerance and conflict between Muslim and Christian communities, and communications and crisis management networks.

The way in which civic cultures and democratic federalism tend to deal with conflict is the subject of chapter 11, which provides insight into their approach to power sharing, symbolism, and leadership. The book concludes with a summary of Nigerian approaches to conflict resolution, an evaluation of conflict models, and some thoughts on the lessons to be drawn from conflict resolution in Muslim civic cultures. Nigeria's experience in this regard is clearly of utmost interest to the international community.

Part I

International and National Contexts

1

Nigeria in the World

Ever since the catastrophic events of September 11, 2001, public interest has focused on relations between the Muslim and Western worlds. Over this period, Nigeria's dealings with the international community, and with the United States in particular, have emerged as key issues.[1] U.S. policy debates have identified several macro-level approaches that might affect relations with Nigeria, including the following measures:

—insist that alliances in the war on terrorism are the litmus test of a coalition or positive bilateral relations or both,

—insist that multilateral relations—in the sense of broad coalitions (rather than unilateral actions)—are the appropriate means of dealing with terrorist threats and other challenges of democratization and globalization,

—focus on the policy implications of failed states and the criminal activities often associated with such states, and

—insist that democratic reforms are a precondition to any future stability and constructive relations.

These lenses through which Nigeria and other states with large Muslim populations are perceived are not mutually exclusive. Yet some sense of priorities is necessary.

In addition, the oil industry brings a range of special interests and policies to Nigeria regarding both the onshore and offshore communities of the Niger Delta. Liquefied natural gas (LNG) reserves in Nigeria, which are among the largest in the world, are also salient. Energy policies within the international community, including relations between the Organization of Petroleum Exporting Countries (OPEC) and consumer nations, are not unrelated to the approaches just mentioned, especially where there may be a breakdown of law

Map 1-1. Islam in Africa

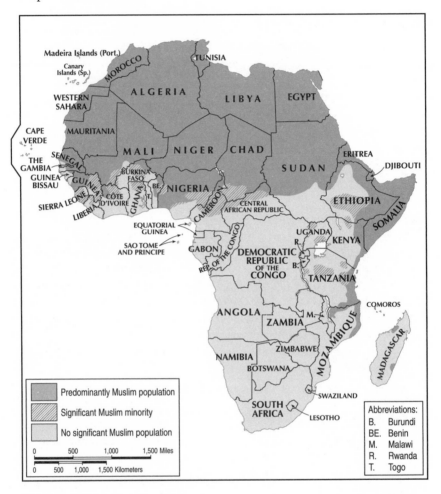

Predominantly Muslim population

Significant Muslim minority

No significant Muslim population

| 0 | 500 | 1,000 | 1,500 Miles |
| 0 | 500 | 1,000 | 1,500 Kilometers |

Abbreviations:
B.   Burundi
BE. Benin
M.   Malawi
R.   Rwanda
T.   Togo

and order or a disruption of democratic governance or where low-intensity violence prevents other development efforts.[2] Also, windfall profits from spikes in oil prices always play a role in international perceptions of concessionary aid or possible debt relief.[3]

The links between Nigerian Muslims and the international Muslim community have been extensive and generally constructive (for an overview of Islam in Africa, see map 1-1). The annual pilgrimage to Mecca, undertaken by Muslims from around the world, and various educational links with Saudi Arabia have had enormous influence on Nigerian Muslim perspectives in recent years. At the same time, Nigeria has had an ambivalent status within the

Organization of the Islamic Conference since 1986, when a crisis over active membership was averted in Nigeria as part of a political compromise between Christians and Muslims. As a non-Arab community, however, Nigerian Muslims have often found more in common with other non-Arab Muslim communities, such as those in Malaysia, and for the most part Nigeria has shown more flexibility in accommodating the issue of local cultures. Within Muslim Africa, Nigeria's long-distance trade has been extensive (its long-distance trade is shown on map 1-2).

Within an African context, Nigeria has provided leadership, along with South Africa, on a wide range of issues, from decolonization to regional peace-keeping, both at the United Nations and in the African Union (AU). Nigeria is often mentioned as a candidate for permanent membership on the UN Security Council.

In the West African context, the ethnoreligious demographic patterns are clear. Interior zones are predominantly Muslim, and coastal zones are predominantly Christian. Hence interfaith conflict mediation or resolution has taken on enormous regional importance in Nigeria. The country's role in the Economic Community of West African States (ECOWAS) has been instrumental in developing a regional perspective on socioeconomic and political matters that cut across anglophone and francophone language zones. The emergence of ECOWAS as a vision comparable to the transnational federation of states in the European Union (EU) means that the experiments with democratic federalism in Nigeria have broader regional consequences.

Nigeria's significance within the international community will only grow as the political, economic, military, social, and religious implications of its transition from military to democratic rule become more apparent on the world stage. That transition was a priority for the Western world, the British Commonwealth, and, indeed, the United Nations, as illustrated by Madeleine Albright's firm desire, while U.S. secretary of state, "to do all I could . . . to help struggling democracies succeed. We could accomplish much on a bilateral basis, so I singled out Nigeria, Indonesia, Ukraine, and Columbia as priorities for our assistance and attention because of their regional importance and the scale of the challenges they faced."[4] President Bill Clinton, Secretary of State Madeleine Albright, President George W. Bush, and Secretary of State Colin Powell have all visited Nigeria since the transition to democratic rule in 1999 and have regarded U.S. interaction with Nigeria as a key bilateral relationship.[5]

Although Western perspectives focused on democracy in the 1990s, the larger concern was how a democratic system based on a U.S.-style presidential and federal model would function in Nigeria in the aftermath of military

Map 1-2. Long Distance Trade Routes across Northern Africa

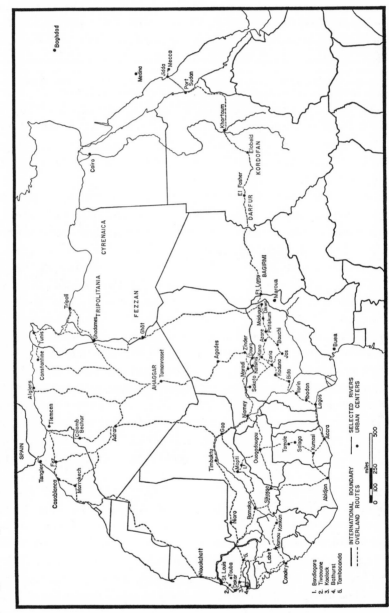

Source: Paden, *Religion and Political Culture in Kano* (University of California Press, 1973).

rule. Given its complex diversity and long history of experiments with federalism, the question was how Nigeria could achieve unity with diversity. As this study argues, key conditions for its stability and development will be a political system that balances ethnoreligious and regional diversity (while at the same time using surrogate designations for such diverse identities). Federalism is a common feature of diverse societies, whether at the more centralized extremes, as in Russia, or at the more decentralized end of the spectrum, as in India or Canada. In the United States, federalism tends to swing between a more centralized form during times of war and a more decentralized form emphasizing states' rights during times of peace.

For Nigeria, which is coming out of a long period of highly centralized military rule, the challenge is to find the right balance in introducing decentralization. The first six years of the Fourth Republic make it clear, however, that centralization is a fact of Nigerian life, much in the tradition instituted by General Charles de Gaulle in the early days of the Fifth French Republic. Given the federal monopoly of resources, a major concern in some Nigerian geocultural zones (for example, in the north and east) is that a single-party system might be imposed from the center, and that it might have little accountability or transparency and be backed by a compliant military and police force. Such a system would pose a serious challenge to the idea of democratic checks and balances inherent in a two-party or multiparty system.

This challenge comes at a time when the international community is trying desperately to avoid what has been called a clash of civilizations. In contrast to the cold war era, when close working relations existed between the Western and the Islamic worlds in common cause against the Soviet threat, the years since then, especially since September 11, have seen these relations come under increasing stress. Clearly, the West and the Islamic world must try to achieve a better understanding of each other rather than allow fringe groups on both sides, or even mainstream interest groups, to poison the atmosphere with wild claims and accusations. Although the current dialogue is focused mainly on the Arab Muslim world, non-Arab Muslim societies may well play a key role in the eventual evolution of more constructive international relations. Indeed, the future of the worldwide Muslim community (*ummah*) may lie in Southeast Asia or West Africa, where the legacy of pluralism and tolerance is more established than in the Middle East.

The death of Pope John Paul II in the spring of 2005 raised the question of whether Roman Catholic relations with the Muslim world would continue to improve. According to the *New York Times,*

John Paul II had a consistent, even ground-breaking strategy for addressing Islam: Talk at all costs, even if there were few concrete results. . . . During his reign John Paul reached out to Muslims like no other pope. He was the first on record to step inside a mosque, in Damascus in 2001, and he apologized for past misdeeds of the church that many have read to include the Crusades.[6]

One of the leading candidates to succeed John Paul II was Cardinal Francis Arinze, of southeast Nigeria. During his eighteen years as archbishop of Onitsha, he built a church that was "devout, unostentatious, deeply conservative on moral questions and distinctly African." When Arinze moved to the Vatican in 1985, he helped pursue the pope's strategy for contact, acting as liaison to other religions. His experience with Islam in Nigeria proved a valuable asset in this regard.[7]

The reaction in Muslim Nigeria to the selection of Cardinal Joseph Ratzinger as Pope Benedict XVI has been positive, not least to emphasize the need for dialogue, rather than a "clash," between civilizations. Observers believe this call for dialogue comes at an opportune time, particularly for Africa and Nigeria:

> Both the two greatest religions of the world—Christianity and Islam—are here as part of the continent's triple heritage. . . . In a world dominated by politics, and in a country, like Nigeria, where politics is dominated by mischief, care must be taken in walking on the tight rope of mutual existence. So thin and delicate is this rope that a word from the mouth of a reckless politician or imprudent leader is enough to cost thousands of lives.[8]

Among the analysts calling attention to the situation in Nigeria are Princeton Lyman, former U.S. ambassador to Nigeria and subsequently director of African Policy Studies at the Council on Foreign Relations, and Stephen Morrison, director of the Africa Program at the Center for Strategic and International Studies. In their view, Nigeria is "by far the most troubling case" on the continent, as its "potent mix of communal tensions, radical Islamism, and anti-Americanism has produced a fertile breeding ground for militancy and threatens to tear the country apart." Nigeria is Africa's most populous nation, they point out, and its Muslim population (69 million) is the second largest in Africa (after Egypt's). The United States, they argue, has failed to "check rising instability there in recent years" despite its close economic ties with Nigeria, which supplies 7 percent of U.S. oil needs. Yet "the U.S. embassy lacks a single American speaker of Hausa, the main language of northern

Nigeria; has no consulate or other permanent representation in the north; and, until recently, possessed only a poorly staffed and unimaginative public diplomacy program. Furthermore, the United States has done little to help Nigeria out of its severe economic depression, which is indirectly responsible for much of the tension in the country."[9] These are powerful accusations and illustrate how important it is for the West (the United States, in particular) to understand the situation in Nigeria.

To this end, the British government has already made some major efforts at engagement, through its British Council programs and other initiatives. These have included tours by British scholars and British Muslims in the far northern Nigerian states, to discuss issues of religious reform and conduct dialogue with counterparts, and some international conferences held in the United Kingdom on topics related to Islam.[10] In addition, British state visits are likely to include Muslim areas as well as Abuja (the Federal Capital Territory) as part of official protocol.[11]

U.S.-Nigerian Muslim dialogue has also increased since the return to civilian rule in 1999.[12] A conference in Kano in January 2003, cosponsored by the emir of Kano and the U.S. Department of State, brought together scholars and policy specialists from both sides with an interest in U.S.-Muslim world relations. In 2002 and 2003 the U.S. Fulbright program supported partnerships between Muslim universities in Africa and U.S. counterparts.[13] And in 2003 the U.S. Institute of Peace began worldwide competitions for research on improving governance in the Muslim world and on conflict resolution. The U.S. Embassy in Abuja also facilitates private scholarship donations, which include assistance for female education in the north, while the U.S. Department of State's annual *Country Reports on Human Rights Practices* focus on a number of challenges regarding "freedom of Religion" in Nigeria.[14]

As for external diplomatic links, northern Nigerian Muslims have served in major Western and international posts, a key one being Washington, D.C.[15] Two other crucial conduits of communication are the high commissioner in London and ambassadorship to the United Nations in New York.[16] In addition, a recent secretary general of OPEC, Rilwan Lukman from Kaduna State, has been involved in extensive negotiations affecting the Western world. During 1999–2003, Lukman served as presidential adviser on petroleum and energy in the Obasanjo government. Other northern Nigerian diplomats have served throughout the Western world, including Eastern Europe and Latin America.[17]

The Muslim world, too, has engaged in dialogue with the elites of Muslim Nigeria at official as well as more informal levels. For many years, the Saudi and Gulf states have provided scholarships and educational opportunities and in general have been a stabilizing force. (Interestingly, the Nigerian-Saudi connection helped create a generally positive attitude in Nigeria toward the United States, since it was clear that the U.S.-Saudi alliance was central to the global economy, and there was a widespread perception in Nigeria that Americans were "People of the Book.") The Nigerian and Saudi sides have also worked together to carefully control the annual pilgrimage and thus prevent major disruptions. Other evidence of cooperation can be seen in the Organization of the Islamic Conference (OIC) based in Saudi Arabia, which represents a wide variety of Muslim perspectives, including West African sufism and Maliki legal jurisprudence, and has a strong policy of working within the existing national state boundary system.[18] For their part, West African states in general, and Nigeria in particular, have had a major impact on Saudi official perspectives since 1960, encouraging a move to a broader view of Islam to encompass sufism, for example. (Shaykh Ibrahim Niass of Senegal, the spiritual leader of Reformed Tijaniyya in Nigeria, was a frequent pilgrim and visitor to Saudi Arabia over the years.)

Furthermore, many of Nigeria's Muslim educated elites have served as diplomats in the Muslim world, not only in the African context, which is extremely diverse and extensive (the West African subregion is particularly distinctive), but in areas ranging from the Middle East to Southeast Asia.[19] Table 1-1 shows a sample of Nigerian ambassadors from the northern states providing links to predominantly Muslim countries during the 1999–2003 period. Many of the ambassadors from such states have played a critical role in communications with predominantly Muslim countries around the world and are aware of the many crosscurrents within the Islamic world. Such Nigerian diplomats are widely regarded as professionals committed to a stable international system and serve as bridges of cross-cultural communication with the Western world, the Muslim world, and other key areas, including China and South Africa.

Of special interest are the links between Nigeria and Saudi Arabia, the major factors being OPEC membership, pilgrimage, OIC relationships, charity contributions for mosques and schools, and cooperation in the war on terrorism.[20] Several of these points, particularly the influence of varieties of the Saudi-based puritanical movement (*Wahhabiyya*) in Nigeria, are discussed in later chapters.[21] Perhaps most salient at the grassroots level are the pilgrimage patterns, including the large number of northern Nigerians who stayed on in Saudi Arabia after the pilgrimage. An account from the 2004 pilgrimage indicates that Hausa is becoming a lingua franca among the ever-growing African communities of Mecca.[22]

Table 1-1. Nigerian Ambassadors from Northern States:
Links to Predominantly Muslim Countries, 1999–2003

Home state	Ambassador	Country
Sokoto	Ladan A. Shuni	Morocco
	Abdulkadir Sani	Guinea
Kano	B. M. Abubakar	Mauritania
	Kabir Rabiu	Algeria
	Abdullahi Muktar	Tanzania
Katsina	Magaji Muhammed	Saudi Arabia
Kwara	M. S. Abdul-Wahab	Lebanon
Yobe	Bukar Mele	Iran
	Lawam Gana Guba	Libya
Kogi	Usman Bello	Sudan
Taraba	A. D. I. Waziria	Pakistan
Kaduna	Shehu Lawal Giwa	Saudi Arabia
	Sule Buba	Senegal
	L. Mohammed Munir	Turkey
Nasarawa	A. M. Bagea	Bangladesh
Borno	Baba Jidda	Burkina Faso
Bauchi	M. M. Bauchi	Chad
	M. A. Humba	Kuwait
Kebbi	Abubakar Udu	Egypt
	Sani Kangiwa	Mali
	Yakubu Kwari	Niger
Gombe	Haruno Wando	Eritrea
	Saidu Mohammed	Indonesia
	Yerima Abdullahi	Sudan
	I. Y. Abdullahi[a]	Malaysia
Zamfara	Ibrahim Wambai	Iraq
	M. Jabbi	Tunisia

a. Individual served as high commissioner rather than ambassador.

Western Public Opinion and Policy Perspectives

Broad Western public opinion of developments in Muslim Nigeria is often event or issue driven. Since 2000 it has focused on reactions to shari'a death penalty decisions in the far northern states, as in the case of a woman whose child was born out of wedlock and who was sentenced to death by a Katsina lower court. The Nigerian high commissioner in London reportedly received over 1 million e-mails and letters protesting the verdict (which was subsequently overturned). Such reactions are especially strong in the European

Union, which has proscribed the death penalty. Significantly, as of 2005 Nigeria has never implemented shari'a capital punishments by stoning.[23] Shari'a codes prescribe the death penalty for several categories of offences besides adultery, including sodomy.[24] Some of these sexual crimes tap into a broader sense of Nigerian multireligious values, which tend to be conservative.[25]

Although several more conservative countries in the Muslim world allow stoning, in practice it is quite rare.[26] In general, Western embassies in Abuja have steered clear of the shari'a controversies, especially in public, because of the general sensitivity on all sides, while still affirming the principle of human rights. (Indeed, on the death penalty issue, there are sharp policy differences between U.S. and European governments.) In general, the U.S. diplomatic response to the stoning issue in Nigeria—which tends to attract the most attention in U.S. popular appeals to the State Department—has been to urge caution regarding due process matters, especially vigilante justice, while stressing the need for political stability. According to an Associated Press wire report, the U.S. State Department expressed concern about the decision to stone a single mother to death for having sex out of wedlock and hoped the appeal process would be "conducted in a manner that affords protection of due process, fairness and justice" to the defendant. However, as the report also noted,

> An Islamic high court in northern Nigeria rejected an appeal ... by the woman, and her lawyers said they planned to appeal to a higher Islamic court. If that fails, they can appeal to the Supreme Court, where the case would force a showdown between Nigeria's constitutional and religious authorities. .... President Olusegun Obasanjo's government has declared Shariah punishments such as beheading, stoning and amputation unconstitutional. Some predominantly Muslim northern states, which began instituting Shariah shortly after civilian rule replaced military dictatorship in 1999, have accused him of meddling."[27]

In addition, Western policy and public opinion have been aware of the event-driven turmoil in Nigeria's Middle Belt areas (including Kaduna State), between Muslim and Christian groups.[28] (Indeed, it is difficult to encourage or retain Western business investment in Kaduna's urban area because of the ethnoreligious polarization.) A single event such as a recent Muslim-Christian student disturbance at Ahmadu Bello University (Zaria) always has the potential to get out of control.[29]

Given the long history of Western evangelical activity in the Middle Belt zone, an additional issue is the role of North American missionaries on the fringes of the northern Muslim culture zones, and the potential for conflict resulting from conversion campaigns along this fault line.[30] The U.S. Commission on International Religious Freedom (USCIRF) discusses such issues in its annual reports, which are submitted to Congress and are publicly available.[31]

In the spring of 2004, extensive Christian-Muslim turmoil in Plateau State—in some instances between cattle pastoralists and settled farmers—left thousands dead and led to reprisal killings in Kano State.[32] A Human Rights Watch report recounts in graphic detail the dynamics of this extraordinary tragedy.[33] In the far north, local religious disturbances involving violence or death are regularly reported in the Western press.[34] Even U.S. evangelical groups with links to Nigeria are growing concerned about some of the chaos accompanying the rapid spread of evangelical churches in Nigeria.[35]

Of course, anything that looks like an Islamic uprising is certain to alarm the international press.[36] How such incidents are interpreted in the context of the war on terrorism may lead to increased U.S. military links with Nigeria, as has already happened in the Sahelian states of Mauritania, Mali, Niger, and Chad.[37]

Another great concern to the international community is the violence between ethnic groups in the oil-producing Niger Delta (for example, between Ijaw and Itsekiri). While this is a predominantly non-Muslim area, much of the federal portion of its oil revenue has gone into the building of Abuja, which some consider to be a northern Muslim initiative.

Further tensions are evident in the urban centers of the southwest, such as Lagos and Ibadan, where northern (Hausa) Muslim migrants have a complex set of relations with indigenous Yoruba communities. Incidents there are always sensitive to political developments at the national level. Similar uneasiness can be seen in far northern urban centers such as Kano, where Igbo-Hausa ethnic relations may take on a religious tone as well. To add to the complexity, there were reprisal killings in the southeast after some shari'a demonstrations in the north in 2000, and in May 2004 the Christian killings of Muslims in Yelwa, in central Nigeria, also met with reprisals (see chapter 10).[38] Since the Igbo no longer dominate key sectors of the northern economy, however, "ethnic market dominance" does not seem to be a key issue in Igbo-Hausa socioeconomic relations in the north.[39]

Equally troubling to many in the West is the concern that since 1999 the government of Nigeria has used lethal force in quelling instances of local turmoil such as the Kaduna riots in 2000 and 2002 (see chapter 7). More broadly, Human Rights Watch has detailed excessive Nigerian police and military actions against dissidents.[40] In the case of the 2004 violence, Human Rights

Watch argues that the police underreacted in Plateau State and overreacted in Kano State.

To some extent, the Sudanese civil war between the Arab-Muslim north in Khartoum and African-Christian south has clouded Western perceptions about Nigeria. (Some otherwise well-informed U.S. opinion leaders are still unclear as to whether Nigerian Muslims are Arabs or Africans!) With the apparent success of international efforts to mediate this north-south conflict in the spring of 2004, the international community has turned its attention to the problems in the Darfur region of Sudan, where Arab Muslim pastoralists and raiders are clashing with largely defenseless African Muslim farmers in what Secretary of State Colin Powell has described as a genocide. This conflict, which came into the spotlight following the confirmation of Senator John Danforth as U.S. ambassador to the United Nations, made clear that in the African context the parties to the dispute could all be Muslim, but there are differences between "African" and "Arab" perspectives.

The public perceptions mentioned earlier feed into the Western policy perspectives that have emerged since September 11. Many of these emphasize sociopolitical stability as an obvious precondition for economic development, along with a variety of other steps to help Nigeria become a constructive member of the international community. The U.S. chargé d'affaires in Abuja, Ambassador Roger Meece, has pointed out, however, that despite the "successful transition to a democratically elected government, the task of transforming a country undergoing economic and social reform is daunting." Nevertheless, "it must be based on an indigenous foundation."[41]

Much of the challenge in this civilian reform is to get economic development and democratic practices in place at the state and local levels, as well as at the federal level. Thus in its 2002 report on Nigerian local government, the World Bank focused on decentralization and ways to strengthen local government.[42] Similarly, the United States has given grants under the Education for Democracy and Democracy Initiative (EDDI) for civic education, especially for nongovernmental organizations (NGOs) with ties to grassroots groups.[43]

This comes, however, at a time when many in the international community are absorbed in the war on terrorism, the global economic slowdown, the reform of the World Trade Organization (WTO), and the situation in Darfur, all of which are matters of national or international policy.[44] Although one of President Obasanjo's high priorities has been to reconnect Nigeria with the international community after its long period of pariah status under the Abacha regime, it is imperative to strengthen the indigenous foundations of democratic civic culture and not wait until macro issues, such as debt relief, are sorted out. Local levels provide first responders and basic security, plus grassroots economic development, in an environment where extremes of wealth and the conspicuous consumption of new elites are potentially desta- bilizing. Another essential task of local government in a federal democracy is to administer the rule of law in multijurisprudential systems, which encom- passes issues of transparency and corruption. These are all part of Nigeria's local civic cultures and practices—in other words, its indigenous founda- tions. A related challenge is to transform its capital in Abuja from a military-style command-and-control center to a genuine federal capital and thereby ensure national and political stability.

However, some in the international community question Nigeria's ability to move toward decentralization or to conduct local policing. They worry that a "warlord" syndrome might develop, with corrupt governors controlling their own local militias, for they see the vigilante movements that have filled the vacuum of local-level security and law enforcement in the southeast, southwest, and north as negative precedents for local policing. On the other hand, limiting police to the federal level has not solved the problem of local security. (Indeed, every time federal police overreact with violence, local com- munities feel more alienated, and some have even accused the national government of being a "warlord" regime.) Nigerians, as well as the interna- tional community, seem to be divided on this issue.[45]

For years, especially during the military eras of the 1990s, the international community discontinued its engagement with Nigeria, except in a few arenas such as oil. (The British Commonwealth even suspended Nigeria after the hanging of Ken Sara Wiwo and others in 1995 by the Abacha regime.) With the transition to civilian rule in 1999, international transition funding flooded in to a wide variety of sectors, although Nigeria's international debt remained unaddressed.[46] As issues of ethnoreligious identities and civic values (plus conflict resolution) emerged during the Fourth Republic, attention again turned to the basic diversity of Nigerian civic cultures and societies and how to achieve national unity without resorting to military rule—which is unpop- ular in both Nigeria and the international community—and to create a level playing field in politics so that incumbents do not invariably win and system breakdowns are not all too common.[47] Military rule also implies human rights abuses and civil strife, which may have religious connotations in the African and international contexts.[48] From a more strategic U.S. foreign policy per- spective since September 11, there are several schools of thought on possible policy toward Nigeria, as already noted.

Some arise from the Bush administration's initial belief that in the war on terror states are either part of the coalition or against it, with no gray areas.[49] On November 6, 2003, President Bush announced that one of his priorities was to establish liberal democracy in the Muslim world; as he explained on November 19, he considers the extension of democracy an antidote to despair, extremism, and terrorism. The second Bush administration has been even more vocal about encouraging "democracy" as a universal goal, although critics maintain that this rhetoric is not matched by policy realities. Nevertheless, the stated policy does represent a strengthening of emphasis.

With Muslim countries as diverse as Indonesia, Morocco, Saudi Arabia, and Turkey feeling the brunt of terrorist anger and destruction, many question how moderate African Muslim countries should function in an era of democratic practices. Specific threats to Nigeria in a 2003 tape purportedly recorded by Osama bin Laden have led many U.S. foreign policy experts to call for a fundamental reorganization of U.S. engagement with Nigeria because of the potential for terrorist infiltration.[50] Some U.S. efforts already under way in the African context, notably in the areas of trade and health (such as anti-HIV and AIDS programs), might benefit Nigeria in the socioeconomic domain, as President Bush noted during his visit to Nigeria in July 2003.

In general, the Nigerian government has been a close ally of the United States in the war on terror.[51] However, preelection ads for President Obasanjo televised about the time of the "battle of Baghdad" pictured him with President Jacques Chirac of France and with the Chinese ambassador to Abuja, both opponents of the war.

Clearly, the war in Iraq has not been popular in Nigeria, in both Muslim and non-Muslim areas, conjuring images of imperial legacies. Despite negative attitudes toward the regime of Saddam Hussein, it is widely believed that the war was less about terrorism than other U.S. priorities.[52] Nigerian Muslims tend to view President Bush's public pronouncements urging tolerance and understanding between Muslims and Christians as a balance to apparent pandering to the U.S. constituency supporting a conservative Christian agenda.[53] It should be added that the United States itself is divided on whether the war on terrorism includes the war in Iraq.[54]

According to former secretary of state Madeleine Albright, who supports another approach, the Bush administration has departed "in fundamental ways, from the approach that has characterized U.S. foreign policy for more than half a century." Bush had concluded, she argues, that hazards to security were so great as to replace "reliance on alliance . . . by redemption through preemption":

The shock of force trumped the hard work of diplomacy, and long-time relationships were redefined. In making these changes, Bush explicitly rejected the advice offered by one senior statesman who warned, "this most recent surprise attack (should) erase the concept in some quarters that the United States can somehow go it alone in the fight against terrorism, or in anything else." So said George H. W. Bush, the United States' 41st president. But his son, the 43rd president, offered his own perspective shortly before going to war with Iraq: "At some point, we may be the only ones left. That's okay with me. We are America."[55]

Albright and other centrist Democrats (such as 2004 presidential candidate John Kerry) have insisted on multilateral rather than unilateral approaches to the challenges of globalization and terrorism. Many also prefer political and diplomatic action to military alliances, especially in building the kinds of coalitions needed to understand the organizational and cultural nature of transnational networks of terrorism.[56] In short, many who advocate a centrist foreign policy (whatever their political party) think the United States should emphasize and support the positive values of democracy (which builds from the bottom up), the emergence of a free media and free expression, and the capacities and cultures of accommodating political pluralism. They are opposed to playing the more short-term game of supporting friends (who sometimes include dictators) and punishing enemies (who sometimes include democratic regimes), a strategy that in their opinion has no regard for long-term institutional reforms and values.

A third perspective—offered by Chester Crocker, who served as assistant secretary of state for Africa under President Ronald Reagan—rests on the view that the real danger to the international community is not state-led regimes but failed or failing states in which "corrupt elites might ally themselves with criminal networks to divide the spoils," thereby undermining and replacing state authority in particular regions and inviting illegal trading operations. Crocker warns: "During transitions away from authoritarianism, state security services might lose their monopoly on the instruments of violence, leading to a downward spiral of lawlessness." He adds,

State failure, inextricably linked with internal strife and humanitarian crisis, can spread from localized unrest to national collapse and then regional destabilization. And unattractive entities—some hostile to U.S. security interests, others hostile to Washington's humanitarian and political goals—may rise to fill the political vacuum. . . . But the challenge is not only to address state failure in the handful of states where regimes get overthrown. It is also to stop and contain the process of failure before it produces worst-case scenarios. In much of the transitional world—those at-risk societies concentrated in Africa, the Middle East, and southwestern Asia—there is a footrace under way between legitimate government institutions and legal business enterprises, on the one hand, and criminal networks, often linked to warlords or political factions associated with security agencies, on the other.[57]

Crocker specifically mentions Nigeria under the Abacha regime as an instance of this syndrome.

Rather than focus on nation-building in general (even of the democratic variety) or more specifically the war on terror, Crocker and others argue, the international community should support those states most at risk of failure as a preventive measure. The key to this approach is to confront corruption and insist on transparency as a way of strengthening legitimate governance.

The Challenges Ahead

The Muslim communities in Nigeria have played a major role in keeping the country together since independence in 1960 and in avoiding outright failure of the national political system. These communities have led the effort to promote democratic federalism as a way of accommodating pluralism and alternative points of view. Because of its complex diversity, however, Nigeria has concentrated on domestic political events rather than external relations with the Middle East or other world areas.[58]

As the United States endeavors to interact more with the Muslim world, it must not fall into the trap of expending diplomatic energy on the coastal zones of Nigeria, to the exclusion of the Muslim or northern zones, as suggested by the slow move of the U.S. embassy and consular facilities from Lagos to Abuja. Indeed, one of the major failings of many Western policy (and academic) establishments is to regard sub-Saharan Africa as organizationally remote and distinct from its neighbors in the broader Muslim world. Such compartmentalization by artificial geographic zones makes it difficult to properly frame the challenges and threats of the twenty-first century or to come to grips with the regional and cultural realities of Africa.

Princeton Lyman has been especially articulate in publicizing the need for the United States to interact with the Muslim communities in Nigeria.[59] As this volume makes clear, the international community should not become preoccupied with personality politics at the national level but should focus on institutional capacity building at all levels, in an even-handed way. There is no mystery as to what needs to be done. The challenge to the international community will be to engage constructively with Nigerians in all regions and at all levels, while observing the motto "Do no harm."[60] It will be necessary to support the institutional strengthening of democratic federalism, despite the pressures of current events and day-to-day politics in this quintessential African state, which, given its ethnoreligious diversity, may or may not be too big to fail.

Clearly, failure could occur at both the national and local levels, as hinted by the ethnoreligious violence of May 2004, which led President Obasanjo to declare a six-month state of emergency for Plateau State and to replace the elected civilian governor with a military governor. As already noted, democratic federalism operates at both national and local levels. Efforts to prevent and detect terrorism must be national and local in scope. Perhaps the emphasis should even be less on the national military and security domain, which is often detached from local realities, and more on the capacity of ordinary citizens to take responsibility for the safety and well-being of their local communities. At the same time, it is important to recognize that all national boundaries are porous, and that the globalization of technologies and communications is the new reality of contemporary life.

The cultural capacities of Nigerians—Christian, Muslim, and traditional—to set an example in conflict resolution will have enormous implications for global society in the years to come. The success or failure of democratic federalism in Nigeria will have even greater consequences. Since democratic federalism clearly depends on grassroots participation, it is essential for local civic cultures to withstand the stresses and strains of economic and political development in the postmilitary environment and not give way to despair, which can only breed instability and disappointment.[61] That is why the international community is beginning to focus on the capacity of grassroots civic organizations and cultures in Nigeria to come to grips with the causes and consequences of local interfaith and ethnoreligious violence. The experience of the Inter-faith Mediation Center based in Kaduna is an example of NGO efforts to build capacities in conflict prevention and mediation.[62] The efforts of an evangelical pastor and Muslim imam are a prototype for many of the secondary school and university "peace committees" already having an impact on conflict resolution efforts in Nigeria.

The first step in conflict resolution and mediation is to analyze the nature and dynamics of the grassroots conflicts, then to assess the human resources available for conflict mitigation, including the capacity of traditional civic cultures to adapt to new conflict challenges. Table 1-2 presents a sample of

Table 1-2. Religious Conflicts in Nigeria, 1979–97

Date	Location	State	Principal source of conflict
October 1977	Zaria	Kaduna	ABU Muslim and Christian students
May 1978	Kaduna/Zaria	Kaduna	I FOUND IT (Jesus Salvation) Christian students demonstration
1978	Kaduna/Zaria	Kaduna	ISLAM ONLY (Muslim students demonstration)
1980	Kano City	Kano	Maitatsine riots
October 1982	Maiduguri	Borno	Bulumkutu riots
October 1982	Rigarsa	Kaduna	Maitatsine riots
March 1984	Yola/Jimeta	Adamawa	Maitatsine uprising
November 1984	Gombe	Bauchi	Maitatsine uprising
May 1986	Ibadan	Oyo	University of Ibadan Chapel, resurrection crisis
1986	Ilorin	Kwara	Palm Sunday conflicts
March 1987	Kafanchan/Kaduna	Kaduna	College of Education, Kaduna religious crisis
March 1987	Zaria/Ikara	Kaduna	Students and community Kafanchan spillover
March 1987	Funtua/Kaduna	Kaduna	Students and community Kafanchan spillover
March 1987	Kankia/Makarfi	Kaduna	Students and community Kafanchan spillover
1990	Bauchi	Bauchi	Muslim and Christian student riots
October 1991	Kano	Kano	Bonke crusade uprising
1991	Katsina	Katsina	Governor Madaki vs. Muslim students crisis
April 1991	Tafawa Balewa	Bauchi	Christian vs. Muslim community conflict

Date	Place	State	Description
April 1991	Bauchi Town	Bauchi	Tafawa Balewa crisis spillover
February–March 1992	Zangon Kataf	Kaduna	Christian vs. Muslim community crisis on market site, plus chiefdom issues
1992	Jalingo Township	Taraba	Muslim and Christian students clash
1993	Kaduna/Katsina	Kaduna/Katsina	Fun Times newspaper, blasphemous article, riots
1994	Ibadan	Oyo	Government schools assembly prayers crisis
1994	Jos	Plateau	Ethnic-religious crisis (indigenes vs. settlers)
December 1994	Kano	Kano	Gideon Akaluka saga
1995	Tafawa Balewa	Bauchi	Second Christian vs. Muslim community conflicts (on Sayawa chiefdom)
May 1995	Sabon Gari Market	Kano	Christian and Muslim (Igbo and Hausa) traders crisis
1996	Ilorin	Kwara	Islamic religious knowledge teaching in government approved mission schools crisis
June 1996	Kaduna	Kaduna	Kaduna Polytechnic student riots
1996	Kafanchan	Kaduna	Second Kafanchan religious crisis
1996	Kaduna/Zaria	Kaduna	Second Kafanchan religous crisis spillover
May 1997	Jos	Plateau	Ethnic-religious (Birom vs. Hausa) community conflicts
1997	Kafanchan	Kaduna	Christians vs. Shi'ah Muslims

Source: Muhammad Nurayn Ashafa and James Movel Wuye, *The Pastor & the Imam: Responding to Conflict* (Lagos: Ibrash Publications Centre, 1999), pp. 87–88.

religious conflicts in Nigeria during the period 1979–97, before the return to democratic federalism in 1998–99. In late 1998, Nigeria began the transition to a civilian Fourth Republic, which brought new conflict challenges. Most significantly, it involved grassroots civil constituencies as well as elected leadership in the attempts to mediate conflict.

Civic Cultures and Conflict Resolution

There are many theoretic and practical approaches to conflict analysis and resolution. These include the well-known hypothesis that when expectations go up and realities go down, violent rebellion may occur.[63] The central concern under this hypothesis is economic conditions, not just in the empirical sense but also in the sense of expected results, which makes relative deprivation a key concept to the analysis. Thus it is assumed that the fact of wealth and poverty may be less important to conflict than the upward expectations and subsequent disappointment of the poor. Other analyses focus more on underlying issues of identity and security, in both the psychological and material sense.[64] They move beyond articulated interests or positions to concentrate on human needs. Still others emphasize the psychological or emotional profiles of key actors and consequently opt for therapeutic approaches to deep-seated conflict.[65] Issues of displacement and mourning become part of the ritual healing.

Various types of conflict have commanded the attention of the post–cold war world, from localized to global confrontations. Some of these are regarded as serious enough to destabilize political systems or even cause a state to fail. Four fundamental patterns of conflict have been identified, each with implications for conflict mediation and resolution:

—In Samuel Huntington's view, serious conflict (clash) tends to occur along cultural or civilizational fault lines.[66] (This suggestion took on new salience in the light of the September 11 events, even for those who reject its basic premises.)

—For Alvin and Heidi Toffler, conflict inheres in the relations between three socioeconomic waves of technological development: agrarian, industrial, and electronic or informational.[67] For example, preindustrial groups and postindustrial networks may enter into alliance to confront the existing order of advanced industrial nation-states.

—Mark Juergensmeyer believes the next cold war will arise between the secular and hyper-religious elements present in every society.[68] As the pace of change in the contemporary world quickens, those who feel their fundamental values are being threatened will find themselves pitted against those willing to adapt to change, even if it means moving their values toward secularism.

—Zbigniew Brzezinski favors a chaos theory model that attributes conflict to the breakdown of old orders and resulting formations and reformations, which may defy current efforts at cluster analysis.[69] This process has been called "pandaemonium."[70] Every major war in modern history has resulted in the dismantling of preexisting empires. Why should the cold war be different? Out of the chaos may come a new order.[71]

These four paradigms may be empirically tested cross-nationally, as Ted Gurr has attempted, by cluster analysis of conflict patterns in the relevant time periods where data are available, especially for the period of transition from the 1980s to the 1990s.[72] An alternative methodology is to undertake penetrating case studies of contemporary conflicts in their historical and cultural context. Such studies, often drawing on participant observation methods, address larger conceptual issues but provide more texture and nuance than cluster analysis. In their pure form, in-depth case studies may test general observations, hypotheses, concepts, and conclusions of broader paradigms by selecting a prototypical case and trying to disconfirm the general theory.

As noted earlier, September 11, 2001, turned global attention to relations between the Western world and the Muslim world. The latter includes more than fifty-six predominantly Muslim countries, plus numerous Muslim minority communities in Western Europe, North America, Asia, and Africa. Yet the focus on tensions there, especially by the media, tends to obscure the fact that pluralistic cultures may have evolved a variety of methods for conflict prevention, mediation, settlement, and even resolution. News analyses of conflict, sometimes done in a crisis mode, are not always the best gauge of realities on the ground, such as the peacekeeping efforts in pluralistic countries.

Values, Identities, and Civic Cultures

Two common concerns of the various approaches to conflict analysis and resolution are values and identities, and linkages and structures. Studies that focus on nation-states as the units of analysis may look at the relationship of values and identities to internal and external linkages and structures.[73]

The types of civic cultures and political values often examined by scholars include a culture's orientation toward the political community, authority and decisionmaking processes and structures, political implementation processes and structures, representation and participation in government, conflict resolution, scope of government, levels of government (including principles of centralization and decentralization), extra-system relations, and system propensity for transformation or change.[74] Orientations to time and perspectives on patterns of temporal sequencing are also key considerations in most cross-cultural studies.[75] Since dual calendars, for example, are a fact of life in the contemporary world, the interaction of solar and lunar cycles deserves more scrutiny than it has received.[76]

I have defined values and identities as follows:

> There is . . . general agreement that by values we mean preferences (in a situation of hypothetical choice), whether these preferences are instrumental (means) or end states (goals). Cultural values and/or national values refer to model patterns of preference which characterize broad segments of a population (whatever the range of deviation from such norms). By identities we mean the in group and out group ascriptions of labels or names to aggregations of people which may have social, political, or economic relevance.[77]

Empirical research in Africa suggests that identities, including situational identities, are much more subject to change than basic core values.[78] Furthermore, situational identities (especially in the African context) comprise a spectrum of at least ten major context categories or situations delineated by locational, clan, ethnic, subnational, ethnolinguistic or larger religious, national, regional, and racial factors.[79]

The Salience of Religion

The relationship of religion to values and identities is salient in each of the major approaches to conflict analysis and conflict resolution. Huntington writes: "Religion is a central defining characteristic of civilizations."[80] The Tofflers' three-wave model clearly identifies secularization as part of the transition from premodern to modern and leaves open the question of re-sacralization in postmodern societies. Juergensmeyer's paradigm and case studies center on the tensions between secular and religious elements in a variety of civilizational contexts. And chaos theory models tend to count religion among the factors that may contribute to the anarchy of systems transformations.

The civilizational clash that Huntington sees (and that is the basis of Osama bin Laden's message) is especially relevant to an assessment of the cultural contours of the world in the wake of September 11 and to an analysis of states that may be divided along religio-civilizational lines. For

Huntington, the most important objective element defining civilizations (that is, cultural identities) is usually religion.[81] Those identities, he argues, "are shaping the patterns of cohesion, disintegration, and conflict in the post–Cold War world."[82] For example, "the West's universalist pretensions increasingly bring it into conflict with other civilizations, most seriously with Islam and China."[83]

One drawback of Huntington's analysis is that it overlooks mechanisms for conflict resolution developed over time by religious identity groups and religions.[84] These may range from interfaith councils to localized roles for elders or community leaders. Very few religiously mixed communities can afford to ignore the issue of interfaith dialogue and the need for regular mechanisms of conflict mediation.

The Idea of Democratic Federalism

Historically, democratic federalism evolved in part as a way of mediating and preventing conflict. The political structure of federalism (in the U.S. case) or even of confederalism (in the Swiss case) was instituted to accommodate the original ethnoreligious pluralism of the component states. Even within highly centralized states, the symbolism of federalism has been used to accommodate ethnoreligious identities (as in the former Soviet Union). Mature federalisms, such as the U.S. example, still find it necessary to reassess their components and civic culture under contemporary circumstances.[85]

The alternatives to federalism in pluralistic communities tend to take one of two forms: either a strong central authority (consisting of a single party or military establishment) or a tendency toward partition. Some sort of partition followed independence in virtually all of the colonial federations set up by the British or French in Africa, the Middle East, and Asia, but the systems failed.[86] This may have been due to the lack of federalist cultures in the metropolitan centers since Britain and France had long operated as highly centralized, unitary states. The postcolonial states were also fragile. One of the few postcolonial federations that did not collapse is Nigeria, but its collective experience since independence in 1960 has been marked by attempts at partition and the stresses of overcentralization.

The Importance of the Nigerian Case

Nigeria is key to assessing the basic arguments about the relationship of religion and civic culture to issues of conflict and conflict resolution within a democratic federalist framework. Moreover, the international community has both an academic and policy interest in the nature and stability of Nigerian federalism.[87]

The Nigerian case has clear implications for the Huntington and bin Laden argument, since it falls into the category of a "cleft" country—that is, one with a civilizational "fault line." As Huntington has pointed out:

> Societies united by ideology or historical circumstance but divided by civilization either come apart, as did the Soviet Union, Yugoslavia, and Bosnia, or are subjected to intense strain, as is the case with Ukraine, Nigeria, Sudan, India, Sri Lanka, and many others. . . .
>
> Cleft countries that territorially bestride the fault lines between civilizations face particular problems maintaining their unity. In Sudan, civil war has gone on for decades between the Muslim north and the largely Christian south. The same civilizational division has bedeviled Nigerian politics for a similar length of time, and stimulated one major war of secession plus coups, rioting, and other violence.[88]

Huntington also notes that Nigeria's size, resources, and location make it a core state within the African context and potentially within the Muslim world. However, its intercivilizational disunity, massive corruption, political instability, repressive government, and economic problems have severely limited its ability to perform this role.[89]

Nigeria stands as the demographic giant of Africa. As one of the major oil producers in the world, it has the potential to be an economic powerhouse. As a military force, Nigeria has participated in peacekeeping missions around the world. At the same time, its vast array of ethnolinguistic groups, which number between 250 and 400, pose an enormous challenge to the idea of unity with diversity. The following pages lay out the full dimensions of this challenge.

2

The Emergence of Democratic Federalism in Nigeria

Nigeria's political evolution from precolonial status to postindependence civilian regimes has been greatly influenced by a legacy of north-south regionalism and its geocultural zones (see table 2-1). The political structure that has emerged represents an attempt to accommodate diversity and facilitate conflict resolution.

The Legacy of North-South Regionalism

Between 1880 and 1905, most of Nigeria was conquered by the British, first in the south along the coast and later in the interior north, with headquarters in Lokoja. Between 1907 and 1914, the British set up native authorities throughout Northern Nigeria under a policy of indirect rule, utilizing preexisting political units for administrative purposes. Just as in Rhodesia, the British chose to rule the northern and southern regions as separate colonies. In 1912 they appointed Frederick Lugard governor of both the Protectorate of Northern Nigeria and the Colony and Protectorate of Southern Nigeria and in 1914 drew up plans to amalgamate the two (see map 2-1). However, it was not until 1946 that Nigerians from these two regions had much administrative or political contact. During the colonial period, a lieutenant governor in Kaduna (the new northern capital) administered the north, a lieutenant governor in Enugu administered the south, and a governor general sat in Lagos. Later, indirect rule also became the colonial policy in the south.

The British identified three distinct political and cultural components in Northern Nigeria: the Sokoto empire (sometimes referred to as the Fulani empire), the Borno empire (or Kanuri empire), and the "minorities" of the

Table 2-1. The Political Evolution of Nigeria: Selected Benchmark Events

Century or period	Event
Precolonial	
11th	Borno (in northeast) established as an Islamic state.
15th	Trans-Saharan trade links establish Hausa kingdoms in the north as nominally Muslim states.
Early 19th	Sokoto Caliphate and emirate states established in most of the far north (excluding Borno) by means of jihad.
Early 19th	Sokoto Caliphate wars with Yoruba states. Subsequent trade links with north and west, and Muslim links. Relative isolation of Middle Belt minority "traditional" cultures.
Mid- to late 19th	Christian missionary activity in west and coastal areas.
Colonial (indirect rule system)	
1880–1905	Most of Nigeria conquered by British.
1903	British conquest of northern Nigeria (including Sokoto Caliphate).
1912	Lord Lugard governor of northern Nigeria; sets up "indirect rule" system.
1914	Amalgamation of northern and southern Nigeria.
1946–60	Period of decolonization.
1950	Ibadan conference of northern and southern delegates.
1953	London conference regarding federal formula.
1957	Constitutional conference.
1959	First national election to set up independence government. Northern domination.
Independence, First Republic (1960–66), and aftermath	
October 1, 1960	Independence from Britain; north and east party alliance. Northerner (Balewa) becomes prime minister.
December 1964	First civilian-to-civilian national election.
January 15, 1966	Attempted coup; assassination of prime minister (Balewa), northern premier (Bello), and others. Countercoup brings Gowon to power.
1966–79	Military rule under Gowon (1966–75); Mohammed (1975–76; assassinated by Middle Belt officers, February 1976); Obasanjo (1976–79).
1967–70	Civil war.
1970–79	Reconstruction after the war and preparation for Second Republic.
1970s	Oil boom takes off.
Mid-1970s	Plans for new federal capital territory (Abuja).
Second Republic (1979–83) and aftermath	
1979	Election of northerner (Shagari) as president; north and east party alliance.
1983	Second civilian-to-civilian election: Shagari reelected.
December 31, 1983	Palace coup; Buhari and military rule.
August 1985	Babangida military coup against Buhari.
April 1990	Attempted coup against Babangida by Middle Belt (Christian) officers.
Aborted Third Republic (1993) and aftermath	
Fall 1992	Two-party system. Primary elections for president, annulled by Babangida.
June 12, 1993	National election, annulled by Babangida. Abiola (Yoruba Muslim) apparently elected president. Abiola jailed in 1994.

Table 2-1. The Political Evolution of Nigeria: Selected Benchmark Events (continued)

Century or period	Event
November 1993	New military government (Abacha).
1993–June 1998	Abacha military rule; Abacha dies in June 1998. Abiola dies in July 1998, on the eve of his release from jail.
Summer–fall 1998	Preparations for civilian rule (under General Abdulsalami), and local elections.
Spring 1999	National elections. Obasanjo elected president.
Fourth Republic: first term (1999–2003) and aftermath (2004+)	
May 5, 1999	Fourth Republic Constitution promulgated.
May 29, 1999	Obasanjo sworn in as president.
2000	Shari'a law established in Zamfara state, and subsequently in eleven other far northern states.
February and May 2000	Kaduna riots between Christians and Muslims over shari'a concerns.
October 2001	Kano demonstrations and street riots as United States attacks Taliban in Afghanistan.
2002	"Miss World riots" in Kaduna, between Christians and Muslims.
April 2003	Third civilian-to-civilian elections in Nigerian history for president and governors.
May 29, 2003	Obasanjo sworn in for second term as president.
Summer–fall 2003	Election tribunals hear petitions.
Spring 2004	Extensive ethnoreligious violence in Plateau State (with reprisal killings in Kano) and federal declaration of state of emergency in Plateau.
Spring, summer, and fall 2004	Petitions opposing presidential election undertake final hearings in Abuja appeals court.
2004	Parties and candidates prepare for 2007 presidential and state elections.
2005	National conference (National Political Reform Dialogue) in Abuja; preparations for census and party congresses.

Middle Belt. Clearly, the Sokoto Calphate, as the framework for the emirate states, was the largest single unit (see map 2-2). They also identified three such entities in the south: the Igbo-speaking areas of the east; the Yoruba-speaking states of the west, and various minorities in the midwest and east. In population, the Yoruba areas were the largest southern zone (map 2-3).

Thus the stage was set for the three major ethnolinguistic groups to dominate the national political landscape. Of the national population, the Hausa-Fulani accounted for about 30 percent, the Yoruba 20 percent, and the Igbo about 17 percent, for a total of 67 percent. Each of these ethnolinguistic groups was located primarily in a specific region, namely, the north, west, and east, respectively (map 2-4).

Map 2-1. Unification of Nigeria, 1914

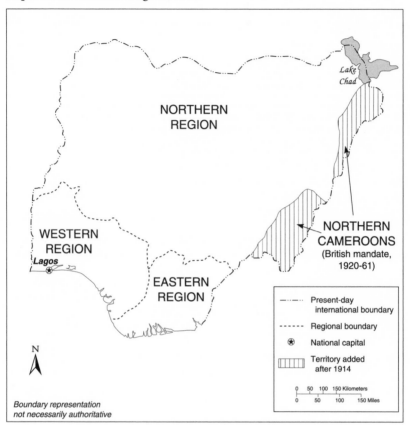

Source: Library of Congress.

During the period of decolonization (1946–60), British officials entered into constitutional disussions with representatives from the northern and southern regions (that is, the eastern and western provinces). At a national conference in Ibadan in 1950, delegates from both regions agreed to let regional assemblies have legislative powers and select some of their members to participate in a central House of Representatives in Lagos. The north insisted on equal representation with the south and proposed a formula for sharing ministerial positions. Elections were held in 1951–52 with political parties forming in each of the three regions. The northern region, with its predominantly Muslim population, prevailed (map 2-5).

A London conference in 1953 agreed on a federal formula for Nigeria that allowed residual powers to remain in the regions. At the Constitutional Con-

Map 2-2. The Sokoto Caliphate, Mid-Nineteenth Century

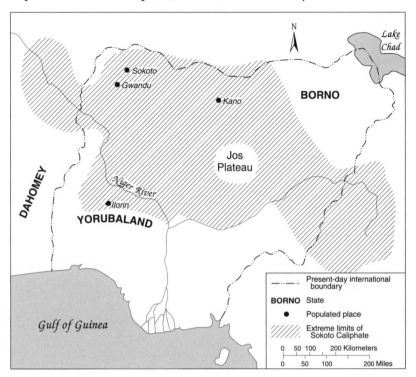

Source: Library of Congress.

ference of 1957, it was agreed that the east and west would become self-governing as soon as possible, and that the north would set its own date for self-government (1959).

Federal elections were held in 1959 to determine the composition of the national government. With independence on October 1, 1960, the major northern party won a plurality (143) of the 312 seats in the federal parliament and formed a governing coalition with the dominant party from the east, leaving the dominant party from the west as the opposition.

During the First Republic (1960–66), the dominant coalition continued to include major elements from the north and east. The civilian-to-civilian election of 1964 (with another in 1965) was flawed, but a north-east alliance appeared to prevail. The boycott and lack of involvement of major elements from the west contributed to the breakdown of the First Republic.[1]

On January 15, 1966, young military officers seized power in a bloody coup in which the major northern political leaders were assassinated. Senior officers

Map 2-3. Yorubaland, Eleventh to Nineteenth Centuries

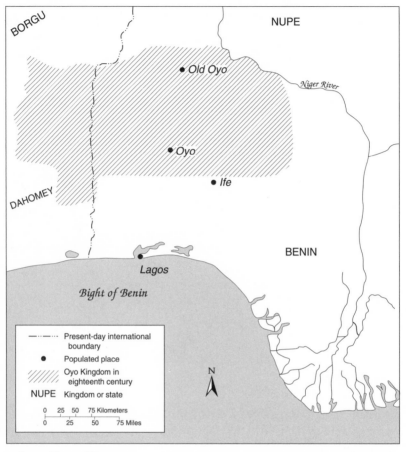

Source: Library of Congress.

then staged additional coups, and from 1967 to 1970 civil war raged between Biafra (in the east) and the other regions of Nigeria. In an attempt to redress the balance between "regions," twelve new states were created and given geographic designations (map 2-6). Subsequently, these twelve states were subdivided into nineteen and later thirty states (see maps 2-7 and 2-8).

During the Second Republic (1979–83), the dominant coalition again comprised major elements from the north and east. The civilian-to-civilian elections of August 1983 were filled with tension. Also again, turmoil in the southwest contributed to the military takeover on December 31, 1983.

During the transition to the (aborted) Third Republic in June 1993, a southwest-based coalition with significant northern linkages appeared to have

Map 2-4. Ethnic Distribution in Nigeria, Post-independence

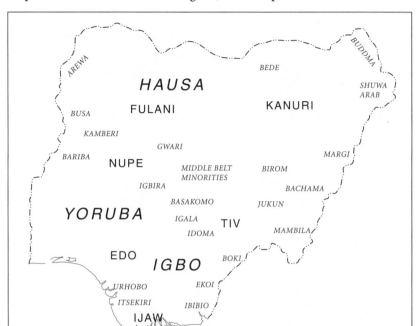

defeated the northern-southeast alignment of the two preceding republics. This alarmed many in several parts of Nigeria (especially minorities in the southeast), who purportedly threatened to secede. The military annulled the election before the official results were announced. After a brief appointed civilian interlude, the military, under General Sani Abacha, again took power. Figure 2-1 provides a summary of electoral patterns from 1959 to 1993.

Thus the "regions" of Nigeria had structural and political relations from the time of independence (1960) to the subsequent iteration of military rule in 1993. On October 1, 1995, General Abacha announced that a rotating "power-sharing" formula had been approved and that "six zones" would be designated the basis for the next transition to civilian rule. In 1996 General Abacha created six new states, bringing the total to the current thirty-six (see the state map in the introduction). All indications were that General Abacha intended to succeed himself as an elected civilian president. But in June 1998 he died of a heart attack, which some Nigerians characterized as a coup from heaven. This paved the way for a transition back to civilian rule under the Fourth Republic following elections in late 1998 and spring 1999.

Map 2-5. Muslim Population in Nigeria, 1952

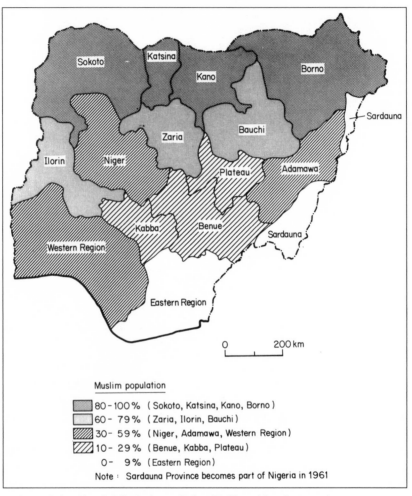

Source: Paden, *Ahmadu Bello, Sardauna of Sokoto* (Hodder and Stoughton, 1986).

Although the regime's new constitution made no mention of the former regions or the six geocultural zones, it mandated a three-tier federalism with thirty-six states and 774 local government authorities as the key units. Nineteen of those states were in the north and seventeen in the south, although the north-south distinction was not formally recognized in the constitution. Politically, however, the north-south reality and even the six geocultural zones were never far from the surface in the calculations of the emergent political parties.

Map 2-6. Nigeria's Twelve-State System, 1967

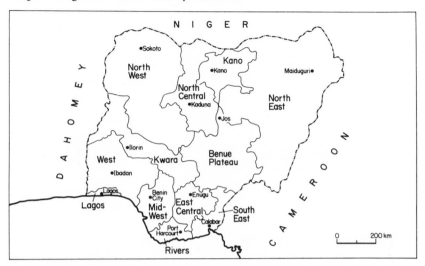

Source: Paden, *Ahmadu Bello, Sardauna of Sokoto* (Hodder and Stoughton, 1986).

The Idea of Geocultural Zones

The six zones envisioned by these parties were the emirate states, Borno State and its environs, the Middle Belt minorities, Yoruba states, Igbo states, and the southern minorities. These coincide with the original zones identified during the British colonial period, which became reified in part because of the indirect rule policy. Their distinctive cultural and historical characteristics have profoundly affected Nigerian efforts at unity and democratic rule.

The emirate states, for example, were part of the Sokoto Caliphate established in the nineteenth century. In the twentieth century they consolidated their northern presence, stretching from Sokoto in the west to Adamawa in the east, and then to Ilorin and Niger in the south. The emirates are, by definition, predominantly Muslim in their traditional political structure, with an emir, or equivalent, as symbolic head of the unit. Although Hausa tends to be their predominant language, the emirate states are a multilingual cluster in which Fulfulde, Yoruba, Nupe, and several minority languages are also spoken. These states often give vent to traditional rivalries (which drove Kano and Sokoto, into civil war in the 1890s). There are many occasions when the cluster does not act as a unified block. Yet it gives the sultan of Sokoto special authority in spiritual matters.[2]

Borno and environs in the northeastern corner of Nigeria constitute the oldest continuous Islamic community in sub-Saharan Africa, dating from the

Map 2-7. Nigeria's Nineteen-State System, 1976

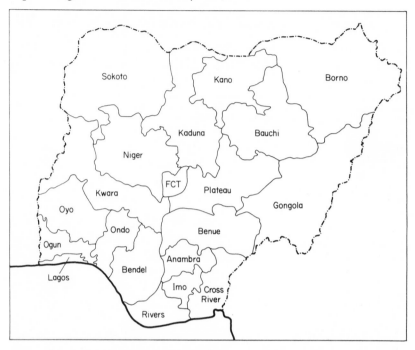

Source: Paden, *Ahmadu Bello, Sardauna of Sokoto* (Hodder and Stoughton, 1986).

eleventh century. Although Borno has the same sort of recognizable Muslim authority structures as Sokoto, Sokoto jihadists of the nineteenth century were unable to conquer it, and its "resistance to Sokoto" became part of the historical legacy. The delicate balance between Sokoto and Borno in the "far north" was an important feature of colonial rule and an important challenge in arriving at postindependence political coalitions. The dominant language group in Borno is Kanuri, although like Sokoto, Borno is home to a multilingual cluster whose lingua franca is becoming Hausa. Other northerners refer to those from Borno as Beriberi, or Bornawa.

The Middle Belt minorities in the "north" are a residual cluster consisting of a large number of smaller ethnolinguistic groups, many of which have historically resisted the large Muslim political powers (such as Sokoto and Borno) of the savanna and horse culture zones. Some of these minorities have hierarchically structured political systems, with leaders such as the *Aku Uku* of Wukari (Jukun), the *Och'Idoma* (Idoma), the *Atta* of Igala, and the *Atta* of Igbirra. Others—such as the Tiv, the Gbagyi (Gwari), the Dass area peoples,

Map 2-8. Nigeria's Thirty-State System, 1991–96

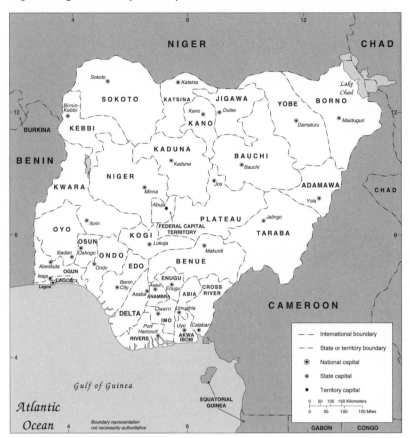

Source: Library of Congress.

the Ningi, and the Bachama—are segmental societies without hierarchical structures. In some of these societies (for example, the Tiv), British indirect rule led to the establishment of central authorities, such as the *Tor Tiv*. In the nineteenth century, these minorities were "traditional" in their religious beliefs, but over the twentieth century, they have been increasingly eroded by both Christian and Muslim groups.[3] Note too that Hausa is now more widely spoken among the Middle Belt minority groups.

In the southwest, the fifty or so traditional Yoruba states share a common linguistic heritage and a political culture of city-states headed by chiefs (*obas*) whose powers tend to be symbolic; decisionmaking is often vested in a council of representatives from the various lineages. A common myth traces their

Figure 2-1. Political Coalitions by Zone, 1959–83 and 1993

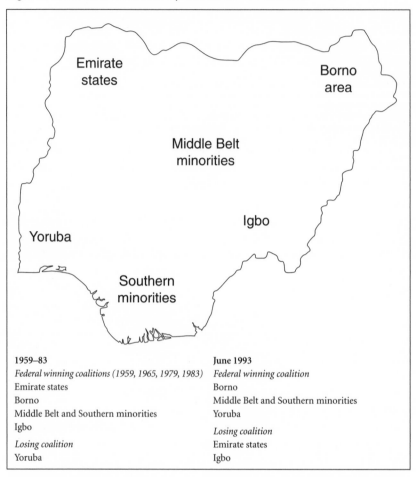

Emirate
states

Borno
area

Middle Belt
minorities

Igbo

Yoruba

Southern
minorities

1959–83	June 1993
Federal winning coalitions (1959, 1965, 1979, 1983)	*Federal winning coalition*
Emirate states	Borno
Borno	Middle Belt and Southern minorities
Middle Belt and Southern minorities	Yoruba
Igbo	
	Losing coalition
Losing coalition	Emirate states
Yoruba	Igbo

origin back to Ile Ife, and much of their cosmology is similar. In the eighteenth century, many Yoruba city-states (except the Ijebu) were loosely united under Old Oyo. They were later split into four states (Oyo, Egba, Ketu, and Jebu). By 1850, after the Sokoto conquest of Ilorin, four new states emerged (Ibadan, Ilesha, Ife, and Ekiti Parapo). With the British conquest, more fragmentation occurred. A certain amount of pan-Yoruba sentiment existed, which was heightened in the independence period by the outsider role of the dominant political factions, at least until the period of the Fourth Republic. The Yoruba states are about half Muslim and half Christian, with strong traditional elements permeating both faiths. Moreover, there have been close intrafamily ties between Christian and Muslim adherents (see chapter 5). The southwest city-state of Abeokuta (Ogun state) gained attention in the 1993 presidential elections, later annulled, as it was the home of the apparent winner (Abiola). The successful presidential candidate in 1999 and 2003 (Obasanjo) was also from Abeokuta.

The emirate state of Ilorin (in the "north") is predominantly Yoruba, although its history of Fulani emirs creates an important overlap in zones. With a strong legacy of Muslim culture, Ilorin (Kwara State) is northern, yet it is also linked to the southwest cultures of the Yoruba.

In the southeast, the Igbo states share a common linguistic identity and a political culture based on decentralized village structures (including age-grade and gender-grade associations). There are numerous locational identities, but the important descriptors are extended families and clan groupings. An important distinction between Onitsha Igbos and others emerged during the twentieth century, although almost all areas came to be associated with Christianity as a result of missionary activity. During the independence era, many of the Igbo political factions associated themselves with dominant groups in the north and hence have been part of governing coalitions. The Biafra secession movement and Nigerian civil war of 1967–70 have underscored the ambiguity of Igbo participation in Nigerian political life.

The cluster of southern minorities forming the residual zone includes large ethnolinguistic groups such as the Edo of Benin, with its powerful history along the Guinea coast, as well as a large number of midwestern and eastern groups, such as the Ibibio, Efik, Ijaw, Itsekiri, and Ogoni. These coastal areas have become Christian to a large extent, although strong traditional cultures persist. Politically, such groups have often been suspicious of their larger southern neighbors (Yoruba and Igbo), and many find themselves in coalition with northern political partners. Much of the oil-producing area is located within this minorities cluster. A significant amount of the violence during the Fourth Republic has been between its groups (for example, Ijaw and Itsekiri), usually over claims to land and administrative status.

The Challenges of Political Structure

The postindependence struggle to find a political formula to deal with such diversity has included attempts at partition, especially during the civil war, in 1967–70.[4] It has also included interludes of centralized military rule (in 1966–79 and 1983–99). Finally, the enduring theme has been experiments in democratic federalism (in 1960–66, 1979–83, and 1999–2005+).

The idea of democratic federalism raises questions about the nature of the component units best suited to Nigeria's realities and the relations between local, state, and federal authorities. The First Republic (1960–66) was by and large a loose federation of three (later four) geocultural components: the north, the east, and the west, with the midwest carved out of the latter. The north prevailed in terms of population and political power. Clearly, there were unresolved issues, including unit balance, the idea of parliamentary government with a presidential component, and regional-center relations. Also, the major challenge turned out to be accommodating cultural diversity, since the country's sociocultural groups had almost no experience working together within a common political framework. A military interlude and the civil war brought an end to this experiment.

The voluntary handover by the military to civilians in 1979, which marked the institution of the Second Republic and a presidential federal system, coincided with the peak of the oil boom. The pressures for centralization in an oil economy were extreme, and the state-center relations were so ill defined that states felt they could mortgage their futures on what seemed to be an endless source of oil revenues. A new federal capital was established in Abuja, at the geographic center of Nigeria, in an attempt to symbolize the idea of equal access to power and revenues. Yet there were few constraints on individual corruption. When oil markets fell and the entire country became overextended, the military again stepped in, launching a senior-level bloodless coup on December 31, 1983, led by General Muhammadu Buhari. This coup was less about "religion" (since the key actors were all Muslim) than about putting a halt to the tidal wave of corruption. In General Muhammadu Buhari's view, however, corruption and injustice were moral issues. Buhari was removed from office in August1985 by General Ibrahim Babangida, who ruled until the summer of 1993, when he handed power to an interim government. In the fall, however, General Sani Abacha took control.

General Babangida's attempt at democratic federalism in 1992–93 included scheduled elections, which were intended to set up a Third Republic. When the election results were annulled in June 1993, a political crisis ensued, and after a brief hiatus the military reasserted itself. The Third Republic was stillborn.

In the 1998–99 attempt to set up a Fourth Republic following the death of Abacha and national elections, the government announced a new constitution, again based on a U.S. presidential federal model. Then in 1999–2003 it moved forward with a number of experiments in democratic federalism. Democratic federalism was challenged during this period by the demands of oil-producing states for a greater share of federal revenues, the establishment

Map 2-9. Nigerian States with Shari'a Law, 2000

in the twelve northern (predominantly Muslim) states of Islamic law (shari'a) in the criminal domain, and the question of regional and religious balance at the presidential level (map 2-9). However, the real test of this Fourth Republic came in April 2003, when civilian-to-civilian elections were held for only the third time in Nigerian history.[5]

Since then, the burning question has been whether legal court challenges to the results (by the All Nigeria People's Party, ANPP) would prevail over other forms of protest. The federal court in Abuja heard the cases in May and June 2004. Results have been appealed to the Nigerian Supreme Court. Court challenges continued until the final ruling, July 1, 2005.[6]

With the reestablishment of shari'a law in the far north plus the global uncertainties stemming from the terrorist attacks of September 11, 2001, and subsequent events, some wonder what the future holds for Nigeria. Will it become a "failed state," moving perhaps toward military take-over, partition, or partial collapse of authority in some regions? Such concerns have focused attention on the large and diverse Muslim community in Nigeria. This comes at a time when the Nigerian Muslim community (*ummah*) is more informed about global trends and events, when classical documents (such as the Qur'an and Hadith) are accessible in vernacular languages, and when Muslim communities worldwide are experiencing a fundamental "reformation." The theory that a "clash of civilizations" is in progress or could occur seems worthy of reexamination, not least because of the al Qaeda challenge to the West.

Muslim Civic Culture and Conflict Resolution

The exact boundaries of culture and religion in Nigeria, although hotly debated, seem less critical in overview than the broad patterns of belief of those who identify as Muslims. Historically, the basic criteria for Muslim identity in Nigeria were the declaration of faith and commitment to the cycle of prayers. Today, however, the debates over the nature of "real Islam" (that is, without cultural contamination) extend into the realm of law and civic culture, given the experiment of democratic federalism.

Since democratic federalism implies an active involvement of civil society, its future in Nigeria depends in part on the nature of the Muslim community and perspectives on civic culture. That is to say, federalism requires political balance between states' rights and central authority; hence grassroots orientations to community, authority, and justice will affect the experiment with democratic federalism.

Nigeria's situation is clearly critical. The alternative of conflict and violence is always close to the surface. Between 1999 and 2003, 10,000 Nigerians reportedly died in one of the world's worst cases of intercommunal violence during this period. Then the government's report of October 2004 counted nearly 54,000 dead in Plateau State alone between 1999 and 2004, which suggests that the violence may be much greater than previously reported.[7] For this and other reasons outlined earlier, Nigeria is an important case in which to study whether diverse social and civic values can be accommodated in a democratic sovereign state. The basic question that needs to be explored is whether cultural or other approaches to conflict mediation or resolution might allow for a transition to a more stable national system, or whether Nigeria is headed for failure, with partition or military dictatorship around the corner.

Part II

Nigerian Muslim Identities and Civic Cultures

3

Variations in Muslim
Identities and Values

As argued in the introduction, the relationship between religious identities and orientations toward authority, community, change (or transformation), law, justice, and conflict resolution helps shape the dynamics of a national civil society. Nationhood, in the sense of a defined independent political community, often derives coherence and momentum from the interaction and transformation of component identities and values.[1] Since independence (1960), Nigeria's search for identity has experimented with subnational regionalism, partition (and consequent civil war), centralized federalism, military centralism, preparations for a three-tier civilian federalism (federal, state, local), and the actual transition to a Fourth Republic. These developments have occurred within a potentially significant transnational regionalism (Economic Community of West African States, ECOWAS). The ways in which community, authority, and processes of change or transition are perceived and articulated in Nigeria's Muslim community are summarized in chapter 6. The emphasis here is on the major subcategories of religious identity in that community.

For potential leaders and their constituencies alike, the quest for leadership in Nigeria has revolved around identity and political values. In part, the political culture, especially in the predominantly Muslim areas, has involved a sense of the potential for the transformation of society. The question of special interest here is what shape and direction such a transformation might take in view of the contours or parameters of subreligious identity in the Nigerian Muslim community. Symbols and the perception of symbols are at least as important to such an analysis as actual programs and strategies of transformation by leaders and potential leaders. It is also essential to consider the

Table 3-1. Nigerian Religious Identity Patterns by State (Estimated)

State	Capital	Religious patterns
Abia[a]	Umuahia	Christian
Adamawa	Yola	Muslim
Akwa Ibom	Uyo	Christian
Anambra[a]	Akwa	Christian
Bauchi	Bauchi	Muslim
Bayelsa[b]	Yenegoa	Christian
Benue	Makurdi	Mixed
Borno	Maiduguri	Muslim
Cross River	Calabar	Christian
Delta[a]	Asaba	Christian
Ebonyi[b]	Abakaliki	Christian
Edo	Benin City	Christian
Ekiti[b]	Ado-Ekiti	Christian
Enugu	Enugu	Christian
Gombe[b]	Gombe	Muslim
Imo	Owerri	Christian
Jigawa[a]	Dutse	Muslim
Kaduna	Kaduna	Mixed
Kano	Kano	Muslim
Katsina	Katsina	Muslim
Kebbi[a]	Birnin-Kebbi	Muslim
Kogi[a]	Lokoja	Mixed
Kwara	Ilorin	Mixed
Nasarawa[b]	Lafia	Mixed
Niger	Minna	Muslim
Lagos	Lagos	Mixed
Ogun	Abeokuta	Mixed
Ondo	Akure	Christian
Osun[a]	Oshogbo	Mixed
Oyo	Ibadan	Mixed
Plateau	Jos	Mixed
Rivers	Port Harcourt	Christian
Sokoto	Sokoto	Muslim
Taraba[a]	Jalingo	Mixed
Yobe[a]	Damaturu	Muslim
Zamfara[b]	Gusau	Muslim
Federal Capital Territory	Abuja	Mixed

a. New state 1991.
b. New state 1996.

intergenerational changes that have resulted from various social disruptions, as well as the larger regional or global context.

Applying the concept of jurisdictional levels (or contexts) to variations within and between different levels and scales of community, one may distinguish between identity and value patterns at the (1) global (or transregional), (2) regional, (3) national, (4) subnational, (5) local, and (6) individual (or family) levels. Table 3-1 shows some of Nigeria's religious identity patterns by subnational states. The parameters of these levels have changed significantly over time. Indeed, many contemporary political identities and values in the Muslim community refer to colonial periods before the creation of the Nigerian state. As noted in chapter 2, the Muslim patterns are dominant in the far north (in the emirates and Borno), with mixed patterns in the Middle Belt, the southwest Yoruba area.

Supranational or transregional identities and links are an important aspect of the way Nigerian Muslims have adapted to the contemporary world. Historically, the links were with West Africa, trans-Sahara, or trans-Sudan. Since the 1970s, they have become more global, and the oil revenues have allowed for extensive links with pilgrimage sites. Internet technology and expanding transportation facilities of the mid-1990s have made these linkages even more widely available.

In Nigeria, as elsewhere, determining "who is a Muslim" is often more than a matter of self-ascription, although self-ascription has been the basis for analysis in this study. During the early nineteenth century, the leaders of *jihad* defined the Habe (Hausa) rulers as non-Muslims, backsliders, or syncretists, even though some of the Habe emirates had been nominally Muslim since the late fifteenth century. The purification movement associated with Usman Dan Fodio has set a Nigerian precedent for claiming that rulers may be considered "non-Muslim" if they are "unjust," even though the rulers may consider themselves Muslims.[2]

Also, since about 1970 there has been a tendency for specific movements or factions within the Muslim community to regard those outside of their group to be non-Muslim (*kafirai*). The charges and countercharges of such groups are partly situational and have changed over time. The tendency in some Muslim groups is to regard those in power as "bad Muslims" or even non-Muslims, although this is related to levels (or context) dynamics and may also change over time.[3]

With Muslim cultures spreading among non-Muslim communities in Nigeria, tolerance toward variations in Muslim culture and style has increased. Many are now willing to accept as a minimalist delineation of a Muslim anyone who (1) makes the declaration of faith and (2) prays in the prescribed manner. Since the 1980s, there has been a nationwide effort to adopt a big-tent definition of the Muslim community and to welcome anyone who makes a genuine effort to self-identify as a Muslim. Nigeria's Muslim community can be divided into four categories of subidentity, which may affect the variations in political values: (1) the sufi brotherhoods, (2) the anti-innovation legalists, (3) traditional ethnic and locational identities, and (4) caliphal/Madina model identities.

The Sufi Brotherhoods

In the nineteenth century, Qadiriyya brotherhood affiliation became part of the identity of the Sokoto caliphal leadership.[4] In the two decades after the death of Usman dan Fodio (1817), Umar Futi and his followers spread the Tijaniyya brotherhood across what came to be Northern Nigeria.[5] Thus the Qadiriyya and the Tijaniyya became the two major sufi brotherhoods in the contemporary northern region, especially in the caliphal areas. By contrast, Borno's leaders and scholars, who had been Muslim for almost a thousand years, were not affiliated with sufi brotherhoods.

During the twentieth century, the Tijaniyya spread extensively in Kano, the commercial and industrial capital of the north. Because their social networks extended out of Kano through the long-distance Hausa trading system, the Tijaniyya spread throughout Nigeria (including Ibadan) and, indeed, throughout West Africa.[6]

Subsequently, a reformed version of Tijaniyya that accommodated many of the modernizations of the post–World War II era emerged. This reformed branch was associated with the leadership of Shaykh Ibrahim Niass of Kao-lack, Senegal, but had its Nigerian base in Kano, under the leadership of Emir Muhammad Sanusi, Tijjani Usman, and others.[7] The spread of the reformed Tijaniyya was due in part to charismatic leadership and in part to the growing transportation networks emerging at that time, plus the use of the vernacular. The Qadiriyya too experienced some reforms associated with Shaykh Nasiru Kabara of Kano. Students from throughout Nigeria would come to Kano to study in his schools and libraries.

In the period leading to independence (1949–60) and immediately after (1960–66), the sufi brotherhoods were the major vehicles for religious identity and values. The system of social networks (*zawiya*) allowed for the broad expansion of the Muslim community and facilitated interethnic contact and mixing. In many cases, these networks blended cultural values with indigenous African traditions and were generally tolerant of diversity. The ultimate legitimacy was the mystical experience itself rather than any legal list of do's and don't's.[8]

For historical reasons beyond the scope of this chapter, the reformed Tijaniyya came to be considered antiestablishment (often anti-Sokoto). In the political realm, the leadership of Aminu Kano identified the Tijaniyya brotherhood, which now had a large mass following, with the progressive opposition political party (Northern Elements Progressive Union, NEPU). While there was some tension between the reformed Tijaniyya and the Qadiriyya, these identity issues caused no major political disruption. In general, sufi brotherhood affiliation was a personal rather than a public matter.

By 1963–64, however, tensions did develop between the brotherhoods and the emerging base of political power in Kaduna, under the leadership of Ahmadu Bello. Plans to set up umbrella organizations of Muslim leaders in the north to accommodate the split between brotherhood members and non-brotherhood Muslims were brought to a halt by the coup of January 1966, which resulted in the formal dismantling of the northern region.

During the period of the First Republic (1960–66), another trend became noticeable: some Muslim scholars—notably the grand khadi of Northern Nigeria, Abubakar Gummi—began challenging the whole concept of sufi brotherhoods.[9] In time, it would take organizational form in youth movements in Hausa named after the Hausa version of Usman dan Fodio's book, *Ihiyaus Sunnah wa Ikhmadul Bidi'ah* (that is, "In favor of Sunna and against innovation"), which came to be abbreviated as *Izala*.

With the oil boom of the 1970s, Nigerian educational opportunities changed dramatically, and many of the younger generation became less interested in brotherhood affiliation than in getting back to the basics of the Qur'an, Sunna, and Hadith. While brotherhood affiliation was still significant, it was superseded in many instances by efforts to strengthen larger and more inclusive identities.

During the military period (1984–99) and in the Fourth Republic, the center for sufi brotherhood activities was Kano. Because of the nature of sufism and its local level of organization, it often served as an alternative to more establishment forms of religion, such as had emerged in Kaduna and Abuja. Sufi attitudes toward authority, community, and change can be summarized as follows:

—On the whole, the sufi brotherhoods did not respect constituted political authority but had strong loyalties to authorities within their particular brotherhoods. Most were detached from political life, except when brotherhood authority lines intersected with political authority lines. The key to legitimacy was direct experience of spiritual life, which transcended mundane affairs.

—Although the sufi brotherhoods include transnational and national forms of community organization, their most intense loyalties are to group or local communities of members; these are voluntary membership communities, open to new recruits.

—The key to change in the sufi brotherhoods is personal discipline and training, with less emphasis on social transformations; however, the reformed brotherhoods are often found among the modernizers and progressives.

The Anti-innovation Legalists

As already mentioned, Abubakar Gummi was an outstanding Arabist and legal scholar.[10] As a student, he was sent by the British to Khartoum for higher education. In 1955 he made his first pilgrimage, along with Ahmadu Bello, whom he had known in Sokoto. Gummi translated for Bello with King Sa'ud and over the next decade served as Bello's key liaison with the Saudi authorities. Shortly after independence, Gummi was appointed grand khadi in Northern Nigeria and as such was responsible for the shari'a legal system as applied in the region. His direct access to the larger Muslim world, especially through his contacts in Saudi Arabia, encouraged him to try to distinguish between "culture" and "religion" in the Nigerian context. Gummi taught many university students who went on to become civil servants and professionals in Northern Nigeria. Hence his influence became extensive in the modern sector.

Within the universities during the 1970s, the Muslim Students Society (MSS) transformed itself and gained widespread support, partly to offset the more radical Westernizing students and partly to reassert the Muslim identity of its own members by recognizing the differences between their local customs and more universal Islamic principles. This process emphasized a return to basics, that is, the Qur'an and Hadith, rather than inherited traditions associated with the Muslim sufi brotherhoods. Although Gummi lived in Kaduna, the major university in the north was Ahmadu Bello University in Zaria, about an hour away from Kaduna. Students from Zaria could easily commute to Kaduna for further lessons with Shaykh Gummi. Many of these students felt they did not have time for the supplemental prayers of the brotherhoods. Also, Gummi was preaching that many of the elements of the brotherhoods were innovations and hence "un-Islamic."

Among the urban youth of the new towns in the north, especially in cities without a brotherhood tradition (such as Jos and Kaduna), social organizations and teaching networks developed under the name of *Izala*.[11] While some of the *Izala* groups were directly influenced by Gummi, others set off in their own direction and followed their own agenda. This led to some confrontations between the *Izala* and the youth wings of the reformed brotherhoods, especially in Kano. The construction of large mosques in places like Kaduna or Abuja was often supported by donations from Kuwait or Saudi Arabia.

Gummi's impact on religious identity and values in Nigeria stemmed in part from his translation of and commentary on the Qur'an into the Hausa language. This provided Nigerians who did not understand Arabic or the foundations of Islamic belief their first direct access to the Qur'an. It also encouraged greater diversity of interpretation. Gummi was often attacked by other Muslims for his interpretations. His reply was always the same: "If you don't like my interpretation, do your own." Gummi was a regular feature on television, especially during the month of Ramadan when reading and commenting on the Qur'an (*tafsir*) became one of the highlights of the year. In these commentaries, he was often paired with Nasiru Kabara (reformed Qadiriyya) and Dahiru Bauchi or Ibrahim Saleh (reformed Tijaniyya). Thus in the 1970s and 1980s a wide television audience followed the historic debate between the brotherhood representatives and Gummi, who based his interpretations on the "Qur'an and Sunna only" and did not hesitate to openly call the brotherhoods innovations or, as already mentioned, imply that they were un-Islamic. Gummi saw his mission as getting Muslims back to basics through a direct reading and interpretation of the Qur'an.

Gummi's death in September 1992 marked the end of an era. His funeral was attended by the Nigerian head of state and many senior dignitaries. Even his adversaries credited him with having led an exemplary life of simplicity and courage. Some of the obituaries suggested that as many as 20 million copies of his interpretation of the Holy Qur'an in Hausa (*Alkur'ani Maigirma Zuwa Harshen Hausa*) had been sold or given away over the years.[12]

The basic pattern had been set for what may be termed a protestant reformation in Nigeria. The primacy of the Qur'an, now available in local languages, allowed individual religious leaders and local communities to arrive at their own interpretations of Islamic faith and belief. In some ways, this hardened the identity of the various Nigerian Muslim groups. After the death of Gummi, the *Izala* movement had no central leadership but rather reflected local leadership patterns, especially in the newer towns. This was the case even in Kaduna.

At the same time, the oil boom and increased opportunities to make the pilgrimage to Saudi Arabia brought Nigerian Muslims in closer contact with the wider world of Islam. Although Saudi religious authorities were initially suspicious of West African sufism—given their own *Wahhabi* traditions—over the decades they developed a clear tolerance for the diversity represented in West Africa in general, and Nigeria in particular.[13] Ibrahim Dasuki's accession to the sultanship of Sokoto further consolidated ties with the Saudis, and the sultan's palace in Sokoto began to take on the look and feel of a Gulf state palace.

The tension between the sufi brotherhoods and the anti-innovation legalists came down to the role of traditional culture in the definition of Islamic identity. To some extent, an increasing number of Nigerians felt more comfortable with the ethnoreligious traditions of their own communities than the transethnic identities of the sufis or *Izala*. There was a need for a West African rather than an Arab model of Islam, and it was clear that outside the Arab world, Muslim communities in Central, South, and Southeast Asia were making efforts to keep the spirit of Islam but allowing for variation in its cultural forms. Nigerian legalist orientations to authority, community, and change can be described as follows:

—The legalists have had a strong respect for constituted authority but have been fearless in criticizing such authority if they felt that moral or legal guidelines were breached. The ultimate authority is the Qur'an itself. However, the interpretation of the Qur'an is a matter for each person to pursue, and for scholars to openly debate.

—The anti-innovation legalists accept nation-state boundaries as appropriate units for international cooperation among Muslims (for example, through the Organization of the Islamic Conference, OIC) but may have a longer-term ideal of transition to a Qur'anic model "in God's time." Many agree that constituted levels of government are appropriate for the administration of a shari'a system, which is the ultimate definer of the community.

—The anti-innovation legalists may espouse changing "back to the future" using classical models, but they are often among the modernizers who oppose "custom" (that is, cultural "innovation" from an Islamic ideal) and seek ways to reconcile modern concepts of science and knowledge with Islamic principles through the use of "analogy" and "consensus."

Traditional Ethnic and Locational Identities

Additional clusters of Muslim communities exist in Borno and in the Middle Belt, which are northern but non-Hausa-Fulani groups and were not really part of the Sokoto Caliphate. Clearly, the former Sokoto caliphal system has greatly influenced the composition of the Nigerian Muslim community. Under the twenty-one states (later thirty and then thirty-six) of the national system, the caliphal areas included the eight states of Sokoto (later Sokoto, Kebbi, and then Zamfara), Katsina, Kano (later Kano and Jigawa), Bauchi, (later Bauchi and Gombe), Niger, Kaduna (including Zaria), Kwara (later Kwara and Kogi), and Gongola (later Adamawa and Taraba). Thus twelve of the subsequent thirty states—or fourteen of the current thirty-six states—have had some direct experience with the caliphal or emirate system stemming from the early nineteenth-century reformist movement of Usman dan Fodio.

Most of the national political leadership of Nigeria since independence has come from the emirate zone, both in the civilian periods (under Ahmadu Bello, Abubakar Tafawa Balewa, Shehu Shagari, and Atiku Abubakar) and in the military periods (under Murtala Muhammad, Shehu Musa Yar'Adua, Muhammadu Buhari, and Abdulsalami Abubakar). Although raised in the new section of metropolitan Kano, Sani Abacha is regarded as coming from a Borno family. Historically, two large geopolitical areas of present-day Nigeria resisted the jihad of the reformers and developed their own patterns of Muslim identity. These were Borno in the northeast (later divided into Borno and Yobe) and some of the Yoruba states in the southwest, including Oyo, Ogun, Osun, and Lagos. In addition, the Middle Belt of Nigeria—including such states as Kogi, Plateau (later divided into Nasarawa and Plateau), Benue, and the Federal Capital Territory at Abuja—has witnessed a significant number of Muslim conversions in the past several decades. The identity of the so-called Three-M groups (that is, Muslim, Middle Belt, and Minority) became highly visible between 1985 and 1993 because President Ibrahim Babangida was from that area. Marriage patterns are more mixed, and the ethnolinguistic diversity patterns are more extensive.[14]

As previously mentioned, Borno has one of the longest traditions of Muslim affiliation in all of Africa, dating back about a thousand years. Through much of the nineteenth and twentieth centuries, Borno was characterized by its insistence on autonomy from Sokoto and by its identification with non-brotherhood forms of Islam. The *shehu* of Borno (that is, traditional leader of Muslims in Borno) is usually ranked as second only to the sultan of Sokoto in national protocol situations.

Many in Borno still do not recognize that the reforms of Usman dan Fodio were central to the subsequent emergence of the Nigerian state. Sokoto's affiliation with Qadiriyya and Kano's with Tijaniyya (especially in the twentieth century) has led many Borno scholars and teachers to insist that they are simply basic Muslims, with no need for reform or brotherhoods. Borno has been at the crossroads of the east-west flows of people, goods, and ideas in the Sudanic corridor, especially West Africans making the pilgrimage to Mecca and Madina. Borno scholars and administrators regard themselves as extremely tolerant and sophisticated in matters of Islamic knowledge and identity.

While the predominant ethnolinguistic group in Borno is Kanuri, the common term "Beriberi" applies to anyone from Borno. Interethnic mixing has been high over the years. The Shuwa Arabs of Borno are the only group in Nigeria that actually use Arabic as their first language, but they are virtually indistinguishable from other Borno people in terms of culture and appearance.[15] Many of the non-Kanuri-speaking Muslim areas of Borno, such as Fika, have long traditions of autonomy and in modern political life pride themselves on being "minorities" and "independents." A number of distinguished northern civil servants have come from Fika (such as Adamu Fika) or from the areas around Potiskum (such as Adamu Ciroma and the late Liman Ciroma).

In short, Muslims in Borno are associated with an edge-of-the-desert (savanna) horse culture that over the centuries has developed its own "no-nonsense" style of life, which in many ways is more similar to some of the Sudanese varieties of subdesert culture than to the emirate structures of the Sokoto Caliphate to the west. Borno Muslims have long regarded Islam as the central organizing principle of their identity and value system. They came to play a greater role in regional and national affairs in the 1980s and 1990s (for example, Baba Gana Kingibe was a vice presidential candidate in 1993), but on the religious front, no one in the Nigerian Muslim community would make the political mistake of assuming that Sokoto religious leadership could speak for Borno religious leadership.

The Yoruba-speaking areas of the southwest also have a history of resistance to Sokoto caliphal domination. Many of the towns in northern Yorubaland were formed to withstand the "Fulani invasion" of the nineteenth-century reform period. Kwara, or at least Ilorin, was a Yoruba-speaking area within the caliphal system, but the political axis from Ibadan to Lagos was resistant to the jihad. During the nineteenth and twentieth centuries, however, many of the Yoruba-speaking peoples in the areas now designated as Oyo, Ogun, Osun, and Lagos did convert to Islam. This was partly an expression of resistance to colonial incursion from the coast and partly the influence of the long-distance Muslim trading networks (via Kano, for instance).[16]

Yoruba patterns of religious identification in the twentieth century were mixed, and even members of the same extended family might be Muslim,

Christian, or traditionalist (see chapter 5). There seemed to be a high level of religious tolerance within families and localities. The city-state was generally regarded as the predominant factor establishing political identity, although this pattern may be changing as locational and ethnic identities are being transcended at the more inclusive levels of *ummah* identity, nationality, or both.

Because of the vigorous legacy of city-state identities among the Yoruba-speaking peoples, there has been no single Muslim leader who speaks for these states. On the contrary, various Muslim leaders in and between localities have asserted their leadership credentials. By reputation, some of the most distinguished Yoruba scholars are from Ilorin, but since this is part of the Sokoto caliphal network, other Muslim scholars and leaders have emerged, especially in Oyo (Ibadan) and Lagos. For example, the *Aare Musulmi* of Yorubaland (Alhaji Abdul Azeez Arisekola Alao) is based in Ibadan and is a significant business and political leader, with close ties to the traditional Muslim leaders and communities in Ibadan.

In Lagos, one of the most distinguished national leaders of the Muslim community is Alhaji Abdu-Lateef Adegbite, a lawyer and constitutional specialist by training. He is secretary of the Nigerian Supreme Council for Islamic Affairs (whose president is the sultan of Sokoto and whose vice president is the shehu of Borno). Hence he is seen as a representative of Yoruba Muslims at the national level.

Unlike the northern Muslim communities (in the Sokoto Caliphate or in Borno), the Yoruba-speaking Muslim communities have a long tradition of locality identities that are unlikely to produce a "Yoruba Muslim spokesman." As in the Hausa-speaking areas, the Qur'an has been translated into Yoruba, although many Yoruba Muslims would probably prefer the various English editions.[17] Having Yoruba (and Western) culture included in the identities and values of the Muslim community makes this a significant case of cultural and religious mixing. Many of the Yoruba political and economic leaders who happen to be Muslim (such as Lateef Jakande or M. K. O. Abiola) tended to be associated with the progressive wings of the political spectrum.[18]

The remaining Muslim zone is the Middle Belt. The Muslim, Middle Belt, Minority (Three-M) ethnic and locational identity may be illustrated by families such as the Attah family of Igbirra, or by individuals such as former president Ibrahim Babangida. The late *Attah* of Igbirra was a distinguished Arabist but insisted that his considerable number of children (boys and girls) have a first-rate Western education. Many have gone on to become national leaders in public and private life, including Mahmud Attah, who was a presidential candidate in 2003 (he passed away in 2005 at the age of seventy). Muslims of this zone are noted for their commitment to national goals and their tolerant attitude toward other religious identity groups.

Also from the Middle Belt, former president Ibrahim Babangida (b. 1941) is of Gbagyi (Gwari) ethnolinguistic background. While in school, he was sent to live with the chief of Minna (in the Nupe-speaking area of Niger State), Alhaji Ahmadu Bahago. His military career put him at the heart of Nigerian politics in the 1970s, 1980s, and 1990s. In August 1985 he became president and commander-in-chief of the armed forces and subsequently presided over economic and political reforms intended to form a transition to the Third Republic. A controversy arose when he annulled the election results on June 12, 1993, and handed power over to an appointed interim government in August 1993, and it has persisted in the Fourth Republic.[19] Yet his capacity to work across locational, ethnic, and religious boundaries and his commitment to establishing Abuja (in the "center" of the country) as a functioning national capital are acknowledged by most observers. His tolerance of interreligious relations is symbolized by his marriage to Miriam Babangida, whose ethnolinguistic and religious background, as noted previously, is Igbo and Christian. In 2003 Babangida was regarded as a crucial political factor in the presidential elections, although he declined to endorse any particular candidate. Since then, he has been considered a factor in the maneuvering for position as a "northern Muslim" candidate in the presidential contest of 2007.

Because the Middle Belt Muslim community is rooted in a more pluralistic context of ethnic and religious diversity, it is closer to the Yoruba pattern of individual affiliation than the state-based Islam of the emirate states and Borno. This is so despite the fact that the Middle Belt was historically part of the north. In short, the distinctive cultural patterns in the emirate states, Yorubaland, Borno, and the Middle Belt continue to influence the forms and variations of identities in the Nigerian Muslim community. The orientations to authority, community, and change in these states are as follows:

—Traditional ethnic and locational identities include (1) the emirate culture, which is highly centralized and hierarchical but has a confederal or quasi-federal vision of authority in the postcaliphal era, that is, between different emirates (the role of the sultan is still emerging); (2) Borno, in which centralized authority resides in the person of the shehu (but with considerable respect for autonomous emirates) and otherwise in scholars; (3) the approximately fifty Yoruba city-states, each with considerable autonomy in terms of authority, but whose chiefs (including many Muslim chiefs) are more symbolic authorities than actual power brokers, although some general sense of rank exists between them and their rivalries are strong; and (4) Muslim, Middle Belt, Minorities authorities, which tend to be segmental rather than hierarchical or pyramidal and are much more influenced by Western authority patterns.

—Traditional ethnic and locational identities include savanna-zone communities (that is, the Sokoto system and Borno), which give low priority to ethnic identities and have a strong sense of broadly inclusive community descriptors; the rainforest and subsavanna-zone communities (for example, Yoruba states), which are more ethnically exclusive; and the Middle Belt Muslim communities, which share the external identity of being a residual zone with a variety of particular traditional types of communities, often small village-based societies.

—These identities changed enormously during the colonial and early independence periods. Initially, the savanna-zone groups such as Sokoto and Borno were resistant to "change" in the sense of Westernization, whereas coastal areas (for example, the Yoruba states) and the Middle Belt had introduced Western education and modernization. Since independence, however, the north has taken significant steps toward both modernization and an international standard of Muslim culture. Universities in the far north have taken the lead in basic research on their own history.

Caliphal/Madina Model Identities

Apart from historical, ethnic, or locational identities, a younger generation of Nigerian Muslims, often well educated and well traveled, has tried to come to grips with the question of what constitutes an ideal Islamic society. This is a nonaffiliational endeavor primarily in the form of academic expositions, debates in the Nigerian press, and postings on the Internet.

There is a fine line between Nigerian Muslims who would like to apply Islamic principles to contemporary Nigerian political life and those who try to identify what an ideal Islamic political system would look like. There is a more pronounced gap between those who reflect on the ideal nature of neoclassical Islamic systems in the contemporary world and those who feel that they should impose such systems on themselves and others. Nigerians tend to look to two sources for an ideal model: some draw their ideas and values from the Sokoto reformation period; others prefer to minimize the Sokoto experience and refer back directly to the prophet Muhammad, using the Madina model as the standard for designing an ideal system. Many Nigerian Muslims blend these two approaches.

Those who favor the Sokoto model argue that the founders of the Sokoto Caliphate were aware of the special circumstances in what was to become Northern Nigeria, namely, its indigenous cultures and realities. (As already mentioned, even the *Izala* movement takes its name from a book by Usman dan Fodio, who thus serves as a reference point for the "return to basics" approach.) The caliphal founders, it is pointed out, selected the balance most suitable and authentic to Nigeria's environment. There are many articulations of the Sokoto caliphal model, drawing on the spiritual, intellectual, and political efforts of such leaders as Usman dan Fodio, his brother Abdullahi, and his son Muhammad Bello.[20]

Many who have studied the Sokoto Caliphate are concerned with its contemporary relevance.[21] There have been many efforts to reprint the writings of the reformist leaders in Arabic, Hausa, and English. As the dialogue on these matters has shifted from a northern regional context to a national arena, the use of publications in English has increased dramatically.[22] Many of the investigations into the ideals and current relevance of the Sokoto Caliphate as well as the early Madina model are taking place at the major universities in today's Sokoto caliphal states, namely, Ahmadu Bello University (Zaria), Bayero University (Kano), and Usmanu Danfodiyo University (Sokoto). Although many of these teachers and students participate in Nigerian affairs in various ways, their classical training always creates a dynamic tension between the realities of the current Nigerian situation and the ideals of an earlier period.

The transnationalism of periods preceding the nation-state era has led many to question the relevance of the concept of "Nigeria" itself, although such speculation is tempered by the realization that in recent decades the Nigerian military has not dealt kindly with any challenge to the idea of the Nigerian state. Nor is a framework of democratic federalism antithetical to the possibility of a shari'a-based polity.

Also, in the shadowy world of dropouts or unemployed students that surrounds these three universities, a mix of idealism and desperation has on occasion ignited a confrontation with the police and military. In the spring of 1991, for instance, some of the Zaria followers of a fringe group burned a newspaper office in Katsina because of some allegedly offensive references. Some in the press and in government blamed the conflict on "Shi'ites" as a symbol of persons outside the boundaries of normal Muslim tolerance, since the basic predisposition of Nigerian Muslims has been to follow the Sunni way.

As for the so-called Shi'ites, some of whose leaders had been trained and financed in Iran, they appeared to relish the labels and symbols of reform or revolution. At the same time, they identified themselves as "Brothers" (*'yan brotha*, or *Ikhwan*) and are clearly in the broader Sunni tradition. They warned the establishment that some day pride and corruption would lead to destruction. Their youthful idealism combined with the desperation of poverty and "injustice" has produced a fringe of nonparticipation or withdrawal from public affairs, but with a propensity to protest in dramatic ways. The symbolism of such protests is amplified by the media and tends to intensify fear in many of the other Muslim (and non-Muslim) communities.

In general, the theorists in quest of an ideal Islamic polity in Nigeria have been part of the establishment and are cognizant of Nigerian realities. The reintroduction of shari'a in twelve northern states in 2000 (and thereafter) has intensified debate about what an ideal Islamic sociopolitical organization would look like in view of the political and national identities that have emerged in the Nigerian public domain since independence and their impact on the Muslim community. These issues are dealt with in chapter 6.

The caliphal/Madina orientations to authority, community, and change have the following traits:

—This model's identities are strongly rooted in classical models of authority. Authority concepts are based on moral and spiritual merit, in accordance with Qur'anic tradition. There is an uneasy relationship with contemporary secular authority, because the model draws on classical ideals for its standards.

—Caliphal/Madina model identities have a strong sense of *ummah*, or community of believers, but with due provision for trust (*amana*) relations with "People of the Book" and for tributary relations with "pagans" (*arna*). The modern national state follows a federalist system with local autonomy, especially for Muslim communities that may want to follow a shari'a model (see chapter 8), and treaty relations with non-Muslims. Sometimes the line between an ideal and a realistic state is not clear.

—Identity groups under this model believe Islamic education is the key to social and individual transformations. Ideas are often articulated in an international language (such as English), although many of the scholars are trilingual (in the vernacular, Arabic, and English) and highly educated. Some of the less educated supporters have used confrontation and public symbol management as a means of expressing their desire for change.

4

Emirate Civic Cultures

The Sokoto Caliphate, established in 1804 in what is now northern Nigeria, was one of the largest political entities in precolonial Africa. By the mid-nineteenth century, approximately thirty emirates had emerged within the caliphate. The British policy of indirect rule during the colonial period (1900–60) kept most of these emirates in place in terms of authority patterns and legal systems. As noted earlier, fourteen of the current thirty-six states in Nigeria have had direct experience with the emirate system, and "royal fathers" (emirs, or their equivalents) are very much part of the political and religious mix in contemporary Nigeria.[1]

This chapter provides a sense of the "ethnographic present" in the emirate states by examining the central tendencies in their orientations to time and destiny, community, authority, civic space, and conflict resolution during the early postindependence period (1960–66). This is before the cultural and political disruptions of military rule, the oil boom, and globalization made their impact on emirate behavior and beliefs. The period is well within the memories of many older citizens and is often referred to in comparisons with more recent turbulent times. Where appropriate, Hausa terms are used to indicate concepts, including abstract concepts, since Hausa is the lingua franca of the emirate states. These emirate patterns imply some role for the state in the administration of law and justice, although emirate civic cultures include a vibrant private sector as well.

Orientations to Time and Destiny

A sense of "time" is an important underlying dimension of emirate civic culture. In politics (as in life), "timing is everything." Frameworks in which event

70

times are calculated can affect larger issues of community identity, approaches to authority and decisionmaking, various perspectives on social change, processes of conflict resolution, and even matters of conflict retribution. Some of these cultural orientations to time are common to other Muslim societies and some specific to the Nigerian emirates.

The Dual Cycles of Calendrical Time

Emirate culture has a dual sense of calendrical time: solar and lunar. This is essentially a unilinear (as distinct from multilinear or curvilinear) concept in that the unit used to measure time is an interval along a time line, such as a day. However, it also reflects the nature-versus-culture dichotomy found in many societies.

Thus the solar calendar is arranged by seasons (*yanayi*), such as the time of cold (late December to mid-February, *lokacin sanyi* or *hunturu*), the time of heat (mid-February to early May, *lokacin zafi* or *bazara*), the time of rain (May to September, *lokacin damina*), and the time of harvest (mid-October to mid-December, *lokacin kaka*). These are the seasons of the sun and the agricultural cycle that follows from the patterns of sun and rain. Appropriately, springtime, before the rains begin, is regarded as a time of hunger, and fall harvest time as a time of plenty. April is sometimes the cruelest month, and political events during that month are often fraught with the potential for violence.

The lunar calendar, by contrast, relates to social and religious activities and is explicitly Islamic. Every phase of the moon is named after the event that takes place during that part of the lunar cycle. Thus certain activities take place during the so-named period, such as the month of pilgrimage (*locakin watan haji*), the month of fasting (*watan azumi*), the month celebrating the Birth of the Prophet (*watan mauladi*, or *watan haifuwar annabi*), or the month of the big festival (*watan babbar sallah*).

Although the lunar calendar had no official standing during the colonial and immediate postcolonial period, it was the basic yardstick for the indigenous political, cultural, and religious activities of the emirate communities. This calendar was sacred. Because it was approximately eleven days shorter than the solar calendar each year and the exact timing of each month depended upon the citing of the new moon, a conscious human effort was needed to interpret and mediate this calendar. The month of fasting (Ramadan), in particular, was a time for spiritual reflection and purification, and traditionally a time to spend evenings with respected teachers who systematically read and interpreted the Qur'an for their communities.

According to some contemporary emirate teachers (*mallams*), the Western calendar has no "Christian" basis. If anything, it refers to earlier pagan times (the months July and August are named after Roman emperors, and March after a Roman god). Hence its use should be discouraged. The general trend in postindependence emirate states, however, has been to insist on the use of a dual calendar, Western and Muslim, in public life.

The daily cycle is a blend of nature and culture in that the time prayers (religion) are said accords with the position of the sun (nature). The basic clock is set by this daily pattern, so it is not divided into equal units between the five cardinal markers but varies with the seasons.

This calendrical dualism reinforces a cosmological dualism between earthly matters (*duniya*) and religious matters (*addini*). Since mystical traditions (sufism) are also strong in the emirate cultures, the line between material and nonmaterial matters may be blurred. The mystical tradition also adds considerably to the number of religious events on the lunar calendar, such as the celebration of saints' birthdays, which increased as the local emirate cultures came into increasing contact with certain types of international Islamic movements.

The mystical traditions of "union with God" (*wusuli*), including nature, also allow for a nonlegalistic interpretation of the preexisting forms of religious experience found in the emirate state. These may be based on the Hausa *bori* traditions, the Yoruba pantheon of gods in Ilorin, or Nupe religion in Niger State. Thus what some legalists might term "syncretism," a blending of new and old sacred ideas, can be accommodated within the broader perspective that "all things come from God."

Although the legalists clearly take a different view of syncretism, the equivalents of harvest festivals do have the sanction of the mystical and customary tradition despite being omitted from the lunar calendar, because these events represent God's bounty. Singers and poets, who have an ambiguous status as teachers, are often the major voices of instruction on matters of local culture.

In the postindependence era, the emirate states have conferred coequal status on the Western solar calendar and the lunar calendar, even in the dating of newspapers. Also, religious holidays are now more standardized and legitimated. Although the English-speaking press is sometimes glaringly insensitive to the legitimacy of a dual calendrical system, at a national political level this has come to be accepted as part of the reality of Nigerian life. Because the lunar and solar calendars are both linear, the systems are basically compatible and congruent, in contrast to the more capricious or apparently random time systems adopted by other indigenous cultures in Nigeria. (For example, the Gbagyi, in the Middle Belt zone, believe in the reincarnation of the body across generations and hence reckon time in a sequential fashion rather than in intervals by generations.)

Cultural and Historical Time

In its historical sense, time implies a basic distinction between past, present, and future, with further distinctions in each of these categories. In addition, time consists of various normative and descriptive cycles (life cycles, political cycles) that are thought to provide an ordering of events.

In the emirate view, past historical time may relate to a particular condition or event (*lokaci*) or to a broad period (*zamani*). The former may refer to a time of hunger (*lokacin yunwa*), war (*lokacin yaki*), prayer (*lokacin sallah*), or fasting (*lokacin azumi*). It may also refer to cycles such as those in the life cycle: childhood (*lokacin yarinta*); youth, from the age of fifteen to thirty (*lokacin kuruziya*); adulthood, from thirty to sixty (*lokacin manyanta*); or old age, beyond sixty (*lokacin tsufa*).

The second use of past time (*zamani*) pertains to historical periods, which, in turn, may be seen as part of a larger pattern of time. Another concept of time past that is not used much locally relates to a pre-Islamic period of darkness or ignorance (*zamanin jahiliyya*), which in Nigeria is called the time of wars (*zamanin yake-yake*) or time of ignorance (*zamanin maguzawa*).

The major event in emirate culture separating periods is the time of Shehu Usman dan Fodio (*zamanin Shehu Usmanu dan Fodio*), which marked the beginning of the caliphal system in the early nineteenth century and supposedly lasted throughout the century. The next period is defined by the coming of the Europeans (*zamanin zuwan turawa*). The postindependence period is considered the time of self-government (*zamanin mulkin kai*), which obviously devolved into the time of military rule (*zamanin mulkin soja*).

The concept of "present" time may vary in length. The terms "now" (*zamanin yanzu*) and "today" (*zamanin yau*) are used interchangeably. The expression "son of today" (*dan yau*) or "son of the modern period" (*dan zamani*) generally refers to young people or to a person who "doesn't think straight." When used by older people, it denotes "changing times," meaning the Westernization or secularization of society, or general breakdown of values.

The future is a more complex concept than the past or present. In emirate culture, the future is in the hands of divine providence. Poets and singers such as Mamman Shata teach that no one brings changes except God (*babu mai zamani ban da Allah*). One can sing of the past and the present, but of the future, who knows? Thus historical time consists only of the past and present. The future may be planned but is something beyond anyone's control.

At the same time, folk custom treats knowing the future (*istahara*) as a legitimate religious art or science practiced by certain categories of learned persons. Since the future is under divine control, anyone who foretells the future is either doing it through a divine message, or has a supernatural touch. Knowledge of the future is revealed through prayer and recitations from the Holy Qur'an and arrives in a dream or sleep. Most emirate traditional leaders, as well as civilian or military leaders from this culture, would pay special attention to *istahara* religious advisers. (The Western equivalent might be astrologers, who advise leaders as to propitious timing.)

The future may also be communicated, according to common folk, through spirits or jinns. There are two types of jinns: white jinns (*farin al-jani*) and black jinns (*bakin al-jani*). White jinns are regarded as religious and therefore harmless entities and may come to a person in human form and talk during prayers. Black jinns, which are part of pre-Islamic Hausa culture (*bori*), can be perceived by men or women. The temporary touch of the black jinn puts people in a state of lunacy and will tell them what they want to know. A person in such a trance speaks and reports what the black jinn says.

Most learned emirate scholars frown on anything to do with jinns or the popular practice of seeing the future through "looking" (*duba*). This is done on the ground, with drawings made in certain ways. "Seeing the future" can also be done with signs and stars, a tradition that goes well beyond astrology to forms of "numerology" (*hisabi*, or *lisafi*). (The infamous cleric Maitatsine was reputedly skilled in these arts.)

The religious approaches to seeing the future—whether the use of prayers for guidance, jinns, astrology, or mystical formulas—and the general sense that the future is unknowable do not rule out future planning (*shiri don gobe*) or preparing for tomorrow, which can be done in the spirit of "God willing" (*in sha Allah*) rather than in the definite sense. There is a general sense that God helps those who help themselves (*Allah ya ce: tashi in taimakeka*); in other words, "Get up, and I will help you." This acts as a balance to the often-quoted expression, "God is here" (*Allah yana nan*). The notion of progress (*chi gaba*) or improvement (spiritual or material) entails aspects of human endeavor.

Probably no emirate zone leader has been without advisers who are knowledgeable in emirate concepts of "seeing the future." Some have a sufi background, others a folk wisdom background. Yet they balance the rational planners and Western-educated bureaucrats in important ways.

Personal Destiny

For the individual, the basic fact of life is that this world (*duniya*) is a preparation for the next world (*lahira*), with its heaven and hell. Thus a person's
actions, faith, and beliefs are critical determinants of the rewards or punishments in the next life. An individual's fate or destiny (*kaddara*) is determined
in every detail. Emirate culture has never stressed the potentially offsetting
beliefs in free will (*basira*) and intelligence (*fasaha*).

Yet the mystical tradition, with its reference to direct communication with
God, provides a balance to the strict legalist tradition, which measures actions
in terms of conformity to a prescribed code. The mystical tradition emphasizes the idea of intention (*anniya or niya*), which has implications for the
moral responsibility of individuals and hence, despite the larger context of a
belief in predestination, suggests individual responsibility and endeavor are
important for they mediate the larger cycles of predestination.

However, intentional suicide, even as an act of war during jihad, is never
condoned. The penalty for taking one's own life is certain condemnation to
hell. The human intentionality of suicide in terrorism events, for example, is
an unforgivable affront to divine providence, quite apart from the fact that
they may kill innocent women and children, which is also strictly forbidden.
A martyr (*ya yi shahada*) is one who dies at the hands of others for one's
faith. It is customary to bury a martyr at the place of death rather than return
the person to a family burial ground.[2]

Regardless of how one's life is finally judged, whether on the basis of intention or strict adherence to codes of behavior, and apart from the mediating
powers of mystical saints and teachers to intercede for individual salvation
(and in some cases to guarantee salvation), the timing of the transition from
this world to the next is always preordained. Thus there are no untimely
deaths in emirate culture, whether the death is caused by a car accident or an
assassin's bullet.[3]

Historical Destiny

Like Christianity and Judaism, Islam recognizes a linear notion of time, with
history moving toward a definite "end-of-the-world" point. This is different
from many other belief systems, including some indigenous to Nigerian cultures, which hold to a recycling concept of history or a more open-ended
notion of historical destiny.

As a result, emirate culture strongly believes that the end of the world is an
ever-present reality, and that the end of the century is a marker of special
salience to historical destiny. The Muslim century ending in 1882 produced

many local expectations in the Sokoto Caliphate, including the idea of an imminent *mahdi*. The century ending in November 1979 also produced important expectations in emirate culture (as it did in other parts of the Muslim world, one such expectation being the revolution in Iran).

Central to future historical time in emirate cultures as in other Muslim communities is the end of the world, or Day of Judgment (*ranar al kiyama*, *ran tashin duniya*, or *ranar hisabi*). Although no particular day has been identified as such, the unfolding of events, especially adverse events, signifies the world is coming to an end. At the time of the actual ending, everyone will die. Today, many followers of emirate religious thought hold that nuclear explosions are inevitable (and hence are not to be feared). It is also widely believed that such an event is likely to happen at the end of a Muslim "century." Since the centuries are named and have been assigned certain characteristics, many have speculated as to which century will usher in the Day of Judgment. Some had calculated that it would come at the end of the fourteenth century AH (that is, in 1979 CE), but since that time has come and gone, new dates are being proposed.

Again, the strong mystical tradition in emirate culture places great emphasis on an eschatological end of human time. The wide popularity of the reformed sufi brotherhoods in the 1950s, 1960s, and 1970s throughout the emirate areas was not unrelated to a sense of messianism, which would produce a *mahdi* and usher in the new era. (The crisis of the Maitatsine episodes in northern Nigeria during 1979 revolved around this symbolism.) The *mahdi* movement per se—that is, the Mahdist movement in Sudan in the late nineteenth century and continuing to the present time—has never had a large following in the emirate areas, partly because of the strength of the sufi brotherhoods and their claims that the *mahdi* would come from their ranks. According to the sufi brotherhoods, especially the Tijaniyya, their own reformers have dominated recent centuries and hence have co-opted the intermediary role at both the individual and societal level.

Partly in reaction to the sufi brotherhoods, new movements that emerged in the emirate areas in the 1970s and 1980s placed more reliance on fundamentals (see chapter 3). They argued that since the sufi brotherhoods all developed long after the time of the Prophet, they could be considered innovations and hence may not be worthy of support.

Each of these dimensions of time and destiny—whether calendrical, cultural, personal, or historical—gives clerics and scholars a central role in mediating issues peculiar to their time and place. In part, those issues relate to the fact that the Sokoto caliphal system—which is behind the idea of emirate states at present—was founded by Usman dan Fodio in the early nineteenth century. Others have to do with the area's relatively brief colonial experience under Britain (between 1900 and 1960); its large number of pre-Islamic cultures, whose "syncretistic" practices are considered a major problem by the Muslim clerics; Hausa agitation for more autonomy from Sokoto control (as reflected in the breaking away of Zamfara State from Sokoto in 1996); the strong tradition of mysticism, often in contention with the equally strong tradition of law; the rapid changes associated with the postindependence era, most notably those related to the civil war and the boom/bust oil economy; and the approach of the end of the Muslim century in November 1979, which was accompanied by severe droughts in the north and the rise of a variety of millenarian Muslim cults and syncretisms.

Orientations to Community

Again, some emirate concepts of community are general to the Muslim world and some are particular to northern Nigeria's Hausa or Fulani society, or both. This section examines some of those basic concepts along with the characteristics of local political communities, national or federal communities, and international communities.

Basic Concepts

The concept of community or people (*jama'a*) is similar to the concept of Muslim religious community (*ummah*), but the idea of peoplehood (*jama'a*) may refer to people of any community and may be used in a religious or non-religious sense. One may refer to people of a home (*jama'ar gida*), people of a ward (*jama'ar unguwa*), people of a village (*jama'ar kauye*), people of a town (*jama'ar gari*), people of a city (*jama'ar birni*), people of a state (*jama'ar jiha*), people of a nation (*jama'ar kasa*), people of Africa (*jama'ar Afrika*), or people of the world (*jama'ar duniya*).

When the concept of people is used in the sense of religious identity, it tends to refer to Muslims (*jama'ar Musulmi*) and hence is coterminous with the concept of Muslim religious community (*ummah*). Christians (*Kiristoci*) and so-called pagans (*arna,* but most often referred to by their local name, *Maguzawa*) are also religious communities. With the introduction of colonialism, the historic designation of Christians and Jews as People of the Book (*ahl kitab*) became common. The caliphal system of the nineteenth century adopted a classical approach to relations with other religious communities: a pact or agreement (*amana*) could be reached with Christians, whereas protection or war was the only course permitted with local non–People of the Book. In practice, after the jihad of the early nineteenth century, the animists (*maguzawa*) and Muslims lived in close contact, although the villages of the animists tended to be isolated.

A major issue in nineteenth-century emirate life was not relations with animists but the definition of a real Muslim and of apostasy, or backsliding, as local Muslim chiefs moved to accommodate pre-Islamic customs in their official political systems. Hence the practice of challenging other Muslims who might have a similar identity but different values became a central matter in intergroup relations.

During much of the colonial period, this issue was temporarily dormant, but in the late colonial and early independence periods—indeed up to the present—the question of intra-Muslim relations has been far more salient than relations between Muslims and animists, or between Muslims and Christians. The sufi brotherhoods became a means of incorporating new elements into the Muslim community, but since they often found it necessary to be flexible in their process of incorporation, they were open to charges of encouraging or allowing practices that were not truly Islamic. After the 1970s, a younger generation with a Western education and more extensive international perspectives challenged the sufi brotherhoods at their very core. These differences were often of a generational, class, and locational nature.

Because Islam was the establishment religion in the emirate states before, during, and after the colonial eras, relations with Christian and even animist groups were highly formalized and based on a set of guidelines that everyone understood. Most notably, Christian evangelization and proselytizing were not to occur among the Muslim populations. Proselytizing among animist populations, by both Christians and Muslims, was allowed and encouraged. Some tension between religious groups developed in the frontier zones (primarily Kaduna, Kwara, Bauchi, and Gongola), whereas in the core states such as Kano, Sokoto, and Katsina the issue arose only occasionally in the urban centers, where residential segregation by ethnoreligious identity tended to be the accepted solution.

While the sense of religious identity was well developed in the core emirate states, such identity was more of an issue in the frontier states, where there were often new converts to Islam and to Christianity. This fed back, even in the core states, into the historic question of who was a true Muslim.

The net result was a widespread pluralism of Muslim identity groups in step not only with the sufi brotherhood but also with local and family traditions.[4] What might have provided an overarching sense of caliphal community identity in the early days—that is, the position of the sultan of Sokoto—came to be associated with administrative appointments during the colonial period and took on more localized significance in the Sokoto emirate sub-system.

In the postcolonial period, various attempts were made to reconstruct the overarching symbols of community solidarity of the early caliphal period. As mentioned in chapter 3, some of these were legalistic in tone and others mystical or emotive. Still others saw no purpose in going back to an earlier form of Islamic community but opted for more contemporary, large-scale community systems that tied together an even broader set of Muslim constituencies.

Because of communication problems in the earlier periods and the difficulties surrounding centralized decisionmaking in a large caliphal system, a general pattern of decentralization developed that recognized the value of the larger Muslim community (based in Sokoto) yet saw the practical necessity of each local emirate having virtual sovereignty in most decisions. Both large and small emirates had the same types of powers, which meant the local emir was able to try cases of capital punishment within his jurisdiction. From a contemporary perspective, this appears to be a quasi-federal or even confederal system.

This quasi-federal system of communities within communities allowed clerics and intellectuals to play a particularly significant role: their primary responsibility was to define communities and the criteria of inclusion in communities, and they were in charge of written communication—in Arabic, Hausa, or Fulfulde—and liaison (or "gateways") between communities.

Local Political Communities

Apart from religious-based communities, those of political significance in terms of administration, law, or representation were kinship or family communities; clan or ethnolinguistic communities; neighborhood, ward, village, or district units, including, in some cases, occupational communities; the emirate communities; and the caliphal system itself.

Kinship had legal implications, and the family was seen as the basic building block of society's communities. Families were by definition "extended" and placed more emphasis on age distinctions (or on experience associated with generational distinctions) than on immediate blood ties. Marriage alliances were the simplest way of utilizing this system to foster community integration. Kinship or clan identities might be a basis for political representation on the emir's council of advisers, and some families had specific responsibilities for key political functions.

Ironically, in light of postcolonial patterns, the emirate's least significant criterion of community inclusion was ethnolinguistic identity. Certain languages might become lingua francas, but their utility was functional and not a basis for political organization, except perhaps in relation to non-Muslim groups. But within the Muslim community, language and ethnic differences were relegated to a low level of legal or political significance.

During the era of national politics, this lack of ethnic salience in emirate political culture caused some confusion on all sides, as Muslim communities tended to see non-Muslim ethnic groups as "non-Muslim" and non-Muslims tended to see Muslims as "ethnic." One of the reasons that emirate culture omitted ethnicity and language from the political framework was that scholars and teachers tended to be among the first classes in society to integrate, in terms of marriage and social networks. Ethnic identity was not irrelevant but was made less important by the long practice of intermarrying into the local populations so as to blur ethnic and kinship distinctions.

During colonial rule, a second level of government (that is, provincial, regional, and national) was built on top of the indigenous emirate structures. Initially, Northern Nigeria was a separate colonial unit, which (as mentioned previously) for all practical purposes was administered as three distinct subregions: the emirate states; Borno (which was Muslim, but not part of the emirate system); and the so-called Middle Belt, at the time, mostly non-Muslim. In the late colonial period after World War II, when the British made a concerted effort to bring the northern and southern regions under a single political system, the former increased in stature because of its primary role in national politics.

At the same time, part of the appeal of the "northern region" was its close association with the earlier caliphal system, which the colonial administration had dismantled in most functional respects. Within this northern regional system, the linkages between the emirate states, Borno, and the Middle Belt states were of crucial political importance. Emirate powers were transferred to the regional level and then reallocated down to the provincial level, so that a regional centralization began to take shape. Later, for all practical purposes these provincial units became the states of contemporary Nigeria.

Under Nigeria's postindependence federal system—which saw the number of component states increase from three to four, then to twelve, nineteen, twenty-one, thirty, and finally thirty-six—the key issue in the emirate zone was the relationship of traditional emirate communities to the evolving federal structures. For the most part, this has taken the form of military rule at the federal level versus civilian authority at the emirate level, with a continuing ambiguity as to the real exercise of authority under these circumstances, despite the formal removal of legislative and executive powers from the emirate level.

National or Federal Level

Because Nigeria's early political system was regional in nature, with strong indirect rule by powerful local communities, the emirate states have tended to see the federation of Nigeria as a set of identifiable communities whose relations are governed by treaties, written agreements, or constitutions, much in the same way that relations between religious communities were regulated by written treaties in earlier eras. Since each of these large communities has some religious identity, it is a natural extension to regard Nigeria at the federal level as a multireligious rather than secular community.

A constitution is considered a treaty that guarantees every community its rights. For many Nigerians, these rights still involve religious obligations and identities. Yet the concept of a nation-state as a community-of-communities is widely accepted in emirate political culture, the reason being that the nation-state characteristic of today's world is said to be a phase in history, and Nigeria has a place in this phase. Eventually, the world will come under one state, which will be an Islamic state and will put an end to the chaos of the world. This is part of the eschatological belief that Jesus (*Isa*) will come back to the world and fight alongside the Mahdi, and this will lead to the Day of Judgment. In short, all of the current communities are a preliminary phase to the period in world history that will climax in the end of the world. Hence there is a close relationship between the sense of community and the sense of historical time, which, as mentioned earlier, is said to be moving toward a preordained destiny.

International Communities

Since Nigeria is seen as a "nation of nations" and the ethnolinguistic aspects of this are not encouraged, the larger community of potential significance is the international Muslim community (*ummah*). Transnational migration is more regulated in today's era of national states, but the idea of migration from one political system under stress to another that might be more conducive to the discharge of religious obligations has a long and honored history in emirate culture.[5]

The idea of receiving those in need who may have migrated from ecologically distressed areas is also well established. During some of the recurrent droughts in Niger Republic, especially in the late 1970s, tens of thousands of refugees migrated to the cities in northern Nigeria looking for work and sustenance. These included not only Hausa, Tuareg, and Fulani refugees but also many others with a Muslim affiliation. (A number of the younger female family members were married into northern Nigerian families, thus creating new kinship alliances.)

Although international travel and communications became somewhat easier during the late colonial and early independence periods, travel and emigration came under more administrative restrictions. Populations from the emirate states that had settled in Saudi Arabia were being challenged on matters of citizenship and passports and visas. Borders between the West African states, particularly along the east-west savanna belt, were more tightly administered. The pilgrimage, while facilitating international exposure, was organized by national groupings. Hence the emirate states grew uncertain and uneasy about the nature of their international identities and obligations within the international Muslim community.

In general, Nigerian authorities at all levels accepted and endorsed the nation-state system. However, some of the major religious leaders in the emirate states were not even Nigerian. (Perhaps the most notable example was Ibrahim Niass of Senegal, leader of the Reformed Tijaniyya. Other religious leaders have come from throughout West Africa and Sudan.) Some of these ambiguities were addressed when Nigeria moved to a system of dual citizenship under its legal code.

Part of the function of emirate clerics and scholars, many of whom have studied abroad, has been to explore the nature of appropriate relations with the emerging international Muslim community. Alliances and identities sometimes formed in the process cut across traditional local identities and communities. The most noticeable clustering, at the international level, has been among those of a more legalistic persuasion. In sorting out culture from religion, they have found natural allies among the *Wahhabiyya* and similar groups in the Sunni Arab world. (The political and financial influence of individuals from Saudi Arabia in this process has been highly significant.)

Those following the sufi brotherhood path have forged closer ties with North Africa (the Tijaniyya, for example, have been especially drawn to Fez, Morocco, where the tomb of Ahmed Tijjani is located) and with other parts of the Arab world (the Qadiriyya, for instance, have strong ties with Iraq). With the collapse of the Soviet Union and the reemergence of sufi-based Islam in central Asia, the benefits of a nonestablishment, grassroots form of Muslim organization in withstanding abusive state power became obvious to all. Those more concerned about modernization found kindred spirits in

Egypt (or the United Kingdom). Many emirate businesspersons and even teachers preferred to spend the month of Ramadan in Cairo because of the more accommodating style of fasting by day and celebrating at night.

The emirate culture's historic bias toward Sunni rather than Shi'ite international relationships reflects its establishment nature and long association with Sunni schools of thought. At the same time, attempts to establish a political community governed by Islamic law (shari'a) within parts of the Shi'ite world (especially in Iran after 1979) has held a certain fascination for many younger scholars.

With increased international travel and telecommunications, the idea of African identity has also gained attention in the emirate states. Until recently, African identities tended to be associated with coastal Nigerians, who have often resisted a continental definition of Africa in favor of sub-Saharan racial definitions. This is a major issue dividing the emirate states and other cultural zones in Nigeria. The emirate states have consistently refused to give political significance to "race" in community formation, and many are profoundly embarrassed and troubled by the idea. Part of the process of Islamization in West Africa has brought the emirate states in close contact with North Africa and the Arab world, and the marriage and family patterns that have ensued have blurred many of the usual racial criteria behind social classificatory systems.

The concept of "humanity" as an ultimate community—that is, the community of the sons of Adam (and Eve) (*al-ummar 'yan Adam*) in a world in which animals and spirits also play their part—with all of its subdistinctions and subcommunities, is legitimated in the Qur'an. A common humanity provides the basic framework for interpreting the historical drama of the world as having a beginning, middle, and end. Younger emirate scholars are asking how their inherited emirate culture, with its religious identities and abiding concern for who is a good Muslim, might be translated into a global perspective. Having met Muslims of all varieties, from Chinese to American, from central Asian to Indonesian, they are beginning to reassess the classical congruence between Arab culture (including political culture) and a more globalized Islamic culture.

Finally, in an era of enormous scientific progress and shrinking global system, some from the Nigerian emirate cultures—especially those associated with universities in Kano, Sokoto, and Zaria—are calling for a complete reassessment of the fundamentals of Islam in a postmodern world.[6] As part of their legacy, the emirate states are still asking the basic identity question, What does it mean to be a Muslim? The context today, however, is global, not regional, national, or subnational.

The way to answer that question, it seems, is to link modern ideas to a reinterpretation of the Qur'an itself, that is, to an Islamic reformation. Because the Qur'an has become increasingly available in indigenous languages, and because of the diversity of local clerics, there are clear parallels to the Protestant Reformation in Europe in the sixteenth century, and to the range of denominations or schisms that emerged from it. In the emirate states since independence, this has been apparent in both the sufi and the legalistic communities.

Orientations to Authority and Decisionmaking

For the purposes of this discussion, authority is viewed in four dimensions: sovereignty and delegated authority, the consultative process, succession to authority and voting, and accountability. An underlying question of concern is the extent to which a concept of decentralized federalism (or proto-federalism) resides within emirate culture, which at first glance appears to be a highly centralized form of authority and decisionmaking.

Sovereignty and Delegated Authority

The emirate system of the nineteenth century had a centralized form of government that placed the ultimate decisionmaking power in the hands of one man, the emir (*sarki*). The emir was the final court of appeal in legal matters and the final authority in the decisionmaking processes. In addition, he was responsible for the implementation of policy and the bureaucratic apparatus of the state. The size of an emirate had no bearing on these powers, even when it came to administering the death penalty. The emirs were the ultimate authorities within their domains. For example, the emir of Kano, with its large population, had no jurisdiction over the ordinary people in nearby Kazaure emirate, with its tiny population and land size.

Under emirate sovereignty, the historic role of Sokoto allowed for appeals in certain types of matters: marriage, inheritance (a crucial issue), and succession to rulership. In return, Sokoto could ask the emirs to contribute money and material for defense purposes. In short, the formal structure of the caliphal system at times had the appearance of a confederal model, although in practice it was a federal model.

The emir delegated authority to territorial administrators, such as district heads (*hakimi*), village heads (*dagatai*), and ward heads (*masu unguwa*), as well as to various functional officials such as chief justice, defense minister, and treasury secretary. At the grassroots level, the ordinary people of a ward or village selected their local representative, and the emir confirmed this appointment.

The Consultative Process

Decisionmaking at all levels usually involved considerable consultation (*shura*), which was part of the required political culture of the emirate states. Learned men (*ulama*, or *mallamai*) played a key role in the consultation process.[7] In many cases, they acted as senior councilors and senators in providing a flow of information and opinion. Some senators were selected by the emir; others had a historic reason for regarding their participation as a kinship right. In all cases, the legitimacy of *ulama* rested with the perceptions of ordinary people, who respected (or did not respect) the knowledge and engagement of such persons in the spiritual, moral, or legal domain.

A regular council of mallams usually participated on an ad hoc basis. The mallams who regularly advised an emir would be the recognized leaders of any major organized sufi brotherhood community, the historic head of the mallams in an emirate, or the imams of the mosques. Sometimes they included a "hidden mallam" who was consulted in private but known to be honest, pious, and just. The reputation for consultation and the reputation of the learned men involved became part of the process for legitimating the emir.[8]

In addition to meeting with teachers and scholars, the emir usually consulted with the leaders of the community, such as businessmen, or with the heads of occupational guilds and various neighborhood communities. As part of the consultative process, the emir listened to all points of view and then tried to articulate a consensus position, if that was possible. The function of the teachers and scholars was to help guide the action in accordance with more abstract principles of jurisprudence and constitutional law, rather than to represent popular opinion. Yet some popular opinion was no doubt reflected in the nature of the consultative process, since the authority and reputation of teachers and scholars depended on their standing in their local communities. Also, learned advisers might articulate their opinions to the emir in written form. Such letters would form part of the emir's private archives and on his death might be burned or left to waste away.

The role of "hidden mallams" (*mallamin asiri*, or *mallamin sarki na asiri*, or *mallamin sarki na boye*) is particularly significant. These are reputedly fearless and very pious individuals who do not want any attachment to the palace or to the government. They may feel that all rulership is a corrupting process, and though willing to advise rulers on a take-it-or-leave-it basis, they do not want to be part of the formal process. No one knows how many hidden mallams there may be at any time, since the emir would not want people to know. Often an emir would visit the home of a hidden mallam at night in disguise. Many of these hidden mallams may look insignificant and appear extremely modest. Others may be key imams of traditional local mosques.

Succession to Authority and the Idea of Voting

In emirate political culture, leadership was based ideally on merit and competition, and leadership preparation was based on education and training. Leaders were chosen by representatives of major segments of society, through an indirect voting system. Leadership had to be acknowledged by the public before it became legitimate. Thus each emirate had a council of kingmakers (perhaps analogous to an electoral college) who at all times kept track of the potential candidates for succession and continued careful scrutiny until the death of an incumbent. In most cases, the kingmakers included the major clan heads, some key public officials, and some judicial leaders.

In most cases, the criteria used in assessing eligibility would include dynastic family ties and relationship to the deceased incumbent. This allowed for a broad pool of candidates. (In a few cases, the first son or some other heir apparent was selected in advance and sometimes designated *ciroma*, but this is the exception.) Beyond family considerations, the personality and performance of the candidates were assessed. Desired qualities might include being kind hearted, considerate, honest, sincere, religious, generous, and well educated. In short, the desired candidate was to be a cheerful person with a kind heart, especially in normal times, where there was no external threat. In general, the older the candidate, the better, since age was highly respected. The selection committee asked how the candidates related to the broader environment, the extended family, colleagues within the establishment, and people from outside the area.

Selectors were expected to tap local opinion on the candidates, especially the view of teachers and scholars and businessmen. (In contemporary situations, the views of Western-educated elites, that is, young educated professionals such as teachers, civil servants, doctors, and students, would also be sought.) Each constituency might have its own criteria, and the electoral college had to take these factors into consideration.

By contrast, at the local level, the village or ward head was usually selected by the people, through some direct system of voting. Formerly, elders would gather and vote by raising their hands. Later, candidates would be assembled by someone of higher authority. The elders would eliminate all except two or three, who would stand up and be placed at opposite ends of the voting area, whereupon people would signal their choice by moving behind their candidate.[9] Following a head count, whoever had the highest number of votes was presented to the emir for confirmation. The emir could overrule this decision only if he received complaints from the community or from the family of the deceased about some interference in the voting procedure. In extreme cases, the emir might send the name back to the elders and state his objection to the selected candidate in writing, on the grounds of some specific character flaw or past record. (In such cases, the emir summoned the chief imam to testify in the dispute.) In short, the emir had the right to refuse to turban a local leader, but in most cases this right was not utilized.

Also, the elders of a local community—usually influential mallams—provided an informal conduit of information between the local area and the emir. In short, those in government and in the mallam class had a vested interest in the stability and workability of the emirate system.

During the military rule of General Ibrahim Babangida (1985–93), as part of the intended "transition" to civilian rule, this system of open voting at the local level was applied nationally in an attempt to reduce voting fraud and increase the legitimacy of the results. Yet, as in more traditional times, the question arose as to who was eligible to vote in a local election, particularly at the village level where many of the young men may have left for long periods to work in the cities. Even challenges to candidacy might arise in this manner, if a migrant family member came back and insisted on being considered. In modern times, this affects the pool of eligible candidates and also the types of persons considered, since anyone with a Western education is likely to have moved away from the village.

People generally know who the legitimate sons (more recently called "indigenes") of a village are, even after several generations of migration to other countries. They rely on written records or the memory of mallams to indicate the elaborate kinship patterns that determine local voting rights and eligibility. In this way, the mallams provide a data bank about the members of the local community over the years.

Accountability

In the emirate system, an office is usually held for life. The leader provides continuity between generations and stability for the community. Can such a system invite abuse or corruption? There are several perceived checks and balances on the outright abuse of power. First, if the selection is handled well, this issue should not arise, particularly if selectors are aware that their own positions would be threatened in cases of such abuse. Second, the general emphasis on reputation and the pressures within the family are such that an abuse could be met with various forms of shunning, shame, or loss of legitimacy. Third, the administration of justice is so central to emirate purposes and administration that if the mallam class and principal judicial officers publicly opposed an emir, he might well be forced to abdicate. In short, the emir is not above the law. He is meant to administer the law. The law itself is what the learned men say it is, but with recourse to argumentation and discussion. Finally, the emir is responsible to God, and any abuse of office would meet with high penalties in the afterlife.

If a serious dispute over succession threatens to divide the entire community, or if the abuses get out of hand, it is possible to appeal to the sultan of Sokoto as a final recourse. In modern times, there have been many other sanctions, and a considerable number of emirs have been deposed for various reasons. The fact that Nigerian military governments had the final right to determine the succession and deposition of emirs brought traditional politics into the modern arena. General Abacha's deposition of the sultan of Sokoto (Ibrahim Dasuki) in March 1996 was unprecedented in independent Nigeria.

As already mentioned, learned men played a central role in this traditional emirate system of authority and decisionmaking, They were instrumental in selecting an emir, they judged the standards of his learning and knowledge, acted as his advisers, and could even challenge his decisions. They were also official and unofficial sources of public opinion in the decision process and repositories of information about local conditions and human populations. If they denied an emir's legitimacy, they could appeal to "higher authorities" to press for his deposition. They could refuse to intercede for his soul, which was the ultimate sanction.

In short, although authority is centralized in the emirate systems, there are numerous checks and balances on the abuse of power, and the processes of consultation are well established. With the stripping of an emir's formal powers during the independence era, the issue of legitimacy now has more to do with personal reputation and symbolic leadership capabilities.

Scope of the State and Civic Space

On the civic side, the emirate states were obviously market friendly, that is, enablers of a market-based system rather than a state-sponsored economy. (Hausa long-distance traders were famous in West Africa, and the Kano market was perhaps the largest in the region during precolonial times.) Furthermore, the state existed to promote "the rule of law." No one was supposed to be above the law. This latter point has affected emirate approaches to conflict resolution and has political significance even today.[10] Emirate orientations to public or civic space, as distinct from private domains, are best assessed by examining the state's defense, economy, and legal system.

The Idea of Public and Private Sectors

Most emirate scholars would argue that in an ideal Islamic polity, the law (shari'a) in its broadest sense would be applied in all aspects of life. In a less than ideal world, shari'a must be applied to the extent possible, although the distinction between what portions of shari'a are the responsibility of the state and what portions the responsibility of individuals is still open to interpretation.[11] The legitimate scope of government is said to encompass three major spheres: defense of the emirate, monitoring of the market system to ensure fair play and to encourage the provision of essential commodities, and application of the legal system.

Defense

The role of the military has changed dramatically over the course of emirate history. During the precolonial period, it had a legitimate place in government. After the colonial conquest, by military means, the local emirate armies had only a ceremonial function, while the national army was expected to enforce overall colonial authority rather than provide defense for the community. This complete reversal in status at the local level may account for some of the ambivalence toward the military in the independence period.

The emir has always had personal bodyguards (*dogarai*). Traditionally, the military (*'yan bindiga*) were under the bodyguards. They were the first to attack in time of war and were the foot soldiers who cleared the way in case of ambush. Next in rank came the "metal hats" (*'yan kwalkwali*), who were to provide protection with bows and arrows or clubs. Third in the hierarchy were those in metal armor (*'yan sulkai*), who were armed with spears. Fourth were the heavy garmented protectors (*'yan lifuda*), with full arms. The officer in charge was the minister of defense (*sarkin yaki*, also called *barade*, or *barde*). In postcolonial times, the title of *sarkin yaki, barade, or barde* was often conferred on those who defended emirate culture in a variety of modern ways, from banking (as in Sokoto) to diplomacy (as in Kazaure).

In addition to the regular army and bodyguards, there was a small army personally attached to the emir, a palace guard. This guard included officers with similar rank to those in the regular army (such as *lifuda*). Others had special rank (for example, *shamaki* or *dan rimi*). In time of war, each group fought at the front in turn. The emir watched, surrounded by his defense men. If there was a particularly dangerous fighter on the other side, the emir might send one of his special officers to fight him. This inner circle of fighters was selected on the basis of merit, and its members could be from any family. The emir was commander-in-chief of the professional army. In wartime, military leaders were highly favored and respected. When the Europeans came, they retired most of these positions. Later, as independence approached, some of these offices were reinstated.

Beyond the professional army, there was a potential reserve, or citizens' army. There were people at every level in the districts who could handle weapons (*masu daji*, *'yan tauri*, or *maharba*) for infantry or conventional fighting. Hunters, for instance, could be archers, and they were conscripted in time of war. Once a call was issued, such people were required to take part in the war effort. Only married men were conscripted. (Unmarried men were considered immature.)

Although war and defense were an important function of the state, the professional military traditionally had the lowest occupational rank, beneath administration, teaching, and business. While mallams might pray for victory in war, they had little or no role in military planning except at the time of the original jihad that led to the establishment of the caliphal system.

The Economy

The emirate states viewed commodities either as items for local consumption (such as grains) or as cash goods locally produced but sold outside or produced outside and imported. The state dealt with consumer items, especially the grains, very carefully since high prices or inflation could threaten its welfare. Hence the state tried to make sure that prices remained at reasonable levels and that hoarding did not occur.

Thus there was a close association between the people handling the grains and the emir's palace. The person in charge of grains, at least in a major emirate such as Kano (which was also a major market), was a female official known as *koroma*. Even in the postcolonial era, the *koroma* hosted the grain merchants and handled the sales. She received commissions generated for the emirate treasury (*baitalmali*). She tried to regulate market prices by influencing supply. She provided sleeping quarters for the merchants and guaranteed their safety and that of their commodities. The *koroma* is a hereditary position but is always associated with a powerful woman.[12] It was assumed that demand was more or less constant and that the state should take responsibility for stimulating supply. The *koroma* served as a sort of secretary of commerce to facilitate imports and exports in grains and also acted as a role model for women in the official market system. In addition, there was a chief of the market (*sarkin kasuwa*) to monitor incoming and outgoing commodities other than grains. He was in charge of market discipline, collected revenues (except for grains), helped stimulate the inflow of commodities, and controlled fighting and disruptive behavior.

The hoarding of grains and other commodities was (and is) considered a serious offense. The *koroma* played a vital role because she knew who bought grain and where it was located. If hoarders were found, the grains were taken back to the market and sold by auction. (The resultant revenues went to the emirate treasury.) The merchant involved could lose everything.

If the inflow of grains and commodities was too great, the state might buy the items and sell them when supplies were low. The goods were stored at the treasury (*gidan ma'aji*) and later sold at a reduced rate (where appropriate) by the *koroma*. Some portion of the grains or commodities was sold to poor people at the treasury building.[13]

In all cases, the state tried to influence prices by regulating supply. The dealers were recognized and accountable. The state took care to license brokers so that cheating would be discouraged. People who were trusted by the state handled the market, although the market mechanism itself set the actual prices. The state's role was to help organize the flow of goods into the market. Normally, the state was not involved in production or in the control of production. The basic market system depended on supply and demand.

Although the emirate state was not involved in the redistribution of income, the general social pressure ensured that voluntary charity was done in the accepted way. The state did not check up on wealthy merchants but left them subject to public opinion. However, since charity (*zakat*) was obligatory, the emir would remind the wealthy of their responsibilities in his public addresses.

In short, the role of the emirate state in the economy was to monitor the market situation and try to ensure that basic needs were met. Food supplies were crucial, and incentive systems were developed to attract trade from other areas. The result was one of the most vibrant market systems in all of Africa, in sharp contrast to some of the later-state managed economies, including those in Muslim areas of the Middle East.

The Civil Service

Emirate civil service or administration was of major importance and in most cases required high degrees of literacy and education. Political loyalty was a secondary factor, but merit was of primary significance. Merit was judged not only by actual skills but also by observational techniques. There were no exams, but observances, vigilance, and public and private reports served as references. Potential candidates did not know if they were being observed. This system was considered highly efficient since it was unobtrusive and focused on attitudes as well as performance.

The emirate civil service required the highest levels of discipline and respect, since it reflected directly on the emir and hence on the inner core of the state system. Because of the hierarchical nature of the civil service, those at higher levels observed those beneath them. If disciplinary action was needed, a superior might call on the person involved and deliver a private warning or reprimand. If this did not work, a public warning would be issued indicating that if the situation did not improve the position would be downgraded. Every emirate civil servant feared the public reprimands, since it was public opinion that put them there in the first place.

In basing selection on merit, the authorities paid particular attention to one's law skill and depth of knowledge, although moral discipline counted even more heavily. It was essential for public opinion to find the person morally sound. Even if candidates were from judicial families, their morals could disqualify them, especially if they had a reputation for womanizing, drinking, making loud noises, having a disheveled appearance, and the like.

A central deputy under the emir was usually in charge of the civil service, but the title for that official varied across the emirates, depending on local traditions. (The term *madaki*, however, is common.) Such an official must have the highest reputation for knowledge, administrative capability, fairness, and honesty. Appointments could be terminated for nonperformance of duties, and it was the responsibility of the emir to monitor this office personally. The advice of the emir's learned men would be important in such monitoring. The emir's knowledge of public opinion would depend on the effectiveness of this officeholder.

Conflict Resolution and Justice

Orientation toward conflict resolution and the central role of law in the emirate model have a direct bearing on conflict mediation and rule of law values in contemporary Nigeria.

Orientation toward Conflict Resolution

In ordinary civil disputes between people, not including criminal matters such as murder or theft, emirate culture has always encouraged working within the broad outlines of the "Islamic way" or shari'a. It was felt that shari'a discouraged going to court, and people preferred not to go to court for civil matters. Conflict resolution was usually the job of the elders. People welcomed mediation from the elders and did not look to the courts as a place to get real justice, but rather as a threat. One went to court if there was no other alternative. People had three main ways to settle a dispute: go to court, seek mediation, or leave it to God, since God is sufficient (*Allah ya isa*).

The ideal and preferred way would have been to leave the matter to God. In practice, informal mediation was the route taken. The elders, both official and unofficial, included learned people, general leaders (*shugabanni*), or simply anyone who was older than the disputants. It was believed that one followed and expected resolution from God, his messenger, and from those in charge of one's affairs. Unofficially, even a person in the street, if elderly, could mediate. The elder (or elders) simply made a decision. He did not have to hear both sides or argue the situation. Before mediating a dispute, he might question members of the crowd to get a sense of the issues and then move in more fully informed. The people would know who was senior and who had the values (*inganci*) that merit deference. If someone with greater values came along, the others would defer. Only if they could not agree did the matter go to the ward head (*mai unguwa*), the next in line of authority.

The ward head learned the details of the issue from the elders. His responsibility was to listen to the two factions and make sure the dispute did not get out of hand. If the disputants became unruly or could not agree, the issue then went to the village head (*dagaci*), or, in an urban context, to the divisional head (*wakilin fuska*). The ward head would listen to the disputants, and if the case merited it, he had the power to arrest them. If it was a minor issue, the authority would not listen to both sides, but simply issue a decision. No police were involved. The matter was settled the same day. Even if a theft had occurred, unless the person involved was a known thief it might not be regarded as a criminal matter at this level. There were no delays. The crowd would follow the disputants up to the level of the village head, then disperse after the matter was settled, almost always feeling satisfied that justice had been done.

If the matter was serious, or disagreement persisted, it might go up to the district head (*hakimi*), whose representative (*wakili*) would deal with it. He would listen to the disputants on the same day. If the matter was urgent, he would relate the details to the district head, who would come out as soon as possible, particularly if there was tension, no matter how late at night. He might do one of two things: if he felt it was a serious civil case, such as adultery or rape, he would weigh the matter; if a crime had been committed, he could ask the emir's bodyguard (*dogari*) who was attached to the district to arrest the person. His next course of action might be to send the matter to a judge (*alkali*) of that district, in which case it would take on "legal" status and he would have nothing more to do with it. If it went to the emir's body-guards, that is, to the emir, it was more serious.

The emir was not only the greater community's leader but also its supreme judge. The emir had high authority and could settle the issue. If it went to the emir, he could punish the perpetrator directly, although it took a longer time, depending on the intensity of the issue, especially if it had aroused consider-able public tension. Usually a letter was written to the head of service (*madaki*), who briefed the emir the following morning. Then the emir called the issue up in court.

The emir held court every day except Friday, which was a greeting or social and religious day. The emir might sit in court from about nine in the morn-ing to noon, or even mid-afternoon. An ordinary case was registered with the emir's court and listed to be heard. The amount of time that lapsed depended on the issue. A heated case might take weeks before it was heard, and the emir might call for witnesses. After the two sides stated their case, the emir would decide if he needed more evidence. He would consult mallams and coun-selors, plus his top judicial officials (*waziri*, or *wali*), and would ask for a "religious" version of the case. If the mallams were attached to the court, they might number about five; in addition, there would be three senior officers (*madaki, waziri, wali*) and the counselors.

The person accused was allowed to give his version of the case, after which some mallams might speak in his defense. Then other mallams might ask questions and interrogate the person. The emir would listen to both sides, per-haps interrupting to ask questions himself, for he could question the mallams or anyone else he wished. A scribe (*magatakarda*) took notes on the entire proceedings, which took place in the courtroom (*fagaci*) of the emir's palace (*fada*).

The judicial reforms of the First Republic introduced an appeals procedure after the emir's court, although earlier tradition also had such a procedure. If a person was not satisfied that he received justice, he could appear outside the emir's palace early in the morning and in a loud voice protest his verdict while the emir's court was in session. The emir was obliged to stop everything and rehear the argument. People believed that anyone who cried out in this way must need help. Thus the emir was the court of last appeal, even for his own court. A crier could petition even if he had been unable to get his case filed with the emir's court.

If a case first went to a local judge, court procedures were followed, even though the case might eventually get to the emir. Next, it would move from the district judge to a city judge, first to a lower judge (*karamin alkali*) and then to a higher judge (*babban alkali*), before finally reaching the emir's court. Criminal cases did not go to the head-of-service (*madaki*) and to the emir directly. A theft, for instance, immediately went before the judge of the ward head, then to the village head, and then to the judge of the district head, through the district head, and eventually to the urban authorities. As discussed in chapter 8, before the criminal code reforms of 1959, criminal cases were regarded as part of the shari'a. These included theft (*sata*), murder (*kashin kai*), and other serious grievances (*koke-koke*). Criminal cases might involve local tension (*tashin hankali*) in the community as well as personal violations, such as rape or adultery. If a rapist was arrested and the parents of the girl did not accept a settlement, the matter became a criminal case. Adultery might become a criminal case if the husband of the adulteress threatened to kill or harm the adulterer, or if the family or ward made a big issue of the matter.

Community tensions at the heart of most civil cases revolved around property disputes, perhaps over farm borders or house boundaries, or the runoff facilities for rainwater, or the trimming of someone else's tree overhanging a yard. Such cases might also deal with marriage, divorce, and inheritance.

Certain criminal cases might have a religious dimension, depending on the status of the person. For a Muslim, drunkenness was an offense punishable by caning (eighty strokes). The actual penalties brought down in criminal cases throughout the twentieth century, before the 1959 reforms to the criminal code, reflected a local sense of appropriate gravity and might change depending on political circumstances. Thus murder was punishable by death or jail. The death sentence, usually beheading, was carried out publicly. Caning was used on fornicators, if unmarried. The penalty for adultery was originally death, which was replaced by jail and caning during the colonial era. The jail term might be two years, but then the person would be expelled from the city for one or two years, in reflection of the strong local taboo on this matter, which would cast lasting shame even on his descendants.

Rape was punishable by beating, or the person might be forced to marry the girl, since he had spoiled the girl's name, and she might never be able to marry "a good person." The marriage was overseen by an authority, to ensure that the man treated the woman kindly.

Cases of theft depended on the amount stolen. In the early part of the twentieth century, the penalty was amputation, but by the 1920s the colonial authorities interfered, and the emirs turned to other harsh penalties, such as ten-year jail terms. In recent times, there has been little public support for amputation but strong support for heavy jail sentences.

A large emirate might have three kinds of jails: some would be for those awaiting sentencing, some would house those sentenced, and some would be reserved for hardened criminals needing maximum security. Traditionally, each prison had a woman's section handled by women warders. There was also a juvenile reformatory. Children would not be sentenced, but if parents felt a child was getting out of hand or had done something serious, they could report it, and the child would be taken away for as long as the parents or the authorities felt suitable.

Before the modern period, when the emir's court was the avenue of final appeal, special procedures were followed for women. They were placed in a small room with windows next to the court. They could peer through the windows and speak but could not be seen.

In late colonial times, many of the above patterns were modified, especially if litigants were Muslim and non-Muslim or differed in some cultural way, although the criminal categories remained much the same. The 1959 Criminal Code of Northern Nigeria was seen as a political compromise modeled on practices in Muslim countries (such as Pakistan and Sudan) but also on a legacy of British colonial rule, with Islamic principles at its core. It was generally agreed that criminal procedures should be removed from the emir's courts, although some debate arose over the abolition of the emir's courts, which became political. But the main reformers were the new breed of Islamic judges who were trained in Western ways as well as in Islamic law. Much of this reflected the new political realities, as power began shifting from the emirs to the regional capital in Kaduna. One of the biggest innovations was the use of lawyers in the magistrate courts, which were not part of the emirs' court procedures. There were procedural and evidential changes as well.

Subsequently, during the First Republic, shari'a courts of appeal were set up in each of the emirate states, so that appeals could be made from an emirs' court. There was also a regional shari'a court of appeal in Kaduna, presided over by the regional grand khadi.

During the military periods of the 1970s, the idea of a national ombudsman emerged, in part based on the emirate tradition of listening to public complaints. The Public Complaints Commission was headed by a former federal minister from Kano State, Maitama Sule (who held the traditional title of *Danmasanin Kano*). He set up offices throughout the federation.[14]

Although the emirate procedures were transferred and modified in the light of postcolonial political realities, they did not fade from the local level.

There the role of elders, mallams, and authorities who knew the litigants remained part of an ongoing emirate culture, and a foundation for expectations of an ideal mode of conflict resolution.

The Central Role of Law

Emirate emphasis on the role of law is central to an understanding of the purposes of the state, the legitimation of power, and the function of clerics and scholars. The main purpose of government is to provide justice (*adalci*), which has a strong connotation of equal treatment before the law, even if such principles were often honored in the breach. No one is above the law. More important, the law is based on divine revelation rather than on natural principles or human-designed precepts. Hence the emirate states were not concerned with how legislators could make laws, but how the vast body of law in the Maliki tradition could be interpreted in the light of the needs of their local people.

Clearly, a formal understanding of Maliki law provides little insight into its application, or lack of application, in the emirate states. They certainly do not apply Maliki law in matters pertaining to the inheritance of property, a major issue in civil law. While the rules of inheritance are well known, the countervailing pressures in an agricultural society with a strong sense of extended family stress the "use" of land rather than ownership. Consequently, a fundamental principle of such a society is that productive land need not be subdivided at the time of inheritance, if that would destroy its productivity. In other words, in this instance local custom has prevailed over a strict interpretation of Maliki law. Another example concerns the legal status of children born out of wedlock, or through concubinage. In general, the emirate states accorded such children full and equal rights enjoyed by other children.

The fact that the emir was the court of final appeal and was seen as the administrator of law was a major part of his legitimation. Yet emirs knew less about law than their chief judicial advisers and the learned men who specialized in the subject. Under this system, the real authorities in society were those who could interpret the law, namely, the learned men.

After the 1970s, when many legal questions arose regarding innovation, the movement "back-to-fundamentals" spread throughout all sectors of the literate emirate community. These fundamentals were no longer found just in the Maliki texts. They were also present in the Qur'an and Hadith, which were the basis for the legal texts. After the 1980s, teachers and scholars spent more time on translating the Qur'an and Hadith into the local languages so that the fundamental sources of faith could guide the entire process of adjusting to the realities of the modern world without going "outside Islam."

At the same time, scholars and teachers have shown renewed interest in the shari'a as practiced during the founding of the Sokoto Caliphate. Mallams have made an attempt, through direct precedent or by analogy, to translate these guidelines and communicate them to a broad public audience. To this end, the mass media have aired the views of senior mallams and contending subsets of mallams.

This process has had a direct impact on modern universities in the emirate states, whose faculties of law now teach and conduct research into both national and Islamic law. A new breed of legal specialist has emerged, namely, the professor of Muslim law. This group has surpassed those under the older system, based at the Kano School for Arabic Studies (KSAS), in conceptualizing the issues, although the KSAS remains the major producer of practicing shari'a court personnel. However, the dual law degree in Islamic and common law offered by Bayero University, Kano, has become very popular, and the Law School at Ahmadu Bello University in Zaria has become a major center for Islamic legal reform. Also, with the emergence of the federal capital at Abuja, the views of key shari'a jurists, such as Justice Muhammad Bashir Sambo, have gained prominence in the national domain.[15] Subsequent chapters turn to the relationship between emirate culture, both in its original and revised form, and other Nigerian Muslim cultures.

5

Nonstate Muslim Variations on Civic Culture

In contrast to the emirate legacy in northern Nigeria, with its pattern of primary state responsibilities in the domain of Muslim religious affairs, other Muslim areas in Nigeria have evolved in ways that reflect more individualized, or nonstate, patterns of Muslim identities and values. In southwest Nigeria, for example, Yoruba ethnic patterns of religious identity are mixed, and even within the same extended family, members may be Muslim, Christian, or traditionalist.[1] Families and localities alike display a high level of religious tolerance. Yoruba city-state identities are generally the predominant factor in political life.[2] This pattern of identity may be changing, however, as locational identities tend to be transcended at the more inclusive levels of religion, ethnicity, or nationality.

The most notable feature of Yoruba Muslim civic culture, in contrast to the emirate cultures, is that the state is not directly involved in Muslim religious affairs. Civic culture tends to be the concern of voluntary associations, whether local mosques, women's groups, or student groups. Yorubaland has an extraordinarily large number of voluntary associations, including religious groups. Since independence, traditional Yoruba leaders, who have come to be known as royal fathers, have played a significant role in mediating intrafaith and interfaith relations.

The Yoruba Muslim Community

Four components of the Yoruba Muslim community are of particular interest here: traditional and religious leaders, women, university students (in

Ibadan and Lagos), and the predominantly Yoruba population of Ilorin, which is an emirate state.

Traditional and Religious Leaders

Over the nineteenth and twentieth centuries, Yorubaland developed an indigenous Islamic culture, especially in the areas that became Oyo, Ogun, and Lagos states.[3] In general, conversion to Islam came from African rather than "foreign" sources.[4] Two major urban centers of Muslim populations are Lagos and Ibadan.[5] The city (and emirate) of Ilorin in Kwara State is a historic component of the Sokoto Caliphate system and has been part of "northern Nigeria" since the time of British rule. Ilorin has a Yoruba society, but it is a bilingual one, with Yoruba and Hausa the predominant languages. Leadership is also mixed, drawing on Yoruba, Fulani, and Hausa populations. Hence Ilorin is a potential bridge (or flash point) between emirate and Yoruba culture zones, a circumstance that has important implications for conflict resolution.

Some of the Fourth Republic's Yoruba city-state leaders (*obas*) in the southwest are Muslim and some Christian. Most continue to observe or preside over the traditional customs and rituals. As in other parts of Nigeria, many consider the evolving role of traditional Yoruba rulers a stabilizing force, both in the political and religious domains. They have defined themselves as "fathers of all" and are often key actors in conflict mediation and resolution. This symbolic position, above partisan politics and religious factionalism, reinforces the centrality of city-state cohesion, since the traditional networks and linkages within the southwest zone cut across religious identity. Over time, they have also played a symbolic role in interfaith reconciliation within a larger Nigerian context.

For example, the *Alafin* of Oyo was the first Yoruba leader of the Nigerian Muslim pilgrimage in 1990. The Oba (*Alake*) of Abeokuta is a Christian but attends the National Joint Muslim Organization meetings of three Yoruba states (Oyo, Ogun, and Lagos). The *Ooni* of Ife is a Christian of the spiritualist variety but opened the Central Mosque at Ife and served as patron of that mosque.

In addition to the multireligious obas, including those who are Muslim, a variety of major Muslim religious leaders who have emerged since the 1970s have adapted traditional symbols and procedures to meet the needs of grassroots urban Muslim populations. Since there is still a healthy competition between city-states, it is not possible to identify any single "Yoruba Muslim leader," although the *Aare Musulumi* in Ibadan is regarded by his followers as leader of the Yoruba Muslims. Before the sultan of Sokoto was deposed in 1995–96, the Abacha regime appeared to recognize the *Aare Musulumi* as the leader of all Nigerian Muslims, thus demoting Sokoto and enhancing the position of Yoruba Muslims, who were considered vital to the general stability of the southwestern zone.

The *Aare Musulumi* (Alhaji Abdul Azeez Arisekola Alao) is a prominent and wealthy business leader in Ibadan, renowned for his local philanthropy. His leadership role in the community is enhanced by the endowment he has given to the new Ibadan mosque and various educational facilities, and by his Friday alms to poor women, who line up outside of his home. He is fluent in English and thoroughly modern. Yet he follows the traditional practice of plural marriage, as well as traditional dress and etiquette. The *Aare Musulumi* is assisted by a chief imam, a deputy imam, and a linguist. He has close ties with other Yoruba Muslim leaders, as well as the local youth wing of the National Council of Muslim Youth Organisations of Nigeria (NACOMYO) and many of the Yoruba Muslim women's groups. In a welcoming address to the author in 1990, the *Aare Musulumi* remarked that Islam has a long history in Yorubaland, having been well established "long before the coming of the British" and Christianity:

> Evidence of the influence of Islam among the Yoruba people abounds in their language and culture. Numerous Arabic loan words, including those relating to *Shari'ah* are found in the Yoruba language. Even those who later became Christians—and their children—use such Arabic and Islamic terms. The Yoruba translation of the Bible contains such words. . . .
>
> The *Shari'ah*, the law of Islam, had been known in Yorubaland long before the Jihad of Shaykh Uthman Dan Fodio. The Yoruba word for just punishment is *Seriya*, which is the Yoruba way of pronouncing *Shari'ah*. The law was practised in many parts of Yorubaland including Ibadan, Ede, Iwo, Abeokuta, Ijebuland, Epe, Lagos, to mention a few. In Ibadan, for instance, *Mufti* were appointed for the sole purpose of giving Islamic legal opinions. And at Ede, the British acknowledged the importance of *Shari'ah* by establishing a Shari'ah Court in 1913. In many towns in Yorubaland, there are families known as *Alikali* families. These are the descendants of the prominent judges and jurists of the *Shari'ah*. All this shows clearly that the recent call for the establishment of Shari'ah Courts in the Southern parts of Nigeria, especially in Yorubaland, was not an attempt to introduce something new. Such demand was made on many occasions even before independence. It also disproves the misconception that the Southern parts of Nigeria are

predominantly Christian. Indeed, Muslims constitute the majority in Yorubaland.[6]

The *Aare Musulumi* is known to promote better understanding between Muslims and Christians and has been instrumental in seeking a common ground on issues involving conflict in the 1990s. According to one report, the Muslim community leaders in Ibadan closely associated with the *Aare Musulumi* were deeply concerned about Muslim-Christian relations in Yorubaland and Nigeria, and the outside world's view of them.[7]

These Ibadan Muslim leaders have stressed the need for tolerance, peace, and patience and are as able to quote the Bible to this effect as well as the Qur'an. They have been concerned about the impact of colonial practices on Yoruba Muslim children, especially the requirement that children change their names and religion in order to get a mission education. They have been concerned about shari'a in the Yoruba states and have argued that family law is needed for those aspects previously covered by customary law, especially in matters of marriage, inheritance, divorce, and the like.

The Muslim community's leaders in Ibadan have been supportive of religious education for both Christian and Muslim children, calling for Islamic Religious Knowledge (IRK) for Muslim children and Christian Religious Knowledge (CRK) for Christian children. Many have worked with the Muslim and Christian peace committees, whose goal is to promote religious tolerance. They have expressed general support for a National Council for Religious Affairs, and most have been involved in the Nigerian Supreme Council for Islamic Affairs.

Ibadan's Muslim leaders have also been supportive of women's education and the women's movement in Islam.[8] They object to politicians who count Christian and Muslim senior government officials, with its implied quota system. Although they believe strongly that Yorubaland is predominantly Muslim, they emphasize the historical continuity of the Judeo-Christian-Muslim legacy of prophets in their poster campaigns and symbolic references.

Yoruba Muslim Women

The Federation of Muslim Women's Associations in Nigeria (FOMWAN) was established to counteract the role of custom in Nigerian Muslim society. In the early 1990s, FOMWAN had 400 member associations, about 300 of which were in Yorubaland. As of 2003, total membership exceeded 500 associations, but Yoruba groups remained preponderant. Many FOMWAN leaders have been from Yoruba areas, although the national leader, or president (*amirah*), is selected through an annual rotational system.

The Yoruba associations within FOMWAN focus on a set of special issues related to the education of Muslim girls and women and have set up nursery and primary schools that provide solid standard education plus religious teaching.[9] Family planning is another issue on their agenda, for many of their members believe that family spacing is covered in the Qur'an through the two-year weaning period. They are also concerned about promiscuity and believe abortion is justified only when the health of the mother is at risk. (They have held national conferences on issues of family planning.)

Some argue that under the cultural circumstances in Yorubaland, shari'a law pertaining to the family and inheritance would strengthen the position of women, since in cases of mixed marriage with non-Muslims it permits an individual to designate 30 percent of discretionary inheritance to non-Muslim heirs. Also, FOMWAN is against early marriage and recommends that girls be at least sixteen before getting married. It supports the injunctions against "unequal" plural marriages in the Qur'an and predicts that with education, in time this will probably lead men to have only one wife. It is felt that women's education at all levels should be encouraged, including university education for married women; education is the key to the awakening in all areas. There should be no sex outside marriage. In addition, FOMWAN believes that women should not be in purdah.

FOMWAN has no counterpart in the Christian Association of Nigeria, but it would be glad to engage in discussions of mutual concern if there were a women's wing. However, the international conference in Nairobi, with its secular agenda, made clear that FOMWAN's concerns were different from those of the National Council of Nigeria Women and the Women in Nigeria groups. Nonetheless, it seeks closer ties with both Muslim and Christian women throughout Nigeria.

FOMWAN was active in encouraging the return to civilian rule during the 1984–98 period. Several of its key leaders (especially from the Lagos area) have been involved in transition politics, serving as peacemakers and conflict resolvers in times of crisis. They have not felt that women need to be central political leaders (as Benazir Bhutto was in Pakistan) and argue that some women enter politics for the wrong reasons (for example, to avenge their fathers). On the other hand, educated Muslim women should help their husbands in government. They do not see themselves as feminists in the Western sense, but as the defenders of a more modern interpretation of the role of Muslim women.

Like FOMWAN, most Muslim women's associations in Yorubaland tend to be in favor of education and against local custom, such as early marriage and wife seclusion. FOMWAN's Yoruba leaders see themselves as Muslim women who are concerned about restoring moral values to society and transcending customs regarding the status and role of women in society. They are quite capable of functioning in Westernized or modernized situations and welcome more contacts with the Western world.

Yoruba Muslim Students

Muslim and non-Muslim students at the University of Ibadan have experienced serious clashes, some involving violence, over issues such as the location of the campus mosque and various Christian places of worship (especially of the inspirational variety). Yet Muslim students have also been instrumental in setting up and working with the peace committees on campus to mediate religious conflict when it arises.[10]

Muslim students are concerned about several issues: the role of women in education, which they strongly endorse, but with modest dress codes; the position of family law, since Muslims in Ibadan were forced to follow customary law in the 1990s; the aggressive use of incentives to persuade people to convert to Christianity (many of the best secondary schools in Yorubaland are connected to Christian churches and may impose religious conditions on prospective students); the activation of the National Council for Religious Affairs and various local peace efforts between Christians and Muslims; the need for more conflict resolution councils (the positioning of the mosque and chapel at universities compounded tensions, until landscaping was undertaken to give each a sense of privacy); and the lack of organization among Christian students and their lack of interest in the peace efforts. On this latter point, many Muslim students feel that several of the student evangelical organizations on the Ibadan campus wanted a confrontation. Also, the hard economic times have spawned hundreds if not thousands of Christian sects in the Ibadan area, which have been visible and assertive.

In general, the Muslim student cohorts have not tapped into the extreme emotionalism, even millenarianism of such despair, perhaps because of traditional societal constraints on Muslim student behavior. Yet some fear that Muslim students might respond with equal vigor to provocation and would accept encouragement or resources from any outside source.[11] In general, the Muslim university students in Ibadan in the 1990s were fully aware of the need for interfaith conflict resolution, and for patience and tolerance in dealing with provocative situations.

At the University of Lagos, where many of the Yoruba Muslim students are from Oyo, Ogun, or Lagos, a major issue has been religious tolerance, with an emphasis on the Qur'anic injunction that "there is no compulsion in religion."[12] Students believe that education is the key to understanding and that Christians need to recognize the five pillars of Islam (including the fundamental reason for pilgrimage, which is not the same in Christian belief). Another concern is whether secondary schools have been forcing Muslims to engage in Christian worship. Christians claim to teach IRK, but sometimes there are no lectures on it at all. Often schools are not closed on Friday afternoons, even though the law states schools should be closed at 12:30 P.M. on Fridays. Some principals simply do not allow this.

Christian propaganda in Nigeria is another serious concern. When some overzealous Christians began preaching on buses, in classrooms, and in schools, these public displays were considered Christian propaganda excesses (for example, nursery schools were obliged to tell only Christian stories). It was also felt that Christians have the upper hand in education, but that Muslims need to learn about the Qur'an and Sunna. Since no Arabic is taught in the university, even as an elective course, students with serious Islamic interests tend to go outside the country for their education.

A further complaint had to do with Nigeria's mass media, said to be controlled by Christians. Reporting was unbalanced and often distorted, spreading negative information about Muslims. International syndicated news deliberately blacked out details about Muslim contributions to development. Western television programming was thought to have a negative effect on society because violence was a central theme. A common concern was that Muslim minors were being corrupted by television.

At the same time, students emphasized that Nigeria is a multireligious country and did not think the government should be pro-Christian or pro-Muslim. However, they wanted the government to reactivate the Religious Affairs Councils, wherein the Muslims were active and the Christians inactive.

In general, Yoruba Muslim students have felt the need for structure in governmental and religious life. The chaos of rapid economic and political changes, often accompanied by an unfettered proliferation of religious cults and sects, has been profoundly disturbing. Patience and tolerance are also necessary, however, and a willingness to engage in peace committees.

The broader spectrum of Muslim youth organizations, especially in the southwest, has been somewhat more assertive, or at least quite articulate in their reactions to perceived political and religious affronts. The National Council of Muslim Youth Organisations of Nigeria, based in Lagos, was particularly upset by the attempted coup of April 1990, against General Babangida, and the attempts of the coup plotters to excise the northern (Muslim) states of Nigeria.[13] More recently, in the spring of 2005, NACOMYO protested the religious imbalance of delegates to the National Political Reform Conference and the population census directorships.[14]

The Special Circumstances of Ilorin

Although officially in the north, Ilorin is a complex emirate shaped by historical factors stemming from Yoruba-Fulani relations in the nineteenth century.[15] Ilorin city itself is a mixture of Muslim and Christian populations, plus a large number of inspirational or syncretist sects. Historically, the emirs were appointed by the sultan of Sokoto and had close ties with northern regional politics. The emir appointed in 1995, however, had a distinguished career as a federal judge and hence was in a position to play a more symbolic role as a national figure, bridging Yoruba and Hausa-Fulani civic cultures.[16] Many members of the Ilorin royal family have a mixture of Fulani and Yoruba lineages, owing to plural marriage patterns.

In the wake of the 1993 political crisis over the annulled election, Hausa-Yoruba tensions intensified, as did the need for gateways or a means of resolving the conflict between the two cultures, even in the respective Muslim communities. One of the diplomatic gateways or liaisons from Ilorin in the international community has been Ibrahim Gambari, who served as the Nigerian ambassador to the United Nations and later UN under secretary and special adviser on Africa for the UN secretary general. Ambassador Gambari is a son of the late emir Sule Gambari and brother to the emir appointed in 1995.[17]

The concept of a gateway (*kofa*) between groups is central to northern emirate civic culture. In the Ilorin context, it is especially salient as Yoruba and emirate civic cultures have been conjoined.[18] The migration of Yoruba businessmen, professionals, and technicians throughout northern Nigeria, especially in the period of the Fourth Republic, has meant that almost every urban area has a significant Yoruba community. Most of the families in such communities have some experience of mixed religious affiliations, that is, Muslim and Christian.

Overall, Yoruba Muslims—whether traditional rulers, religious leaders, women, students, or diplomats—tend to eschew religious confrontation, preferring peace committees and conflict resolution instead. The political crisis following the annulled presidential election in 1993 of M. K. O. Abiola (originally from the Egba city-state of Abeokuta) did not represent a Christian-Muslim split but a Muslim-Muslim split. The Yoruba Muslims' affinity for patience and conflict resolution may have played a role in the relative tranquility in most parts of Yorubaland after 1993, despite the disappointment of those who had hoped for a Yoruba Muslim president. (The influence of Yoruba Muslims on the conflict resolution efforts of the Fourth Republic is considered in part 3.) Significantly, the various peace efforts of Yoruba Muslims represent more of a voluntary association approach rather than a statist approach. In short, Yoruba civic culture encourages a separation of church or mosque and state and a religious pluralism, even though the traditional indigenous culture remains strong.

The Yoruba Blend: Christians and Traditionalists

The most recent Nigerian census (1991) did not include religious identity as a category. This was understandable politically. In the Yoruba-speaking areas, the line between the mainstream Protestant churches and their various off-shoots is blurred, and this Christian overlay blends with a strong substratum of Yoruba indigenous beliefs. While it may be politically incorrect to refer to Yoruba "animists and syncretists" rather than "indigenous congregations," the fact remains that part of the religious tolerance in Yorubaland stems from the nonexclusivity of religious identity categories and the situational use of religious identities. This appears to be more a characteristic of the Protestant Yoruba churches than the Muslim community. In addition, the general lack of Roman Catholicism in Yorubaland (in contrast to Igboland) has lessened possible external influences on church structure and dogma. It has been suggested that Yorubaland's complex religion reflects the "subjugation of village life within larger polities":

> These city-states produced a theology that linked local beliefs to a central citadel government and its sovereignty over a hinterland of villages through the monarch. The king (oba) and his ancestors were responsible for the welfare of the entire state, in return for the confirmation of the legitimacy of the oba's rule over his subjects. . . .
>
> In Oyo, for example, there were a number of national cults, each with its own priests who performed rituals under the authority of the king (alafin) in the public interest. Shango, god of thunder, symbolized the power of the king and of central government; Ogboni represented the fertility of the land and the monarch's role in ensuring the well-being of the kingdom. In 1990 these indigenous beliefs were more or less openly practiced.[19]

In a literary account of indigenous Yoruba culture, *Death and the King's Horseman,* Wole Soyinka—originally from the Egba city-state of Abeokuta—

illuminates Yoruba metaphysics.[20] The play focuses on the death of an *oba* and the crisis that ensues when the king's horseman is unable to commit suicide to join his monarch on the journey into the afterlife. The cycle of life includes a powerful symbiotic relationship between the living, the unborn, and those who have passed on.

The dynamics of contemporary southwest Nigeria have been greatly affected by the Yoruba wars of the nineteenth century, which transformed Yorubaland and led to the collapse of Oyo after 1817. New centers of power emerged in Ibadan, Abeokuta, and elsewhere.[21] As the wars continued through much of the nineteenth century, Ibadan became the major center positioned to offset the rising power of the Sokoto Caliphate to the north. British church groups and missionaries then entered the picture, especially the Anglican Church Missionary Society (CMS). Meanwhile, Catholic missionaries became active in the southeast, especially among the southeastern Igbo-speaking areas.[22] When a liberated slave became the first Anglican bishop of Niger, the idea of an indigenous religious leadership was firmly planted.[23] Indigenous congregations then began breaking away from the orthodox churches, blending the experiences of the cultural past with the new European-based Christian approach:

> Christianity had been active in Nigeria for approximately forty years when the first visible signs of an indigenous response to this new religious phenomenon began to emerge. Early movements took the form of independent churches, motivated by the desire to cast off the yoke of white domination in religious affairs. Known as "the African Churches," they seceded from the major Protestant missions in Lagos (Anglican, Methodist and Baptist) from the 1880s until 1971. The major schisms, such as the Native Baptist Church, the United Native African Church and the United African Methodist Church, were characterized by a desire to retain the polity and liturgy of their parent mission churches, while advocating African leadership and acceptance of polygamy for both clergy and laity. This accounts for the designation of these churches as "separatist" or "orthodox independent."
>
> It was left to the wave of revival movements which arose in the early part of the twentieth-century, in both western and eastern Nigeria, to make a more radical stand against western missionary Christianity. The majority of the movements professed Christian orientation, but sought a more African way of worship, in terms of symbolism, music, dance

and a more direct religious experience characterized by dreams, visions and spirit possession, and spontaneous emotionalism.[24]

The new blended Yoruba churches came to be known as *aladura*, or "praying people."[25] Nativistic churches, which were concerned explicitly with the revival of traditional practices, also increased in number:

> They distinguish themselves from traditional cults by adopting new forms and ideas as part of the revitalization processes. For instance, the Ijo Orunmila (Church of Orunmila), founded in the 1930s by Yoruba Christians seeking to re-establish links with their traditional religious heritage, drew on a Christian liturgical framework to promote the worship of Olodumare (the supreme deity) through Orunmila (the deity of divination) and the use of Ifa divination.[26]

A leading scholar of Yoruba new churches has suggested that their highly complex evolution from the 1930s owed much to a charismatic emphasis on healing, ritual calendars, personal rituals, and competition with rival churches.[27] By the mid-1990s, the growth of inspirational or even nativistic churches had come to be of concern to a number of government officials and others in Nigeria. The loss-of-hope atmosphere had prompted the rise of Pentecostal churches, often promising jobs and wealth in exchange for loyalty and personal resources. According to one magazine account, "Churches have sprung up in the warehouses that used to be built for storage during the booming Eighties. Their owners and the pastors now flaunt private jets, flashy cars and choice estates."[28] These "health and wealth" churches have had a profound effect on interfaith relations in Yorubaland and throughout the Nigerian federation.[29]

The extreme pluralism of religious groups in Yorubaland among the Christian, syncretist, and animist groups, not to mention the propensity for large numbers of Yoruba Muslim associations (such as those affiliated with FOMWAN or NACOMYO) might seem likely to generate high levels of conflict. Rather, the situation is closer to a *pax Yoruba* that promotes accommodation between mainstream Protestant and Muslim groups.

A fault line exists, however, between the establishment churches and mosques, on the one hand, and the creative chaos of nativistic, syncretistic, and traditional forms of religious expression, on the other. This same fault line—between establishment religious organizations and free-wheeling challengers—informs some of the conflict in other geocultural zones, such as the Middle Belt and northern cities (see chapter 10 on national interfaith issues).

Yoruba Civic Values and the Capital City Issue

Yoruba civic values and political culture are reflected in the structure of the zone's city-states. Its leading city, Lagos, was the capital of Nigeria until various factors forced a move to Abuja, outside the Yoruba zone.

Yoruba Civic Values

Basic community identities or loyalties in Yorubaland have been to city-states, and within city-states to lineages. There were often intense rivalries between Yoruba city-states. These city-states had a symbolic head, without real executive powers, and a representative council of lineage heads who handled most decisionmaking. In anthropological terms, Yoruba societies are pyramidal (representational) rather than hierarchical, as in emirate culture, or segmental (participatory by age and gender), as in Igbo culture.

Yoruba civic life revolved around particular city-states. The political leader (*oba*) was at the center of this civic culture, but more as a figurehead rather than an actual ruler. The council in charge of the actual decisionmaking for the city-state had its roots in clan structure.[30]

During the independence period, intercity and interclan rivalries in Yorubaland translated into factions that might support or oppose alliances with non-Yoruba partners in the east or north. Political turmoil in Yorubaland has been constant but normally does not reflect religious identities. Thus some non-Muslim factions have allied with the "Muslim north," while some Muslim factions have allied with non-Muslims in the east.[31]

Close working relationships across religious lines were perhaps exemplified by the long-term alliance of Olusegun Obasanjo (a Yoruba Christian from Abeokuta) and Shehu Musa Yar'Adua (a Hausa-Fulani Muslim from Katsina), both former generals. After the head of state, General Murtala Muhammad, was assassinated in 1976 by disgruntled Middle Belt officers, Obasanjo became head (1976–79) with Yar'Adua as his deputy. In 1995 Obasanjo and Yar'Adua were jailed for allegedly plotting against the Abacha government. While Obasanjo survived to become president during the Fourth Republic, Yar'Adua died in prison. Yet his political organization became the backbone of the People's Democratic Party, which supported the Obasanjo presidential bid in 1998–99 and 2003.

The Capital City Issue

In 1975–76, during the regimes of Murtala Muhammad (from Kano) and Olusegun Obasanjo (from Abeokuta), a decision was made to move the capital of Nigeria from Lagos to Abuja. The ostensible reasons were the rapid population growth of Lagos, which was doubling every ten years, and the extraordinarily poor ecological conditions in Lagos, which was originally built on a swamp. Because huge pylons would have to be sunk into the ground to support any future construction, the costs of building a modern city in Lagos were felt to be prohibitive.[32]

A political reason for transferring the capital was the need for a location that was equally accessible to all six geographic zones in the country and that could serve as a bridge between northern and southern Nigeria. Moreover, other geocultural zones were uncomfortable with the fact that Lagos was a Yoruba city. Although key planners for the new capital in Abuja included distinguished Yoruba professors, such as Akin Mabogunje, much of the actual construction and land-use planning was controlled by the political powers of the day, which reflected a north-southeast (that is, emirate-Igbo) alliance.[33]

The transition to Abuja was slowed down during the oil-bust period of the 1980s, but by the mid-1990s all of the ministries had been transferred and the facilities put in place for the civilian government structure. Many older Yoruba civil servants, who dominated the national civil service in Lagos, retired rather than move to Abuja. Some of the lower-level government employees found themselves without jobs in the new "federal character" workforce in Abuja.

Many in the economic axis between Lagos and Ibadan felt threatened by the gradual transfer of powers to Abuja. With the economic downturn in Nigeria and the realities of the transfer setting in, some vocal Yoruba personalities, such as Wole Soyinka, complained that the Abuja project was "the soured, arid dream of a symbol of national unity, situated in the center of the country and the exit valve from the heart of a national treasury."[34]

Others, however, including many Muslim women, students, and religious leaders, were strongly supportive, arguing that it would reduce congestion in Lagos and help link the nation together more securely.[35] Also, few seemed to fear northern Muslim domination, since each of the Muslim Yoruba groups had good working relations with their northern counterparts.

In the spring of 1993, with the prospect of a presidential election on June 12, many in Yorubaland and throughout Nigeria seemed to think that a vote for a Yoruba Muslim (Abiola) would ease the transition to Abuja. Part of the subsequent frustration in Yorubaland was due to the feeling of marginalization this process caused. Not until well into the Fourth Republic, under the presidency of Obasanjo, has there been a sense that Abuja could represent Yoruba interests as well as those of other zones. As a new city, without traditional ethnic or religious civic cultures, Abuja was unlike indigenous cities.

The question was whether it could represent all Nigerians, and whether the emergence of a new civic culture in Abuja could accommodate the ethnoreligious diversity of the country in a constructive way.

Yoruba Family Values and Religious Mixing

Family law issues in the Muslim Yoruba areas came into sharper focus when the Fourth Republic introduced shari'a law in both the civil and criminal domain in the twelve far northern states. Increased efforts were made to set up alternative legal structures in the Yoruba states for civil matters, and lobbying increased for shari'a civil courts. Significantly, unofficial judicial panels along these lines were established on a voluntary basis, without waiting for the blessing of the state.

Independent panels were set up under the Supreme Council for Shari'a in Nigeria. Yoruba Muslims who had been taking family law matters to the common law or customary courts had the option to use the nonofficial shari'a. Such courts began to handle divorce, contracts, inheritance, and other civil issues.

In Oyo State, an independent shari'a panel set up at the Oja-Oba mosque in Ibadan in May 2002 heard more than 500 cases in its first year. In Lagos, an independent shari'a panel was set up at the Abesan Estate Central Mosque, Ipaja, in December 2002 and also at the 1004 Estate Central Mosque, Victoria Island, in March 2003. Ogun State had less success in this regard because of opposition from some imams in Abeokuta.[36] According to one report, "The non-recognition of the independent Sharia panel by governments in the Yoruba states where they have been established still constitutes a major impediment to the smooth operation of the panels."[37] Even so, nonrecognition by the local states did not stop the process.

An even more controversial issue arose in Ibadan in October 2002 when "a 29-year-old self-confessed fornicator, Suleiman Shittu, who had insisted on being punished in accordance with Sharia law, was ordered to be given 100 strokes of the cane by the Sharia panel at Oja-Oba Central mosque. The eventual public caning of Shittu had attracted criticism from the opponents of shari'a who maintained that the panel had no legal authority to adjudicate on the criminal aspect of shari'a since it is a private initiative."[38]

Some of those who argue for shari'a in the civil domain in Yorubaland contend that Muslims there never did abandon the Islamic legal system entirely, particularly in matters of marriage and inheritance, even though it was officially abolished under colonial rule:

As far back as 1923, the Lagos Muslim community had petitioned the colonial administration for the creation of Sharia courts. The Muslim communities of Ijebu-Ode and Oyo also demanded the reintroduction of Sharia from the colonial masters in 1940 and 1944 respectively. The Nigerian Muslim Council (NMC) led by Senator Hassan Fasinro had mounted vigorous pressure on the then military administrator of Lagos State, General Buba Marwa, to create civil Sharia courts in Lagos.[39]

To add to the complexity of the Yoruba Muslim family law system, families adopting it have extraordinarily high levels of interfaith mixing. With family and kinship networks dominating social relations in Yorubaland, many families have active identity adherents from traditional, Christian, and Muslim communities. Such interfaith mixing in family patterns may help to depoliticize religion. For example, President Obasanjo is widely regarded as a born-again Christian, yet a number of his family members are Muslim. When Chief Olabode George (retired navy commodore, former military governor of Ondo State, and active supporter of President Obasanjo) was asked about his (and the president's) capacity to work with Muslims, he said:

> Let me now tell you what we have in the South-West. My immediate elder sister is a Muslim. She was born a Christian, she married a Muslim from Lagos State. I gave her money to go to Mecca. She is today an Alhajia. She is still my sister. When there is need for her to come to the family house for anything, she comes of course. She was brought up a Christian; she will sing all the songs. But you see, her husband and her children, they are Muslims. . . . That's my immediate elder sister. I am a Christian. I have another younger brother who married a Muslim from Lagos State. She is now so converted that she preaches the Bible. But all her family in the area are still Muslims. So to us, it's nothing. There is hardly any Yoruba family you will go [to where] you won't find a Muslim or a Christian in the South-West. There is hardly anyone.[40]

Referring to President Obasanjo, or "*Baba*," Chief George continued: "*Baba's* sister, the only sister *Baba* has is a Muslim. . . . In fact, they look like twins. But will he throw her away? You see, such things are important but they shouldn't play to the top, otherwise, you will start to send different signals. *Baba's* first child, Iyabo, is married to a Muslim. Her husband is a Muslim. So why should he hate Muslims? . . . [H]istory will judge him."[41]

Clearly, the pattern of religious identity in the southwest differs from that in the emirate states of the north. Yet the fact that M. K. O. Abiola, a self-identifying reformed Yoruba Muslim, was able to carry large sections of the north in the 1993 presidential election, and that a Yoruba Muslim such as Tunde Idiagbon (from Ilorin) served as deputy head of state to General Muhammadu Buhari, suggests that the Yoruba experience with religious identity and community values may have wider salience in the Nigerian context.

6

National Muslim
Identities and Values

Ethnic and religious-based political parties have been banned from recognition and participation in elections in Nigeria since before independence. Hence the various political parties and nongovernmental organizations tend to be associated with public perspectives, which range from conservative to progressive. This has been the case even in the predominantly Muslim areas during both civilian and military periods.

Progressive Identities

In the transition to independence in 1960, a number of young men in northern Nigeria who had both an Islamic and Western education provided political leadership as well as guidance in interpreting Islamic principles in a modernist context. They were often from distinguished Muslim families but sought to differentiate between tradition and principle by utilizing some of the ideas of the global modernist movement and filtering such ideas through Qur'anic and caliphal primary sources. In addition, many had traveled abroad and were aware of developments in other Muslim areas, such as Egypt and Turkey. In fact, some of them were initially called "the young Turks" because they insisted on getting rid of the customs and habits of traditional life in the northern emirate states.

Led by Aminu Kano (1920–83), who is better known simply by his title "teacher" (*mallam*), these young men insisted "the common man" (*talakawa*) should be able to participate in government, women should participate fully in economic and political activities, education (Western and Islamic) is central to development, and honesty is essential in personal and public affairs.

They made the bold assertion (at the time) that "kingship" (that is, the emirate system as it had evolved in Northern Nigeria) had no place in Islamic thought, and that "kings" had arisen merely out of "custom" as part of a feudal legacy that should be scrapped.[1]

The Aminu Kano movement was organized during the First Republic (1960–66) as the Northern Elements Progressive Union (NEPU). During the Second Republic (1979–83), NEPU was incarnated as the Peoples' Redemption Party (PRP). In the interim military period (1966–79), when Nigeria experienced enormous changes as a result of the oil boom and the development of educational and infrastructural facilities, Aminu Kano played a significant role in government. Perhaps more important, he continued teaching at his home in Kano, which was always filled with students and ordinary men and women from the city and the rural areas who would come to hear his commentary on the Qur'an or his lectures and speeches. Aminu was from a legalist family in Kano, and he also had close ties with the Reformed Tijaniyya, although he always claimed he did not have time to perform the voluntary prayers and rituals. Virtually the entire cohort of educated youth in northern Nigeria during the 1960s and 1970s came to regard Aminu Kano as an ideal spokesperson on issues of ethics, sorting out Islamic principles from traditional culture and recognizing the need to take personal responsibility for transforming society.

As the flood of young people who were continuing their education overseas began to return in the mid-1970s and as the excesses of the oil boom became more apparent, a split developed between those who believed the emirate structures were capable of progressive "reform" and those who considered the "struggle" a product of class-based contradictions. Students taking a hard line became known as the "Abubakar Rimi faction," after the young man who ran for Kano State governor in 1979 and was elected on the PRP ticket.

Until his death, Aminu Kano himself believed that education was the most revolutionary form of power and worked tirelessly to extend educational opportunity (Western and Islamic) to groups previously bereft of such opportunities (especially women and poor people). Thus the PRP itself split into the Aminu Kano faction and the Rimi faction. The former won the governorship in Kano in 1983—after the death of Aminu in April 1983—but the split in the party reduced its potential national impact.

Since 1983 Aminu Kano's ideas have spread, as print and visual media facilities have improved. During the development of the Social Democratic Party (SDP) in 1990–93, however, many of the old PRP fissures reappeared, between the supporters of a multireligious Nigeria as a moral, progressive, reformist endeavor and those who saw the state as a repressive instrument of class interests. Many of the young professionals in Kano State and other northern cities still identify with these two points of view. The front runner for president from the SDP in 1992—before the annulment of the primaries—was General Shehu Musa Yar'Adua, who had been number two to General Obasanjo in the military regime (1976–79) that succeeded General Murtala Muhammad. Yar'Adua, considered a more moderate member of the progressive faction, was an outstanding organizer and mobilizer of people. He continued to draw the verbal fire of the Rimi group in part because of his combination of effectiveness, popularity, moderation, and progressiveness.[2]

With the return to democratic federalism in 1999, Bayero University, Kano, established the Centre for Democratic Research and Training in November 2000, located in the residence of the late Aminu Kano, in Kano City, known as Mambayya House. The center is dedicated to the scholarly furtherance of democracy and good governance, in the spirit of Aminu Kano. It has converted Kano's original house, including his library, into a political museum. The center serves an outreach function, in terms of community education, conferences, and publications. The home is also the site of the tomb of Aminu Kano, which continues to be a locus of pilgrimage for his followers.

Today Aminu Kano is considered the founding father of progressive thought in northern Nigeria and has become an inspiration to a cohort of younger scholars and activists.[3] Aminu Kano's passion for women's education and the involvement of ordinary citizens in the processes of government is balanced by his reputation as a *tafsir* scholar, who could recite and interpret the Qur'an in light of modern realities. His legacy of progressive orientation encompasses authority, community, and change:

—The progressive thinkers challenged constituted authority, but because of strong reformist tendencies among such challengers, factions or polycentric authority patterns tended to emerge.

—Although progressives are usually open to all like-minded persons, in some cases they are identified with political resistance communities (that is, pockets of autonomy within larger communities of constituted authority). Many Western-educated individuals have strong links to global modernist communities.

—Progressive identity groups are strong supporters of "modernization." They promote change in individuals as much as in societal conditions, including the status of women. The means of change may range from education to political coercion.

Progressive-Conservative Identities

The political spectrum in Nigeria is not unlike the shades of religious identity in the Muslim community. To some extent the spectrum reflects different age-group perspectives and orientations, but with political and religious identities cutting across generations. It consists of three basic groups: a conservative, progressive, and middle faction. The conservative cluster wishes to conserve many of the cultural structures of the emirate (or chiefdom) systems. The argument, often unarticulated, is that people need some stability in the face of rapid changes, and the traditional system, by being above politics, can serve as a stabilizer and shock absorber as other changes occur. In short, too much change can be disruptive: better not to throw out the baby (of lifetime tenured "fathers-of-the-people") with the bath water of natural, incremental changes in "customs." Many of the "traditional rulers" (Muslim emirs and chiefs) have been educated in the West and think they should play a spiritual as well as social role. The overtly legal and political functions were stripped from emirs and chiefs during the military reforms of the mid-1970s.

An example of a modern emir in the well-educated public service tradition is the late *Etsu Nupe* in Niger State.[4] Others still preside over Muslim festival occasions in their domains and carry primary spiritual authority in their emirates. The normal rules of succession are some variant of dynastic succession, although such guidelines may be broadly interpreted to include any male relatives of the deceased.

At the opposite point on the spectrum is the progressive clustering described in the preceding section. This cluster tends to attack the kingship basis of traditional rule, not to mention the abuses of power that might come from such traditions.

The third group, the middle-ground clustering, has actually formed the center of Nigerian political life since 1960 and may be termed progressive-conservative (in the Canadian sense). It tends to be incrementalist, or moderate, rather than radical. It is associated with free-market approaches to the economy and to political reform (for example, it supports the extension of voting rights and a constitutionally tuned political system, with respect for the rule of law). The group basically favors modernization but also wants to conserve the "best of the past." As for religious overtones, the progressive-conservatives have tended to be identified with the moderate centrist Muslim political leaders who headed Nigeria's civilian regimes during the First and Second Republics.

Under the Fourth Republic, many of the northern progressive-conservatives have joined forces with the social democrats in the People's

Democratic Party (PDP), while others have been aligned with General Buhari in the All Nigeria People's Party (ANPP), which has a strong base in the far north. (It should be noted, however, that Buhari's political emphasis on "justice" and "integrity" and his challenge to establishment complacency toward grassroots suffering is reminiscent of the Aminu Kano message.)

During the First Republic, the national leadership of Abubakar Tafawa Balewa (prime minister) set a tone of tolerance within and between religious groups. His Muslim identity was not broadcast, although it was apparent to all. His "moderation in all things" and personal austerity, plus dedication to development of the whole nation, created a model for some of his younger cabinet ministers (such as Maitama Sule or Shehu Shagari) and also for many younger northern Muslim students, who, like Balewa (and indeed Maitama Sule), had come from "servant" family backgrounds rather than from the upper crust of northern society. Education was the key value for this group, and there was considerable overlap between some of its members and those who followed Aminu Kano.[5] (Ahmadu Bello, premier of the Northern Region during this period, was also one of the "definers" of progressive-conservatism, although he was clearly from the Sokoto royal family and the leadership style in his regional role was very different from the style of his party cohorts at the national level.)[6]

During the Second Republic, the role model for progressive-conservatism was President Shehu Shagari, a former teacher from Sokoto.[7] His capacity for tolerance—an essential skill in building a national coalition—turned out to be a liability when it came to the financial accountability of national party leaders. But the modesty and sense of service that characterized Shagari's personal and professional life restored his image as a Muslim identity model in the abortive transition to the June 1993 elections and afterward.[8]

As the transition to a Third Republic unfolded, the major competitors for the presidency from the National Republican Convention (NRC) included several Muslim candidates clearly of progressive-conservative persuasion. One of the leading candidates was Adamu Ciroma, originally from a minority area (Fika) in Borno, who held the honorific title of *Dallatun Fika*. Ciroma was born in Potiskum, Yobe State, in 1934. He attended Barewa College, Zaria, and Nigerian College of Arts and Science before going on to University College, Ibadan. Later he became governor of the Central Bank of Nigeria, a member of the Constituent Assembly, secretary of the National Party of Nigeria, and minister of industries, of agriculture, and of finance. Although he was probed after the fall of the Second Republic, there was no official indication of impropriety. In general, he has been in the Balewa or Shagari tradition of public service and personal austerity and modesty. (During the first PDP term of the Fourth Republic, Ciroma served as federal finance minister.)

In an interview with the *African Guardian* in 1992, before the annulment of the primary elections, Ciroma was asked how he would respond to those who had accused him of being anti-south and an Islamic fundamentalist. Ciroma replied:

> I have been one of the lucky people who went for a university education in Nigeria when there weren't so many universities, and we lived, we learnt and interacted with Nigerians from all over the country. Most of these students were from the South. We got on well. I made friends with students of my generation. I worked in the northern civil service but I also worked in the federal civil service. I did not turn out as someone intolerant or incapable of being just. In fact, just the opposite is the truth. I worked as Governor of the Central Bank when there were few people from the North working in the bank. Ask the people who worked there. I had full respect because I was fair and equitable. I worked as minister in various positions. Nobody knew me as being anti any group. . . . As minister I am prepared to serve all Nigerians. . . .
>
> My view is that if this country is made up of Christians who are living according to Christian precepts and Moslems who are living according to Moslem precepts there will be no confusion. It is people who are trying to live in-between, [who] are neither here nor there, who are bringing in all this religious confusion. The proper Christian is a decent man. He will not go against the 10 commandments. He will not deviate from behaving well towards his fellow men. That also is the position of a good Moslem. So all this talk about fundamentalists, well, so what am I supposed to do? Not to live as a Moslem?[9]

In the same interview, Ciroma emphasized the qualities he represented, particularly his honesty and experience, which made him a suitable, "morally clean" candidate who was "not going into government to lie" but "to act."[10] Ciroma was responding to the public's concern with "character" in Nigerian public (and private) life. The relationship between character and religious or moral foundations has often been an issue with progressive-conservatives, who maintain (at least in ideal terms) that reforms are possible and progress achievable only if the moral foundations of religious and personal responsibility can be developed in individuals, who can then make an impact on society. The original party slogan of the Northern People's Congress (NPC) during the First Republic was "Work and Worship." This is in the "faith, family, and freedom" tradition of political values, which gives religion an important place in public life.[11]

In the June 12, 1993, aborted elections, the candidates for president and vice president from the SDP, M. K. O. Abiola and Baba Gana Kingibe, and those from the National Republican Convention (NRC), Bashir Tofa and Sylvester Ugoh, were all in the progressive-conservative tradition. The presumed winner was Abiola, a Yoruba "renewal" (*tajdid*) Muslim from Ogun State. He was a big businessman and drew support from throughout the north, as well as the south.[12]

As already noted, the progressive-conservatives have been modernizers, but with a commitment to conserve the best of the past. For many years, they have served to define Nigeria's moderate approach to both politics and religion. With the emergence of the PDP as the dominant party in the Fourth Republic, it clearly took on an umbrella role, for it included radical progressives (such as Abubakar Rimi), moderate progressives (Atiku Abubakar, in the Yar'Adua tradition), and progressive-conservatives (such as Adamu Ciroma). The group's orientations can be summarized as follows:

—Progressive-conservatives have been the backbone of civilian authority in Nigeria since independence, with partial exceptions during the military periods; they have a strong respect for constituted authority and support "change with stability."

—Progressive-conservative identities often have a strong sense of federalism and a tradition of power sharing between communities.

—Their identity groups tend to believe in transformation through a combination of Western education and classical Islamic education. The progressive component seeks modernization; the conservative component wishes to preserve the best of the past.

Military Identities

On July 29, 1975, General Murtala Ramat Muhammad emerged as the first Muslim military head of state in Nigeria. For the next six months, he made a powerful impact on the national and international political worlds with his decisive actions and his image as a smart, strong leader driven by a sense of social justice. Following his assassination on February 13, 1976, he was revered as a hero and charismatic figure. "Ramatism" became a popular ideology, especially among semieducated youth in the large northern cities. Books idealizing his memory appeared, and his home city of Kano established a mosque and prayer ground around his burial site, now a pilgrimage destination for those who respect his memory.[13]

Murtala's emphasis on youth and social justice resonated with the public at a time when the oil boom in Nigeria was producing millionaires overnight and the question of principles appeared irrelevant to the quest for money. When the young Kano soldier who appeared fearless in "speaking truth to power" lost his life, many in the Muslim community considered him a martyr.

Murtala was succeeded by his second-in-command, General Olusegun Obasanjo, a Christian from the southwest. For the next three and a half years, before the return to civilian rule in 1979, he worked to continue many of the "progressive" policies of his predecessor. His next-in-command was Shehu Musa Yar'Adua, the dynamic personality who also represented progress and patriotism to many young people in the north.

Shehu Musa Yar'Adua was born in 1943 into a distinguished titled family in Katsina. He had inherited the traditional title of *Tafidan Katsina*. His father was a First Republic minister. Shehu Musa attended Nigerian Military School in Zaria, the Royal Military Academy in Sandhurst, England, and Command and Staff College in the United Kingdom. Having completed his military training in England before the civil war, he was among the first northern Muslim officers to work closely with colleagues from throughout Nigeria and to experience the tragedy of the civil war firsthand.[14]

After the transition to the Second Republic, Shehu Musa Yar'Adua retired from the military and launched a successful career in agribusiness and farming (as did Obasanjo). He retained his close personal links with Obasanjo during the Second Republic and the successor military regimes of Muhammadu Buhari (from Daura) and Ibrahim Babangida (from Minna). Shehu Musa served on a number of corporate boards and was part of the emerging Nigerian national business community. He appeared to be a symbol of cooperation between northern and southern Nigerian business leaders, and many of his close associates were from the southern parts of the country.

In the transition period to the Third Republic, Shehu Musa Yar'Adua declared his candidacy for the presidency through the SDP. In the primaries, he emerged as the party's leading candidate. Articulating his views on public values and social programs, he fended off challenges from the Rimi wing of the old PRP and seemed the successor to a no-nonsense social justice program in the Murtala Muhammad and Aminu Kano populist tradition. He had become an icon for those who wanted social change and some "progressive" transformation of Nigerian society. He had good organizational skills and commanded the loyalty of those who served with him.

During the Abacha military regime—after November 1993—Shehu Musa was accused of plotting to overthrow Abacha and was subsequently jailed (as was his colleague, Olusegun Obasanjo). In December 1997, Yar'Adua died in prison under mysterious circumstances and was buried in Katsina.[15]

The brief regime of Major General Muhammadu Buhari (1984–85), before the takeover of Ibrahim Babangida, favored a form of austere and disciplined religious simplicity associated with the extreme far north in Nigeria, in this case, Daura, on the edge of the desert. Ironically, Buhari's honesty, straightforwardness, and insistence on probity in government affairs bothered many in his regime and in the emerging upper classes, particularly when he tried to root out corruption through draconian measures. At the same time, he was widely admired by ordinary people, especially in the north. The next regime, under Babangida, was far more receptive to the free-wheeling business atmosphere of the oil era.

However, Buhari reemerged in public life as the head of the Petroleum Trust Fund (PTF), set up in October 1994 to manage surplus income from the increased prices of petroleum and to provide a domestic intervention aid function. Some considered the PTF an alternative government, but the key point was that Buhari had the trust of a broad base of Nigerian constituencies.[16] During the Fourth Republic, Buhari became the presidential candidate for the All Nigeria People's Party and after the elections in 2003 remained the most active challenger to the Obasanjo government.[17]

The ethnoreligious profile of General Ibrahim Babangida has already been mentioned. Basically, he is considered a Middle Belt Muslim without deep roots in his religious legacy.[18] In the run-up to the 2007 elections, however, Babangida has sought to strengthen his religious credentials.

The accession to power of General Sani Abacha in November 1993 kindled some controversy, in view of the ambiguity surrounding his ethnoreligious background. His father was from Borno but moved to Kano as a soldier in the British colonial forces. Sani Abacha was born in the Kano urban area, in the "new northern district" (Fagge). He received his education in Kano and in many respects was a combination of Kano and Borno influences. Because of his migrant status in Kano, however, he had less contact with the traditional emirate or religious elites and more with the new modernizers, including the commercial classes of Kano and the educated elites. Yet his religious identity was firmly rooted in his Borno heritage, which gave him a no-nonsense, no-frills confidence in his ethnoreligious identity.[19] In general, however, he was regarded as a secular ruler, who, after his death in June 1998, came to widely epitomize the personal aggrandizement and corruption of the Nigerian state.[20]

With the transition to civilian rule in 1999, many of the northern military officers who had held political office under military regimes were involuntarily retired. Some have become engaged in party politics (with the PDP or ANPP), while others have moved to the business sector or otherwise serve as counselors to various groups.

In sum, Muslim military identities at the senior level have ranged from progressive radicals (Murtala Muhammad) to moderate progressives (Yar'Adua), progressives or progressive-conservatives (Buhari), and secular-leaning individuals (Babangida, Abacha). Because of their influence on public life in Nigeria, they have served as different types of role models within the national Muslim communities. Though diverse, military orientations to authority, community, and change can be summarized as follows:

—Having a strong sense of hierarchical authority, military identities display strong centralization tendencies; military command structures tend to be the model of decisionmaking.

—These identities also have a strong sense of national community, with little patience for subnational demands for autonomy. They often have strong links with transnational professional communities, including counterparts in the Western world.

—Those in support of the military model tend to use power to achieve change. They are impatient with consultative approaches to consensus building and prefer to rely on technology and organization to effect transformation.

Women's Organizational Identities

On the whole, Muslim women in Nigeria reflect the ethnolinguistic cultures of which they are a part. Over the past century, most urban women in the predominantly Hausa-Fulani emirates have been secluded, depending on their status in society, with women of higher status being more secluded.[21] (Rural women have not really been secluded, owing to the circumstances of their agrarian life.) Muslim women in Borno tend to be less secluded and in recent years have been very active in educational and commercial activities. Muslim women in Yoruba societies have not been secluded and are virtually indistinguishable from non-Muslim Yoruba women in many cultural matters. In the Muslim Middle Belt minority areas, more women have been educated and have no tradition of seclusion.

Within the emirate sufi brotherhood societies, women have been part of the reform movements and have sometimes even achieved high status as sufis. In contrast, the more legalistic subcultures of emirate society favor a more classical ideal of womanhood, which entails restricted legal rights for women.

Many of the distinctions between "progressive," "progressive-conservative," and "conservative" movements among Nigerian Muslims pertain to the role of women. More progressive groups favor a more equal and open role, with corresponding opportunities in education and economic life, whereas more conservative groups espouse a traditional view of women (whatever the cultural view happens to be).

In the mid-1980s, education began to have a clear impact on Muslim women, encouraging some to become even more Western. Some Muslim women participated in organizations such as Women in Nigeria (WIN), widely regarded in Nigeria as "feminist."[22] Others, equally educated (through secondary or university level), began to reclaim their own sense of Muslim identity. One result of this trend was the organization of the Federation of Muslim Women's Associations in Nigeria (FOMWAN, see chapter 5) following a meeting of the Muslim Sisters Organization (MSO) in Kano.[23] FOMWAN was to give coherence to Muslim women's organizations throughout Nigeria and focus on counteracting the role of custom in Nigerian Muslim Society.

As noted in chapter 5, by the early 1990s, FOMWAN had about 400 member organizations throughout Nigeria, but with the majority in the Yoruba-speaking areas.[24] Each state selected representatives to a national committee, which published a magazine (*The Muslim Woman*) and held annual conferences on a topic of special concern to Muslim women. Using English as the main language of communication, FOMWAN acts as a liaison with other national and international Muslim women's groups.[25]

One issue of special concern is women's lack of education. In response, FOMWAN has set up nursery and primary schools that provide solid, standard education plus religious teaching. The organization is also concerned with various shari'a issues, concentrating on matters of family law. It is against early marriage and wife seclusion. The women are articulate and engaged in public life, as well as involved in raising their own families. FOMWAN has close ties with the Nigerian Supreme Council for Islamic Affairs (NSCIA) and shares an interest in both Islamic and Western education. The leadership tends to come from the educated establishment.[26]

Throughout the 1990s, FOMWAN was particularly interested in the "widespread political, economic and intellectual immorality which is an obstacle to progress in our society. Such immorality (includes) abuse of power, maladministration, embezzlement of public funds, fraud, unjust economic policies that bring hardship to the people, and distortion of religion to satisfy selfish desires."[27] One of its special services during the 2003 national elections was to provide election monitors throughout the country. From its base in Abuja, FOMWAN has developed into a well-recognized nongovernmental organization with national reach and a moderate outlook. Many of its state-based leaders are wives of establishment figures.[28] All in all, women's organizations are noted for the following approaches to authority, community, and change:

—Most women's organizations follow traditional models similar to culture zone parameters, although some women's models are diverging from those of male counterparts, in the reformist tradition of reinterpreting tradition through education. Women's umbrella organizations tend to rotate authority and leadership among the federal components, that is to say, the country's thirty-six states.

—Visions of community coincide with many of these components, although a sense of national community is also emerging, especially through FOMWAN's federalist structure. FOMWAN also has extensive international contacts with counterpart organizations in both the Western and Muslim worlds.

—Women in gender-based identity groups offer many significant examples of how organizational, communicational, and educational approaches can be used to achieve change. Some also follow approaches similar to those of other identity groups discussed in this chapter. FOMWAN is an umbrella organization that focuses on education (in both classic religious knowledge and a standard curriculum), with an emphasis on language skills (Arabic and English). It maintains strong links to the international community as well as the mainstream Muslim organizations. Women's organizations have often been successful in lobbying for changes on specific policies or programs, such as creating space for women inside the new mosque at Abuja.

National Umbrella Organizations and Identity

Muslim identity became a prominent issue in December 1980, when a violent conflagration sparked by an itinerant "syncretist" preacher, Muhammad Marwa (also known as Maitatsine), in Kano City left thousands dead.[29] For the Muslim community, this event made clear that the interbrotherhood (sufi) rivalries and the brotherhood/nonbrotherhood (sufi/*Izala*) confrontations were less important than the extreme syncretism emerging in its midst. (Maitatsine appeared to blend Hausa *bori* customs with selected versions of Islam.)[30] As was widely recognized, it was essential to broaden the scope of acceptable orthodoxy to include all of Nigeria's mainstream Muslim communities, many of which had a different legacy from that of the Sokoto caliphal reformers.[31]

The early Muslim ecumenical movement of the 1960s, especially the northern-based Society for the Victory of Islam (*Jama'atul Nasril Islam*/JNI), broadened its scope to the national arena, mainly through the activities of the NSCIA.[32] As mentioned earlier, the head of the Supreme Council was the sultan of Sokoto. The vice president was the shehu of Borno, and the secretary a leading Yoruba Muslim lawyer, Alhaji Abdu-Lateef Adegbite.[33] In a sense, this format reflected the emerging establishment's ties to the political, economic, and military arenas in Nigeria.

An event of further significance to national umbrella organizations was the death of the elderly Sultan Abubakar III in November 1988. During his long illness, there had been a subtle positioning for succession between two branches of the descendants of the original founder of the Sokoto caliphate (Usman dan Fodio).[34] The immediate family of the deceased sultan felt his eldest son, Muhammad Maccido, should be named successor. The rival candidate from the Buhari family was Ibrahim Dasuki, born in December 1923, in Dogandaji, Sokoto. Dasuki's cause ultimately prevailed among the kingmakers, and he was appointed the new sultan in 1990 by the governor of Sokoto State, although not without considerable turmoil in the Sokoto community.

Part of the significance of the Dasuki succession was his close association with the NSCIA and its traditional leaders.[35] He had been the de facto leader of the Muslim delegation to the National Council for Religious Affairs (NCRA) even before his succession. Thus in 1987, in the aftermath of the Organization of the Islamic Conference (OIC) controversy, Federal Decree 30 established the National Council for Religious Affairs, which, in modified form, ultimately came to have twelve Christian leaders and twelve Muslim leaders. They were to meet to discuss matters of mutual concern and report directly to the Ministry of Interior. The symbolic leader of the Muslim delegation was the sultan of Sokoto, although in practice it was his representative, Ibrahim Dasuki.[36]

Thus Dasuki came into his sultanship with a weak base of support in Sokoto but a long history of experience at the national and international levels. This included serving as Nigerian "pilgrim officer" in Jeddah (Saudi Arabia) from November 1959 to August 1960. When Nigeria achieved independence, he became the first secretary and head of chancery in the Nigeria office in Khartoum. Throughout the 1960s, 1970s, and 1980s, he worked to formulate and strengthen the various umbrella organizations that would bind the Nigerian Muslim *ummah* together. The Nigerian Supreme Council for Islamic Affairs was a balanced endeavor that used the existing subnational state system to see that Muslim groups and interests throughout the federation were given fair representation.

With Dasuki's succession in 1988 (the final installation was not until March 1990), he intensified his quiet diplomacy among the various Muslim communities in Nigeria, ranging from traditional emirs to modern women's groups. In essence, he moved the symbolism of the sultanship from an emirate or caliphal base to a national base. Various Muslim circles and conferences outside Nigeria came to regard him as the chief spokesman for Nigerian Muslims.

The image of a modern and effective sultan was a double-edged sword, since many within the Muslim community and outside feared that his powers (or rather, authority) might be too great. On the morning of April 22, 1990, certain junior military officers in Lagos tried to mount a coup and assassinate the head of state (Babangida). They took over the broadcast facilities in Lagos to announce, among other things, that they were expelling the five far northern (predominantly Muslim) states and insisted that the sultan of Sokoto, Dasuki, resign in favor of his much more locally oriented rival from the incumbent's family, Maccido. Although the government restored order quickly, it soon became clear that the coup-makers had Christian first names and appeared to be from the Middle Belt or the south. This set off alarm bells in the Nigerian Muslim community and had the effect of consolidating support for the head of state and Dasuki.

In March 1996, however, Sultan Dasuki was deposed and jailed by General Abacha, on vague charges of financial irregularities. The political fact, however, was that Dasuki had been appointed by Babangida, partly under the influence of Dasuki's son, Sambo Dasuki, who was Babangida's *aide de camp*. Hence Abacha found himself working closely with the rivals of the Dasuki/Babangida faction, especially Shehu Malami and his protegeé, Muhammad Maccido. Another significant point, Sambo Dasuki had been charged with attempting to overthrow Abacha but was living outside Nigeria.

In Dasuki's place, Abacha appointed Muhammad Maccido, the major contender for the title in 1988. Since Maccido was popular in Sokoto but virtually unknown outside the local context, the move was considered an attempt to diminish the national base of the sultanship, especially in relation to Kano and Borno, and to neutralize a potential rival (Dasuki).

Yet during the Dasuki sultanship, the NSCIA, with its somewhat "progressive-conservative" (establishment) image, had to deal with the full range of Nigerian Muslim identities and values, plus try to serve as an effective liaison with the counterpart Christian Association of Nigeria (CAN). In the politicized atmosphere surrounding the local elections of 1990, the state elections of 1991, the national primary elections of 1992, and the national elections of 1993, some of the old north-south issues and intra-Muslim rivalries resurfaced.

How the Nigerian *ummah* would handle such challenges remained to be seen, but the national-based umbrella organizations provided one means of communication across the other cleavages of ethnicity and location. Clearly, Sultan Dasuki was comfortable with the outcome of the June 1993 election, since he had worked with M. K. O. Abiola over the years on a variety of Muslim projects.[37] After his deposition and subsequent jailing on vague charges of financial improprieties, Dasuki eventually settled quietly in Kaduna and made no effort to reclaim the title of sultan following the death of Abacha.

Thus being identified as a "Nigerian Muslim" is in many ways more relevant outside of Nigeria than inside. Yet with the significant number of pilgrims each year and the large number of Nigerian students who are abroad, the existence of national-based organizations to promote and mediate Muslim interests and identities serves important functions, including the reinforcement of national identities.

The national Muslim groups tend to fit into the existing nation-state international system and are often seen as an intermediate step toward closer cooperation of the Muslim community (*ummah*) at the global level. This acceptance of the nation-state system sometimes puts them at odds with the challengers to the nation-state system in the international arena (historically, Iran and Libya) and draws them closer to the Saudi-backed Organization of the Islamic Conference model of cooperation.[38] Nigeria's status within the OIC has been the subject of heated debate within Nigeria, and opinions may vary depending on whether there is a Muslim head of state. In any case, Nigeria has kept a low profile on OIC matters.[39]

A major challenge for the umbrella organizations in Nigeria was how far to extend tolerance within the Muslim community. As already mentioned, the Maitatsine affair in 1980 (and thereafter) helped shape the boundaries of acceptable doctrine and behavior. In turn, this affair was affected by the general expectation among Muslim communities in West Africa that the *mahdi* would return at the end of the Muslim century, that is, in 1979 CE (1400 AH). Subsequently, that expectation diminished and may remain low at least until the turn of the next Muslim century. The challenge for the sultan of Sokoto (that is, the president of the NSCIA) has been to balance all of the competing identities and values in the Nigerian Muslim community and to promote tolerance in the multireligious fabric of Nigerian society.

The NSCIA's role in conflict resolution is considered in more detail in part 3. Significantly, as elections in the Fourth Republic became more partisan and violent, the NSCIA followed the precedent of FOMWAN and the Muslim League for Accountability—an association of young Muslim university men—who monitored the 2003 elections as accredited nongovernmental organizations. The NSCIA began this monitoring in the local government elections of March 27, 2004, in hopes of ensuring fair play and avoiding violence.[40]

National umbrella organizations can be said to have the following orientations toward authority, community, and change:

—Umbrella organizations are consensual and representational, but with a central hierarchy of traditional religious figures. They tend to be establishment oriented and often find themselves challenged by younger reformist elements. The role of the sultan of Sokoto may partly depend on the qualities and inclinations of the incumbent. Basically, the umbrella organizations are "federal" in design and practice.

—During the First Republic, these groups developed a sense of northern regional organization; during the Second Republic, there was a growing sense of national community. In the transition to the aborted Third Republic, the nation-state was recognized as the main organizing principle in the international system. In the Fourth Republic, these organizations have tried to mediate across the three-tier federal structure. At the same time, they are providing a link to broader transnational communities.

—Umbrella organizations tend to focus on "change with stability" (that is, incremental change rather than radical change); they use organization (including finance), media, and education to bring about change. In this respect, they are as much a part of the mainstream establishment as the progressive-conservatives. However, they are also a representational body and hence reflect the full range of orientations found in Nigerian Muslim society.

Summary: Patterns in Muslim Civic Orientations

As outlined in chapters 3 and 6, Nigeria has nine Muslim identity groups with distinct orientations to authority, community, change, and conflict resolution.

Orientations to Authority

With the shift from Arabic to indigenous language sources (and more recently, English-language sources), local interpretations of the primary sources are serving as the basis for the legitimation of a wide variety of authority structures. To some extent, such reformations may be said to have started with the

Sokoto reformers of the early nineteenth century. (In addition to writing in Arabic, many of the reform scholars and leaders wrote and preached in Hausa, Fulfulde, and other indigenous languages.)

The reformed sufi brotherhoods of the twentieth century were successful partly because they legitimated the use of vernacular languages in their poetry of praise and in other brotherhood (*tarika*) rituals. Thus perhaps a second reformation occurred, especially after World War II, which had the effect of incorporating many local shaykhs into new combinations of religious identity structures and opening the door to more grassroots participation.

A third reformation occurred in the 1970s and 1980s during the oil boom (and bust) period in Nigeria, when international contacts and mass media equipment and technology made audiovisual communications a grassroots phenomenon. The anti-innovation, back-to-basics approach of Abubakar Gummi was convincing to many, especially a younger generation who did not read Arabic but who were capable of communication in Hausa and English. This reformation challenged virtually every preexisting category of authority, from sufi brotherhoods to emirate constituencies and modern youth. This reformation has had a profound effect on the Sokoto caliphal authorities, and even on the Nigerian Supreme Council for Islamic Affairs. At the same time, the reformation has made the Muslim community aware of the need for tolerance within the *ummah* and within other Nigerian religious communities (such as Christian ones), which should be trying to understand the historic changes that are under way. Almost all categories of Nigerian Muslim authority are beginning to sense that authority patterns are changing, and that tolerance and patience are prerequisites to a peaceful transformation. Orientations toward authority in each of these categories have a strong age or intergenerational bias. Also, many of these categories overlap, in which case the salience or tendency of the pattern is strengthened.

Orientations to Community

Clearly, some of the Muslim identity groups are associated with different community levels in Nigeria. Thus the sufi brotherhoods and anti-innovation legalists tend to have more local or grassroots interests. The political progressives and progressive-conservatives tend to work at both the state and federal levels. The military model is mainly appropriate at the national level. The umbrella organizations work at national, state, and local levels. The caliphal/Madina models, of course, are theoretical alternatives or ideals, which in some cases may challenge the whole notion of modern nation-states, especially of a secular variety.

Orientations to Change and Transformation

There is a strong sense of generational change among the age groups in Nigeria's Muslim community. The tension between the progressives and the progressive-conservatives is by and large associated with struggles for authority between those of a younger age (between twenty and thirty-nine) and those who are forty and older. Thus responsibilities for stability increase with age, whereas pressure for change comes from society's youth.

This intergenerational tension also comes from differences in education. The enormous jump in secondary and university education enrollments in the 1970s and into the 1980s and beyond has affected all parts of the country, including the predominantly Muslim areas. The tension between "culture" and "religion" (between "innovation" and *sunna*) was in part a result of the wave of young people (men and women) who were pulled into the educational slipstream and who challenged the wisdom of their parents and elders. With the economic downturn of the 1980s, jobs were not available for many of these graduates. Their commitment to realistic career stakes in the national system gave way to another range of emotional strategies, from despair to idealism. During the repressive rule of the Abacha period, many of the educated elites found jobs abroad. While southern Nigerians migrated mainly to the United States, Britain, or South Africa, northern Muslim professionals also found opportunities within the oil-rich states of the Middle East.

The process of change in Nigeria has been extreme in its fluctuations, with the 1970s exhibiting high rates of urbanization and growth, and the 1980s and 1990s bringing austerity and largely negative growth. The spike in oil prices during the First Gulf War (1990–91) to about $40 a barrel resulted in a $12 billion windfall for the government of Nigeria, but much of this revenue was "off budget" and seemed to disappear.[41]

The return to civilian rule in 1999 did not immediately turn these economic realities around, although there was hope in some quarters for a "democracy dividend" in terms of job opportunities. The next spike in the price of oil, to well over $40 a barrel during the Iraq War (2003–05), created pressure to make sure some of this wealth got to the state and local levels. In face of the economic despair at the grassroots level, on one hand, and the get-rich-quick attitudes of those in power, on the other, younger northerners grew intent on finding solutions to the country's problems. These fluctuated from the quick-fix military solutions of the Murtala Muhammad period to strong calls for "social justice" (which formed the base of the Buhari political movement in 2003; as already noted, Buhari's reputation for integrity and his passion for "justice" won him a younger generation of followers throughout the country).

The spike in oil prices immediately before and after the Second Gulf War has given the Nigerian government some respite, although it came at a time when "money politics" crept into the 2003 elections. (As mentioned earlier, during the first nine months of 2004, a windfall of $20 billion accrued to the federal budget from oil revenues, that is, more than $2 billion a month. This pattern has continued in 2005.) The glaring disparities in wealth and charges of bribery and corruption in the elections seem to suggest that the elites are getting richer and the masses are getting poorer.

All age groups in Nigeria have experienced both negative and positive change, and all frequently discuss and express concern about the process of change itself. Remedies that would transform the lives of individuals, groups, and society as a whole range from fatalistic incrementalism to radical interventionism. It is not clear whether the Muslim community's solutions differ from those of other groups in Nigeria. However, some of the tensions surrounding negative change are being released through the manipulation of religious symbols, while some segments of the population are asking whether Nigeria should even stay together as a nation.[42]

Significantly, most of the pessimism about the survival of Nigeria as a nation does not come from Nigeria's Muslim community, but rather from its southern and Christian community. In general, Muslims believe their future lies with a united Nigeria. (This thinking may be based on the logic of oil revenues, which derive from the Delta areas.) Thus discussions of "change" within the Muslim community do not often dwell on partition or secession as a strategy for improving society. Many Muslim educated elites argue that a clean division of Nigeria is impossible, because of people's high mobility and intermarriage patterns.

Although some followers of a caliphal model might counsel withdrawal into the private worlds of religious communities, many of the articulate spokespersons for neoclassical Islamic models are part of university systems or other educational systems that are national in their funding and orientation. The topic of "change" within the Muslim community inevitably comes back to a discussion of leadership.[43] That community has clearly shifted its identities and values from subnational regionalism and localism to more national and international orientations. This is in part a reflection of changes in education and communication, which have important implications for confidence in national communities, that is, the vision of Nigerian Muslims providing the backbone of society, both within the clusters of states where they are demographically significant (Borno, the Sokoto caliphal areas, the Middle Belt, and several of the Yoruba areas) and within the nation as a whole. Implicit in this vision is the need to work closely with Christian communities in Nigeria. (The status of "traditional religion" is something of a taboo subject among most establishment Muslims, given the nonpreferentialist national model that seems to be emerging and the constitutional recognition of "customary law.")

Several broad patterns of transformation in the Nigerian Muslim community may well affect identity and nationhood. One such pattern relates to intergenerational differences, with educational level or access being a key variable. As a result, Muslim religious movements have experienced dramatic shifts associated with age groups and a growing tension between youth and "elders." Second, the Muslim community is developing a sense of tolerance on the national level, recognizing that stable relations with non-Muslims are a first step to other changes and values. Third, individual and societal conditions are clearly changing both for better and for worse. "Justice" has become a major concern, along with fluctuations in international economic conditions. "Justice" refers in part to how the national cake is divided up. The federal model has worked well enough for horizontal distributive purposes, but what to do about the extremes of wealth and poverty has not yet been resolved. Corruption is another major concern, although almost everyone in Nigeria has his or her own definition of "corruption." Fourth, many argue that it is time to come to grips with "ethnicity" and cultural issues stemming mainly from "traditional" rather than Christian culture or educated groups. (Popular Western culture is seen as a threat to the youth but is considered a separate issue.) Fifth, societal transformation generates new groupings and regroupings. The progressive-conservative center appears to maintain its hold in Nigerian society, partly because it draws in younger progressive elements. At the same time, there is a national tendency, also reflected in Nigerian Muslim society, to swing between more consensual models of decisionmaking (that is, civilian) and military models, both of which are headed by authority figures.

The Nigerian Muslim community continues to take new shape as modern print and electronic media allow vernacular languages and languages of wider communication to provide authority and community structures within expanded levels. The models of nationhood that may emerge from this may reflect as much the intense Nigerian interest in current European experiments in nationhood or in the republics of the former Soviet Union as in the historic legacy of communities in West Africa or in the contemporary Muslim world. As of 2005, Abuja has become the real political, military, and economic center for thinking and planning for the Economic Community of West African States, and West African parliamentarians hold regular meetings in designated facilities at the International Conference Center.

Orientations to Conflict Resolution

Clearly, some sort of communication between religiously diverse groups is necessary if conflict mediation and resolution is to occur. This is true within the Muslim community as well as between Muslims and Christians. As mentioned earlier, some leadership patterns are already evident in the Nigerian Supreme Council for Islamic Affairs, with the sultan being the major spokesman and mediator.

In recent years, traditional authorities, many of whom have a religious as well as a cultural position in Nigerian society, have also become an essential node in the crisis management and conflict resolution system. At times, they have provided important leadership, alone or in concert with other traditional authorities of different religious identities, to mediate religious riots, student demonstrations, or other forms of direct confrontation. As lifetime appointees (pending good behavior), traditional leaders tend to be local diplomats facilitating catharsis and encouraging a "forgive-and-forget" approach to local conflict, particularly of a religious nature.

The sultan of Sokoto, the emir of Kano, and the shehu of Borno are all playing active and constructive roles, as are many of the smaller emirate leaders. For example, given the extreme tension between the emirate zone and the Yoruba zone in the post-1993 period, the mediating role of the new sultan, Muhammad Maccido, was watched closely. In October 1996, the sultan traveled to Akure, in Ondo State (one of the predominantly "non-Muslim" Yoruba states), to meet with two traditional rulers from the state: the *Osemawe* of Ondoland (Oba Festus Ibidapo Adesanoye) and the *Deji* of Akureland (Oba Adeboboye Adesida). According to one account, Sultan Maccido "urged the people to promote peace, unity and stability for the country to move forward."[44] Maccido also said that "the nation's abundant natural and human resources could only be tapped under a peaceful atmosphere. According to him the forces that held the nation together were stronger than the differences which could also be reduced by co-operation and understanding among the nation's over 250 ethnic groups."[45]

Whether such mediating activities, both within the Muslim community and with other traditional leaders of Nigeria, are sufficient to address the concerns of younger elements or "new breed" elements should not obscure the fact that elders can contribute to the conflict resolution processes. Formally or informally, they will play a key role in promoting religious tolerance and preventing instances of religious intolerance.[46]

Part III

Challenges of Nigerian Democratic Federalism

7

Challenges of the Fourth Republic (1999–2005)

Military rule in Nigeria came to an end on May 29, 1999, with the swearing in of President Olusegun Obasanjo and the establishment of a Fourth Republic.[1] Between 1999 and the undertaking of elections in April 2003 (and their aftermath through 2005), important issues and precedents were set regarding democratic federalism.[2]

With the return to civilian rule in 1999, after fifteen years of centralized military rule and the trickle-down logic of an oil-driven economy, the basic challenge was how to decentralize the country without moving to partition or to those variations of confederation that might be a prelude to partition. The political compromise was clearly some form of democratic federalism, although what such federalism would look like in the Nigerian context was a matter of ongoing debate.[3] An underlying issue was the reform, or "re-professionalization," of the military, especially since many of the retired "political officers" came from the Muslim north.[4]

These domestic developments have a global context as well. It has been marked by a general increase in democratic participation, an interconnected global economy in which comparative advantage may reward both small and large nations, the decentralizing impact of information technologies on forms of human organization, and, since September 2001, new forms of security cooperation across all levels. Security concerns, in particular, require first responders to be especially effective at the grassroots levels.

Perhaps less obvious, but equally important, has been a global trend that transects all these issues: the evolution and implementation of forms of federalism as a way of decentralizing political power and locating more decisions at local or subnational levels. This trend has also provided a template for newer types of transnational regional organizations.

Thus Nigeria's experiment in democratic federalism under the Fourth Republic occurs not only in the light of previous political experience but also in a changed global context. Nigeria's 1999 constitution, with its 160 pages of provisions, closely approximates the 1979 constitution and the aborted 1989 (1993) constitution in outlining the structures and responsibilities of federal, state, and local governments.[5] How the constitution would function in practice was of concern to Nigerians as well as the international community. The National Political Reform Dialogue (NPRD) was established in the spring of 2005 to examine constitutional issues, with the exception of the "no-go" areas of federalism and national unity.

Emerging Issues of Nigerian Federalism

As noted previously, Nigerian "military federalism" is a contradiction in terms, since major state and local appointments came from above, not from below, and decisionmaking showed little sign of decentralization. Hence the military periods in Nigeria—from 1966 to 1979 and 1984 to 1999—do not qualify as experiments in federalism, despite the state-level reorganization and establishment of a new federal capital territory (Abuja) during these periods. Indeed, under the military regimes the political culture of Nigeria hardened into a strong centralized system. Nonetheless, the more limited civilian periods—1960 to 1966 and 1979 to 1983—saw the birth of certain patterns and expectations (see chapter 2).[6]

In the first term of the Fourth Republic (1999–2003), the presidential/federal model was in theory (constitutionally) based on a separation of powers between the executive, legislative, and judicial branches of government. In practice, this emerged as a strong presidential model, along the lines of the system in both France and Russia. In 1999 the major issue was the transition from military to civilian rule. The winning party coalition won the support of five of the six zones, that is, all except the southwest. When both major parties selected their 1999 presidential candidates from the southwest, the move was considered a concession to marginalization problems in that area following the annulled 1993 election and the shift of the federal capital from Lagos to Abuja.

This winning coalition seemed to come apart after the 1999 elections, as the "democracy dividend" did not fully materialize and strong tensions developed between the legislative and executive branches, both dominated by the People's Democratic Party (PDP). At the same time, states' rights advocates set up shari'a law in the criminal domain in the twelve far northern states. The federal government was now fully based in the new federal capital at Abuja. With most government revenues coming in through the federal level—a result of oil royalties—a new issue to consider was the proper balance of state and local authorities versus federal authorities. Under military rule, local government authorities had been severely weakened, but now attention turned again to their role as well as that of traditional rulers (the so-called royal fathers).[7]

The 1999 presidential/federal model, with "federal character" balances enshrined in the constitution, left unclear how the thirty-six states would act as surrogates for regional and subregional identities in the federal establishment. The six-zone formula for representation had not been legally articulated, yet it continued to play an informal role in the political coalition-building processes. A larger issue was the increased alienation of the north.

Another concern was overcentralization, a legacy of oil and military rule, especially since the Second Republic. It has generated counterpressures for decentralization, confederation, and even partition. Since political coalitions were weak or shifting, it was still the military that guaranteed the integrity of the country. Furthermore, the shift from a command-and-control center to "federal capital" has not been smooth, and balance has not yet been achieved in the three-tier federal structure. The role of the federalized police has been problematic in situations where state and local security first-responders belonged to a party or faction that was different from the president's, or simply were incapable of "serving and protecting" local populations. Also, since most revenues came from oil and gas at the national level, the distribution formula to states and local governments was still not in political balance, especially in the oil-producing areas.[8]

Finally, as noted above, the presidency was looking more like a Fifth French Republic (as envisioned by General Charles de Gaulle) rather than a model that balances the role of the federal legislature with the federal executive, especially on budget issues. Although the legislature's impeachment efforts against the president in 2002 appeared to have subsided, the challenge remains how to offset overcentralization at the federal level and in the presidency.[9] In the spring of 2005, the National Assembly again tried to implement impeachment procedures against President Obasanjo.

Second, national leadership, as distinct from state and local leadership, has tended to come from the military ranks, even in a civilianized or retired military guise. A big challenge was how to encourage national civilian leadership that did not simply reflect regional political constituencies. Some of the provisions for a national base in federal elections tried to address this issue, but there were still weaknesses in the political recruiting system.

Third, crime and corruption undermined even well-meant efforts to provide good government. There was no obvious solution to this problem, other than leadership by example, since political culture in Nigeria had increasingly allowed for a wink-and-nod approach favoring high-ranking individuals over ordinary citizens. Consequently, local violations of law and order were endemic, which again raised the prospect of a federalized police force as opposed to a community service entity. Clearly, security and police forces needed better training in conflict prevention and crisis management at all levels.

Fourth, the judiciary continued to play a weak role partly as a result of long-term military rule. Political interpretations of the constitution tended to rely on power politics rather than judicial precedent. Ideally, the issue of multiple legal systems at different levels of government would have been handled in ways that strengthened institutional and legal capacities, rather than undermined them.

Finally, national elections had always been problematic in Nigeria, given the high stakes in a winner-take-all partisan environment, where preelection coalitions dissolved in the aftermath of elections and personalities tended to dominate. The elections also witnessed the emergence of ethnic youth organizations, which sometimes had strong separatist tendencies or were not above using localized "terrorism" to achieve their goals. Such vigilante groups have multiplied since the return to democratic federalism in 1999, leaving Nigeria with a potential Achilles heel as it experiments with civilian rule. Not least, they seemed to justify the federalizing of all police activities, lest the police be co-opted by local notables and interest groups, or worse, that a local "war lord" syndrome might emerge.

In the immediate aftermath of the 2003 elections, the losing parties and coalitions chose to appeal the results through election tribunals. Tensions continued to rise through the summer and fall of 2003, however, in some cases taking on an ethnoreligious tone as allegations increased that the Obasanjo government was biased against Muslims.[10] In the former northern region, only four of the nineteen governors were "Christian" (in Benue, Taraba, Adamawa, and Plateau). Of these four, the election of the Adamawa governor (Boni Haruna) was successfully challenged in court (although later overturned on appeal) and the Plateau governor (Joshua Dariye) was replaced during a six-month emergency decree issued by President Obasanjo in May 2004, after ethnoreligious violence broke out in the state.[11]

Politics and Federal Character

The three-tier elections in late 1998 and early 1999, which ushered in the civilian regime, implemented a "federal character" electoral provision. Thus a successful candidate for president was required to have "not less than one-quarter of the votes cast at the election in each of at least two-thirds of all the States of the Federation and the Federal Capital Territory, Abuja."[12] As noted earlier, the Nigerian idea of "federal character" was based on a formula of parity between the thirty-six states in virtually all areas, from elections to executive appointments. The Federal Character Commission was constitutionally mandated in 1999 to be made up as follows:

> One person to represent each of the States of the Federation and the Federal Capital Territory, Abuja, and to (a) work out an equitable formula subject to the approval of the National Assembly for the distribution of all posts in the public service of the Federation and the states, the armed forces of the Federation, the Nigeria Police Force and other government security agencies, government owned companies and parastatals of the States; (b) promote, monitor and enforce compliance with the principles of proportional sharing of all bureaucratic, economic, media and political posts at all levels of government.[13]

Clearly, there was a historic local incentive for the creation of states, both in terms of access to budget allocations and representation in all executive branches. But the rush to statehood, often devised as a management mechanism by military regimes, left considerable disparity in strength between the states and, in fact, consolidated national control over them, since during military periods all appointments were made by the central command. Yet, as mentioned earlier, the geographic zonal balance was important both locally and nationally.

In the 1998–99 elections, the three major political parties—the PDP, All Peoples Party (APP), and the Alliance for Democracy (AD)—put various coalitions together depending on the level of government. Hence some states might have different patterns at the state and local levels, as distinct from the national elections. Since these coalitions were all forged hastily given the need for a rapid military-civilian transition, it is difficult to say much about the zonal voting blocks, other than that the PDP was dominant in five of the six zones, the exception being the southwest, as in earlier historic patterns.[14] This occurred despite the fact that presidential candidates of both major parties were from the southwest.

State party patterns arranged by zones (table 7-1) show the AD dominant in the six southwest states, the APP dominant in some of the northwest and northeast states, and the remainder strongly PDP. Even in the northwest, Kano and Katsina (PDP) balanced off Sokoto and Zamfara (APP). In the northeast, Yobe and to some extent Borno (APP) balanced off the traditional emirate

Table 7-1. Party Strength by States and Zones, with Number of Local Government Authorities (LGAs), 1999–2003

Zone and state	Number of LGAs	Dominant political party
Northwest		
Sokoto	23	APP
Zamfara	14	APP
Kebbi	21	APP & PDP
Kano	44	PDP
Jigawa	27	APP
Katsina	34	PDP
Kaduna	23	PDP
Total	186	
Average per state	27	
Northeast		
Borno	27	APP & PDP
Yobe	17	APP
Taraba	16	PDP
Bauchi	20	PDP
Gombe	10	PDP & APP
Adamawa	21	PDP
Total	111	
Average per state	18.5	
Middle Belt		
Benue	23	PDP
Kogi	21	APP
Kwara	16	APP
Nasarawa	13	PDP
Plateau	17	PDP
Niger	25	PDP
Total	115	
Average per state	19.2	

states (PDP). In part, this pattern reflected personality politics: the APP vice presidential candidate was from Yobe and Sokoto, and the PDP vice presidential candidate was from Adamawa. These results reflected more enduring regional politics, however. There was a strong PDP showing in the north, southeast, and south-south, with Kwara (APP) tilting toward the AD/southwest.

Subsequently, in the April 2003 national elections, the PDP appeared to do well in all areas, although many results remained in legal contention. (It is beyond the scope of this study to analyze the exact transformation of the

Table 7-1. Party Strength by States and Zones, with Number of Local
Government Authorities (LGAs), 1999–2003 (continued)

Zone and state	Number of LGAs	Dominant political party
Southeast		
Anambra	21	PDP
Ebonyi	13	PDP
Imo	27	APP & PDP
Enugu	17	PDP
Abia	17	PDP
Total	95	
Average per state	19	
South-south		
Bayelsa	32	PDP
Cross River	19	PDP
Delta	21	PDP
Edo	18	PDP
Rivers	23	PDP
Akwa Ibom	31	PDP
Total	144	
Average per state	24	
Southwest		
Ekiti	16	AD
Lagos	20	AD
Ogun	18	AD
Ondo	18	AD
Osun	30	AD
Oyo	33	AD
Total	135	
Average per state	22.5	

Source: World Bank, *Nigeria: State and Local Government in Nigeria*, Report 24477-UNI (Washington, 2002), p. 67.

PDP as a party formed basically in the north and victorious in 1999 in the north into more of a southern and Middle Belt party.) In overview, the major shift in 2003 was in the southwest, from the AD party to the PDP (with the exception of Lagos), which added to the impression that the incumbent PDP had swept the field.

Yet election results in the southeast, south-south, and in parts of the north have been contested by the All Nigeria People's Party (ANPP) and the twenty-eight minor parties, and election tribunals were activated to adjudicate these matters.[15] In March 2004, the election tribunal in Adamawa State declared the

Table 7-2. Governorships by Party and Zone: Post-2003 Elections

Zone	AD	ANPP	PDP
Southwest	Lagos		Ekiti, Ogun, Ondo, Osun, Oyo
Southeast			Abia, Anambra, Ebonyi, Enugu, Imo
South-south			Akwa-Ibom, Bayelsa, Cross River, Delta, Edo, Rivers
Northwest		Jigawa, Kano, Kebbi, Sokoto, Zamfara	Kaduna, Katsina
Northeast		Borno, Yobe	Adamawa, Bauchi, Gombe, Taraba
North-central			Plateau, Nasarawa, Benue, Kogi, Kwara, Niger
Total	1	7	28

Source: A. Carl LeVan, Titi Pitso, and Bodunrin Adebo, "Elections in Nigeria: Is the Third Time the Charm?" *Journal of African Elections* 2, no. 2 (2004): 40.

gubernatorial vote invalid and called for new elections, although, as noted, this was later overturned on appeal. In the north, the major shift at the gubernatorial level was in Kano State, from PDP to ANPP. Table 7-2 shows the official results of gubernatorial elections in 2003 by official zone and party.

Since federal balance meant alternating between north and south at the presidential level, by the summer of 2003 there was widespread speculation as to who the northern Muslim presidential candidates would be in the elections of 2007. The three major candidates appeared to be Atiku Abubakar (vice president, from Adamawa State), Muhammadu Buhari (leader of the ANPP, from Katsina State), and Ibrahim Babangida (former military head of state, from Niger State and the Federal Capital Territory).[16] Long-shot possibilities included Abubakar Rimi (former governor of Kano State), Ahmed Mu'azu (governor of Bauchi State), Brigadier-General Buba Marwa (former military governor of Borno and Lagos states, originally from Adamawa), and Ahmed Makarfi (governor of Kaduna State).[17] In 2004 additional candidates emerged, including Governor Bafarawa of Sokoto. The role of Muhammadu Buhari was particularly critical, since he was the acknowledged leader of the major national opposition party and coalition. Atiku Abubakar had both the advantages and disadvantages of vice presidential incumbency. He has tried to convey his strong opposition to the dictatorship of Sani Abacha, his own humble origins, and the need for continuity of government reforms.[18]

States' Rights and Shari'a Law

In January 2000, the governor of Zamfara State (Ahmed Sani) implemented legislation authorized by the state assembly establishing shari'a law in the criminal domain applicable to all Muslims in the state. This enactment was based on two interpretations of the 1999 constitution. First, the precedent for dual (or multiple) legal systems based on Muslim affiliation was clearly established in the domain of civil law, that is, family law, including marriage, divorce and inheritance, as per the 1979 and 1999 constitutions. Second, legislation that was not specifically prohibited in the 1999 constitution and that was a matter of state concern was appropriate for state-level action, provided it did not contravene fundamental constitutional rights.

Subsequently, eleven other far northern states also passed some form of shari'a criminal law, applicable to Muslims only. It should be noted that certain aspects of the shari'a legislation, such as the banning of alcohol and prostitution, were applied to all citizens in those states that held to a stricter interpretation of the law.

As previously noted, the legacy of shari'a law in northern Nigeria has always been based on the Maliki school of jurisprudence. During the colonial period (1903–60) the British system of indirect rule kept the Maliki system at the emirate level but modified it in regard to certain punishments (such as amputations and beheadings), which were considered repugnant. This modified Maliki system remained in place until the reforms of 1959, when criminal laws were consolidated into a northern regional code, in preparation for national independence in 1960. At that point, the northern region adopted a dual legal system, distinguishing between Maliki law in the civil sphere (for Muslims only) and criminal law in the common domain, with emirates losing virtually all of their legal powers.

The key figure in the First Republic's northern region legal system was Abubakar Gummi, who served as grand khadi. Since he also served as a key liaison with Saudi Arabia, the stage was set for a reevaluation of the historic legacies of both the Maliki and sufi traditions in northern Nigeria. As discussed in chapter 3, Gummi focused on going back to the original sources in the Qur'an and was one of the first to interpret the Qur'an into the Hausa language. Until his death in 1992 he served as a symbol for challenging the cultural legacies of Islam in northern Nigeria, insisting on Qur'anic-based reformation. Many of the younger generation of educated northerners became his loyal students, and Kaduna, as capital of the northern region and a "new" city, became identified with his *Izala* (anti-innovation) movement. Since Gummi was also a key link to the Saudis—intellectually and through the pilgrimage—this link strengthened Nigerian ties to the custodian of the holy places and weakened those with the traditional West African roots of Islamic culture.[19]

During the long periods of military rule, the issue of shari'a was by and large dormant. The transition to the Second Republic in 1979 did see heated debate and a compromise on the shari'a civil law issues, leaving the question of Muslim civil law up to each state, for example, without an overall national shari'a court of appeals (but with provision for Islamic scholars on the Supreme Court). With the return to civilian elections in the fall of 1998, Ahmed Sani, the APP candidate for governor of Zamfara State, ran on a platform of establishing shari'a in all domains. On his inauguration, Zamfara became the first state to institute shari'a law in the criminal domain. The published statute was clearly a mixture of several different sources of Islamic jurisprudence and reflected the input of northern university scholars as well as traditional mallams.[20]

Since each of the twelve northern states had to pass its own version of shari'a law, the key questions they faced were what range of interpretations to adopt, what procedures to establish for consulting with the learned Islamic legal scholars, and how to handle appeals. Zamfara opted for hard-line interpretations of the law and its punishments, while states such as Kaduna applied a looser interpretation, and then only in the predominantly Muslim local government authorities.

As of 2003, Kano was the only state based on the principle of consensus by the learned scholars that explicitly linked theft with embezzlement by public servants. In other states, this category usually came under public trust provisions, which carried lighter penalties. As the patterns of the twelve shari'a state interpretations emerged, several contextual traits became clear:

—The states created more recently, in 1991 and 1996 (Zamfara, Kebbi, Gombe, and Jigawa, some carved out of the larger traditional emirates), had less experience with the scholarship and interpretation of shari'a law and were more inclined to be somewhat eclectic in their mixture of jurisprudential principles.

—Because of their historic roles, Sokoto, Kano, and Borno (and Katsina) had special weight and standing.[21]

—Kaduna was clearly a twentieth-century political hub, but without historic roots, other than Zaria emirate in the northern part of the state.[22]

—All twelve states had significant populations of non-Muslim migrants, especially from southern Nigeria and frequently located in "new towns" within the major cities. During the colonial and postcolonial eras, non-Muslim populations were not subject to Muslim law.

Profiles of the Shari'a States

The twelve shari'a states in the far north are located in four clusters: Sokoto, Kebbi, and Zamfara in the northwest; Katsina, Kano, and Jigawa in the north-central area; Borno and Yobe in the northeast; and the middle tier consisting of Bauchi, Gombe, Niger, and Kaduna. The relevant characteristics of these states are summarized in table 7-3.

Profiles of Non-Shari'a Northern States

By contrast, the non-shari'a northern states clearly have more mixed ethnic and religious identities. The seven remaining northern states, which were part of the former Northern Region, are Adamawa, Taraba, Plateau, Nasarawa, Benue, Kogi, and Kwara. Two of these non-shari'a states (Adamawa and Kwara) were part of the Sokoto caliphal system. The relevant characteristics of these states are shown in table 7-4.

In the case of Plateau, many Christian evangelical missionaries set up their bases in Jos, and tensions developed as Muslim migrants settled in. (As already noted, in 2004 these tensions exploded into massive ethnoreligious violence.) In states such as Benue, tension had long existed between Tiv peoples and northern Muslim leaders. In recent years, the conflict in Benue has crystallized between two predominantly non-Muslim peoples, the Tiv and Jukun. Although a number of efforts have been made to resolve conflict in this seven-state area, for most of the twentieth century these states were part of Nigeria's "Northern Region" and have historic links with northern politics.[23]

Perspectives on Shari'a

As of January 2003, when the major political party conventions were held in Nigeria, the timing of the electoral cycle had already fueled competition within and between the two major parties in the north, the PDP and APP (later ANPP), which had about equal strength in the twelve shari'a states.[24] One issue, especially at the local level, revolved around interpretations of the shari'a.

In general, residents of the Muslim north lean toward four public political perspectives. First, some prefer a secularist, progressive modernist approach to politics, one that separates religion and politics, for example, but allows the option of applying shari'a law in the civil domain, that is, in the area of family law and inheritance. A second group would like to see greater links between religion and politics, including full implementation of shari'a in criminal and civil domains at the state level for Muslims only. A third is aware of the problems of implementing shari'a in the contemporary Nigerian system, especially in a multireligious context, but still treat shari'a as an ideal. Fourth, some believe the current implementation of shari'a is flawed, owing to corrupt practices or political favoritism. In each of these cases, shari'a is considered a powerful goal, despite ongoing debates about what it means.

Table 7-3. The Twelve Shari'a States

State[a]	Capital	Population[b]	Religious identity	Ethnicity and context
Sokoto	Sokoto	n.a.	M	Hausa-Fulani; seat of Sokoto Caliphate
Kebbi (1991)	Birnin Kebbi	2.6	M	Hausa-Fulani; historic rival w. Sokoto; minorities include Dakarkari, Kabawa, Gungawa, Kambari
Zamfara (1996)	Gusau	2.2	M	Hausa-Fulani; minor commercial hub; rival w. Sokoto
Katsina	Katsina	2.9	M	Hausa-Fulani; historic center of scholars; close ally of Sokoto
Kano	Kano	5.6	M	Hausa-Fulani; historic commercial capital of West Africa; strong sufi legacy; large southern Nigerian migrant population
Jigawa (1991)	Dutse	2.9	M	Hausa-Fulani; was part of Kano Emirate
Borno	Maiduguri	2.6	M	Kanuri, Shuwa, Babur; resisted Sokoto Caliphate in nineteenth century; oldest continuous Islamic state in Africa; Kanuri speaking; "shehu" is Islamic leader
Yobe (1991)	Damaturu	1.4	M	Formerly Borno minority areas; Fulani, Kanuri, Kare-Kare, Bade, Hausa, Ngizm, Bolewa
Bauchi	Bauchi	3.3	M	Hausa, Fulani, Jarawa; borderline emirate with Middle Belt
Gombe (1996)	Gombe	1.8	M	Hausa, Fulani, Tangale, Terawa, Tula; borderline emirate with Middle Belt
Niger	Minna	2.5	M	Nupe, Gbagyi (Gwari), Hausa, Kaduna, Fulani, etc.; borderline emirate with Middle Belt
Kaduna	Kaduna	5.0	Mix	Hausa, Gbagyi (Gwari), Kurama, etc.; a new city; former capital of northern Region; includes Zaria emirate, and Christian minority

n.a. Not available.

a. Dates of new states in parentheses.

b. Estimated millions in 1991. As noted previously, the last Nigerian census was in 1991. In 2005 the figures were considerably higher. Thus Kano State is estimated by Governor Ibrahim Shekarau to be around 12 million (personal discussions, April 9, 2004, Washington, D.C.). The figures in this table demonstrate approximate proportionality among the northern states and are taken from the campaign publication by the PDP in 2003: Sidi Ali, *Why the North Must Vote Obasanjo & Atiku* (Nigeria: Diametrics Limited, 2003).

Table 7-4. Profiles of Non-Shari'a Northern States

State[a]	Capital	Population[b] (millions)	Religion	Ethnicity and context
Adamawa (1996)	Yola	2.2	Mix	Seat of Lamido of Adamawa (Fulani) minority borderline; Higgi, Bwatiye, Chamba, Lunguda, Mbula, Kilba, Marghi, Yandang, Hausa
Taraba (1991)	Jalingo	1.5	Mix	Minority borderline; Fulani, Mumuye, Chamba, Yandang, Mambilla
Plateau	Jos	n.a.	Mix	Minority center; strong Christian missionary influence
Nasarawa (1996)	Keffi	1.3	Mix	Minority center; Hausa, Eggon, Tiv, Alago, Fulani, Gbagyi, Kanuri, Jukun
Benue	Makurdi	2.8	Mix	Minority center; Tiv, Idoma, Jukun, Hausa
Kogi (1991)	Lokoja	2.1	Mix	Minority center; Igala, Yoruba, Idoma, Egbira, Ugori
Kwara	Ilorin	1.5	Mix	Emirate, but predominantly Yoruba (and Nupe, Bar)

n.a. Not available.
a. Date of new states in parentheses.
b. 1991 census estimate.

If states' rights in the criminal domain (including shari'a laws) were to be tested and challenged through constitutional review procedures, clearly the shari'a states' attorneys general would have to argue that they were not "establishing" a state religion but continuing a legacy of dual systems, depending on religious affiliation; that the system does not apply to non-Muslims, and hence non-Muslims do not have "standing" in the appeals process; that due process has been followed at the state level in setting up such laws; and that the penalty phase, especially in capital crimes, did not violate indigenous norms of justice, despite colonial era modifications.

The counterarguments would depend on the particular case, but the issues would likely pertain to vigilante justice; due process in terms of women's legal rights; processes of appeal; the "cruel and unusual" nature of some penalties; the apparent conflict with certain constitutional provisions, such as the right of individuals to change religion; and the question of whether some states have overstepped their writ in matters such as issuing *fatwas*.

An even more pressing question was how the states' rights approach to the criminal law domain would emerge from the federal legal system and whether such a fragile national system could accommodate the crosscurrents of multiple perspectives on this matter. The framers of Zamfara's shari'a code tried to be careful not to violate the "no establishment of religion" clause in the constitution by focusing state legislation on the criminal code and using the precedent of the shari'a civil code in applying the new code "to Muslims only."

The first round of legal protests, often by non-Muslim nongovernmental organizations, failed partly because the defendants did not have standing. Subsequent appeals, often involving cases of theft or adultery, have attracted closer legal scrutiny at the appeals court level, and many lower court decisions have been reversed. By the end of its first term in office (May 2003), the federal government had not introduced the shari'a issue into the federal court system. (The implementation of shari'a in the twelve far northern states is discussed further in chapter 8.)

The constitution of 1999 contains several provisions that might be referenced if this federal-state issue were to reach the Supreme Court, including Fundamental Rights (chap. IV), plus sections on the scope of police activity and the judiciary, plus the whole area of states' rights. Some shari'a states consider "apostasy" an offense, even though the constitution (sec. 38) says that "every person shall be entitled to freedom of thought, conscience and religion, including freedom to change his religion or belief." By 2003, however, all twelve shari'a states were dropping any prosecution of apostasy cases, although some cases had been brought to the shari'a courts earlier.

At the same time, the constitution of 1999 clearly established federal police as the only legitimate police force. By contrast, most other federal governments also allow for police capacities at state and local levels. This vacuum at the state and local level was being filled throughout the federation by state-sanctioned vigilante groups, often youth groups with only a modicum of oversight.

Federal police in Nigerian states live in separate barracks and are exempt from the "no alcohol" rules of local authorities. Many police do not even speak the local languages. As discussed in chapter 10, when the police fail to quell local disturbances, the army may be called in, in which case conflict may escalate to an even more obvious federal level.

During the 1999–2003 period, about half the members of the Supreme Court were Muslim, some of them learned in shari'a law and familiar with future prospective cases. Nonetheless, a pressing concern was how ordinary Nigerian Muslims at the grassroots level viewed legal issues from the perspective of their own civic cultures.[25] This raised the further question of how to solve the states' rights issue politically before it destabilized the federation. At least one precedent was available in this regard, the compromise of the

Penal Reform Laws in Northern Nigeria in 1959, which took into account local needs while recognizing a national interest.[26]

Aftermath of the 2003 Elections

Scholarly assessment of Nigeria's 2003 election points to many flaws, both intentional and unintentional.[27] Legal challenges were still under way into 2005. Underlying economic problems that were so central to the election and its aftermath continue to be a matter of domestic and international concern.[28]

An informal political alliance after the election between Muhammadu Buhari's ANPP in the north and Odumegwu Ojukwu's All Progressive Grand Alliance in the southeast blunted some of the Hausa-Igbo tensions arising from the earlier introduction of shari'a in the far north.[29] Indeed, the selection of an Igbo/Christian ANPP vice presidential candidate (Chuba Okadigbo) in 2003 also served to downplay religious differences. The death of Senator Okadigbo in September 2003, however, raised "conspiracy" concerns, focused on the government of President Obasanjo in Abuja, and especially on the role of the police.[30] The tragedy seemed to bind the northern and eastern factions of the ANPP even closer together.

With a number of political issues still unresolved following the 2003 elections, the Buhari Organization (TBO) urged supporters to use the election tribunal system for appeals. Buhari himself toured other African countries, trying to make the case that election fraud was no more acceptable in Nigeria than it was in Zimbabwe. On his return to Nigeria, Buhari called on his supporters to protest in a nonviolent manner. The large Buhari rally in Kano, on September 23, 2003, although unauthorized by the police, included Governor Shekarau and indicated widespread Buhari support at the grassroots level.

The previous weekend, in an address to the conference of Nigerian Students in Defense of Democracy at Arewa House, Kaduna, Buhari made a strong appeal for tolerance and restraint: "As the elections have come and gone, we have chosen the path of tolerance and pragmatism to protest the usurpation of your right to determine your leadership. It is not as if we did not know other faster and more effective methods for resisting the imposition of dictatorship, but, as always, uppermost in our minds is the fate and progress of our country."[31] In short, Buhari had become a key factor in encouraging moderation in political protest, rather than violence. His calls for "mass action" against the flawed elections of 2003 have taken the form of nonviolent protests, at least as of 2005.[32]

To partly deflect TBO anger, in September 2003 the government conferred on Buhari (and Babangida) the highest national honor of Grand Commander of the Federal Republic (although as of 2005, Buhari had yet to acknowledge the legitimacy of Obasanjo's election and has made every effort not to meet with him). Other initiatives by the president's office have been more controversial, including the broadcasting of Obasanjo's religious devotions from the presidential palace each week.[33]

Other key notables in the north have also tried to steer grassroots disaffection toward constructive endeavors. Governor Shekarau of Kano has proposed introducing science and technology courses in the Islamic schools of Kano. He has also set up a public works project, for youth, especially in areas of urban sanitation.[34] The sultan of Sokoto has introduced scholarships for Muslim students studying science in higher education.[35] In Katsina, a Katsina Islamic University has been planned, which is to offer courses in computer science.[36] The whole issue of *madrasas,* or Islamic schools in the north, and how to steer students (*almajiri*) away from "begging" toward practical education began to emerge as a potential political issue.[37]

At the federal level, a major development since the 2003 election has been the creation of a thirty-member National Commission on Peace to deal with various issues of conflict resolution (both political and ethnoreligious).[38] The commission chair is Alhaji Shehu Malami, a close ally of the sultan of Sokoto and former ambassador to South Africa.[39] The antecedent to the commission was a nongovernmental organization first established by a wealthy Yoruba businessman and later expanded by a wealthy Igbo businessman.[40] Although the commission has set up branches in each of the states, it remains to be seen how such a federal mechanism might relate to more traditional or grassroots conflict mediation efforts, and how it might fit into the overall politics of the post-2003 election era.

The question of local government reforms and the possible enhanced role of traditional "royal fathers" (including in conflict resolution) was to be addressed by a technical committee on local government reforms. This committee was initially headed by the *Etsu Nupe.* After he passed away in September 2003, the government appointed as chairman Liman Ciroma, a distinguished elder statesman and former civil servant, originally from the Borno area.[41] The creation of this committee raised concerns in some quarters that the position of "royal fathers" would be strengthened, and in other quarters that the "third tier" would be undermined (and possibly even abolished) by the federal government.[42]

In November 2003, the committee submitted its report, with two key recommendations: the 774 local councils should be retained; the system of selecting local chairmen should shift from a "presidential to parliamentary system."[43] Thus the councils would select their chairs after elections, rather than allowing governors to appoint chairs or allowing for direct election of chairs.[44]

As noted previously, the two major political features of the postelection period have been the role of election tribunals in contested elections and speculation as to who the likely northern political candidates for president will be in 2007. In 2005 three major issues with political consequences emerged: National Political Reform Dialogue (NPRD), also known as the National Political Reform Conference (NPRC); the projected census, scheduled for November 29–December 3, 2005 (which could reallocate political representation patterns); and the projected party congresses, scheduled for late 2005, in which candidates would vie within parties. The NPRD was especially salient in giving voice to a wide-ranging set of opinions, such as the proposals by the Kano Emirate Council for a return to more of a First Republic parliamentary model, including a role for state and local police.[45]

ANPP insistence on judicial process and the "rule of law" after the 2003 election has focused attention on the role of the Supreme Court. Indeed, by constitutional law, if the presidential election was voided and rerun, the acting presidency would normally go to the president of the Senate and then the speaker of the House. Since both of these individuals were under election tribunal challenge, however, the acting presidency legally would go to the chief justice of the Supreme Court, Muhammadu Uwais, who would then supervise new elections within three months.[46] This was the scenario the ANPP hoped for, although by early 2005 it was clear that this would not happen.

With regard to the 2007 elections, since Obasanjo cannot constitutionally succeed himself, the next president is widely expected to be a northern Muslim. A "permanent campaign" by key individuals and organizations, especially at the informal levels, had already begun by the fall of 2003.[47] Discussions as to the candidates' religious observances, integrity, character, resonance with civic cultures, and conflict resolution skills became part of the campaign. As noted previously, the three obvious northern (Muslim) contenders were Atiku Abubakar (PDP), Ibrahim Babangida (PDP), and Muhammadu Buhari (ANPP).[48]

While candidate perspectives on shari'a law were less emphasized in the public discourse, most northerners were aware that Buhari (from the northwest zone) was sympathetic to the shari'a law initiatives in the far northern states that were based on democratic principles, but that he also needed alliances in the southeast and south-south. Abubakar (from the northeast zone) was identified more with the Obasanjo regime's skepticism of shari'a. Babangida (from the Middle Belt zone), as usual, remained circumspect, although clearly he would have to compete for the PDP nomination and that party has tended to downplay the shari'a issue. By 2004, however, much of the initial flurry over shari'a-related issues had died down. Yet there was widespread concern that the issue could surface again, depending on state and local incidents. The shari'a issue is discussed in more detail in chapters 8 and 9.

Underlying all of these political crosscurrents was the widespread Muslim concern (especially in northern Nigeria) that Muslims were being marginalized by the Obasanjo regime. In June 2005, the emir of Gwandu (Mustapha Jokolo)—second in protocol rank to the sultan of Sokolo—confronted Obasanjo directly on this matter in the presence of other emirs. Apparently the president's office then called the governor of Kebbi State and insisted that the emir be deposed. Thus by mid-June 2005, Jokolo was in "exile" in Nasarawa State, and a new emir had been appointed. The implications remain to be seen.

8

Challenges of the Shari'a Issue

With civilian rule emerging in the fall of 1998, following the death of General Sani Abacha in June, the issue of "law and order" became a prime concern in many local minds, especially in the north. In a larger sense, this had to do with the rule of law. As noted earlier, a gubernatorial candidate from Zamfara State (Ahmed Sani) capitalized on this sentiment, promising to set up a shari'a-based penal code extending to criminal matters. Sani's success at the polls prompted other northern governors to introduce state legislation setting up broad and extensive shari'a codes, but with application to Muslims only. These governors argued that they were working within the framework of the Fourth Republic's constitution (1999), which recognized the principle of shari'a law in certain domains and allowed state assemblies to pass needed legislation, unless explicitly prohibited by the constitution. Hence there was a clear return to a multiple jurisprudential framework, much in the British colonial tradition.[1]

The twelve northern states continued experimenting with shari'a law in the criminal domain throughout the first four-year term for officeholders. In the state and national elections in the spring of 2003, "shari'a" became a political (or at least background) issue in some instances, especially in Zamfara, where the People's Democratic Party (PDP) accused the government of playing politics with shari'a.[2]

An additional dimension to the shari'a issue, in terms of its national implications, is how the constitutional question of "federal character" in the twelve shari'a states (that is, the requirement that each state be represented at the cabinet level and also in other executive branches) may serve as a mediating system of checks and balances in states where the governor and president

157

belong to different parties. The federal cabinet members from each state may serve as "gateways" between federal and state levels and may contribute to conflict prevention and mediation. (Alternatively, these appointments may be a source of tension.) The representation of the federal government abroad by professional diplomats from the shari'a states is another potentially mediating influence on extreme or provocative applications of shari'a, as shown in table 1-1.

In terms of influence, the "big three" northern city-states—Sokoto, Kano, and Borno—are historically Muslim, but each has its own character.[3] Katsina is unique in serving as a historic balancer between Sokoto and Kano. During the colonial period, the "bargain" reached was that non-Muslim migrants could settle outside of these traditional cities and not be subject to Muslim law, while British administrators worked "indirectly" through the traditional authority structures. Since independence, the "traditional rulers" of these large far northern states have been vital connections between central administrations and grassroots peoples, and as "conflict resolvers" both within the Muslim community and between the Muslim and non-Muslim communities.

The middle tier of shari'a states—especially Bauchi, Gombe, and Niger—have straddled the Muslim/non-Muslim demographic divide in Nigeria and have had to devise mechanisms for accommodating such diversity. Kaduna State is a special case, with its "new city" serving as capital of the former northern region. Kaduna, known as "everyone's city," is unique among the twelve shari'a states in not having a "traditional ruler," although for some purposes of protocol, the emir of Zaria (about forty-five minutes north of Kaduna) serves this function.[4] (The original premier of Northern Nigeria, Ahmadu Bello, resisted the temptation to establish a "traditional ruler" for Kaduna, arguing that such an office would be a contradiction in terms.) The northern part of Kaduna State is predominantly Muslim, the southern part predominantly Christian or traditional.

The Politics of Shari'a in the North

With the return of party politics in 1998–99, the two major northern parties—the People's Democratic Party (PDP) and the All People's Party (APP)—agreed to a power-shift strategy to try to bring the southwest back into the mainstream, and the issues were more local in nature. However, the APP vice presidential candidate (Umaru Shinkafi) was originally from Yobe and later moved to Sokoto, where he became a title holder (*Marafa*) and son-in-law, posthumously, to the Sardauna of Sokoto, Ahmadu Bello. The PDP

Table 8-1. Party Politics in the Shari'a States, 1999-2003

State	Dominant party, 1999-03	Governor, 1999-03	Dominant party, post-2003	Governor, post-2003
Sokoto	APP	Attahiru Bafarawa	ANPP	Attahiru Bafarawa
Kebbi	APP	Moh. Adamu Aleiro	ANPP	Moh. Adamu Aleiro
Zamfara	APP	Ahmed Sani	ANPP	Ahmed Sani
Katsina	PDP	Umaru Yar'Adua	PDP	Umaru Yar'Adua
Kano	PDP	Rabiu Kwankwaso	ANPP	Ibrahim Shekarau
Jigawa	APP	Saminu Turaki	ANPP	Saminu Turaki
Borno	APP/PDP	Mala Kachalla	ANPP	Ali Modu Sheriff
Yobe	APP	Bukar Abba	ANPP	Bukar Abba
Bauchi	PDP	Ahmadu Mu'azu	PDP	Ahmadu Mu'azu
Gombe	PDP/APP	Abubakar Hashidu	PDP	Moh. Danjuma Goje
Niger	PDP	Abdulkadir Kure	PDP	Abdulkadir Kure
Kaduna	PDP	Ahmed Moh. Makarfi	PDP	Ahmed Moh. Makarfi

vice presidential candidate (Atiku Abubakar) was from Adamawa State and had been elected governor before relinquishing his post to compete for the PDP nomination.[5] Table 8-1 shows the successful gubernatorial candidates in 1999 and 2003.

Muhammadu Buhari, presidential candidate for the All Nigeria People's Party (ANPP), was hoping to carry all twelve shari'a states in 2003. The three crucial states were Kano, Kaduna, and Katsina. These were battleground states in part because Buhari was from Katsina State but living in Kaduna State. Kano State had a long history of progressive politics. Only Kano provided a major win for the ANPP and since then has become a center of antigovernment and anti-PDP sentiment.[6]

Although Katsina is the home state of Muhammadu Buhari, the incumbent governor (Umaru Yar'Adua) was popular and part of the Yar'Adua family political organization, which was committed to supporting Vice President Atiku Abubakar and the PDP. The Buhari Organization, recognizing the popularity of Governor Yar'Adua, counseled its followers to split their votes, if need be, supporting Yar'Adua for governor and Buhari for president. In a highly contested election, the PDP incumbent won the governorship, and the ANPP the presidency. The PDP incumbent governor also won in Kaduna, although among allegations of rigging and intimidation.

The shari'a issue faded to the background in the PDP-ANPP contests in the twelve shari'a states, but in Zamfara, the PDP candidates specifically criticized the ANPP governor for the way in which shari'a was implemented. In general, the issue of shari'a worked to the populist advantage of the ANPP in the Muslim areas. Subsequently, Kano emerged as an ANPP center, raising expectations in some quarters that shari'a would be enforced more rigorously under a Shekarau administration.

The ANPP swept the gubernatorial races in the far northern states with one exception (Katsina), providing seven of the eight governors. At the same time, the PDP swept all four governorships of the middle-tier states, which are characterized by more of a Muslim and Christian demographic mix. However, Buhari won the presidential contest in Bauchi and Gombe, as in Katsina. In nine of the twelve states, the incumbent governors appeared to have won reelection, although legal appeals continued throughout the summer and fall of 2003, throughout 2004, and into 2005.

The Impact of Federal Character Appointments

The 1999 constitution, in parallel with the 1979 constitution, established a "federal character" provision, requiring that each of the thirty-six states be represented at all levels in the federal executive, including the cabinet. This was intended to provide a structural guarantee that no state was left out of the national game. For all its appearances of being too bloated to be workable, the mechanism has proved critical to both a sense of fairness and a level playing field, and to a conflict prevention capacity, should the need arise. Table 8-2 shows linkages between shari'a states and federal ministers. One of the notable linkages was between the national security adviser and Zamfara State. There was special federal concern about the politics in that state, including possible external linkages, since the governor was associated with a back-to-basics perspective on shari'a.

Even in the domain of diplomacy and foreign affairs, there has been an attempt to draw senior Nigerian personnel from all states, including the far northern states. Many of the ambassadors from such states have played a critical role in communications with predominantly Muslim countries around the world and are aware of the many crosscurrents within the Islamic world (a sample was shown in table 1-1).

The elections in April 2003 were highly contested, especially that between the ANPP team, which tried to link the north with allies in the south-south and southeast, and the PDP team. The latter tried to hold its incumbent advantage in the north, knock out the regional party in the southwest (the Alliance for Democracy), and prevent the ANPP from continuing its historic

Table 8-2. Federal Character in Shari'a States, 1999–2003

State	Minister	Ministry
Sokoto	Muktar Shehu Shagari	Water Resources
Zamfara	Aliyu M.Gusau	National Security Adviser
	Bello Usman	State, Education
Kebbi	Bello H. Mohammed	Communications
Katsina	Sani Zangon Daura	Agriculture
	Moh. Kabir Said	Environment
	Lawal Batagarawa	State, Defense (Army)
Kano	Musa Gwadabe	Labor, Employment, and Productivity
	Aisha Ismail	Women's Affairs
Jigawa	Sule Lamido	Foreign Affairs
Yobe	Adamu Ciroma	Finance
Borno	Moh. Abba Gana	Federal Capital Abuja
	Ibrahim Kida	Intergovernment Relations and NDDC
Bauchi	Mahmud Y. Ahmed	Head of Service, Federation
	Isa Yuguda	State, Transport
Gombe	Murtala Aliyu	State, Power, and Steel
Niger	Jerry Gana	Information and National Orientation
	Mustapha Bello	Commerce
Kaduna	Rilwan Lukman	Presidential Adviser on Petroleum and Energy
	Garba Madaki Ali	State Works and Housing

alliances with the south-south and southeast. These two zones witnessed much of the violence and obvious rigging.

As already mentioned, the main contests in the shari'a states were in Kano, Kaduna, and Katsina. With the PDP losing Kano to the ANPP, the new administration in Abuja appointed the former (defeated) governor of Kano (Rabiu Kwankwaso) to the key post of federal minister of defense, although he has no background in military affairs. The PDP in Zamfara is represented at the cabinet level by a retired military officer, Colonel Bala Mande. These moves appear to be part of a checks-and-balances strategy by the federal government (see table 8-3).

Notably, Colonel Bala Mande (PDP), from Zamfara State, was a harsh critic of Governor Sani (ANPP) for his implementation of shari'a during the 2000–03 period. According to Colonel Mande, shari'a was used to punish political opponents, and the "spoils" of office were going to ANPP supporters regardless of merit. Shari'a, he argued, had become "politicized." His new position allowed him to check on the potential developments in Zamfara. Clearly, the PDP cabinet appointments from the shari'a states after the 2003

Table 8-3. Federal Character in the Shari'a States, Post-2003

State	Minister	Ministry
Sokoto	Muktar Shehu Shagari	Water Resources
Zamfara	Bala Mande	Environment
Kebbi	Samaila B. Sambawa	State, Foreign Affairs
Katsina	Magaji Mohammed	Industries
Kano	Rabiu Musa Kwankwaso	Defense
Jigawa	Sale Shehu	State, Works
Yobe	Lawan Gaba	Cooperatives and Integration
Borno	Bintu Ibrahim Musa	State, Education
Bauchi	Isa Yuguda	Aviation
Gombe	Musa Mohammed	Sports Development
Niger	Abubakar Tanko	Internal Affairs
Kaduna	Nenadi Esther Usman	State, Finance

elections were intended to place a check on the ANPP governors, especially in Kano and Zamfara.

Processes of Shari'a Implementation

Shari'a emerged in the criminal domain between 1999 and 2003 (see chapter 7), the initial impetus coming from the governor of Zamfara State. Within a matter of months, the Zamfara penal code became a template for the other eleven shari'a states, although there have been significant variations in structure, process, and content. Leaders in the twelve states recognized that it was politically impossible to be "against" shari'a.

In essence, shari'a is a concept of justice that is central to Islamic faith. The question in Nigeria was how to interpret and implement it in a contemporary context. The intellectual interpretations in the shari'a states ranged from a shock therapy approach ("just do it") to a gradualist approach. Some also argued that shari'a was a political tool to keep poor people in line and exempt leaders from accountability, a suggestion that requires a class analysis of the uses of shari'a but is beyond the scope of this work.[7]

In examining the common elements in the implementation of shari'a and the particular challenges of representative states, the first point to mention is that after its initial social impact in 2000–01, the issue took on a lower profile.[8] During the preelection and election period in 2002–03, however, the implementation and interpretation of shari'a became a serious matter within the Muslim community in some states. In general, the community was divided on what came to be called "political shari'a," with some arguing for a strengthened shari'a system, and for a more pragmatic approach to the issues.[9] Opinions varied from one state to another, with Zamfara following a strict constructionist approach, whereas Kaduna pursued a minimal approach in light of the backlash and violence, and then did so only in the predominantly Muslim local government authorities. The key aspects of shari'a implementation between 1999 and 2004—in practice and not necessarily in ideal theory—are shown in table 8-4.

Patterns of Implementation in Shari'a States

States varied somewhat in their implementation of shari'a. The following overview touches on the major differences.[10]

Northwest States (Sokoto and Zamfara)

In Sokoto, when Governor Bafarawa signed the shari'a bill, he promised the construction of courts, recruitment and training of staff, and respect for the rights of non-Muslims. He set up a shari'a implementation committee to link with the Judicial Service Commission in the recruitment of judges.

In evaluating implementation, the Sokoto State Information Commissioner, Alhaji Ibrahim Gidado, noted that the "crime rate has reduced drastically which is the essence of shari'a" and cited the closing of two major cinema houses, one of which was converted to a mosque.[11] Steps were also taken to close brothels, bars, and other such establishments, to monitor marketplaces, and to build more mosques and Islamic schools in the state. A sheikh at the Islamic Science Institute, Sokoto, complained that it was not enough to "flog" those who committed adultery or were found drinking alcohol. Although many agree that crime has been reduced along with prostitution and alcohol consumption, the general impression of proponents of shari'a in Sokoto is that it has been poorly monitored:

> There should be the introduction of what we call Hisba, those who are responsible for the arrest of those people who commit some of these offences or vices. They are supposed to be in place parading many corners of this metropolis and the state to arrest and hand people over to the police who will then introduce them to the judges for appropriate punishment.

> This has not been done in Sokoto. You can see that nobody is responsible for arresting people who contravene the Islamic penal code like before. Maybe they regard it as no more necessary or they are playing

Table 8-4. Key Elements of Shari'a Implementation, 1999–2004

Structural	Major legal domains	Due process	Equal treatment	Training, facilities	Realtions with non-Muslims
Ulama (scholars) Council Government appointed or Independent	*Family law* Marriage, divorce, inheritance, and the like	*Hisba groups* Arrest suspect Take to police or alkali (khadi)[a]	*Shari'a* Applied to Muslims only, whether state citizens or passing through Social order laws (e.g., alcohol, prostitution), since enacted by state assemblies, apply to all in the state, in theory	*Codes* Many codes drawn up by younger, educated elites from northern law schools; hence mixture of Maliki law plus international influences Increase in pilgrimages since the 1970s brought new interpretation Mixture of experiences makes it hard to judge cases Wide range between "strict constructionist" and modernist interpretations –Councils final arbiters States developing own case law National council of Shari'a trying to coordinate	*Muslims in any recorded case* However, alcohol prohibition meant to be statewide Some Hisba have tried to close bars, even non-Muslim hotels in non-Muslim areas Non-Muslims feel like second-class citizens *Apostasy*: next likely explosive issue in the north
Hisba ("voluntary" enforcers, at local level) Government appointed or Independent	*"Serious" crimes* Murder, theft, adultery, rape	*Seriousness judged* Case moved to appropriate alkali court	*Shari'a criticisms* Political opponents claim to be victimized "Royal" family members seem exempt Most applications focus on ordinary people Little done to address official or business corruption	*Proponent complaints* Training facilities and courts inadequate No real infrastructure to implement shari'a	

Judicial system	Social order crimes	Islamic rules of evidence
Shari'a court judges[a]	Alcohol, prostitution, in some cases "drumming" (especially at weddings), mixed gender in public transport	Applied
Other court judges		Initial judgment
Police	Social welfare enforcement	Appeals process
All police are federal, not local	Alms (zakkat) collection and distribution	Up to state level if appropriate
	Welfare for widows and orphans	
Political leaders	Corruption	
State governors	Official	
Others	Business	
	"Apostasy"[b]	

a. Court judges called alkali or alkalai (plural); often transliterated as kadi or khadi.

b. In this context, apostasy means renouncing Islamic identity to become "Christian"; so far, this transgression has not made its way into the shari'a legal system, but in theory it is a capital crime.

politics. The weakness in the entire issue depends on the non-introduction of Hisba or the aid group like those in Zamfara and some other places. If Hisba is introduced in Sokoto, shari'a would achieve more purpose than now.[12]

In Zamfara State, the early euphoria over the reintroduction of shari'a has begun to subside, and signs of backsliding are evident. In addition, a "disquieting cloud" has been darkening the governor's relationship with the Hisba and Islamic scholars (*ulama*), even though his second term had been based on a shari'a campaign:

> The prohibition on the free mixing of the sexes has drastically slackened, so that motorcyclists now carry Muslim women passengers even as young men and women could be seen hugging each other at night without the slightest fear of apprehension by the now-reluctant members of the Hisba. And in spite of the restriction on the sale of alcoholic beverages to specified spots, drunks are seen these days roaming the streets of Gusau virtually unhindered. As if this is not enough, a local brothel also operates less than 50 metres away from the offices of the Directorate for Shari'a Implementation behind Labin-Labin Motor Park in Gusau town. Reports of forceful acquisition of land and other properties of the less-privileged by those in authority, particularly village and district heads, have also reached an alarming proportion around the state.[13]

In response to these allegations, Alhaji Mohammed Attahiru Bello, secretary to the Zamfara state government, noted that "Zamfara State has the lowest number of criminal cases in the country" and denied a rift between the governor and the *ulama*.[14]

Another aspect of shari'a in Zamfara has been the effort to address the issue of students who attended Islamic schools and made their living by begging. One of the religious nongovernmental organizations in Zamfara—the Global Network for Islamic Justice (GNIJ)—argues that what once was an honorable tradition has become debased by the economic poverty that is driving it. The GNIJ holds the federal government responsible for such poverty.[15]

North-Central States (Katsina, Kano, Jigawa)

A growing problem in Katsina has been confusion over "who has the legal power to control and supervise courts between the newly created Shari'a Commission led by the state grand khadi and the already established State Judicial Service Commission led by the chief judge of the state." In addition, some questioned whether the state government was really serious about enforcing shari'a inasmuch as vice was reappearing, and perhaps in much worse degree than before. Some blamed the enabling legislation for this state of affairs, but others claimed the state government had deliberately "pulled down the structure it had earlier established":

> The state chairman of the Supreme Council for Shari'a implementation in Nigeria and a renowned cleric in Katsina, Sheikh Yakubu Musa Hassan, . . . noted the strangulation of shari'a enforcement bodies namely Hisba and Da'awah committees whose power of apprehension of offenders were curtailed by the government. He said the Katsina State government later accused the Hisba of taking laws into their hands and issued a directive to the courts to stop accepting cases from them, while giving the police the exclusive right to apprehend and prosecute shari'a offenders even without any constitutional mandate, thereby rendering the two committees useless.[16]

In October 2003, a committee for the implementation of shari'a in Katsina was inaugurated with the deputy governor and commissioner for religious affairs (Alhaji Abdullahi Garba Aminci) as chair. The emir of Katsina, Alhaji Muhammadu Kabir Usman, attributed the lack of progress in implementation to "polarisation of the Muslim ummah along sectarian lines," and to "the jostling for supremacy among the many Islamic sects."[17]

Kano, with its long history of sufism, as distinct from legalism, faced a similar issue when serious political tensions arose between the sufi brotherhoods—namely, Qadiriyya and Tijaniyya—and the "legalists" (for example, *Izala*). The brotherhoods favored a postlegalist interpretation of shari'a and resented being eclipsed and preached to by the legalists.[18] In the spring of 2004, members of the Qadiriyya staged a major urban demonstration protesting their alleged exclusion from or underrepresentation in the state shari'a councils.

According to Ustaz Abubakar Rabo Abdul-Kareem, secretary of the Independent Shariah Implementation Support Committee in Kano, however, the obvious changes in people's moral and social lives indicated that "shari'a is very much functioning and working in Kano State." Furthermore, "social problems within our communities are no more going to the police or courts, because they are now being solved at ward levels, at various levels in the state. This was done through the Shari'a Guidance and Councils, Da'wah Committees and through Hisba sub-committees in each and every ward, village and local council." Abdul-Kareem also called on the government to give shari'a full support, so it could "take its due course, which is not brutal or cruel":

Shari'a as a total way of life will not leave anything untouched. In respect of any issue, whether naming or wedding ceremonies, shari'a has its own way of doing it. We are not saying there should not be gatherings during ceremonies within our communities. But rather, in what manner should such activities be conducted? . . .

For the non-Muslims, they should conduct their ceremonies in their private environments and they shouldn't disturb peace in the society. The way that we are interfering into such cases was to assign our elderly people living in the area where such events take place to meet the organisers of the ceremony for proper solution, and sometimes, we just report them to the police. We are not taking laws into our hands at all.[19]

Other assessments of shari'a implementation in Kano during the 2000–03 period (before the administration changed) focus on the "tug of war between the Independent Shari'a Implementation Committee led by ulama and the state government-appointed Shari'a Implementation Committee led by the state's deputy governor, Dr. Abdullahi Umar Ganduje, himself a strong shari'a protagonist."[20] The system was also surrounded by controversy in Jigawa State, even though the government there had established various organs "to ensure its sustainability, enforcement and awareness. The government introduced shari'a courts, appointed shari'a judges and other paraphernalia associated with the conditions for the proper implementation of the legal system."

Jigawa also established a ministry to ensure strict compliance with shari'a and was the first state to appoint a special adviser to the governor on "religious matters, à la shari'a." Despite these steps and the use of Hisba, the system did not run smoothly. In fact, Hisba angered the Dutse royal family when one of its members was arrested and sentenced to eighty lashes by a shari'a court. Some took this as an affront to the emirate and launched a "verbal war" that eventually left the legal system with little power in the state.[21] One imam agreed that the Hisba had exceeded their legal authority: "Islam does not allow you to arrest anybody on mere suspicion and that was just what they were doing. That is why a new Hisba has been established and are being trained to work in accordance with Islamic values and orientation."[22]

Northeast States (Borno and Yobe)

In Borno and Yobe, few specific adjustments were deemed necessary to accommodate shari'a because of the long experience with Islam in those areas. There may have also been a sense that the more recent shari'a movement was something associated with the Sokoto Caliphate areas. In addition, no law had been proposed to enable the application of shari'a in the state.[23]

Middle-Tier States (Bauchi, Gombe, Kaduna)

In Bauchi, implementation of the law came to involve the *Izala* leaders, who commended the state for working to cleanse itself of all societal ills. They also asked the government for plots of land for the construction of schools, noting that the Izalatul group was operating nursery, primary, and postprimary schools at Tilden Fulani, Bauchi, Ningi, and Jama'are in rented apartments and needed assistance to construct permanent sites.[24] One perplexing issue for the state was how to handle outside visitors to hotels in Bauchi, although strictly speaking such arrangements were within the mandates of the shari'a law.[25]

By contrast, Gombe State appeared to have done little beyond passing the shari'a bill into law. Hence the system never seemed to get off the ground there, even though many believe it "represents the essence of every Muslim's life on earth."[26]

In Kaduna, as mentioned earlier, the shari'a system has been applied only in the predominantly Muslim local government authorities. Kaduna has also been the site of major conflicts between Muslim and Christian communities (see chapter 9).[27] In addition, loud clamoring both for and against the legal system and the resulting crisis eventually led the Kaduna government to establish a tripartite judicial system

> that provides for the establishment of shari'a courts, customary courts and common law courts . . . supposedly wide enough to accommodate the varying demands of the people in the state. Convictions of the people are now the major determinants of their own individual or collective choice of courts as and when the need arises. According to the provisions of the law establishing the system, shari'a is now enforceable in such areas where there is dominant Muslim population. And local government councils in such areas, most of which are located in the northern part of the state, are responsible for the enactment of by-laws that will primarily prohibit the existence of brothels and liquor stores.[28]

Many complained, however, that Kaduna State had not even established an agency to ensure that people observed at least the basic tenets of shari'a. In response, Governor Ahmed Mohammed Makarfi assured the public that "he would direct the chairmen of the care-taker committees of those local government areas where shari'a is meant to take off to ensure that the demand for the proper implementation of the legal code is met."[29]

Clearly, the clash of multiple interpretations of shari'a has been played out primarily within the Muslim community. The question of who controls the Hisba has also plagued some states. In Kaduna, the shari'a question has even fueled riots between Muslim and Christian communities. The political cross-currents and tensions in implementing shari'a in the twelve far northern states have led some of the more idealistic younger generation to try to set up shari'a local communities based on "flight" (*hijra*) or withdrawal from the larger society. Thus a community of about 3,000 persons was set up in Niger State and has lived there peacefully for several years. In Borno and Yobe states, however, young networks of self-described *taliban* have had serious clashes with federal, state, and local authorities (see chapter 10).

Shari'a in the Financial Domain

In the business law domain, shari'a-compliant banking is under federal rather than state jurisdiction. Although this topic is too broad and complex to go into detail here, it should be noted that Nigeria's first Islamic bank, JAIZ International, was set up in October 2003. The organizers of the bank included the chairman of the First Bank Plc (Umaru Mutallab), the governor of Zamfara State (Alhaji Ahmed Sani, who had worked in the Nigerian Central Bank before becoming governor), a major Kano businessman (Aminu Dantata), the secretary general of the Nigerian Supreme Council for Islamic Affairs (Chief Abdu-Lateef Adegbite), the *Aare Musulumi* of Yorubaland (Arisekola Alao), and an engineer (Bunu Sheriff Musa). To dispel fears that the bank's central purpose was to promote Islam, Governor Ahmed Sani (*Yerima*) stated that it would serve Muslims and Christians alike and follow standard business practices except for being "based on Islamic principle of non-interest banking," adding that "similar banks exist in 45 countries including where more than 50 per cent of populations are non-Muslims, such as U.S.A. and Switzerland."[30] The organizers of the bank are working closely with the Islamic Development Bank (IDB) in Jedda, Saudi Arabia, which will appoint the managing director and the initial management team. Because Islamic banking is voluntary and well established in many countries, including those in the West, this issue has not produced high levels of non-Muslim concern in Nigeria.

To summarize, the implementation of shari'a in the northern states of Nigeria has taken a variety of forms and raised constitutional issues such as the role of the police and magistrate courts. Its most basic impulse was to return these areas to some recognizable form of rule of law and to counter the trend of criminal lawlessness that had emerged. Yet the symbolism of shari'a has been so powerful, both in the Muslim and non-Muslim communities, that it has stirred up a number of unintended consequences, including the violent conflicts in Kaduna State.

9

The Shari'a Issue and Sociopolitical Conflict

Kaduna is not the only site of shari'a-related violence. There have been vigilante incidents in Kano, and even Sokoto has witnessed turmoil. In addition, the extreme ethnoreligious violence in Plateau State (a non-shari'a state) may have been influenced by perceptions of shari'a-related issues in other northern states. However, by far the most serious sociopolitical conflict of the shari'a states has occurred in Kaduna.

The violence in Kaduna City in February and May 2000—the so-called shari'a 1 and shari'a 2 riots—left at least 2,000 dead, and perhaps as many as 5,000.[1] In November 2002, another 250 people were killed, and tens of thousands of persons were relocated in what may be termed ethnoreligious cleansing. This came from the so-called Miss World riots. Events in Kaduna shifted the focus to Muslim-Christian relations rather than intra-Muslim relations. In the crisis atmosphere in November 2002, at the end of Ramadan and as a prelude to the national elections in 2003, many other issues emerged, such as which Muslim notables were entitled to issue legal opinion decrees (*fatwas*). Kaduna was on high alert during the 2003 national elections. By June 2004, a sense of calm had returned to the urban area, in part because of the active programs of nongovernmental organizations (NGOs) such as the Inter-Faith Mediation Centre.[2] Also, political leaders such as Muhammadu Buhari took an active role in trying to keep calm among urban educated youth after the 2003 elections.

The lessons learned from this ongoing sociopolitical conflict in Kaduna go to the heart of the police system, the mobile military, the role of the judiciary, and the role of state and national leadership. A related issue is the apparent breakdown of conflict resolution mechanisms in times of crisis, both governmental and nongovernmental.[3]

Kaduna Riots: "Shari'a 1," "Shari'a 2," and the Aftermath

The city of Kaduna, one of the more developed cities in Nigeria's northern region, is the capital of Kaduna State but is also considered the symbolic capital of the north because of its history and large size. Both the city and the state have attracted a large population of Christians from many ethnic groups. This mixture has become volatile at times, the most serious outbreaks occurring in 1987, 1992, and 2000. The first dispute to get out of hand started in the southern town of Kafanchan, between students from different ethnic and religious groups there, and then spread to several other areas. Subsequently, the relocation of a market ignited the 1992 clashes in Zangon-Kataf between the Hausa and the Kataf (a predominantly Christian ethnic group), which left many dead. Again, the hostilities spread to several other parts of Kaduna State.[4] In 2000 the contentious issue was the state's decision to introduce shari'a, which brought two main waves of violence (called Shari'a 1 and Shari'a 2), with much death and destruction among both the Muslim and Christian factions. Many fear that the perpetrators and their organizers will never be prosecuted.[5]

Following this latest bout of violence, large parts of the population were displaced and communities segregated in some areas: "By 2002, residents were describing particular areas of Kaduna town as '100 per cent Christian' or '100 per cent Muslim. . . .' Christians and Muslims increasingly moved to areas which were dominated by people of their own faith in the hope of finding safety there."[6] In recognition of the large Christian population in the state, the governor agreed to by and large exempt Kaduna's Christians from restrictions on social activities such as the consumption or sale of alcohol. In addition, the state waited another year before applying shari'a to criminal law or creating shari'a courts. Although the new penal code provides for harsh sentences such as death by stoning or floggings, Kaduna has not yet followed that path, unlike some other northern states.[7]

Whether there was an ethnic base to some of the violence in Kaduna is less clear, although many of the small non-Muslim ethnic communities in southern Kaduna State had long-standing grievances over matters of land, market locations, and chiefdom appointments. Hausa Christians (a small minority), who are mainly in the Zaria emirate areas (for example, Wusasa), have developed historic patterns of accommodation with their Muslim Hausa neighbors. But the extent of ethnic differentiation in the Kaduna riots remains to be determined.

The "Miss World Riots" and Their Aftermath (2002)

With the growing tension in August 2002, the governor of Kaduna State (Alhaji Ahmed Mohammed Makarfi) convened key Christian and Muslim leaders in Kaduna to sign "The Kaduna Peace Declaration of Religious Leaders" and distributed it in poster form around the city.[8] Validated by the names and signatures of the religious leaders and governor, the declaration prayed for peace in Kaduna State and expressed a commitment to ending the violence and bloodshed, and to punishing "any individual or group found breaching the peace . . . in accordance to the due process of the law":

> According to our faiths killing innocent lives in the name of God is desecration of His Holy Name, and defames religions in the world. The violence that has occurred in Kaduna State is an evil that must be opposed by all people of good faith. We seek to live together as neighbors, respecting the integrity of each other's historical and religious heritage. We call upon all to oppose incitement, hatred, and the misrepresentation of one another.

The declaration also called on Muslims and Christians of all tribes to "respect the divinely ordained purpose of the creator by whose grace we live together in Kaduna State, such ordained purposes include[ing] freedom of worship, access to and sanctity of places of worship and justice among others," also "to refrain from incitement and demonization, and pledge to educate our young people accordingly," and "to explore how together we can aid spiritual regeneration, economic development, and inward investment."

Pledging to work with security forces in keeping the peace, the declaration also announced the establishment of a permanent joint committee to implement its recommendations and encourage dialogue between the two faiths. The good intentions of the interfaith committees were soon swept aside, however, when the Miss World contest scheduled for November 2002 sparked even greater violence, even though it was postponed to December 7, so as not to coincide with the Muslim holy month of Ramadan.

Any hope for a peaceful event quickly dissipated when a journalist writing for one of Nigeria's main daily newspapers suggested that the Prophet Mohammed would not only have approved of the Miss World Contest but "in all honesty, he would probably have chosen a wife from among them." Muslim outrage provoked public protest against the content of the article, which "was hijacked by a group of people who were apparently intent on causing trouble, and the demonstration quickly turned to violence.[9]

In all, 109 churches, 39 mosques, and hundreds of buildings in Kaduna were destroyed in 2002. The devastation prompts many questions. Where were the police and military? Where were the special police "strike force" units set up in 2000 to prevent such communal violence? Where was the leadership? Where was the judicial process after the violence? Where were the conflict resolution mechanisms? Why was the violence in Kaduna allowed to spill over to Abuja? To what extent were senior political leaders (on various sides) involved in stirring up trouble? Would a nonbiased government inquiry provide some answers to these questions?

It appears that about 350 people were arrested, mostly young boys accused of looting. Christian defendants appeared before magistrates' courts, and Muslims appeared before shari'a courts. Virtually all were released by the government. Senior instigators were not apprehended, in part because the government had to appear evenhanded or religiously neutral as the country lurched toward the 2003 national, state, and local elections. The role of the police was particularly crucial, since there is evidence that many police shot and killed large numbers of rioters. The efforts of the few NGOs that tried to resolve the conflict were simply overpowered by events.

The attitude of the Christian Association of Nigeria (CAN) hardened into what may be described as a war mode. This situation was further inflamed when the deputy governor of Zamfara issued a *fatwa* condemning to death the author of the offending newspaper article. This was countered by the *Jama'atu Nasril Islam* (JNI), which stated that the deputy governor had no right to issue a *fatwa*. Within Kaduna, the Muslim elites were visibly shaken, as street youth of whatever identity threatened to burn their houses down. The relations between Christians and Muslims, and within the Muslim community, had clearly reached a state of crisis.

The "Miss World riots" were an accident waiting to happen, and the early warning signs were clear. The timing was inauspicious, with Ramadan and the upcoming elections creating an atmosphere of heightened religious and political awareness. The inability of the police to handle the crisis raises questions about the relations of state and local government to a nationalized police force in a federal system. Another major concern is how the judicial system—which is in a state of flux not only because of the shari'a issue but also because of the transition from military to civilian rule—will adjust to the demands of partisan political pressures. A related issue is how NGOs, both in the religious and secular domains, can encourage a rule-of-law approach in resolving conflicts.[10] The role of a "free press," which is often unrestrained in "shouting fire in a crowded theater" raises questions about sensitivity training, particularly in the Muslim areas, regarding such emotive symbols as the Qur'an, the Prophet Muhammad, and indeed, the shari'a.[11] An overarching issue is how to understand and strengthen the legacy of conflict resolution within the shari'a states and apply such insights to contemporary intra-Muslim relations, as well as Muslim-Christian relations. The following pages provide some perspectives on this challenge.

Conflict Resolution in Shari'a States

The shari'a states mediate conflict through a number of channels, notably "gateways" (liaisons), state leaders, ecumenical bodies across states, the judicial system, the police, occasionally the media, universities and educated elites, NGOs, and federal policy.

Gateways

The traditional northern way of mediating conflict is to establish formal or informal gateways, or liaisons between various authorities and their counterparts in the opposition.[12] Thus even at the height of political tension, leadership of competing parties would maintain back-door contact, to ensure that situations did not spiral out of control. This implies a certain amount of trust and sense of common overall purpose. Since a gateway (*kofa*) was meant to be a back channel, it was not always apparent at the time whether the process was working or not. Some recent evidence suggests that the gateway system is still working within the northern Muslim community, which is significant, given the tensions between the PDP and ANPP. In a place like Kano, the emir would have gateways to each of the ethnic and religious factions in the emirate. (Note, however, that today's traditional leaders have only a fraction of their former official powers and resources.)

Within the shari'a states as a whole, it is not clear whether Muslim-Christian relations have reestablished workable sets of gateways. In general, northern Muslim cultures prefer to work through recognizable authority structures, which makes it difficult at times to determine how to work with some of the Christian groups, other than Roman Catholics and mainstream Protestants.

Evangelical and Pentecostal groups predominate in places like Kaduna, which do not have much traditional Muslim authority but more localized *Izala* Muslim groups. Such contexts present special challenges. (Like Kaduna City, Plateau State lacks traditional Muslim authority but has numerous segmental ethno-Christian groups and has been the site of much ethnoreligious violence.)

Leadership

Although Kaduna does not have senior "traditional leaders" in its state capital, the emirs (or their equivalents) in the emirate north have considered one of their major responsibilities to be conflict mediation.[13] With the increased secularization of state governments since the 1970s, the governors have created an alternative center for power and leadership. Yet governors in a civilian system are always aware of the need to position themselves for reelection. In a military system, governors serve at the whim of the central government and hence have less incentive to use mediation rather than force in preventing or resolving conflict. Traditional leaders, whether in the emirates or in the non-Muslim areas, tend to be lifetime appointments, much like supreme court justices, and can take a longer-term view of the need for security and stability. For example, the *lamido* of Adamawa, although not in a shari'a state, celebrated his fiftieth year on the throne in August 2003. The emir of Kano, who is well known for his efforts at conflict resolution, came to the throne in 1963. The emir of Zaria, who lives in the shadow of Ahmadu Bello University and in a religiously mixed demographic environment, has been effective within Zaria Emirate but does not have any responsibility for the Kaduna urban area.

The post-2003 election administration in Abuja asked the (late) *Etsu Nupe* (in Niger State) to chair a commission evaluating the role of local governments. Within this domain, the role of "royal fathers" seems to be important in addressing the issue of grassroots stability.

Also, the establishment in September 2003 of a National Peace Commission (see chapter 7) under the chairmanship of Shehu Malami (and hence, indirectly, linked to the sultan of Sokoto) is an attempt to channel the efforts of traditional and modern leaders toward effective conflict mediation. Many of the emirs have modern credentials as well. Thus the emir of Ilorin (Sulu Gambari) was a former federal judge. Such experience and leadership could be focused on issues of conflict resolution.

To some extent, the northern governors of the Fourth Republic have replaced the "royal fathers" in having the primary potential for managing conflict resolution. This is a basic question of leadership and the sensitivity of symbols. Some of the younger, technically trained or business-oriented governors have focused more on "development," since the constitution clearly reserves "security" issues—police and military—to the federal government. The ability of Muslim governors to reach out to their Christian citizens is crucial in preventing conflict in the shari'a states. In more religiously homogenous states, such as Zamfara, with its strict constructionist view of shari'a, this may take a less accommodating form, especially on issues of alcohol or shop closings during prayer times. In a diverse state such as Kaduna, Governor Makarfi clearly was caught in the middle, and his efforts at reconciliation seemed to please neither side.

In a large metropolitan state such as Kano, a promising example of trying to bridge religious communities was the incoming governor (in 2003) Ibrahim Shekarau, a strong proponent of shari'a. When interviewed by the *Kaduna Weekly Trust* in July 2003, he replied in a modest way:

> [My] understanding of shari'a is putting God first in anything one does.
> ... Every good Muslim will like to deal with a good Christian, likewise every good Christian will like to deal with a good Muslim. I did not choose to come from a Muslim family nor do you choose to come from a Christian family; these were accidents of birth. But God chose to create us that way so that we may know each other and live with one another in peace. Who am I to challenge God's wisdom in this respect?[14]

The Kano governor has been trying to articulate symbolic ways of bridging the Muslim and Christian communities of the state, by emphasizing the tradition of People of the Book (*ahl kitab*). He also sees a strong need for cooperation on issues of education and development.[15]

Trans-State Ecumenical Bodies

As noted previously, Nigeria has two major Muslim ecumenical umbrella bodies: the Nigerian Supreme Council for Islamic Affairs (NSCIA) and the Society for the Victory of Islam (*Jama'atu Nasril Islam*, or JNI), which is based in Kaduna. Both the NSCIA and JNI draw their members from a wide range of Muslim groups, from traditional "royal fathers" (emirs) to representative sufi brotherhood leaders (especially the Tijaniyya and Qadiriyya), plus the anti-innovation legalists (*Izala*). The JNI was originally a northern Nigerian body, set up in the First Republic by Premier Ahmadu Bello. Subsequently, it extended its concerns nationwide.

The NSCIA has much the same membership as the JNI but is more inclusive nationally, with the sultan of Sokoto as president, who has expressed increasing concern about domestic security matters and civil disorder.[16] Often the NSCIA meets at Arewa House in Kaduna.[17] In recent years, Arewa House has been active in conflict mediation efforts throughout the north, even in non-Muslim areas such as Tiv versus Jukun.[18]

In addition, since 2000 the Supreme Council for Shari'a has focused on legal issues around the country. The major women's umbrella group, the Federation of Muslim Women's Associations of Nigeria (FOMWAN), which addresses current issues of concern to Muslim women, has taken seriously the themes of tolerance and conflict mediation. Numerous Muslim youth organizations also exist in different parts of the country, although at times they have been on the cutting edge of confrontation rather than conflict mediation.

The Inter-Faith Mediation Centre in Kaduna provides a different model, yet does not have the national reach to be effective outside its immediate area. Since the 2004 riots, it has become active in training and mediation efforts in Plateau State and may link up with conflict mediation efforts in Kano State. As for broader reach, the Mediation Centre works closely with the JNI and CAN.

In times of crisis, it is usually the NSCIA that acts as a counterweight to the Christian umbrella group, CAN. As already mentioned, CAN includes Roman Catholics, mainstream Protestants, evangelicals, Pentecostal or inspirational churches, and African churches with a Christian legacy. Unfortunately, the politics of unity within CAN and NSCIA often preclude a real capacity for conflict mediation. At their best, these trans-state ecumenical bodies can serve as potential conflict resolution liaisons. In potential conflict situations such as Kaduna, both the JNI and CAN are seen as "part of the solution rather than part of the problem."[19]

At a more secular and cultural level, the Arewa Consultative Forum (ACF) and the committees of northern elders serve to bring together Muslim and non-Muslim leaders from throughout the north for discussions of mutual interest. Since 2003 the ACF has been led by Chief Sunday Awoniyi, a northern Yoruba Christian, closely associated with the earlier northern civil service, who maintains personal ties with all major northern factions.[20] The ACF has been a key factor in the National Political Reform Dialogue in 2005.

Judicial System

The potential of the legal system for conflict resolution is clear, even with its three-legged base (common law, shari'a, customary law). Unfortunately, the dominant magistrate court system is still so rooted in British common law that it seems unwieldy and slow in a Nigerian context. Also, the judiciary has been weakened over time by military rule. Something as basic as election appeals, which are taken to the federal tribunals, are a clear alternative to mass protests (and possible turmoil) on the streets. Such courts must be seen to be evenhanded—the essence of "rule of law"—yet the number of complaints, especially with the election tribunals, seems to be increasing exponentially.[21] In a few cases where the court has ruled against an apparent election victor—usually from the dominant incumbent party—there has been little enforcement capability, and appeals can drag on (or reverse lower court decisions), while frustrations mount. There is also a widespread perception, especially in the north, that "equal treatment" is not being followed with regard to suspects from the north who are remanded, as distinct from those in the southwest. Such perceptions of "selective justice" may contribute to future violence rather than defuse conflict.

Police

The slogan painted on the Nigerian police vehicles in 2004, and indeed official policy, has been "operation fire-for-fire." That is, if violence was perpetrated on police, they would return fire. (This slogan changed in 2005, after the forced resignation of the federal inspector general on grounds of embezzling US$100 million.) The fact that the constitution (1999) designates all police as federal, with no state or local counterparts, has meant that every local conflict may become a national issue. Quite often, since the police cannot handle such conflicts, the military is called in, again a federalizing of all conflict. The heavily armed mobile military patrols in places like Kaduna before the 2003 election became a national source of additional conflict between the political parties.[22]

Although police are assigned to states for service, they are only responsible to a federal inspector. They are exempt from many local laws—including shari'a law—which often creates the impression of a double standard. Thus police live in separate barracks, where alcohol may be served. The kind of grassroots challenges to law and order that are emerging may require first responders to be more in the "serve-and-protect" tradition, rather than the "fire-for-fire" tradition.

Media

Over the years, Nigeria's media have more often been a source of conflict than a mediating influence. Quite simply, violence sells newspapers. Photos (sometimes doctored) of gross interethnic (or interreligious) violence have precipitated panic and flight, and more violence.[23] Given the presumption of a free press, however, the way to address the issue is better training of journalists, better editorial guidance, and the creation of more balanced prototypes.[24] Note, however, that some effort has been made to establish procedures for vetting rumors on sensitive matters, such as the role of the sultan of Sokoto.[25]

The use of television is significant, and in the wealthier northern homes satellite dishes pick up global sources. Within the Muslim north, there has been a TV and radio tradition over many decades airing different points of view on issues as basic as the interpretation of the Qur'an (that is, *tafsir*) presented every night during the month of Ramadan. Christian radio and television still tend to present denominational or parochial perspectives, without the interactive debates typical of Muslim media. Still less common is dispassionate media coverage of Christian-Muslim dialogue.

Universities and Educated Elites

The four major far northern universities—Ahmadu Bello University, Zaria; Bayero University, Kano; Usman Danfodio University, Sokoto; and the University of Maiduguri—have over the years produced generations of well-educated men and women who often provide the intellectual depth for discussions regarding shari'a, constitutionalism, rule of law, and conflict resolution. The Internet and the northern press are full of serious contributions to the religious, political, or socioeconomic debate.[26]

In addition, northern universities have developed conflict resolution approaches and mechanisms that might have wider significance.[27] As in the cases of universities in Ibadan and Lagos, the "peace committees" on every university campus are essential to the prevention or mediation of violence.[28] In addition, major traditional and civil authorities have become more involved in such university conflict resolution efforts, especially in Zaria.

However, the university systems in the north are struggling financially and for the most part have little contact with universities or scholars outside of Nigeria.[29] When they are short of budget or human resources (or are closed by the government), the frustration levels are high, and almost predictably there will be violence, especially in the spring when the weather is hot and the annual budgets have expired.

During the military periods, universities were seen as a threat and a seat of opposition. With the return to democratic federalism, more constructive policies are required, as well as a clear appreciation of the need for peace committees on campus as shock absorbers in the seemingly endless student conflicts over religious and secular issues. (Alcohol, of course, is both.)

Nongovernmental Organizations

Nigeria has several conflict resolution NGOs, a prominent one being Academic Associates/PeaceWorks, based in Abuja but active in Muslim-Christian dialogue programs in Kano and Kaduna, for example.[30] Another is the Inter-Faith Mediation Centre in Kaduna, already mentioned, which works closely with a number of local government authorities in Kaduna, Bauchi, and

Plateau, as well as with international NGOs. Other NGOs, such as BAOBAB, which is a Muslim women's human rights group, are directly involved in the shari'a issue in the north.[31] They have provided appeals counsel to women accused of adultery in some of the high-profile cases.[32] FOMWAN is very active, of course, as it serves as a network among various Muslim women's groups.

Not all NGOs are capable of serving as conflict mediators, however. Some that come out of the antimilitary period are more confrontational than mediational. Others, such as the Transition Monitoring Group (TMG), an umbrella network of hundreds of NGOs, have provided valuable services in monitoring election sites throughout the nation and may develop capacities for conflict mediation as well.

Federal Government Policy

A wide range of federal governmental policies, sometimes incorporated as constitutional provisions, serve as conflict mediation mechanisms. A case in point is the formula for ensuring broad support for candidates and parties (the requirement that 25 percent of the vote come from two-thirds of the states), or federal character provision of the constitution, covering all domains in the executive branch.

In interpreting "federal character," the tendency in some quarters has been to apply religious identity criteria (rather than state of origin) and to argue for an interpretation that reflects religious as well as ethnic (that is, state) balance.[33] A more obvious principle, although not in the constitution, has been to have a presidential and vice presidential balance reflecting the north and south. Since President Obasanjo is from the south, it is widely expected (especially in the north) that the president in 2007 will be a northern Muslim. The PDP chair (Audu Ogbeh, a Middle Belt Christian) announced his commitment to this principle in 2004, although his subsequent forced resignation by President Obasanjo has raised alarm bells in the north. Any deviation from this expectation of a northern-led ticket in 2007 would have serious consequences for stability in Nigeria.

Some other federal policies or initiatives should also be mentioned: the relocation of the federal capital to Abuja, thus giving each cultural zone a sense of equal access; the National Youth Service Corps program, whereby graduates are sent to work in another state for a year (and usually to another cultural zone); the scheduled census in 2005 (and possible redistricting); the training of the military for appropriate civil-military relations, including civilian control of the military; issues of "justice" and corruption, which were a major point of contention in the 2003 elections; issues of multiple judicial systems; and the roles of traditional leaders and local governments.[34] The idea of a national conference to consider amendments to the constitution (that is, the NPRD) has already been mentioned. In short, almost every issue can be related to conflict mediation or resolution in the larger context but also has the potential to increase conflict if perceived to be unfair.

The Challenges of Mediating the Shari'a Issue

Regardless of the political motives of individual actors, the reestablishment of a broad spectrum of shari'a law in the twelve far northern states of Nigeria was a reaction to the previous fifteen years of military rule, sometimes capricious and abusive, and the need to return to a recognizable "rule of law."[35] Ironically, the attempt to establish shari'a in parallel with the Nigerian common law tradition, applicable to Muslims only, was initially met with suspicion and conflict both in the Muslim community and in the Muslim and Christian communities of the north. Kaduna experienced some of the worst violence since the end of the Nigerian civil war, but with the elections of 2003, much of the anxiety regarding shari'a was transferred to the political arena, particularly in the far north. However, the PDP links in the north and the ANPP links with parties in the southeast muted the shari'a issue. In the aftermath of the election, the opposition parties have decided to take their grievances to the election tribunals, that is, the courts, rather than the streets. Whether the courts can act as evenhanded conflict mediators remains to be seen.

The debate surrounding the meaning and role of shari'a in Nigeria will undoubtedly remain. It is largely an intrafaith issue, although questions about interfaith relations are not far from the surface. In addition, some large challenges remain in clarifying the roles of the police, the courts, the traditional leadership, the NGOs, the media, the universities, and the ecumenical bodies (both Christian and Muslim). A fundamental framework issue is whether the Nigerian constitution (1999), which was designed as a conflict-mediating document, will be interpreted in ways that promote peace and reconciliation rather than set off more violent conflict, which could threaten the foundations of the Nigerian state.

10

Religious Tolerance and Conflict Resolution

The central issue within the Muslim community of Nigeria for the past two hundred years has been what degree of tolerance is necessary to sustain unity with diversity, without letting syncretism or cultural mixtures run riot in the local traditionalist communities. There have been several categories of serious intra-Muslim conflict during this time frame.

Tolerance and Conflict within the Muslim Community

A prime concern of the jihad of Usman dan Fodio was whether the establishment authorities—Muslim Hausa chiefs—were really "good Muslims" (as distinct from unjust rulers). By confronting those authorities with intellectual, political, and eventually military force, the jihad movement established that the legitimacy of reform rested on being able to persuade the community that the limits of tolerance had been breached by various unjust practices or customary cultural behavior. In short, being a good Muslim meant not being tolerant of unjust practices.

Yet what complicated the situation for emirate authorities after the jihad was the need to accommodate a variety of indigenous communities with traditional cultures. The standard way of dealing with such communities was to work through a local chief and to allow non-Muslim communities to continue their practices without interruption. However, any local community that claimed to be Muslim could be held accountable to a set of standards connected to a Muslim code of conduct, namely the Maliki law as interpreted in Sudanic West Africa.

Because the leaders of the Sokoto Caliphate were also identified, at least in the public mind, with a particular Muslim sufi brotherhood (Qadiriyya), another important question even in the nineteenth century was whether the example of the reform leaders also extended to affiliation with a sufi brotherhood. By the late nineteenth century, the polarization within the Sokoto Caliphate between Sokoto and Kano (the major commercial capital of the caliphate) had reached the point where the Kano civil war for succession to the position of emir revolved around Kano's willingness or unwillingness to assume a subordinate position to Sokoto. The anti-Sokoto faction prevailed in Kano.

Early in the twentieth century, the emirate leaders of Kano came to follow an alternative sufi brotherhood (Tijaniyya), identified in northern Nigeria as a new type of reform movement. The rivalry and religious tension between Kano and Sokoto—and later between Kano and Kaduna—sometimes spilled over into localized violent confrontations between those Muslims who followed Qadiriyya and those who followed Tijaniyya, especially the reformed version associated with Shaykh Ibrahim Niass of Senegal.

This occasional lack of interbrotherhood tolerance was particularly intense in the 1950s and 1960s, as the transition to self-government and independence raised challenges to traditional authorities and also to the natural order of Sokoto's preeminence within the caliphal-emirate system. The symbolism of praying with arms crossed (reformed Tijaniyya) versus arms at the side (Qadiriyya and traditional Tijaniyya) fueled tension not only in local communities but also throughout the northern region.

Yet another source of conflict developed after the Nigerian civil war in the 1970s, with the oil boom under way, when the enormous investment in education and human resources in the far north enabled an entire generation of young northern Muslims to obtain a Western education for the first time. Many of these young men and women found they did not have time for the supplementary prayers of the brotherhoods, and once again the question of what was necessary to be a good Muslim became a central issue.

As mentioned earlier, new Muslim organizations developed in nontraditional cities such as Kaduna and Jos, which were anti-*tarika* (that is, "anti-innovation") and often lumped under the name of *Izala*. Clashes between *Izala* and the youth wing of the reformed Tijaniyya became a serious problem, especially since the relations between Kano and Kaduna were still uneasy. Kaduna's Shaykh Abubakar Gummi—the father figure to a whole generation of young northerners who wanted to confront innovation, including the brotherhoods, and return to fundamentals—never sanctioned direct confrontation or violence. However, he was unswerving in his insistence that much of the sufi legacy in West Africa was based on culture and not religion, and that the Qur'an itself was the only true guide to appropriate Muslim behavior. He interpreted the Qur'an in Hausa and printed the first major bilingual edition of the Qur'an in Arabic and Hausa. He was skilled in using the media, especially radio and television, and was willing to debate with others.

Also during the 1970s, the Muslim Students Society developed widespread support within the universities, partly to offset the more radical Westernizing students and partly to reassert their own Muslim identity and to try to educate themselves as to the differences between their local customs and more universal Islamic practices. As part of this process, the emphasis was on basics, that is, the Qur'an and Hadith, rather than on inherited emirate traditions. In the ensuing turmoil, several northern university facilities that served alcohol were burned down, and the tension between "secular" and "religious" student groups grew more serious.

In addition, during the oil boom of the 1970s, with its high urbanization rates (and perhaps with the end of the Muslim century approaching), fringe cults appeared ready to challenge all aspects of Muslim establishment authority. The violent conflagration sparked by an itinerant "syncretist" preacher (Muhammad Marwa, also known as Maitatsine) in Kano in December 1980, with thousands of resulting deaths, served to demonstrate to the Muslim community that interbrotherhood rivalries and the confrontations with non-brotherhoods were less important than the question of extreme syncretism. The authorities handled the Maitatsine cult first by negotiation, mainly through the office of the Kano governor (Rimi), and later through direct police and army intervention. The death of the leader (Maitatsine) did not stop the spread of the movement, and further violence occurred in areas ranging from Lagos to Gombe and Borno.

The oil boom, with its expanded road linkages and increasing contact with other Nigerian Muslims, also raised anew the question of emirate zone relations with Muslim organizations throughout Nigeria, whose legacy differed from that of the Sokoto caliphal reformers. The early Muslim ecumenical movement of the 1960s, especially the *Jama'atu Nasril Islam* (JNI), was broadened to a national arena, mainly through the vehicle of the Nigerian Supreme Council for Islamic Affairs (NSCIA).

Although tension within the JNI and NSCIA did not appear serious, some Muslim elements were deeply suspicious of each other, and the fact that they were meeting at all is, in part, a tribute to the diplomatic skills of Ibrahim Dasuki, both before and after he became sultan. Dasuki was especially sensitive to the need to work with Borno Muslim authorities and Yoruba Muslim leaders (especially Abdu-Lateef Adegbite), and the need to work with women's groups such as FOMWAN.

One Muslim community that did experience a serious split was that in Sokoto. The dispute in this case was over the sultanship succession in the late 1980s. The tensions between traditional forms of Islamic or emirate culture in Nigeria and more modern forms reached a peak with the death of Sultan Abubakar III in November 1988. Abubakar had been sultan for more than fifty years; he was appointed in the 1930s by colonial administrators, who preferred him over his younger Western-educated rival, Ahmadu Bello.[1] Even before the death of Abubakar, a succession competition developed between two branches of the descendants of the original founder of the Sokoto Caliphate. The immediate family of the deceased sultan felt entitled to the succession and supported Muhammad Maccido, the sultan's eldest son. The rival candidate, from the Buhari family, was Ibrahim Dasuki, who ultimately prevailed and was appointed the new sultan by the governor of Sokoto State. There was considerable turmoil in Sokoto, and Dasuki's home and some properties were burned. He required heavy personal security protection, which continued even after his public confirmation.

Part of the significance of the Dasuki succession was his close association with the Nigerian Supreme Council for Islamic Affairs. In his new role as sultan, he was now president of the Supreme Council. The rival candidate, Muhammad Maccido, was a soft-spoken, pious, well-liked "local," who had been at his father's side throughout some long illnesses. (As mentioned earlier, Maccido was appointed sultan after Dasuki's deposition in 1996.)

Thus in 1988 Sokoto seemed to be regaining its preeminence within the Muslim community of Nigeria, perhaps at the expense of Kano, but it achieved this by emphasizing the need for tolerance and patience both within the Muslim community and between the Muslim community and the Christian community. Tensions between Christians and Muslims had increased in 1986 over the issue of Nigeria's membership in the Organization of the Islamic Conference (OIC).

Yet another cause of tension or occasional confrontation arose in the late 1980s and 1990s between the various branches of the Muslim establishment and the younger generation of semieducated and better-educated youth, who had grown uneasy because they had no employment prospects in the austere economy of the times. This economic downturn was due largely to a drastic drop in oil prices, gross mismanagement and corruption by some officials, and the structural adjustment policy being used to reshape the Nigerian economy.

Prohibited from protesting by a military ban on all political activities, some of these young men used Muslim reformist symbols to articulate their displeasure with government policy and the establishment. (This clearly finds a parallel in other parts of the Muslim world.) Issues of social justice surfaced on university campuses, and young unemployed urban dwellers began to follow leaders who challenged the authorities. Some of the fervor of the Iranian revolution served as inspiration, and posters of Ayatollah Khomeini were put up in many northern homes. The main thrust of these youth movements, however, was the legacy of reform in northern Nigeria. The press, and even those in authority, often referred to such austere puritanical calls for reform as a "Shi'ite" conspiracy.

Hence the conflicts, sometimes violent, as in Katsina in the spring of 1991, came to be blamed on "Shi'ites." Such symbolism was meant to suggest that youth were outside the boundaries of normal Muslim tolerance, since Nigerian Muslims followed the Sunni way. The so-called Shi'ites relished the labels and symbols of Islamic revolution, warning the establishment that someday they would be destroyed by pride and corruption. This simmering confrontation reached a peak in 1996 when the Zaria leader of the challengers (Mallam Ibrahim Zakzaki) was jailed by the Abacha regime, and his followers threatened reprisals. (A subsequent confrontation between "Shi'ite" and emirate authorities occurred in June 2005, in Sokoto City, when the youth groups demanded access to the central mosques.)

An additional number of confrontations shook the Muslim community during the Fourth Republic with the inception of the shari'a systems in the far northern states. As mentioned earlier, some Muslims preferred a direct, "just-do-it" approach to shari'a, whereas others favored a gradual pragmatic approach. Still others insisted that conditions in Nigeria were not right for the constitutional structure to accommodate shari'a. Sometimes these differences spilled over into the streets. Traditional leaders, such as the sultan of Sokoto, and civilian leaders, such as Vice President Atiku Abubakar, were given a rough time when they tried to mediate. Even the Muslim women's legal groups, such as BAOBAB, were hassled when they tried to make legal representations in Zamfara.

In the aftermath of September 11, 2001, and the U.S. attacks on the Taliban in Afghanistan, some of the youth in Kano demonstrated against the United States and in support of Osama bin Laden. This was an obvious taunt to the establishment in the Muslim community, who, following the unanimous lead of the OIC, had condemned terrorism and the killing of innocent civilians. As usual, street demonstrations in Kano led to Muslim-Muslim and Muslim-

Christian violence.[2] Such demonstrations raised questions about stability and security in Kano Emirate, which had long been a center of Qur'anic and higher Islamic learning for migrant youths, especially in the many schools throughout the urban area.[3]

The violent confrontation between a *hijra* group in Yobe State—called Taliban in the media—and the federal police and military in early 2004 has already been mentioned. The group appeared to be an idealistic faction of postgraduate students who had returned from studies in Sudan and were migrating to set up an ideal Islamic community. Although the circumstances of this event are not yet clear, they again raise the possibility that establishment authorities may have mishandled the situation. As of 2005, the self-styled Taliban movement had grassroots networks in major cities throughout the far north. The Taliban, according to local reports, argued that Nigerian Muslim authorities had been corrupted and hence were illegitimate.

Other demonstrations and challenges, between urban Muslim street youth and emirate or northern Muslim governors in 2003–04, suggest there is a potential for class violence between wealthy Muslim northerners (and their security protectors) and those who have been left behind economically. This is the most frightening specter of chaos that haunts many in the educated and prosperous sectors of the Muslim north and has prompted people to devise a variety of strategies for protection. These range from direct charity to schools and mosques, "for blessing," to more gated and secured compounds with private militia or security arrangements.

In Kano, after the transition to an ANPP government in 2003, the Qadiriyya brotherhood demonstrated against state authorities over the issue of appointments to the shari'a boards. There were signs of politics in this, since the Qadiriyya leadership was said to be closer to the previous PDP government. In the spring of 2004, the police halted some of the traditional Qadiriyya religious processions in the aftermath of crises in Plateau State, and the subsequent crises in Kano. At the same time, tensions between PDP stalwarts and the new team of ANPP politicians in Kano contributed to the turmoil in the spring of 2004.

Tolerance and Conflict in the Christian Community

Since the overall stability of Nigeria depends in part on amicable relations between Muslims and Christians, tolerance takes on added importance in the Christian communities. The Nigerian Christian community can be divided into five main branches: Roman Catholic, mainstream Protestant, evangelical

Protestant, inspirational groups or churches (including Pentecostal), and African syncretist churches (including Aladura). To the extent that Christian denominations have been associated with particular ethnic groups, the intrafaith relations have been part of the larger fabric of society.

As mentioned in chapter 5, much of the British impact in the port city of Lagos and in the surrounding Yoruba areas was reflected in early forms of mainstream Protestant denominations—especially Anglican and Methodist (plus Scottish Presbyterian)—incorporated into the educated elite culture of southern Nigeria. British mainstream Protestantism also formed the baseline for Western-educated elites during the colonial and postcolonial eras. The breakaway churches developed from this baseline. Some, such as the Aladura, focused on faith healing through prayer. Others were guided by a particular vision of a founding father (or mother). Most inspirational churches arose by "breaking" from the mainstream Protestant churches and then drawing their constituencies from the common people. Orthodoxy had no arbitrators other than the willingness of people to follow or participate in religious groups or practices. Since mainstream and inspirational African churches differed in socioeconomic status, they tended to live peaceably, except where some of the more extreme forms of group therapy or traditional culture represented by these groups generated tension.[4] The idea of "secret societies" or "cults," which are constitutionally banned in Nigeria (a ban often enforced on university campuses), may be seen as a mainstream attempt to curb the extreme autonomy of some syncretist churches associated with occult practices and enforcement procedures.

British dominance in Nigeria was partly offset by the missionary work of a number of Roman Catholic priests from Ireland, often in education and health services. For complex historical reasons, the spread of Roman Catholicism among the Igbos of eastern Nigeria seemed to provide an ethnic and geopolitical counterbalance to the dominant Protestant forms of religious allegiance among the Yoruba. The occasional tension between Irish priests and British administrators may mirror the tensions between Igbo and Yoruba communities in the 1950s and 1960s. During this time, party coalitions were formed that linked northern Muslims and eastern Roman Catholics against the "Protestant" Yoruba in the west.

During the civil war of 1967–70, there was a realignment in which northern and western Nigerians confronted the secessionist state of Biafra, with its predominant Igbo population and strong ties to the Roman Catholic Church within and outside of Africa. One of the intriguing aspects of the civil war was the effort of Catholic and Protestant church leaders and other religious-based Western groups to try to mediate the human tragedy of the civil war.[5]

Even years after the civil war, Catholic groups in Nigeria and their Protestant counterparts have many barriers to transcend. The Roman Catholic archbishop of Lagos (Okogie) became the outspoken head of the Christian Association of Nigeria (CAN) for almost ten years.[6] Yet many Anglicans felt he did not speak for them.[7] (When Bishop Sunday Mbang of the Methodists succeeded Okogie, he initially took a more moderate tone in relations with Muslims.[8])

The competition between Roman Catholics and Anglicans (and other mainstream Protestants, such as Methodists) was heightened over the question of what kind of Christian "cathedral" to build in Abuja as a counterbalance to the national mosque. In the end, the Christians decided to build an ecumenical center with multifaith facilities, although its completion was delayed for years. As of 2005, it was still far from completed.

The issue of churches on public space has also been debated on university campuses. In an effort to treat Christians and Muslims nonpreferentially, the government usually reserves space or building facilities for each major religious group in appropriate public projects. Even so, the various churches have seldom been able to agree on common ecumenical endeavors. To add to these pressures, Muslims insist that there be equal space for Christian and Muslim facilities, and they object when the schisms so evident among the Christian groups are used to justify reserving additional space for Christian groups.

Of the evangelical Protestant groups, many originating in North America have been engaged in missionary activity in the Middle Belt zone, mainly the states of Plateau (and later Nasarawa) and Benue, but including Taraba (formerly southern Gongola) and Kogi (formerly western Kwara). Schools and clinics attracted those residual ethnic populations who had resisted advances of the Muslim horse culture from the savanna zone.

The Sudan Interior Mission (SIM), based in Toronto, had extensive facilities and headquartered many of its activities in Jos, high on the plateau, which was cooler than the rainforest to the south or the savanna zone to the north. Bible literature was translated into local languages, and many local churches began to develop indigenous leadership. When the government took over all private (that is, parochial) schools in 1975 and many of the expatriate missionaries retired, the first generation of indigenous evangelical leaders assumed control and tried to work out new relationships with the religiously mixed urban authorities. SIM and other groups such as the Sudan United Mission reorganized into the Evangelical Church of West Africa (ECWA). Subsequently, the term "ECWA" was used to describe a wide variety of autonomous evangelical Protestant churches. Because of the opportunities for

Western education, many of the Middle Belt Christians had a disproportionate representation in institutions of higher education and in the military.
Being situated in the northern Middle Belt and having an ethnic base there,
many of the ECWA groups have at times collided with the northern Muslim
establishment.[9]

As for the southern Christian groups, the evangelical churches along the
southern fringe of the northern Muslim zone have very little cohesion and are
less likely to participate in Christian ecumenical activities than the mainstream churches. There are literally hundreds of separate evangelical churches
in the Middle Belt zone, as there are hundreds of inspirational breakaway
churches in the southern part of Nigeria (and in the ethnic ghettos of the
northern cities). In the case of both the evangelical and the inspirational
churches, the principle of local autonomy is part of the message that appeals
to their constituencies, including the use of local languages in services.

Like the Muslims, the Christians had their national organization, CAN, which
had its roots at Ahmadu Bello University in Zaria but quickly spread to all parts
of Nigeria after the country's membership in the Organization of the Islamic
Conference (OIC) came up in 1986. The following year, Federal Decree 30 established the National Council for Religious Affairs (NCRA), composed ultimately
of twelve Christian leaders and twelve Muslim leaders, who were to review matters of mutual concern and report directly to the Ministry of Interior.

The Christian leaders in NCRA included representatives from Roman
Catholic churches (especially those in Lagos, Onitsha, and Jos), Anglican
churches, Baptist churches, inspirational churches (for example, Aladura),
and evangelical churches (for example, ECWA). As mentioned earlier, the
archbishop of the Roman Catholic Church in Lagos was the chairman of
CAN. The fear of Muslim domination in Nigeria provided some of the glue
for CAN, although on practical matters of interfaith Christian dialogue, there
was a long legacy of fear and intolerance. At a structural level, the more hierarchical churches (Roman Catholic and mainstream Protestant) had more
resources at their command, including human resources, to try to effectuate
channels of communication.

Ironically, many of the "traditional rulers" in the south had come to be
associated with the inspirational churches, partly to accommodate their broad
constituencies. The net result, however, was that traditional rulers have been
able to facilitate intra-Christian (as well as Christian-Muslim) dialogue
because of their symbolic significance as "fathers of their people."

With the institution of shari'a in the far north in 2000, the Christian
groups, sometimes under the umbrella of CAN, became vocal critics of this

development. As mentioned earlier, it was the Christian protests and demonstrations that sparked the Kaduna riots in February 2000. At the same time, the shari'a issue has provided a bond among the Christian groups. Thus as differences sharpened between Muslims and Christians during the Fourth Republic, the Christian groups became increasingly aware of the need for cohesion. When President Obasanjo declared himself a "born-again Christian" (Baptist), he became a national symbol of "difference," emphasizing the complex relations between Muslims and Christians. (Note that by 2005 Vice President Atiku Abubakar had dropped his title of "Alhaji," that is, someone who has made the Muslim pilgrimage, to deemphasize his religious identity and strengthen his "national" identity.)

Tolerance and Conflict between Muslims and Christians

During the colonial period, there were relatively few instances of direct Muslim-Christian confrontation. With the rise of "new towns" in the major northern areas and the arrival of southern immigrants with English-speaking skills, tensions developed over a combination of economic, social, and religious factors, and groups vied for political advantage. Similar tensions had surfaced in southern cities with northern migrant quarters.

An early example of interethnic and interreligious strain that got out of control was the violence in Kano in May 1953, following a federal budget session in Lagos during which northern delegates had been harassed by street mobs. The violence in Kano focused on the Igbo community, which appeared to dominate the new market system.

Another case of violence, during the early independence period (1960–66), involved various factions of the Yoruba community in the west (including Christians and Muslims). Political issues were the primary cause here. Violence also erupted in Benue Province at this time, between certain elements of the Tiv community and the Muslim-led regional government based in Kaduna.

A complex set of factors led to the assassination of government leaders in Kaduna, Ibadan, and Lagos in January 1966 and the subsequent violence, between May and October 1966, that preceded the Nigerian civil war (1967–70).[10] That war claimed perhaps as many as 3 million lives, including casualties due to famine and the breakdown of food and medical systems. Although religious symbols—Christian and Muslim—were manipulated on both sides, this was not strictly speaking a "religious war," since it pitted five highly diverse geocultural zones against the Biafran secessionists.[11]

The postwar reconciliation and reconstruction was quite remarkable by global standards, as conflict resolution teams worked diligently throughout the country, and Igbos were reintegrated in most sectors (except in the senior ranks of the military). The oil boom in the decade following the civil war (1970–80) provided opportunities to link up sections of the country with little previous contact. Road networks were the most visible sign of this linkage, as was the decision to locate the new capital in the center of the country at Abuja. Indeed, much of the construction in Abuja was done by Igbo contractors, which further strengthened their integration into the national endeavor.

Postwar reconstruction was made possible not only by the infusion of petrodollars but also by the concerted effort of Nigerians at all levels to heal the wounds of war. The northern Christian head of state, General Yakubu Gowon, was instrumental in this process. Churches were rebuilt. Economic opportunities were opened up to large segments of the population. Rapid urbanization brought large numbers of young rural dwellers to the cities. Part of the transition to urban life was facilitated by the urban churches and mosques.

Clouds of religious fear appeared for a while in the mid-1970s, when leadership patterns changed following the assassination of Murtala Muhammad by Middle Belt "Christian" officers in February 1976. Confidence was restored, however, after the smooth succession to General Obasanjo. The economy was still strong, and there seemed to be opportunities for all areas and sectors of the economy.

The return to civilian rule in 1979 coincided with the end of the oil boom. The 1980s were years of austerity, as the realities of Nigeria's place in the global economy and years of neglect of the agricultural sector began to take their toll. The national elections of 1979 and 1983 revived concerns about ethnoreligious and political balance within the country.

The coup that put the military back in control at the end of 1983 did not at first pertain to religious intolerance, since the new military head of state (Buhari) was of the same religion (Muslim) and ethnicity (Hausa-Fulani) as his civilian predecessor (Shagari). However, increasingly tight controls on the economy and on civilian dissent began to take on regional overtones and hence had ethnic and religious implications. (Buhari's second-in-command was a Muslim Yoruba, and some may have felt that Christians were being neglected.)

The senior officer coup against Buhari in August 1985 (led by Babangida) resulted in a realignment of regional forces in the country. The religiously mixed areas of the Middle Belt came to have a central place in the symbolism of religiously diverse leadership and increased tolerance for diverse views.

Shortly after the 1985 coup, Nigeria's membership in the OIC became public and the news polarized Muslim-Christian sentiment. The Babangida government attempted to provide channels of communication between the Christian and Muslim communities (for example, by establishing the National Council for Religious Affairs), but by 1989 the Christian members of the council had stopped attending and the group became dormant.

On the morning of April 22, 1990, some junior officers in Lagos tried to mount a coup and assassinate the head of state (Babangida). They took over the broadcast facilities in Lagos to announce, among other things, that they were expelling the five far northern (predominantly Muslim) states and insisted that the sultan of Sokoto (Dasuki) resign in favor of his more locally oriented rival from the previous incumbent's family.

The government restored order quickly and denied that the attempted coup was religious in nature. Yet the fact that the head of state was Muslim, that the perpetrators of the coup were disgruntled about internal Muslim affairs in the far north and many of them seemed to be from the Middle Belt or south, sounded a serious alarm within the Nigerian Muslim community.

A national debate ensued on the power-sharing formula, which was joined by the leader of CAN (Archbishop Okogie of Lagos) and many of the northern newspapers. Some counted the number of Christians and Muslims at the senior appointment levels, and there were intimations that a "federal character" quota system for Muslims and Christians was emerging.

Meanwhile, plans continued for the transition to a civilian Third Republic. A two-party system was introduced at the grassroots level. As much as anything else, this dispelled the idea that the two-party system would encapsulate the religious polarization that was being headlined in the media almost every day.

As economic austerity continued and political life slowly returned, Christians and Muslims clashed in a number of local incidents. One occurred in Katsina, over the publication of an article deemed to be derogatory to the Prophet Muhammad; another occurred in Bauchi, over a local government matter that had Muslim-Christian overtones.

Then in August 1991 the government announced that it was creating nine new states, which involved partitioning the three largest predominantly Muslim states: Sokoto, Kano, and Borno. The message seemed to reinforce the government's pledge that politics as usual would not be allowed to reemerge. With gubernatorial elections pending in the states, attention turned to the new types of coalitions needed to govern both at the state and national levels.

One thing was clear: both parties would have to forge new alliances that bridged the chasms between the Muslim and Christian communities. To this end, there was widespread reassessment of ways in which tolerance between religious communities could be enhanced and conflict resolution could be encouraged at all levels, between ethnic, religious, political, economic, and generational groups.

As mentioned in chapter 7 (and appendix A), the 1993 election saw a realignment of the usual religious and political forces. The National Republican Congress nominated a Muslim candidate from Kano and a vice president from the Christian east. The Social Democratic Party (SDP) nominated a Muslim Yoruba from Ogun State (Abiola) and a Muslim from Borno State (Kingibe). The apparent success of the SDP team and the subsequent election annulment strained relations throughout the country, but especially in Yorubaland. Significantly, this zone of disaffection cut across religious lines, with some of the strongest support for recognizing the "June 12" election coming from Yoruba Christians.

The Abacha regime established in November 1993 dealt with the religious balance issue through a careful co-optation of both Christian and Muslim political leaders from throughout the country. The subsequent political unrest came primarily from the Yoruba zone and did not follow religious lines.

The presidential elections of 1999 saw a voluntary power shift from the (Muslim) north to the (Christian) southwest. This was intended to heal some of the geopolitical wounds stemming from June 12 while allowing for the first elected Christian president (Obasanjo). The principle of "federal character" was to provide an approximate ethnoreligious balance at the national level.

As mentioned in previous chapters, the shari'a issue tended to exacerbate tensions between Christians and Muslims during the Fourth Republic. However, in the actual elections of 2003 and their aftermath, the shari'a issue took a back seat to other concerns.

The ethnoreligious crisis in Plateau State since 1999, in which a reported 54,000 people have been killed, can be attributed to a number of factors. These include tensions between "indigenes" (ethnic minority/"Christian" communities) and "settlers" (mainly Muslim Hausa) in the cities; tensions between farmers and pastoral (Muslim Fulani) cattle herders; local authorities and chiefs, who had to make land decisions (including locations of churches and mosques); and access to government positions. The heavy influence of evangelical Christian groups, and the nontraditional nature of the Muslim community (for example, *Izala*) has been mentioned. There may also have been higher-level political manipulation of symbols and violence in

2004, possibly involving maverick (or retired) military elements, since military automatic weapons were apparently used in some of the massacres of Muslim Fulani pastoralists by local "indigene" groups. (The reprisal killings of Christians in Kano by Muslim urban youth mobs were mentioned earlier.) The federal declaration of a six-month state of emergency in Plateau State (May–November 2004) clearly indicated that state-level civilian politicians were unable (or unwilling) to manage or resolve local level ethnoreligious conflicts.[12]

An official "peace conference" was convened in Plateau State in 2004, to try to get to the root of some of the land controversies and determine the "rights" of different ethnic groups. In October 2004, the conference publicly "laid to rest" Hausa-Fulani claims to ownership of Jos, Yelwa, and Shendam:

> Delegates to the peace conference declared the Birom, Anaguta and Afizere natives as owners of Jos. They also ruled that Yelwa and Yamini towns in the Shendam Local Government belong to the Goemai natives. The Administrator, Major-General Chris Alli (rtd), said . . . the issues pertaining to ownership of Jos and Yelwa towns were thoroughly debated at the peace conference before the conferees reached a consensus on the ownership of these towns based on historical facts and presentations at the conference. The administrator, who adopted 23 resolutions at the conference for immediate implementation . . . said resolution No. 1 of the conference considered the usage of the term "settler" in the state as offensive, discriminatory and against the collective quest for effective integration, assimilation and development.[13]

How these official pronouncements in Plateau State will affect the ethnoreligious tensions locally remains to be seen. Clearly, issues of "settlers" and "indigenes" need to be resolved, within a rule-of-law framework. Leadership at all levels is critical.

In this brief summary of relations between Muslim and Christian communities, much emphasis has been placed on the political context and the public policies related to this issue. Significantly, the Muslim-Christian polarization of the post-1986 period seemed to have been partially dissipated following the 1993 election and its annulment. The religious identity of the apparent victor (Abiola) turned out to be less important than his regional and ethnic identity. At the same time, this outcome was partly the result of an election system that attempted to minimize the role of religion in public life. Subsequently, the Abacha regime was prepared to jail prominent Muslim leaders (for example, Shehu Musa Yar'Adua and Ibrahim Dasuki) and prominent

Christian leaders (for example, Olusegun Obasanjo) who were thought to be challenging the Abacha regime.

As already mentioned, ethnoreligious relations in the Fourth Republic have been exceedingly complex. Significantly, the presidential election of 2003, between the two major contenders (Obasanjo and Buhari) could have polarized religious communities, especially since Obasanjo seemed negative toward shari'a and Buhari positive. Because of the political alignments and coalitions during the election, however, the polarization did not occur. Indeed, the decision of Buhari to channel the election protests through the courts and not the streets was seen as a conflict avoidance strategy.

Communications and Crisis Management Networks

Clearly, some sort of communication between religiously diverse groups is necessary if conflict mediation and resolution is to occur. Whether such communication and mediation can be achieved by national councils of religious affairs remains to be seen. Such councils may be an important experiment in democratic conflict resolution. Yet, as other observers have noted, the councils tend to turn into "religious trade unions." Thus senior religious leaders are expected to articulate and defend their faith and may or may not be skilled at interfaith communication or mediation. Furthermore, it is unlikely that any single set of national religious leaders will be able to speak on behalf of all religious groups in the country. Even within CAN, there is a wide gap between the Roman Catholic and Anglican bishops, on one hand, and the localized inspirational and evangelical group leaders, on the other.

Likewise, the Nigerian Supreme Council for Islamic Affairs shows some clear leadership patterns, with the sultan as the major spokesman. Yet there is probably as much diversity within the Nigerian Muslim community as within the Nigerian Christian community. (In addition, the differences in personality between Sultans Abubakar III, Dasuki, and Maccido have raised questions about the subsequent directions of the NSCIA.)

The idea of locating a National Council for Religious Affairs under the Ministry of Interior has not proved fruitful. (The impact of NIREC, set up in 1999 in Abuja, remains to be seen.) The occasional meetings of senior Christian and Muslim religious figures in the capital may provide symbolic assurances at the elite level but has not translated into effective action at the state or local levels and sometimes produces headlines that are counterproductive.

Of more symbolic political importance, the pattern of religiously balanced (that is, Muslim/Christian) pairs of senior government leaders at all levels seems to have been more successful in mediating between religious leaders and communities under crisis management circumstances. Symbolic management in the media of a level playing field and a sense of access through gateways are probably more important than formal interfaith structures. In practice, national interfaith religious councils are often highly dependent on personalities and may be counterproductive in terms of conflict mediation. At the state level, however, interfaith peace and reconciliation committees may be useful on an ad hoc basis.

Secondary and postsecondary schools, where many of the problems of religious intolerance have surfaced in recent years, have formed peace committees consisting of lecturers and staff from various religious persuasions, who maintain a communication network and an alert system in case of potential crisis. These have been remarkably effective, although their ad hoc nature and dependence on local leadership is sometimes problematic. Since many potential crises of religious intolerance are avoided or contained by such peace committees and they keep a low profile with behind-the-scenes efforts, the general public is often unaware of their existence, except on those occasions when the committees fail to prevent violence. Hence there is no sustained demonstration effect that might help such committees become more effective and widespread.

There are numerous indications that informal national peace committees have also been set up. Such groups along with crisis management networks make every effort to counsel patience and tolerance even under circumstances of extreme provocation.

In recent years the role of traditional authorities, who often have a religious as well as a cultural position within Nigerian society, has evolved into an essential node in the crisis management system. If there are religious riots, or student demonstrations, or other forms of direct confrontation, many of the traditional authorities, acting not just in their own capacities but also in concert with other traditional authorities who may have different religious identities, have provided leadership within the emerging religiously pluralistic societies of Nigeria.

As lifetime appointees, pending good behavior, traditional leaders tend to be local diplomats, facilitating catharsis and encouraging a "forgive-and-forget" approach to local conflict, particularly of a religious nature. As mentioned previously, the emir of Kano and *Ooni* of Ife are widely recognized to be effective conflict resolvers, both within their respective domains and across domains.

The fundamental constitutional question for the Nigerian state is which of two paths it will follow with regard to state and religious issues. The first path is to try to enforce a strict separation of religion and state, not just on the issue of denying an "establishment" of religion, but also to create a firewall upholding the view that it is unconstitutional for government (at any level) to support any form of religious endeavor. In its extreme form, this may prohibit the use of phrases such as "under God," or "in God we trust," or opening public meetings with prayer, or employing chaplains in the armed services. In the Nigerian context, it would raise serious questions about the use of shari'a in any domain.

The second path holds that the government may not establish any particular religion or prefer one religion over another but must treat all recognized religions equally. (In the United States, this constitutional approach is called "nonpreferentialism.") Thus in Nigeria if public meetings are opened with a Christian prayer, they must be followed by a Muslim prayer. If Christian chaplains are available in the military, then Muslim imams must also be included. If pilgrimages to Mecca are subsidized for Muslims, then pilgrimages to Jerusalem for Christians must also be subsidized. The same logic applies to certain forms of family law, which have a religious or canonical basis.

The distinction between the strict separationists of religion and the state and the even-handed nonpreferentialists often translates into the debate between a secularist versus a multireligious interpretation of the Nigerian constitution. In practice, the Nigerian state has consistently chosen the multireligious (nonpreferentialist) route, despite pressures from secularists, on one hand, and those who might wish to impose a single state religion, on the other.

Thus from colonial times to the present, the Nigerian state has faced issues of impartiality among religions (especially between Islam and Christianity), both in practice and in perception. Two particularly difficult questions have been whether these should include traditional religions or even syncretistic "cults" and whether the government should actively intervene in the interfaith mediation process. Many would argue that the grim alternative is to wait for violent crises to arise and then send in an ill-equipped police force or army. But the involvement of the federal government in interfaith mediation again raises the question of centralization and decentralization. Increasingly, what goes on in Abuja has symbolic political value but little impact on state and local affairs.

Part IV

Conclusions:
Muslim Civic Cultures
and Conflict Resolution

11

Civic Cultures and Conflict Resolution

The discussion of civic cultures or political values in this volume has highlighted orientations to community, authority, change, and conflict resolution, plus some orientations to time and the scope of the state. The question remains, does congruence or incongruence of civic values across culture zones within Nigeria promote or impede conflict and conflict resolution?

Effect of Civic Values on Conflict and Its Resolution

On the issue of community boundaries, there is a clear difference between cultures for which ethnic affiliation is crucial (even to the point that one is born into an affiliation and cannot opt out) versus those for which community boundaries are flexible and may expand or contract depending on personal affiliation. One of the great conceptual divides in Nigeria is between people (including scholars) who argue that ethnicity is the central fact of political life and those who see coalition building (through marriage, personal affiliation, or political alliance) and permeable boundaries as the mainstay of the Nigerian experiment. In the latter category would be those who place religion rather than ethnicity at the center of their value system, particularly the universal religions of Christianity and Islam, rather than the localized ethnoreligions. A considerable number of Nigerians have shifted their primary community identity to Islam or Christianity during their own lifetimes, or at least during the times of their parents. It is difficult to imagine that in all cases such shifts represent radical breaks with the past, although the born-again evangelicals and the enthusiastic newly minted Muslims do represent a vigor and commitment that is characteristic of the converted.

In the more established Muslim and Christian communities, there has been a public effort since the time of British rule to promote the concept of People of the Book, that is, to foster the congruence of Muslim and Christian values in contrast to localized animist cultures. In the postcolonial era, many of the elders in both Christian and Muslim communities believed in the idea of tolerance and natural alliance of monotheism as opposed to polytheism.

Nigeria's three major ethnic groups are in less agreement on the centralization or decentralization of authority. The Hausa-emirate culture tends to favor hierarchical decisionmaking. Yoruba culture is representational, or pyramidal, with councils making decisions and an overall authority representing the symbolic unity of the community. Igbo culture, which has not been elaborated on in this volume, is essentially segmental, or based on full participation by age and gender.[1] Thus the culture shows wide differences in expectations about how decisions should be made.

When these ethnic patterns are compared with authority patterns of the universal religious affiliations, there is a curious counterbalance between the two. The sufi tradition in the emirate states in many instances favored a decentralized, grassroots authority, emphasizing "no king but God" (*ba sarki sai Allah*). Also, the basic federal structure of the nineteenth-century Sokoto caliphal system suggests a counterbalance to the apparent hierarchy within each emirate. (If anything, it was the central authority of the colonial period that set the stage for postcolonial authoritarian regimes.)

In Igboland, the Roman Catholic tradition was hierarchical, although blended with the Irish propensity for challenging British authority. Furthermore, because the Igbo emphasized respect for age, their system accorded elders more decisionmaking authority than the young men or the middle-aged cohorts.[2]

In Yorubaland, the mixture within families of Muslim, Christian, and traditional identities suggests a representational approach to religion, which preserves Yoruba political culture but is flexible on the matter of identities. Also, as a culture of city-states, the representational patterns within each community set the stage for loose affiliation with other city-states, much in the manner of the mainstream Protestant forms of organizational structure (especially Methodist, Presbyterian, and Baptist, as distinct from Anglican).

In short, the sharp edges of ethnic orientations to authority become blurred when religious affiliation is taken into account. The result is a form of representational authority that is certainly congruent with modern forms of federalism, assuming the symbolism of the overall national community is legitimate.

With regard to cultural perspectives on change, Nigerian cultures have built-in stabilizing mechanisms, especially the strong lineage systems that characterize all culture zones. Even the emirate states, with their legacy of nineteenth-century Islamic reformism, took only one generation after the death of the founder to reassert the dynastic principle in terms of succession to leadership.

Despite this lineage-stabilizing factor, other aspects of change are usually accepted as natural, and in some cases inevitable. Several traditional ethnic cultures have a recycling concept of time in which "the more things change, the more they stay the same." Yet both major universal religions, at least in their Nigerian permutations, have a strong sense of linear time, with a beginning, middle, and end. This presumes a day of judgment, which "in God's time" will bring an end to human existence as we know it. The idea of "God's time" provides a common bond between Muslims and Christians in a multireligious society. It is, of course, differentiated from a secular modernist view of time, which provides cross-cutting perspectives within both Muslim and Christian communities. Thus a chasm separates secularists, of whatever ethnoreligious backgrounds, and the People of the Book, of whatever ethno-religious backgrounds.

With regard to cultural perspectives on conflict resolution, the emirate and Yoruba cultures, the central concern of this book, both gave traditional leaders the ultimate responsibility for conflict mediation and resolution in their respective communities. The patterns of intercommunal conflict resolution are less clear historically, since a state of war existed between the emirate states and the Yoruba states in the nineteenth century. During most of the colonial period, there was relatively little contact between emirate and Yoruba cultures until after World War II. Yet in the postcolonial era, the political turmoil between the "north" and "west" was offset by an alliance of emirate and Yoruba states during the civil war with "Biafra." (Curiously, many political leaders in the Igbo community blame the Yoruba for not supporting them.) The alliance between the north and the east has been an enduring fact of political life from the first independence election of 1959 through the annulled election of 1993. It has been a major element in the challenge of the All Nigeria People's Party to the People's Democratic Party in 2003–05.

Conflict resolution between culture zones in Nigeria remains problematic in many respects. However, a basic argument of this volume is that the civic cultures of Nigeria's grassroots communities are predisposed to conflict resolution mechanisms, both within and between cultures. Also, it is argued that the legacy of a proto-federalist approach will provide part of the solution to the challenge of conflict resolution.

Democratic Federalism and Conflict Resolution

Federalism in Nigeria has two dimensions: horizontal and vertical. Horizontal refers to the balance of "federal character" issues associated with the nature of the units in the national state system. Vertical refers to the relations between federal, state, and local levels.

Much of the political energy in Nigeria in the post–civil war era has gone into experimenting with the nature of the horizontal components of the state system. The lopsided federalism of the First Republic, in which the north demographically dominated the federation, was modified during the run-up to the civil war to include six northern states and six southern states. Later, this was modified to ten northern states and nine southern states. This set of nineteen was later transformed into twenty-one, thirty, and thirty-six, all numbers divisible by three, which was necessary to the political balancing mechanisms.

The type of horizontal federalism Nigeria is likely to adopt depends on the nature of the component states. Recognizing the southern fear of the "big three" northern Muslim states (Sokoto, Kano, Borno), General Babangida, for example, subdivided each of these units in his 1991 reorganization. Thus Sokoto was divided into Sokoto and Birnin Kebbi, Kano into Kano and Jigawa, and Borno into Borno and Yobe. The fact that this division was done by a Middle Belt Muslim made it slightly more acceptable to the far north than if it had been done by a southern Christian. During the Abacha regime, Sokoto was further downsized by the excision of Zamfara.

Yet because of the transethnic nature of emirate states (not just Hausa and Fulani but also Nupe, Yoruba, and minorities), the resultant northern cluster of states was not so much bounded by ethnic composition as by other historical realities. There has been no effort to create a "Hausa-speaking state" in Nigeria, except, perhaps, in the imaginations of certain non-northern secessionists or partitionists.

Likewise, the southern states established after the First Republic did not group Yoruba and Igbo into specific states but applied other historical or city-state principles to determine political divisions. Nor has there been any effort to balance the number of Hausa, Yoruba, and Igbo states, since the demographics are disproportionate.

Much of the pressure to create new states has come from southern minorities (or from Middle Belt minorities) who do have an ethnolinguistic base to their claims. The 1996 review of claims to new states contained a total of 72 requests for new states, 2,369 claims for local councils, and 286 claims for boundary adjustments.[3] As mentioned elsewhere, many of these minorities have had political alliances in the past with the emirate states to counterbalance the Yoruba and Igbo states.

The Abacha regime shifted the concept of horizontal federalism to a zonal clustering of states within six broad geocultural zones. These six zones were given geographical designations as surrogates for cultural groupings. A partial exception has been the clustering of Borno with some of the northeast emirate states in order to reduce the emirate zone's usual dominance. Also, the number of minorities in a "frontier" emirate area such as Adamawa is much larger than in most of the core emirate states.

In short, the federal components of Nigeria are usually based on historic patterns and a sense of pragmatism rather than an explicit encapsulation of religion or ethnicity. This frequent cross-cutting of ethnic and religious lines is intended to ensure that when ethnoreligious conflict does arise it will be handled at the local and state levels, rather than escalate to the national level. This puts additional pressure on the state and local levels in the federation to develop capacities for conflict mediation or resolution.

This three-tier vertical federalism has been carefully crafted through a constitutional design that includes formulas for distributing budget resources (in the form of block grants) from the federal government to each state. In practice, the legacy of military rule in Nigeria has undermined any real semblance of vertical federalism, but it has created opportunities for redesigning horizontal federalism. There has been a divide-and-rule quality in the creation of states and local government authorities, and military regimes often managed grassroots politics by holding out the hope of creating more local units, which in turn would receive federal subventions.

At the same time, military rule was based on hierarchical chain-of-command decisionmaking. Governors were appointed by the federal government. Indeed, top-down federalism is a contradiction in terms. The constitutional experiment with three-tier federalism was reintroduced after the transition from military to civilian rule in 1999. However, the legacy of military rule, reinforced by the centralization of major sources of state revenue (oil royalties), provides a powerful counterbalance to the achievement of real vertical federalism.

Military regime experiments with horizontal federalism included the interim six-zone design introduced for political purposes and the vision of rotational offices. Yet it became clear that this mechanism might cause more stress than relief in balancing horizontal federal character, especially since zonal rotations of national leaders would produce unrealistically long cycles of inclusion and exclusion. The zonal framework did serve as a virtual backdrop or fourth tier in the vertical layering of decentralized government after the return to experiments with democratic federalism in 1999. The complexity of the six-zone solution, however, may have resulted in an informal return to the de facto use of north-south regionalism as an operational principle in politics.

Power Sharing, Symbolism, and Leadership

Choosing national symbols of leadership in a multireligious country is certainly a complex task that usually involves some elements of perceived power sharing. The criterion used with effectiveness in Nigeria since the time of the civil war has been to consider "federal character" in selecting cabinet appointments and other national political leaders. Each state is expected to have at least one representative at the senior executive level. Although cumbersome, the thirty-six states form the basis of this formula in an implicit context of six zones and a north-south framework.

As a guideline, federal character was never intended to be an exact quota system, despite the fact that many observers keep score and make lists of Muslim and Christian appointments. If federal character were to include all aspects of ethnoreligious identity applied in a mathematical manner, it would be unworkable. The fact that federal character was intended to use the state system as a surrogate for ethnicity as well as regional and local identities means that it may not be as well suited to balancing Muslim and Christian religious communities as expected. Furthermore, the real diversity of religious identity in Nigeria cannot be duplicated at the senior political level.

The idea of civilian or democratic politics normally balances out religious identity factors without introducing hard rules or procedural requirements. In the Nigerian presidential system, the vice president has always been from a zone that balances that of the president. The Second Republic (the early experiment in shifting from a Westminster model to a presidential model) had a Muslim president and a Christian vice president. The Fourth Republic had a Christian president and a Muslim vice president.

Even the military regimes have tried to keep an ethnoreligious balance at the top. A partial exception was the Buhari military regime, headed by two Muslims, although one was Hausa-Fulani and the other an Ilorin Yoruba. The Babangida military regime paired a Middle Belt Muslim with a southern minorities Christian. The Abacha military regime was somewhat unique in not having a highly visible second-in-command, although the nominal number two, Oladipo Diya, was a southern Christian. Also, cabinet appointments were reasonably balanced in terms of federal character.

In an apparent extension of the federal character principle, Abacha shifted to a six-zone rotational presidential system to succeed his regime and announced that other top political positions would be balanced according to the six-zone formula. The next regime, led by General Abubakar Abdulsalami (a Muslim from Niger state), was clearly an interim transition to a civilian regime.

More important than the actual mechanics of power sharing in a multireligious society is the management of multiple symbols, so that all major sections of the country feel some identification with national leadership. In a military regime, the style of dress tends to be uniform and hence blurs overt identities. In a civilian regime, civilian dress is common and may denote religious or ethnic identity. The management of visual symbols on tour or on television is a skill that denotes sensitivity and also is a necessary prerequisite for successful leadership.

One of the challenges of national leadership in Nigeria is how to allay the fears of minorities. It is probably natural for identity concerns to shift from an ethnic to religious sphere as larger-scale systems emerge and national community building occurs. Many of the mechanisms developed in Nigeria during the First and Second Republics were designed to accommodate ethnic pluralism. Although still an issue, ethnic identity may turn out to be less salient than religious identity in the Fourth Republic. Religious minorities may include many of the subgroups within the Christian and Muslim communities. An awareness of these patterns and a sensitivity to symbol management may help allay the fears of the minorities.

Finally, the role of elder statesmen may need to be reconsidered in light of the often-constructive role being played by former presidents, including Yakubu Gowon, Shehu Shagari, and Muhammad Buhari, or even former ministers, such as Maitama Sule (who at one point served as national ombudsman). Nigerian cultures tend to value the role of elders, not just because they can provide advice but also because they play a symbolic role in the continuity of communities. The need to incorporate younger elements should not obscure the importance of senior contributions to conflict resolution processes. Whether formally or informally, elders may play a key role in promoting religious tolerance and preempting instances of religious intolerance.

12

Nigeria in International Perspective

In the evolving culture of conflict resolution in Nigeria, two counter-vailing tendencies are notable: the active engagement in mediation and arbitration and the legalistic take-it-or-leave-it approach. Both have strong antecedents in Nigerian Muslim civic culture.

The Culture of Conflict Resolution

Within emirate culture, the ideal form of conflict resolution is consultation (*shura*) and patience (*hakuri*). When conflicts arise, every effort is made to prevent them from degenerating into violent events. "Socially binding" arbitration by elders is most common, but with appeals to higher authorities. The central purpose of the traditional leader was to act as a final arbiter in cases of serious conflict. Beyond that, there might be an appeal to God for justice, or there might be emigration or "flight" (*hijra*) from the land of "injustice."[1]

The concept of flight as a means of resolving conflict is a legacy of the West African Sudanic zone, where succession disputes or dynastic rivalries were often resolved by the losing side moving away. Historically in the Muslim communities, this meant moving east toward the "holy lands" of Mecca and Madina. (Frequently, it meant getting stranded in Sudan and settling there.)

The concept of involuntary exile—whereby an emir may be deposed and then live out his life in a neighboring emirate, or a religious leader might be told to leave a jurisdiction and not return—also has a long legacy in northern Nigeria. Surprisingly, in most cases this exile does not result in violent conflict but a sense that destiny is at work, and "God's will is being done."

The contemporary pattern of jailing opponents and later releasing them (at least until the time of the Abacha regime) follows the cultural code of not doing irreparable harm to the principals in a conflict situation. In a society where lineage ties are strong in all cultural zones, there is a keen awareness that blood feuds might go on for generations if real physical harm (as distinct from temporary incarceration) became the norm. Consequently, senior political prisoners often continued to manage their economic and political affairs from prison, although Nigerian prisons are notoriously dangerous to an individual's health.

In modern times, emigration or flight for Western-educated Nigerians has meant resettling in the United Kingdom or the United States, both English-speaking catchment areas. For Arabic-speaking or more religiously integralist individuals, emigration might be to Egypt, Sudan, or Saudi Arabia, although such a move may be hampered by bureaucratic regulations. All the same, a Nigerian Muslim diaspora, especially of the professional classes, has developed in response to the economic austerity and political turmoil in Nigeria through the 1990s and beyond.

Yoruba cultures are more likely to rely on elders and symbolic traditional leaders to resolve conflicts, although to a more limited extent than is done in the emirate states because of the lack of overall hierarchical authority patterns. Yoruba Muslim culture follows some of the same patterns of patience and consultation, while non-Muslim Yoruba cohorts rely on a strong lineage system and its internal dynamics to try to avert violent conflict. The fact that religious and political pluralism is at the center of Yoruba cultural life suggests a high degree of tolerance for identity differences and a strong preference for conflict resolution.

In the Abacha era, the rate of emigration of Western-educated professionals from Yorubaland was high. The 1995 estimate for Nigerians living in the United States, for example, was about 1 million, with most coming from southern Nigeria, that is, Yoruba and Igbo areas.[2] Many U.S. cities became home to Yoruba doctors, lawyers, journalists, professors, architects, and administrators. The impact on conflict resolution capacities in Nigeria is difficult to assess with a large number of professionals living abroad, but emigration clearly depleted the potential for a middle-class mediating influence on Nigerian conflict resolution. Whether such middle-class professionals would return during the Fourth Republic has been an ongoing question.

Despite these cultures of conflict resolution, there are frequent breakdowns in mediation, and legal systems are often used to try to resolve larger societal issues that are not amenable to juridical solutions. When legal systems prevail but the outcome is considered unjust, the parties concerned may seek more activist solutions, such as demonstrations and even physical violence. This has been true in both emirate and Yoruba zones and is partly due to the lack of experience in dealing with the increased pluralism associated with urbanization and demographic mobility in the postcolonial era. Precisely because of these frequent breakdowns, there have been renewed attempts to create mechanisms to address these issues.

Mechanisms of Conflict Resolution

The idea of councils of elders is not new. A Northern Elders' Committee was established in June 1987 "to deliberate on the inter-religious conflict and crisis which erupted in certain parts of the northern states."[3] Counterestablishment councils have also been used to resolve conflict, such as the Council of Ulama set up in 1986 in Zaria.[4] The *Jama'atu Nasril Islam* and the Nigerian Supreme Council for Islamic Affairs were both established to serve as conflict resolution mechanisms within the northern and national Muslim communities, respectively. The only interfaith council to mediate conflict was the National Council for Religious Affairs, set up in 1986.

The limitations of such interfaith councils clearly reflect the problems of mediation in an environment where the political or constitutional aspects of pluralism have not been defined. The various attempts at national constitutional conferences, which usually consist of notables of one kind or another, have often ended in gridlock, which the military has then used as evidence of the shortcomings of the political class. The calls for a national conference to discuss constitutional issues of the Fourth Republic went unanswered during the first term (1999–2003) and in any case have been highly controversial, in part because they might stir up more conflict than they resolve.

As noted earlier, in March 2005, a National Political Reform Dialogue was set up in Abuja. For the most part, delegates were nominated by state governors, thus giving the People's Democratic Party a predominant role. (Some parties and interest groups have boycotted the conference, while others, such as the Buhari Organization, have sent senior stalwarts of the All Nigeria People's Party to participate.) The conflict resolution peace committees that have emerged at universities (and even institutions of secondary education) are important mechanisms for mediating disputes and creating an atmosphere of restraint to help conflicting parties avoid eruptions in situations of real turmoil. These peace committees have been especially concerned with religious conflict, although the issues considered often have an ethnic component as well.

As yet, no legal guidelines have been established for addressing press and free speech issues. Under Nigeria's military regime, clumsy and often overreactive attempts were made to curtail such human rights. The Fourth Republic is experimenting with free speech, but in a cautious and reactive manner, after an event blows up.

Nigeria seems to have put its major conflict prevention effort into creating rotational national authorities and a system of balanced federalism. The Abacha regime, despite its harsh treatment of dissidents, appeared willing to undertake a schedule for responding to horizontal conflict. Because of the subsequent disdain for the Abacha period (in all but a few quarters), the formalities of zones and rotation have been relegated to the background.

Evaluating Conceptual Models

The introduction to this volume raised questions about appropriate frameworks for analyzing propensities for violent conflict in the world since the end of the cold war and the events of September 11. The four paradigms (or more modestly, models or even hypotheses) mentioned were Huntington's civilizational-clash model; Toffler's three-wave socioeconomic model; Juergensmeyer's religious-secular model; and something that might be termed a chaos model. How does the Nigerian case relate to such models?

Civilizational Clash?

If Samuel Huntington's model of fault lines and cleft states is correct, conflict in Nigeria should be most noticeable along such lines. As discussed in this volume, however, there is not a straight horizontal line dividing Nigeria into north and south, or Muslim and non-Muslim zones. Nigeria's test case would have to be Yorubaland in the southwest, whose population is about 50 percent Muslim and 50 percent Christian. Yet Yorubaland has not been the site of a primary fault line in politics or religion. Nationally, the pattern of political alliances would not pair the emirate states with the Christian Igbo states. (Nor should there be an alliance of emirate states with the southern minorities.) Yet these very patterns have been consistent since before independence. (The temporary aberration was during the civil war, when an emirate-Yoruba-minorities coalition prevailed.)

Within the northern emirate states, there have been pockets of localized religious conflict, sometimes between Muslims and Christians. However, they were based on ethnic or land-use disputes, which mitigate against a strictly religious or civilizational interpretation. Indeed, religious conflict within the emirate states has been more pronounced as an intrafaith phenomenon, that is, between sufi brotherhoods, or between the legalists and the sufis. (There has been an equivalent amount of religious pluralism within the evangelical Christian communities in the emirate states, and between many of the components of the Christian communities at the national level.)

However, conflict in Nigeria has seldom been related to such a fault line perhaps because of the evolving policies and practices of horizontal federalism. By relying on nonethnic criteria to define the component states, the federal balance has kept religious conflict localized. Even so, the potential for a serious religious split is always present when national leaders from emirate states may be assassinated by non-Muslim elements, as occurred in 1966 and 1976. Indeed, the purpose of the attempted coup in April 1990 may have been to split the country along ethnoreligious lines. Its failure and the calm throughout the country afterward are a tribute to Nigerian management of the potential crisis and general public support for a united Nigeria. The voluntary power shift from the north to the southwest in 1999 was also clearly an attempt to bring the southwest back to the national mediation table. No one would deny the seriousness of religious politics in Nigeria. The point is that to date, policies and practices have bridged such fault lines wherever and whenever they have arisen.

The Huntington argument for a "clash of civilizations" does have an ominous ring, however, when examined in the light of al Qaeda and other efforts to divide the world (and certainly countries such as Nigeria) into Muslim and non-Muslim camps. At the same time, the lack of success in Nigeria, even in difficult zones such as Kaduna, bodes well for interfaith accommodation.

The Three-Waves Clash Model?

Alvin Toffler's expectation that civilizations will clash along techno-economic lines rather than religious-civilizational lines may have some relevance in the Nigerian case because of the extraordinary range of developments that have taken place following the large infusions of oil revenue after 1970. The scale of urbanization in Nigeria—calculated to be among the highest level in the world during the oil boom—meant that agriculture no longer predominated economically or politically. As small- and large-scale industrialization forged ahead in the major urban areas, educational investments climbed, and an urban-based middle class arose to challenge the traditional political cultures. However, the economic downturn of the 1980s and 1990s eroded the underpinnings of the middle class, hitting employees on a fixed salary much harder than their rural counterparts because of the freeing of the market in agricultural products and resultant increase in cost of living for urban dwellers. Even so, the potential for a clash between agricultural sectors and urban/industrial sectors has never emerged as a systematic phenomenon.

Indeed, one of the obvious reasons for the lack of a techno-economic "wave clash" has been the pattern of professional or middle-class emigration. Many of the professionals living abroad may also be considered a postindustrial class that represents a globalization of technologies and communication patterns. Such overseas Nigerians had clashed with elements in Nigeria over the role of the military during the Babangida and Abacha periods. That is to say, the Nigerian professional diaspora represented a major source of opposition to military rule.

Yet because of the status and nature of professional immigrant groups in advanced industrial (or postindustrial) societies, it seemed more effective to lobby against military rule within the foreign policy frameworks of the industrial host countries than to face the risks of direct confrontation in Nigeria. This strategy placed the conflict in the traditional category of interstate relations rather than between "waves" within a particular national state. As mentioned elsewhere, the overwhelming preponderance of southern Nigerians in the United States and United Kingdom meant that there are ethnoreligious underpinnings to this techno-economic wave theory.[5]

Religious-Secular Conflict?

Mark Juergensmeyer anticipates, and chronicles, a number of fundamentalisms in a variety of civilizational contexts, including the Muslim Sunni world, the Muslim Shi'ite world, the Western Christian world, the Buddhist world, the Jewish world, and Japan. A common characteristic of such fundamentalisms is their aversion to secular society, whether it is one inherited from colonial rule, developed during the modernization phase of an economic upswing, or generated by Western doctrines advocating the separation of church and state. The idea of state secularism, which historically arose to accommodate religious pluralism, is under attack from both premodern and postmodern elements in society.

In relatively homogeneous societies, the pattern of "back to basics" (or return to fundamentals) may reflect disillusionment with the promises of modernization. In religiously heterogeneous societies, the challenge of multireligious frameworks—that is, the nonpreferentialist legal model—is a powerful counterbalance to a secular-nonsecular confrontation.

In the Nigerian context, the rapidity of change since independence has meant that secularism is most often associated with educated individuals, who were usually the ones to emigrate and remain external dissidents. Yet the Western constitutional models that have served Nigeria since independence all make a point of enshrining religious freedom, including the freedom not to believe. The fragility of such constitutional frameworks is clear, given the history of military rule in Nigeria and the powerful forces of shari'a that followed it in the Fourth Republic.

The integrated nature of the Nigerian military and its essentially secular perspective on Nigerian national life creates the unusual profile of a military establishment defending secularism against a clearly multireligious society. The fact that in the presidential elections of 2003 the major candidates were former military generals (Obasanjo, Buhari, Nwachuku, Ojukwu), plus the extraordinary political influence of General Babangida, meant that the line between military and civilian politics was blurred at best.

This potential clash between secularism and nonsecularism finds its most fertile ground in institutions of higher education, and possibly in the military itself. Yet the law-and-order advocates are clearly not disposed to allow a backlash against a secular national framework to undermine the state itself. Indeed, the state defines as off limits "secret societies and cults" that may be broadly interpreted to include "religious fanatics" who threaten "public order." Harsh measures have been used against such groups—recall the Maitatsine episode—although it is fair to add that suppression of religious sects and factions by physical force is seldom successful in the long run.

A Chaos Model?

Two common Nigerian popular expressions are "No condition is permanent" and "Nigeria is accident-prone." A full chaos theory model would probably focus on the Nigerian state itself and question the stability of the inherited boundaries. This is not a north-versus-south, or Christian-versus-Muslim, or city-versus-countryside, or religious-versus-secular, or civilian-versus-military model. Rather, it suggests that the various lines of cleavage within society—generational, economic, religious, ethnic, occupational, and so on—may conjoin or reinforce each other in ways that may produce new combinations or unexpected results.

In terms of "catastrophe theory," a particular circumstance—in natural science it might be a heart attack, or nervous breakdown, or earthquake—will precipitate the nonlinear sequence. Complexity theory often uses the metaphor of grains of sand piled on top of each other until the whole pile collapses. (In monotheistic metaphysical or theological doctrines, the coming of a *mahdi* or messiah presages the end of the world.)

To return to the Nigerian case, it is not clear who, what, why, when, how, or where such a collapse or reformation might occur. Critics of excessive external pressure, including serious sanctions, have suggested that one unintended outcome of such pressure might not be a change of regime but a collapse of society or state. A variety of internal incidents could also be "the straw that breaks the camel's back," whether of the human volitional sort (such as assassinations or attempted coups) or economic pressures, or desertification, or HIV/AIDS, or other disease pandemics.[6] The chaos resulting from the collapse of society and state plus the probable scale of refugee floods would be monumental both by African and by global standards. Needless to add, failed states are also the breeding ground of desperation and terrorism, which are often transnational in nature.[7]

In part, the fear of chaos is what drove the military to retain its stern grip on Nigerian society. The chaos of democracy or the chaos of free markets, so the argument went, would undermine state structures. On the other hand, according to critics of the military, the controls imposed by military rule in themselves may precipitate chaos. The conflict scenarios anticipated by a chaos model are multidimensional and do not fit any of the single-factor explanations.

Since 1999 the Fourth Republic has recorded more than 10,000 deaths from group violence, and possibly as many as 60,000, given the official reports (2004) of the situation in Plateau State. Under these circumstances, one may well ask whether the democratic federal system is able to allow for local chaos without descending into a failed-state syndrome.

A Nigerian Model?

Many of the early Western and indigenous social scientists working in Nigeria functioned within a national integration paradigm. Among other things, they looked at congruence and incongruence of civic values in the component culture-bearing units of Nigeria and elsewhere in Africa.[8] Thus Nigeria presented an extreme example of apparently incongruent orientations to authority, notably of the hierarchical, pyramidal, and segmental type. Other African countries with extensive language and ethnic identities, but with congruent political cultures, such as Tanzania, were at the other end of the spectrum. Yet empirically, the incongruence of political cultures does not seem to have differentiated levels of violent conflict in African countries. One is therefore led to ask whether there is a Nigerian model of conflict, and whether there is a Nigerian approach to conflict resolution.

The components of a Nigerian model would include rapid rates of change, because of the country's place in the international economy, especially its membership in the Organization of Petroleum Exporting Countries (OPEC). Some other components would be Nigeria's extreme ethnolinguistic and religious pluralism and diverse civic cultures; its various attempts at federalism, which, significantly, do not include encapsulating ethnic or religious differences; and its various experiments in civilian rule, but with recurrent military intervention and mixed military-civilian regimes. The idea of federal character, which in its mid-1990s' incarnation revolved around the six geocultural zones of Nigeria and the idea of balanced representation, was the fundamental vision of how to accommodate pluralism and diversity. In addition, the idea of a national federal capital that was not part of any major cultural zone was an experiment in conflict prevention. In the Fourth Republic, the federal character issue has reverted to the thirty-six-state solution and the proximate balance between north and south. Also, rotating the presidency between south and north seems to be emerging as a norm.

In short, the Nigerian model is one that tries, through political means, to link up the components of the nation. Since militarism is not a long-term solution, the experiment with democratic federalism—including vertical decentralization—will be the test of the Nigerian model. The tension between centralization (via legacies of military and oil revenues) and decentralization (via the variety of civic cultures at the grassroots level) may be the ultimate source of conflict in any Nigerian model.

Implications for Conflict Resolution

In the Huntington model of conflict, it seems nothing can be done in a cleft state to improve the chances of avoiding the inevitable clash. Similarly, the Toffler model suggests the clash of techno-civilizations is inevitable, both within and between countries. Insofar as the third (postindustrial) wave is in conflict with second (industrial) wave, the whole idea of a nation-state itself is part of the drama, as the global economy moves toward a "borderless world." Part of the global economy model recognizes the importance of subnational units, and hence some form of decentralization—often via federal or "devolution" mechanisms—that alleviates the tensions between a nation-state and the global economy.

In the Juergensmeyer model, conflict resolution focuses equally on premodern and postmodern challenges to secularity. A variety of mediation practices, including political co-optation, seem to be utilized, although police or military force tends to predominate.

In practice, the chaos model includes all of the preceding models and seems to warrant a multimethod approach to conflict resolution. However, most collapsed states are not oil-producing members of OPEC, and it is more likely that chaos in such a situation would be met with more military rule.

The Nigerian model explicitly rejects the "nothing-can-be-done" inevitability of various clash models. The "something-can-be-done" approach in Nigeria, which is an extreme case of multiple cleavages, has focused on political solutions, especially various forms of horizontal federalism. Even military regimes seemed to have the sense to recognize that federalism can only be part of the solution to conflict resolution if it is democratic, that is, vertical (bottom up and not top down) as well as horizontal. Thus every military regime has tried to legitimate itself as a transition to more successful versions of democratic federalism. Many of these visions remained vague until the experiment of the Fourth Republic. Its challenges are clearly to respect the diversity of civic cultures, draw on the cultural resources of indigenous communities, establish federal mechanisms to accommodate diversity, and manage conflict resolution in a way that strengthens rather than weakens the commitment to a national endeavor.

Muslim Civic Cultures and Conflict Resolution

The introduction to this volume posed two basic questions. First, in a national context of extreme ethnoreligious diversity, and after a postmilitary shift to democratic federalism, will indigenous civic cultures in predominantly Muslim areas provide reinforcement to efforts at conflict resolution, or will they undermine such efforts? Second, what is an appropriate role, if any, for the international community in reinforcing efforts at conflict resolution within and between such conflict zones?

As this volume has suggested, Nigeria's Muslim civic cultures can be divided along state-based and non-state-based lines. The most striking example of a state-based legacy is found in the emirate states (plus Borno), while the non-state-based legacy is typified by Yorubaland (plus Middle Belt). The coexistence of these two types of civic cultures, plus their interactions and modifications, may hold some broad lessons for the contemporary Muslim world.

Several points are clear. First, there is nothing inherently antidemocratic in Nigerian Muslim civic cultures. Second, there is a long tradition of proto-federalism in both the statist and nonstatist examples. Regarding democratic principles, Muslim Nigeria's emphasis on consultation, patience, and accountability was sometimes honored in the breach, but traditional rulers of all sorts were aware that there were many sanctions if they abused their powers. In the statist model, such power was usually a combination of executive and judicial functions.[9] Legislative powers were less well developed, since shari'a was concerned more with interpreting religious law. Yet shari'a was mainly a matter for individual citizens to undertake, interpret, and fulfill in their religious obligations. The state was hardly all-powerful in this regard.

With the British practice of indirect rule in Northern Nigeria, plus the introduction of British forms of legislative council functions in the late colonial period, not to mention the intense regional and national politics of the postindependence era, the experiences of legislative councils and assemblies took on a life of their own. Because of the active engagement of traditional rulers and their sons in the process, initially through a regional upper house, the legislative and executive functions became conjoined. Thus Nigerian Muslim culture, especially in the north, came out of the era of indirect rule much as India had done, with a strong commitment to elected legislatures. Later, in the Second Republic, these executive and legislative functions would be separated, as in the U.S. presidential tradition.

Apart from "justice," a broader and even more practical function of the emir and council was to work for the peace and harmony of the emirate. Thus the formal and informal conflict mediation and resolution functions were central to the integrity of the state. The institutional forms might vary, but the legitimacy of the regime demanded peace and prosperity.

In the late colonial era, with the emergence of non-Muslim migrant populations in the major northern urban areas, the idea of a dual legal system emerged, with Muslims responsible under Islamic law, and non-Muslims responsible under British magistrate law. As independence approached, the sharp disjunction between criminal and civil law was agreed to as the price of national unity and peace, with criminal law subsumed under a national code. In practice, there were many instances in which traditional judicial authority continued to act in a gray zone, although the fact that local emirates found themselves under a regional system of justice was made palatable because many of the regional political leaders were from emirate leadership backgrounds. In short, there was no abrupt disjunction between indigenous civic cultures and the new independence forms of civic principles.

All of this changed with the assassination in 1966 of northern leaders by junior officers, mainly from the southeast. Even as the shock of this potential chaos was still reverberating, and certainly before it was widely known that Nigerian oil reserves were abundant, the north decided that Nigeria was the community of destiny and joined with the southwest to "keep Nigeria one." (The political crisis in 1966 may have involved elements in the southeast that were aware of the petroleum potential. But such an "oil" impetus for the north was less obvious at the time than in subsequent decades.)

The alternating military and civilian rule, drawing on a wide range of Nigerian Muslim leaders, did not differ much on the ultimate goal of a representative democracy within a federal framework. As the oil revenues began to surge through the federal coffers, however, much of the spirit of civic cultures as legitimating administrations dedicated to justice and conflict mediation was replaced with an extraordinary pursuit of wealth by individuals and groups.

The challenge of the Fourth Republic is clearly not just to achieve a smooth transition from military to civilian rule but also to reclaim the heritage of civic cultures, where the rule of law and conflict mediation could create the conditions for economic prosperity based on the traditional values of merit and hard work (including long-distance or international trade), rather than nepotism and corruption.

At this point, the debate over shari'a in the Nigerian Muslim community comes into play. Clearly, the idea of a moral way of life, rooted in a religious tradition, would be an ideal for most. Yet the way in which such moral principles are derived or interpreted in a world of high technologies and globalization, with the demonstration of oil wealth all around and with a deep chasm developing between rich and poor, has intersected with the increased access to the traditional sources of moral behavior, namely, the Qur'an and Hadith.

Thrown into this mix of reformation is an extraordinary number of voices, increasingly in English, as well as Hausa, Yoruba, and Arabic, and a variety of minority languages. The Muslim community's experience in the postindependence era suggests general agreement that a big-tent approach is the only viable strategy with which to avoid intrafaith violence and promote the general good of the community. National umbrella organizations are crucial to this endeavor, which has the potential to bridge language, ethnic, and regional identities. Such organizations, at their best, can also serve as bridges to the Nigerian Christian communities, and others.

The memory of the civil war, and the early sacrifices of the military to keep the country together, created a new sense of national civic culture in Nigeria, centered in a federal capital and committed to working out differences by peaceful rather than violent means. This interdependency of national elites has created a sense of common destiny. At the grassroots levels, however, there are still tensions and violence, which, despite occasional threats of partition, have not yet escalated in a major way into the national arena.

The challenge for the national authorities is to strengthen the capacities for conflict resolution at all levels, especially the local levels, since there is no guarantee that local tensions and violence will not reach national crisis proportions. The key to success will be to build on indigenous or grassroots legacies of justice and conflict resolution. Another challenge at the national level is to trust the state and local cultures and institutions, which have been eclipsed by extreme centralization, and to encourage the evolution of vibrant civic cultures that can combine the best of the past with the needs of the future. In this process, the Nigerian Muslim community has always taken a lead in terms of commitment to a national endeavor, a rule-of-law ideal, and a capacity for coalitions that link various regions.

Nigeria and the International Community

There is no shortage of international experience (good and bad) in addressing the challenges of "unity with diversity." Some countries, such as France and Russia, come out of a long tradition of extreme centralization and have tried to find ways to accommodate diversity, including the large number of Muslim cultures within their broader societies. (With Russia, the partition option always seems to rise to the surface as a challenge to central authority. Also, in an era of perceived "terrorism" the tendency to recentralize is increasingly evident.) In both France and Russia, the idea of a strong executive presidency, or French Fifth Republic model, stands as an alternative to the U.S. presidential federal model. This strong Gaullist executive model, with legitimacy for declaring a state of emergency, often postpones facing the more difficult task of engaging diversity in a constructive way at the grassroots level. In global perspective, both Russia and Nigeria stand in the ranks of countries with high diversity. Whether the five-tier federalism in Russia or the three-tier federalism in Nigeria can be made to work in a framework of strong centralization remains to be seen.

In the case of China, with its fifty-five official minorities and highly centralized government, the pressures for decentralization are being driven largely by economic forces at present, although village elections are also creating a new dynamic. Again, the crisis of Muslim (Uighur) partition movements in northwest China is largely being dealt with by a state-of-emergency mode. Other large diverse countries with Muslim populations, such as India, have found that democratic federalism is a formula that allows for a more stable political evolution. Switzerland stands as perhaps the oldest democracy in the world, and without a loose federal (even confederal) structure, it is unlikely that Switzerland would have survived the religious wars of the postreformation period.

In the domain of international relations, Nigeria has historically played a constructive and moderate role. To a large extent, the Nigerian Muslim leaders who have steered this course have reflected their own sense of civic culture, which prizes harmony and conflict mediation over confrontation and disruption.

In the current atmosphere of global concern with terrorism and with the challenges and diversity of Muslim populations of the Middle East, the international community should do what it can to ensure that Nigeria is not plunged into anything approaching a failed-state syndrome. The means to achieve this goal is clearly to encourage a stable form of democratic federalism, which Nigerians themselves have fought and died to sustain. Without appropriate governance and conflict resolution mechanisms in place, the capacity of Nigeria to play a constructive international role is compromised. There is no simple formula for the international community to achieve this goal, other than the obvious, "Do no harm."

For international organizations—including the British Commonwealth, the World Bank, the Organization of the Islamic Conference, the United Nations, the African Union, the Economic Community of West African States, the Organization of Petroleum Exporting Countries, the World Trade Organization, and the like—the key is constructive engagement at all levels, but not to the point where Nigerian sensibilities and perspectives are overlooked. There is often a tendency not to focus on flawed elections or excessive internal violence if a country is strategically significant, or friendly.

In bilateral relations between the United States and Nigeria, with special reference to issues related to Muslim civic cultures and conflict resolution, the key, again, is "Do no harm." It is imperative that the United States remain neutral on matters that impinge on the religious domain, including interfaith relations in Nigeria. Now that global communications are becoming widespread and instantaneous, Nigerians are aware that evangelical voting blocks are well organized and active in U.S. domestic politics. It is a challenge to any U.S. administration to maintain a separation of church and state in the foreign policy domain. In Nigeria, the issue of Muslim-Christian relations is far more salient than the issues of Israel or the Middle East. It is essential to appear evenhanded in Muslim-Christian relations in order to avoid an unnecessary clash of civilizations, with all of its negative implications.

Part of the challenge for the United States in this regard is the long legacy (in both the academic world and government) of making an arbitrary separation between sub-Saharan Africa and other parts of the Muslim world. This institutional vision is blind to the realities of the contemporary world, where socioeconomic, political, and religious ties often transcend the traditional geographic categories. More precariously, the emphasis on sub-Saharan Africa tends to relegate Muslim West Africa, which includes many interior as well as coastal zones, to a lower priority in terms of engagement.

West African forms of Muslim culture have many distinctive characteristics, including a long history of tension between sufism and legalism, and between modern and traditional forms of culture. At the same time, the overlapping of African and Muslim culture has produced unique blends of accommodations with civic cultures, ranging from the strong role of Muslim women in Yorubaland to the edge-of-the-desert mysticism and puritanism of the far north, to the vibrant merchant trading networks in commercial cities, to the centuries-old judicial scholarship associated with certain families. The European overlay of British and French cultures completes this historic blend of cultures. With the globalization of communications and technologies, combined with oil wealth (however unequally distributed), the question in Nigeria Muslim communities is "Can the center hold in terms of cultural continuity"? The porous nature of West African borders, and the ebb and flow of current events, make this problematic. Yet there are clear indications that the cultural centers of gravity do hold, however much the fringes of society may fluctuate.

If the goal of U.S. policy toward Nigeria is constructive engagement on a wide range of issues, it faces some very basic challenges here. For one thing, the United States needs to be at full diplomatic strength in Nigeria, in both its physical and human resources. (Since Hausa is the major indigenous language in Nigeria and the lingua franca of the emirate northern areas, an obvious goal for the diplomatic community should be to develop its capacity for the language.) Ensuring secure but efficient visa opportunities for travel to the United States is a global challenge under current circumstances, but one that is especially hard for northern Nigerian Muslims to meet who may have to travel 800 miles to Lagos and then wait long periods of time for visas for the mutually rewarding endeavors of enrolling in higher education or attending academic conferences in the United States. Whatever long-term technologies and procedures may emerge in the visa domain, efficient and effective practices are sorely needed, so that the flow of legitimate human interaction may continue at this critical time. It is equally important not to humiliate Muslim students and scholars with clumsy security regulations once they have arrived in the United States.

Second, the weakest link (so to speak) in the transition to democratic federalism is clearly the role of the police, the judiciary, and the media. There is no reason why nongovernmental or professional organizations could not assist in strengthening these capacities. The opportunities in higher education and women's affairs could also be strengthened by engaging NGOs, including American Muslim groups.

Clearly a major concern of the U.S. public at present lies in the judicial realm. The United States should resist the temptation to lecture Nigerian Muslims on some shari'a provisions and punishments, or to ally with non-Muslim anti-shari'a advocates. If political solutions are not forthcoming, at best the United States should hope for the involvement of the Nigerian Supreme Court in a timely manner, so that judicial institutions are strengthened, not weakened or sidestepped by the increasingly powerful executive branch.

Recognizing that some basic legal issues pertaining to state and religion are explosive and divisive—as they have been in the United States over time—the alternatives of civil war or partition may well hang in the balance if these matters are not handled with care. The issue of states' rights is clearly a matter that Nigerians need to sort out internally, if democratic federalism is to prevail.

Third, the U.S. government should focus on constructive engagement with the institutions of democratic federalism, rather than with the personalities who might inhabit the political spaces at any given time. One key step to this end is to encourage local governments to take more responsibility for their own destinies. Needless to add, the professionalization and transparency of block grants to local governments is essential to the viability of local government. Another important measure is to recognize the legitimacy of a two-party or multiparty system as a means of ensuring accountability, rather than endorsing the gradual slide to a single-party system.

It is also essential to prepare for the day after the full transition from military to civilian rule, when there is a larger pool of national leaders. The overdependence on former military leaders at the federal level may be an inevitable part of transition but suggests that leadership training and experience for the next generation needs to be addressed at this time. In part this is an educational challenge, even at the midcareer level, and in part a matter of Nigerian experiential engagement in the broader international community. It is also a matter of respecting the diversity of ethnoreligious talent pools within Nigeria.

Fourth, with specific reference to conflict resolution, this volume has suggested that a wealth of experience exists within the Nigerian communities. The peace committees in the educational sector, the interfaith councils (especially at state and local levels), the faith-based organizations, the informal grassroots cultures of conflict mediation, and the political leadership are all elements that could be strengthened. The ambiguous but crucial role of traditional leaders should not be overlooked in the rush to engage with the next generation, or with particular segments of society. How the international community responds to capacity building in these domains will have a multiplier effect on local efforts at conflict resolution and may well help to legitimize such initiatives.

Fifth, the opportunity and danger surrounding the current war on terrorism should not be allowed to create an overreaction to the possibility that fringe groups in huge metropolitan conurbations (in places like Kano) may provoke fear and hysteria, which can undermine more rational forms of constructive engagement. The major challenge is to achieve better understanding of and communication with mainstream elements that have every incentive to avoid violence.

In short, democratic federalism is a means of avoiding state failure and of addressing the threats of terrorism effectively. The frustrations and despair generated by overcentralization and partition will simply breed violence and chaos. Clearly, the highest priority for the international community is a workable democratic federalism in Nigeria.

The implications of this democratic federalism model in Nigeria for other parts of the Muslim world are profound. Especially in the non-Arab countries, if indigenous civic cultures can reinforce conflict mediation and resolution approaches, then other priorities such as economic development and the free exchange of ideas may emerge, rather than violence and destruction. A globalizing world requires that we build bridges, not walls.

Selected Electoral Patterns: The First Three Republics

The First Republic (1960–66), Second Republic (1979–83), and "Third" Republic (1993) all represented attempts to engineer vertical and horizontal structures and processes that would keep Nigeria as one federal system. Political parties, of necessity, had to establish coalitions across zonal and regional boundaries.[1] The administrative nature of the component parts in Nigeria has undergone several transformations over the years, from regions to provinces, to states, to the idea of six geocultural zones, to a combination of states within implicit regional and geocultural zones. These component units and their electoral patterns are shown in tables A-1 to A-4.

Although Nigeria is persistently analyzed in north-south regional terms, an equally enduring reality is a six-zone cultural division, which can be traced to earliest British perceptions. This zonal vision surfaced later in the proposals of General Sani Abacha in October 1995, although it was not formalized in the subsequent constitution of 1999. The persistence of a north-south set of perceptions and the realities of relations between geocultural zones are illustrated in the electoral patterns during the first three republics.

In the First Republic, under a parliamentary federal system, the ruling coalition involved components from the north and east. In the Second Republic multiparty elections of 1979 and 1983, the final coalitions occurred after the elections rather than before (as in a two-party system). The parties that won 50 percent or more of the votes in the 1979 presidential elections are shown in table A-2, by state, arranged by geocultural zones. The three northern-based predominantly Muslim parties (NPN, PRP, GNPP) won majorities in all of the three northern zones: emirate states (NPN), plus Kano (PRP), and Borno (GNPP); that is, the dominant party, NPN, lost in Kano and Borno.

Table A-1. Overview of Federal Units and Regime Types

Year	Number of regions or states	Extent of regional or state autonomy	Regime type
1914	2	Very high	Colonial
1954	3	Very high	Colonial
1963	4	High	Democratic
1967	12	Low	Military
1976	19	Low	Military
1979	19	Medium	Democratic
1991	30	Low	Military
1996	36	Very low	Military
1999	36	Medium and rising	Democratic

Source: World Bank, *Nigeria: State and Local Government in Nigeria*, Report 24477-UNI (Washington, 2002).

The two southern-based predominantly Christian parties won in their respective zones: Yoruba areas (UPN) and Igbo areas (NPP). The UPN was able to win only one state outside its zone, that is, the neighboring state of Bendel. The NPP split the vote in Plateau (with a near win of 49 percent) but did not capture any state outside the Igbo zone.

The only party with a significant showing outside its zonal base was the northern-based NPN, which won in the Middle Belt (Benue) and among southern minorities (Rivers and Cross River). To some extent this represented a coalition of emirate states, Middle Belt and southern minorities, that is, a northwest to south-south axis, with clear cross-religion (Muslim-Christian) linkage implications.

After the 1979 election (perhaps because the presidential and vice presidential team represented an emirate and Igbo ethnoreligious alliance) and with the close cooperation of the GNPP (Borno), the only "outsider zone" was the Yoruba area. Meanwhile, the splits in the PRP in Kano into a hard-line faction and an accommodating faction made it possible for certain Kano elements to cooperate with the NPN.

In the 1983 presidential elections, the northern-based party (NPN) again won majorities or pluralities in six of the seven emirate states. In Kano, the race had tightened between the NPN and PRP, with the latter winning a slight plurality.[2] Yet neither of the two northern smaller parties (PRP in Kano, GNPP in Borno) won a majority in any state. As in 1979, the NPN won majorities in minority states of Benue, Rivers, and Cross River and after the election worked in coalition with Igbo and Borno elements. The NPP won the Igbo areas, and the UPN won the Yoruba areas, plus Bendel, with a strong showing in Kwara (see table A-3).[3]

Table A-2. Presidential Elections, 1979[a]

Sociocultural zone	NPN	UPN	NPP	GNPP	PRP
Emirate states					
Sokoto	x				
Bauchi	x				
Kwara	x				
Niger	x				
Kaduna	x				
Gongola	34%			34%	
Kano					
Borno area					
Borno				x	
Middle Belt					
Plateau	35%		49%		
Benue	x				
Yoruba areas					
Oyo		x			
Ogun		x			
Lagos		x			
Ondo		x			
Igbo areas					
Anambra			x		
Imo			x		
Southern minorities					
Bendel		x			
Rivers	x				
Cross River	x				
Total	8.7	5	2.5	1.3	1

Source: Author's calculations.

a. Parties with 50 percent of votes cast per state, except as noted. Blanks indicate insignificant portion; "x" indicates majority vote in that state.

The prelude to the annulled June 1993 elections was the series of presidential primary elections within the two officially designated parties in the fall of 1992: the Social Democratic Party (SDP, "a little to the left") and the National Republican Convention (NRC, "a little to the right"). These primaries were canceled in November 1992 by the Babangida military government, in a way that clearly reflected the unease with the apparent continuation of northern political dominance. Thus by October 1992 the primaries had resulted in strong leads for Shehu Musa Yar'Adua (from Katsina) of the SDP and Adamu Ciroma (from Borno) of the NRC. President

Table A-3. Presidential Elections, 1983[a]

Sociocultural zone	NPN	UPN	NPP	GNPP	PRP
Emirate states					
Sokoto	x				
Bauchi	x	45%			
Kwara	49%				
Niger	x				
Kaduna	x				
Gongola	44%				
Kano	32%				37%
Borno area					
Borno	49%			25%	
Middle Belt					
Plateau	45%		43%		
Benue	x				
Yoruba areas					
Oyo	38%	x			
Ogun		x			
Lagos		x			
Ondo		x			
Igbo areas					
Anambra	33%		x		
Imo	25%		x		
Southern minorities					
Bendel	41%				
Rivers	x				
Cross River	x				
Total	7(+)	4.5	2.5	0	0

Source: Author's calculations.

a. Parties with 50 percent of votes cast per state unless otherwise indicated. Blanks indicate insignificant portion; "x" indicates majority vote in that state.

Ibrahim Babangida (originally from the Federal Capital Territory [FCT] area) pointed to instances of voting irregularities, but there was also a clear concern that both leading candidates were from the far northern part of the country, and the issue of regional balance was not far from the surface.

The two parties were asked to generate new candidates through a process of bottom-up nominations for presidential candidates by means of a series of primary elections within each party. Presidential candidates then selected vice presidential candidates. This process culminated in national elections on June 12, 1993, between the SDP team of M. K. O. Abiola (from Ogun State, in the southwest) plus Baba Gana Kingibe (from Borno State, in the northeast) and the NRC team of Bashir Tofa (from Kano State, in the northwest) plus Sylvester Ugoh (from Imo State, in the southeast). All four team members were carefully vetted prior to the election to ensure their eligibility.

The results of the June 1993 presidential election were not announced officially, and shortly thereafter, the elections were annulled. Yet the unofficial results gave the SDP 58.5 percent of the votes to the NRC's 41.5 percent. The SDP appeared to have won the election in nineteen states, and the NRC in eleven.

A central question is whether the distribution of these votes reflects patterns that are clearly different from previous Nigerian federal elections (1959, 1964, 1979, 1983). These patterns are ascertainable from an assessment of the apparent electoral strength of the SDP and NRC in each of Nigeria's six major geocultural zones, as indicated in table A-4. The voting patterns cut across the two major religious zones (Muslims, mainly in the north, and Christians, mainly in the south). Were religious identity patterns reflected in the results? Both presidential candidates were Muslim, so there is no obvious religious pattern.

The crosscurrents within the Muslim community were significant. Of the four major ethnocultural groups within the Nigerian Muslim community—former Sokoto caliphal states (that is, the "emirate states"), Borno, Yoruba communities, and Middle Belt "minorities"—the SDP won in the latter three zones and made clear inroads into the emirate states.

In short, the NRC won the emirate states (except Kano, Jigawa, Kaduna, and Kwara) and the Igbo-speaking areas (except Anambra). The SDP won the Yoruba-speaking areas, the Borno area, the Middle Belt (except Kogi), and the southern minority areas (except Rivers). This was a fundamental shift in coalition alignments, but one not based on religious identities.

In July 1993, the military government (National Defense and Security Council) along with the SDP and NRC considered the idea of an interim government with both the SDP and the NRC participating. The NRC wanted 50 percent of the positions and an interim president other than Chief M. K. O. Abiola. Abiola would not agree and insisted that he was the duly elected president of Nigeria. He continued to make his case within the international community during August, September, and October. By November, he appeared supportive of the idea of military intervention, and a government of national unity. (Baba Gana Kingibe actually joined the new military government.) Then in June 1994, Abiola reasserted claims to the presidency and was arrested and detained.[4]

Table A-4. Presidential Elections, 1993[a]

Sociocultural zone	SDP	NRC
Northern emirate states		
Kebbi		x
Sokoto		x
Niger		x
Katsina		x
Bauchi		x
Adamawa		x
Kano	x	
Jigawa	x	
Kaduna	x	
Kwara	x	
Borno area		
Borno	x	
Yobe	x	
Middle Belt minorities		
Plateau	x	
Taraba	x	
Benue	x	
Kogi		x
Yoruba-speaking areas		
Oyo	x	
Ogun	x	
Lagos	x	
Osun	x	
Ondo	x	
Igbo-speaking areas		
Abia		x
Enugu		x
Imo		x
Anambra	x	
Southern minorities		
Edo	x	
Delta	x	
Akwa Ibom	x	
Cross River	x	
Rivers		x
Federal Capital Territory	x	
Total	20	11

Source: Author's calculations.

a. "x" indicates estimate: party won state.

APPENDIX B
Selected Biographical Summaries

Sources for this appendix include standard résumés (widely available), press accounts, books about the individuals, miscellaneous sources, and the author's observations.

Ambassador Ibrahim Agboola Gambari

An official abbreviated biography is contained in his prospectus for *The Savannah Centre for Diplomacy, Democracy and Development,* 1995:

> Born in Ilorin, Nigeria, in November 24, 1944, Ibrahim Agboola Gambari attended Kings College, Lagos as well as the London School of Economics, obtaining a B.Sc.(Econs) degree in Political Science with a specialty in International Relations. At New York's Columbia University, he earned his M.A. (1970) and Ph.D. in Political Science/International Relations (1974).
>
> From 1969–74, he taught at the City University of New York and later at the State University of New York (Albany) 1974, then returned to his home in Nigeria to teach at Ahmadu Bello University, first as Senior Lecturer (1977–1980), later as Reader, then promoted to Professor (1983).
>
> He was appointed Director-General of the Nigerian Institute of International Affairs in October 1983, a position he held before his appointment as the Minister of External Affairs of Nigeria following the December 1983 military change of government. His tenure ended in August 1985, whereupon he returned to Ahmadu Bello University to continue teaching. Between 1986–1989, he was visiting Professor at the

School of Advanced International Studies, Johns Hopkins University, Baltimore, Maryland in U.S.A., and he also taught at Georgetown University and Howard University, Washington, D.C.

As Nigeria's Permanent Representative to the UN, he had chaired the UN Special Committee against Apartheid, which successfully saw the demise of that long-standing social injustice and the establishment of democratic rule in South Africa. He has led several United Nations Missions, in particular those of the Special Committee against Apartheid as well as those of the Security Council to South Africa, Burundi, Rwanda, and Mozambique. He has also served twice as President of the Security Council of the United Nations (May 1994 and October 1995). Currently, he chairs the UN Special Committee on Peace-keeping Operations.

Widely traveled, Professor Gambari is a leader, pioneer, scholar, and diplomat. His diplomatic and scholarly careers have been distinguished and productive.

Etsu Nupe (Umaru Sanda Ndayako)

See "LG Reforms Chairman, Etsu Nupe, is Dead," *Lagos and Abuja ThisDay News,* September 2, 2003.

The Niger State Government has announced the death of Alhaji Umaru Sanda Ndayako, the Etsu Nupe and Chairman of the State Council of Traditional Rulers. Ndayako, who passed on at 66, was until his death the chairman of the Technical Committee on the Review of Local Government Structures set up by the Federal Government in July.... Born in Bida, his hometown, on February 19, 1937, Ndayako spent 28 years on the throne, as he was appointed and turbanned as the 12th Etsu Nupe in 1975, at the age of 32 years. The Etsu Nupe, the chancellor of Obafemi Awolowo University, Ile Ife, attended the East Elementary School, Bida in 1945 and entered the Middle School, Ilorin before joining Barewa College, Zaria, in 1951. He was a product of University College, Ibadan, where he graduated with a Bachelor of Arts degree in English language in 1962. On completion of his education, the paramount ruler joined the defunct Northern Region government as an assistant secretary, Ministry of Local Government, Kaduna, between 1962 and 1964. He became the assistant district officer in charge of Tiv division in 1962 before he was posted to Kano in the same capacity until 1965. He later transferred his services to the federal civil service in

1966 as principal assistant secretary, Ministry of Housing, Lagos. He was promoted to the rank of the Deputy Permanent Secretary (Political) in the Cabinet Office Lagos, where he doubled as the principal personal secretary to the former military head of state, Gen. Yakubu Gowon. . . .

The late Etsu was buried in Bida yesterday after a short prayer led by the chief imam of the town at about 4 pm amidst tears from his subjects, family members and members of his emirate council.

Justice Muhammad Bashir Sambo

Justice Sambo was born in Zaria in 1931 and graduated from the Kano School for Arabic Studies in 1951. He pursued a diploma in Arabic and Islamic studies at London University (1956–57) and taught at Barewa College, Zaria. He was acting principal of Barewa College and became khadi of the Kaduna State Shari'a Court of Appeal (1975–85). He was appointed grand khadi of the Shari'a Court of Appeal of the Federal Capital Territory, Abuja, in 1985. He retired as grand khadi in 1996, before being appointed chairman, Code of Conduct Tribunal, Abuja, in May 1996. He has served on the Nigeria Inter-Religious Council (1999) and on the Executive Council, Nigerian Supreme Council for Islamic Affairs.

Umaru Shinkafi

Shinkafi was born in 1937 in Kaura Namoda, Sokoto State. (His father immigrated there from Yobe State.) He also attended Barewa College, Zaria, before proceeding to the Police College, Ikeja, in 1958. He graduated from the law program at University of Lagos in 1973 and went into the national police service. Subsequently, he was appointed federal commissioner (later minister) for Internal Affairs in 1975. He became head of the Oyo State Police Command in 1978, before joining the Shehu Shagari government as director general of the National Security Organization. (In terms of Sokoto politics, he was appointed *Marafan* Sokoto and married the daughter of the late Ahmadu Bello in 1984.) He is regarded as a "progressive conservative," with a strong commitment to Nigerian national goals, and with a capacity to work across religious and ethnic boundaries. In the 1999 elections, he was the vice presidential candidate for the All People's Party.

Ibrahim Badamasi Babangida

Babginda was born August 17, 1941, in Minna, Niger State. He attended Government College, Bida; Nigerian Military Training College, Kaduna (1962–63); Indian Military Academy (1964); the U.K. Royal Armoured Centre (1966–67); Advanced Armored Officers' Course, U.S. Army Armored School (1972–73); Command and Staff College, Jaji (1977); Nigerian Institute for Policy and Strategic Studies, Kuru (Jos); and Senior International Defense Management Course, U.S. Navel Postgraduate School (1980).

He was appointed commanding officer, Reconnaissance Squadron (1964–66); commander, 44th Infantry Battalion (Rangers) (1968); instructor and company commander, Nigerian Defence Academy (1970–72); commander, Nigerian Army Armoured Corps (1975); director, Army Staff Duties and Plans (1981–83); chief of army staff (December 31, 1983); member of the Supreme Military Council (August 1, 1975–October 1979, and December 1983–August 1985); president, commander-in-chief of the armed forces (August 27, 1985); and chairman, Armed Forces Ruling Council (AFRC) (August 27, 1985–July 1993).

As of June 2004, Babangida was campaigning actively for the PDP presidential nomination in the 2007 elections, complete with campaign literature and an activated cadre of supporters.

Abdu-Lateef Oladimeji Adegbite

Adegbite was born March 20, 1933, in Abeokuta, Ogun State. He attended Methodist School, Abeokuta; St. Paul's School, Abeokuta; King's College, Lagos; University of Southampton (1959–62); Law Society College, Lancaster Gate, London (1962–63); and School of Oriental and African Studies, London (1962–65). He served as lecturer, Faculty of Law, University of Lagos; commissioner for Local Government and Chieftaincy Affairs (Western State); attorney general and commissioner for justice, Western State (1973–75); pro-chancellor and chairman, Governing Council, University of Maiduguri; president, Nigeria Olympic Committee (1972–85); member of Council and Executive Committee, Lagos Chamber of Commerce and Industry. In addition, he was co-founder and first national president, Muslim Students Society of Nigeria, and later served as grand patron, Muslim Students Society of Nigeria. He has served as chairman of the Ogun State Pilgrims Board and member of the National Pilgrims Board. He continued his legal practice in Lagos, focusing on business law, while serving as legal adviser and secretary general of NSCIA.

Olusegun Obasanjo

Obasanjo was born March 5,1937, in Abeokuta, Ogun State. He attended Baptist Boys' High School, Abeokuta, and then Mons Officers Cadet School, Aldershot, United Kingdom. He continued at the Royal College of Military Engineering, Chatham, England, and Indian Army School of Engineering, Poona. He served in the 5th Battalion, Nigerian Army, Kaduna, where he had close interaction with many of the first generation of northern officers and learned to speak basic Hausa. He served in the UN Force in Congo. He was in Kaduna during the assassination and coup attempt by junior officers but was given safe haven to Maiduguri (Borno) by northern civil servants who felt he might be at risk from the junior officers.

During the Nigerian civil war he was commander of the garrison, Ibadan, and then general officer commanding (1967–70) 3rd Infantry Division. During 1970–74 he was commander, Engineering Corps. He was appointed federal commissioner (now minister) for Works and Housing January–July 1975 and chief of staff, Supreme Headquarters, Lagos, in 1975–76. He became head of state and commander-in-chief of the Nigerian Armed Forces in February 1976 and retired voluntarily from the Nigerian Army in October 1979.

Subsequently, he returned to farming in Ogun State and served on numerous international commissions until his jailing by Abacha in 1995. He was released from jail after the death of Abacha in June 1998. During his time in jail, he is reputed to have become a born-again Christian, as his only allowed reading material seems to have been the Bible.

After his release in the summer of 1998, he was chosen by the PDP as its presidential candidate and with clear northern backing was successful in 1999, with about 62 percent of the national vote. His reelection in 2003 was confirmed by the Supreme Court in July 2005.

Muhammadu Buhari

Buhari was born December 17, 1942, in Daura, Katsina State. He attended Katsina Middle School and Katsina Provincial Secondary School. On entering the military, he attended Nigerian Military Training College, Kaduna (1962); Mons Officer Cadet School, Aldershot, United Kingdom (1962–63); Defense Services Staff College, Wellington, India (1973); and U.S. Army War College (1979–80).

He was platoon commander, 2nd Infantry Battalion, Abeokuta (1963), and UN Peace-Keeping Force in Congo in the early 1960s. During the Nigerian civil war, he was commander, 2nd Infantry Battalion. He was acting director,

Transport and Supply, Nigerian Army Corps of Supply and Transport Headquarters, 1974–75.

He served as military governor, North-Eastern State (now Borno), during 1975–76; federal commissioner for Petroleum and Energy, 1976–78; chairman, Nigerian National Petroleum Corporation, 1978–79. He was military secretary, Army Headquarters, and member of the Supreme Military Council, 1978–79. Subsequently, he served as general officer commanding in Ibadan, and then in Jos. He was appointed head of state and commander-in-chief, Nigerian Armed Forces, January 1, 1984, until August 26, 1985. He was ousted on August 27, 1985, in a putsch led by General Babangida.

He was in political detention from August 27, 1985, until December 14, 1988, when he was released. Later, under the Abacha regime, he served as director of the Petroleum Trust Fund between 1996 and 1999.

After the presidential elections of 2003, contested by Buhari on the ANPP ticket, he was awarded the Grand Commander of the Federal Republic (GCFR). But he "failed to show up to be decorated with the tag of GCFR bestowed on him by the Obasanjo administration because, according to him, the government was an illegitimate one and he could [not accept] an award from such a government" (*Sunday Independent*, October 31, 2004).

Buhari married Safinatu Yusuf in 1971, and they have four daughters.

Chief Chukwuemeka Odumegwu Ojukwu

Chief Ojukwu was born November 4, 1933, in Zungeru, Niger State. He attended St. Patrick's Primary School, Lagos; King's College, Lagos; Lincoln College (Oxford University), United Kingdom; and Joint Services Staff College, Camberley, England. He enlisted in the Nigerian Army and was posted to Zaria (1957). He was deputy assistant adjutant and quarter-master general, Kaduna (1961). After serving with the United Nations in the Congo, he became commander, 5th Battalion, Kano (1964–66), and was appointed military governor, Eastern Region (1966–67).

He was proclaimed head of state and commander-in-chief, "Republic of Biafra" (May 1967–70), during the Nigerian civil war. He was granted asylum in Côte d'Ivoire after the defeat of Biafra in January 1970. He was granted a state pardon and came back to Nigeria on June 18, 1982.

He joined the National Party of Nigeria (1982–83) during the Second Republic. His traditional Igbo title is *Ikemba* of Nnewi. Other traditional titles include *Dikedioramma Ndi Igbo, Ochi Obi* of Onicha-Ugbo, and *Ugo Chinyee ndi Igbo*. In the 2003 election, he ran for president on the AGPA ticket.

Chuba Okadigbo

Okadigbo was born December 17, 1941, in Ogwashi-Uku, Bendel State. He attended St. Patrick's College, Asaba (1955–57); Our Lady's High School, Onitsha (1958–59); and Catholic University of America, Washington, D.C. (1968–72). He served as associate professor of philosophy, University of the District of Columbia (1970–75), and director general, Centre for Inter-Disciplinary and Policy Studies, University of Nigeria, Nsukka (1975). He was a member of the National Party of Nigeria (1978–79) and special adviser for political affairs to President Shehu Shagari (1979–83). His traditional Igbo titles were *Ekwueme* of Ogbunike and *Ikenga Igwedo*. In the 2003 election, he was the vice presidential candidate for Muhammadu Buhari, on the ANPP ticket.

Chief Justice Muhammadu Lawal Uwais

Uwaus was born in 1936, in Zaria, the son of the Chief Alkali and later Waziri of Zaria emirate, who was famous for his blunt and fearless legal advice to Emir Ja'afaru. Uwais was educated at Barewa College, Zaria, and the Institute of Administration, Ahmadu Bello University. Thereafter, he studied at the University of London (1961–62), Inns of Court School of Law, and was called to the Bar, Middle Temple, London, in 1963.

He was solicitor-general and permanent secretary, Ministry of Justice, North-Central State (1971–73), and judge, High Courts, North-Central and North-Eastern States (1974–47). He was appointed justice of the Federal Court of Appeal (1977–79), and justice of the Supreme Court of Nigeria in August 1979.

Cardinal Anthony Olubunmi Okogie

Okogie was born June 16, 1936, in Lagos. He attended Holy Cross School, Lagos; St. Patrick's School, Sapele; St. Gregory's College, Lagos; St. Peter and St. Paul's Seminary, Ibadan; Urban University, Rome. He was ordained Catholic priest in 1966 and assigned various parishes in Lagos and Oyo.

He was appointed Roman Catholic archbishop of Lagos in May 1973 and served as vice president, Catholic Bishops' Conference, 1985–89. In November 1988, he was elected president, Christian Association of Nigeria (CAN), a position he held for almost ten years. He was appointed cardinal by the Vatican in September 2003.

Sunday Coffie Mbang

Mbang was born August 26, 1936, in Idua, Eket, Akwa Ibom State. He attended Methodist Boys' High School, Eket (1951–56); Methodist College, Uzuakoli (1956–58); University of Nigeria, Nsukka (1966–67); Harvard University (1974–78).

He served as Methodist minister, teacher and chaplain, and lecturer, University of Ibadan (1978–79). He was consecrated bishop of Tinubu, Lagos (1980–84), and patriarch and head, Methodist Church of Nigeria, in 1985. He succeeded Archbishop Okogie as the president of CAN.

General Sani Abacha

Abacha was born September 20, 1943, in Kano. He attended Provincial Secondary School, Kano; Nigerian Military Training College, Kaduna; and Mons Defence Officers Cadet Training College, Aldershot, United Kingdom. He was promoted general officer commanding, 2nd Mechanised Division, 1984–85, and major-general, 1984. He was promoted to lieutenant-general in October 1987. He became head of state in the fall of 1993 and remained in that office until his death in June 1998.

Notes

Introduction

1. Ted Robert Gurr, *Why Men Rebel* (Princeton University Press, 1970).

2. Nigerian authorities have been quick to assert that there are no al Qaeda cells in Nigeria and to pledge full support in the war on terrorism. According to a presidential spokesperson, "The President of the Federal Republic is a core player in the global fight against Terrorism and he has ensured that all of the security agencies have taken measures to root out any element that may want to disturb peace here." See "No Al-Qaeda Cells Here," *Lagos and Abuja ThisDay News*, March 9, 2004.

3. A 2004 survey of people's religious beliefs in the United States, the United Kingdom, Israel, India, South Korea, Indonesia, Nigeria, Russia, Mexico, and Lebanon suggests that "Nigeria is the most religious country in the world." See *BBC News*, World Edition, February 26, 2004. More than 90 percent of the Nigerian respondents indicated they believed in God, prayed regularly, and would die for their beliefs. All Nigerians surveyed said they believed in God or a higher power, whereas the figure was 80 percent or so in most of the other countries, reaching 91 percent in the United States but dipping to 67 percent in the United Kingdom. Whereas 91 percent of Nigerian respondents said they regularly attended a religious service, the figure was a mere 21 percent in the United Kingdom and averaged only 46 percent across the ten countries surveyed. As for the subject of prayer, 95 percent of Nigerians claimed to pray regularly, compared with 67 percent in the United States.

4. Various analysts have explored these relations, most notably Don Ohadike, "Muslim-Christian Conflict and Political Instability in Nigeria," in *Religion and National Integration in Africa: Islam, Christianity and Politics in the Sudan and Nigeria*, edited by John O. Hunwick (Northwestern University Press, 1992), pp. 101–23. See also Matthew Hassan Kukah and Toyin Falola, *Religious Militancy and Self-Assertion* (Aldershott: Avebury, 1996); Jacob K. Olupona, ed., *Religion and Peace in Multi-Faith Nigeria* (Obafemi Awolowo University, 1992); Simeon O. Ilesanmi, *Reli-*

gious Pluralism and the Nigerian State (Ohio University Center for International Studies,1997); Pat Williams and Toyin Falola, *Religious Impact on the Nation State: The Nigerian Predicament* (Aldershott: Avebury, 1995); S. P. I. Agi, *The Political History of Religious Violence in Nigeria* (Calabar: Ushie Printing and Publishing, 1998).

5. For in-depth discussions of these legacies, see J. F. Ade Ajayi and Bashir Ikara, eds., *Evolution of Political Culture in Nigeria* (Lagos: University Press Limited, 1985); Peter B. Clarke and Ian Linden, *Islam in Modern Nigeria: A Study of a Muslim Community in a Post-Independence State 1960–1983* (Munich: Kaiser, 1984); and Richard Olaniyan, ed., *Nigerian History and Culture* (London: Longman, 1985).

6. On centralization under the military, see Olatunde Odetola, *Military Regimes and Development: A Comparative Analysis in African Societies* (London: George Allen & Unwin, 1982); and Jimi Peters, *The Nigerian Military and the State* (London: Tauris, 1997). The oil economy is discussed by Sarah Ahmad Khan, *Nigeria: The Political Economy of Oil* (Oxford University Press, 1994); and David L. Goldwyn and J. Stephen Morrison, *Promoting Transparency in the African Oil Sector: Recommendations for U.S. Policy* (Washington: Center for Strategic and International Studies, March 2004).

7. For a discussion of conflict management in Africa, see T. A. Imobighe, *The OAU (AU) and OAS in Regional Conflict Management: A Comparative Assessment* (Ibadan: Spectrum Books, 2003).

Chapter One

1. For background on U.S.-Nigerian relations, see Robert B. Shepard, *Nigeria, Africa, and the United States: From Kennedy to Reagan* (Indiana University Press, 1991).

2. See David L. Goldwyn and Stephen Morrison, *Promoting Transparency in the African Oil Sector: Recommendations for U.S. Policy* (Washington: Center for Strategic and International Studies, March 2004). The authors note, "The Nigerian government's oil earnings between 2004 and 2010 will likely exceed $110 billion.... In Nigeria, an elected government is in its second term, with leadership rhetorically committed to fiscal reform, anticorruption, and modernization of the petroleum sector. But Nigeria's performance has yet to match its declarations." For insight into the Niger Delta conflicts, see Niger Delta Youth, *Report of the Niger Delta Youth Stakeholders Workshop,* Port Harcourt, April 15–17, 2004. Also, Oronto Douglas, "The Road to Justice and Prosperity in the Niger Delta," *PeaceWorks News,* vol. 4, no. 4 (September 2004).

3. The Nigerian federal budget for 2004 was calculated on a price of oil in the neighborhood of $23 a barrel. By September 2004, with oil prices well above $40 a barrel, a "windfall" of approximately $20 billion had accrued to the Nigerian 2004 budget. The federal budget for 2005 was premised on oil prices in the range of $30–32 a barrel, at a time when actual oil prices were well above $50 a barrel. What to do with the "windfall profits" has been an on-going question in Nigeria and the subject of litigation by some states.

4. Madeleine Albright, *Madam Secretary* (New York: Miramax Books, 2003), p. 443.

5. Clinton and Albright visited Nigeria in October 1999, Bush and Powell in July 2003. Powell was an international monitor for the presidential elections in Nigeria in 1999. Albright has served as chair of the National Democratic Institute for International Affairs, which aims at promoting democracy around the globe.

6. "Issue for Cardinals: Islam as Rival or Partner in Talks," *New York Times,* April 12, 2005. See also "Vatican Is Rethinking Relations with Islam," *Washington Post,* April 15, 2005, which notes that Nigeria's Cardinal Francis Arinze urged more "contact with other believers" as a means of strengthening Catholicism, as it would teach Christians "what great gifts, for example of wisdom, holiness of life, love of others, self-gift to others and asceticism God has given to some people who are outside the visible boundaries of the Church."

7. Nigeria's Spiritual Rainmaker Is Eyed at Vatican," *Washington Post,* April 27, 2005.

8. Aliyu Tilde, "Pope Benedict XVI and Dialogue" (aliyutilde@yahoo.com; AmanaOnline.com [May 24, 2005]).

9. Princeton N. Lyman and J. Stephen Morrison, "The Terrorist Threat in Africa," *Foreign Affairs,* January/February 2004, pp. 75–86.

10. See, for example, Ibrahim Ado-Kurawa (who is from Kano), "Negotiation Identity and Representation: A Review of British Council International Seminar on Representing Islam," a nineteen-page report on the seminar held at Hunton Park in Watford, June 22–27, 2003 (majekarofi@yahoo.com [September 25, 2003]; www.gamji.com). See also Ado-Kurawa's account of his travels in the United States as part of an international visitors program, "United States Society and the Muslim World," January 5, 2005 (see www.gamji.com).

11. Queen Elizabeth II opened the Commonwealth Heads of Government Meeting in Abuja, December 5, 2003. She was scheduled to visit Kano, but this apparently posed a challenge to Nigeria's security services, and the Kano visit was canceled at the last minute. See "Atiku Heads Committee on Queen's Visit," *Abuja Daily Trust,* October 7, 2003. Also, "Why Queen's Kano Trip Was Cancelled, by Aide," *Lagos and Abuja ThisDay News,* December 2, 2003; "CHOGM: Security Beefed Up As Queen Arrives Today," *Abjua Daily Trust,* December 3, 2003.

12. For example, in May 2000, the governor of Zamfara State, Ahmed Sani, articulated his views about shari'a in the state at a Voice of America conference in Washington, D.C. See also Ado-Kurawa, "Negotiation Identity and Representation."

13. In 2003 Bayero University, Kano, was awarded a Fulbright grant to further research and exchanges with an American university in the field of criminal sociology.

14. See, for example, "US Awards N6M Scholarships to Borno Students," *Lagos and Abuja ThisDay News,* March 2, 2004. Also, U.S. Department of State, *Nigeria: Country Reports on Human Rights Practices* (Washington, February 25, 2004), p. 11 ff.

15. In Washington, these include Ambassador Zubairu Kazaure, from Jigawa State, and Ambassador Jubril Aminu, from Adamawa State. Aminu played a key role

in cross-cultural communications in Washington in the difficult period after September 11, until returning to Nigeria in the spring of 2003 to compete for the senate.

16. Alhaji Abubakar Alhaji ("Triple A") served as high commissioner in London. Originally from Sokoto, he was selected to be the Sardauna of Sokoto after the death of Ahmadu Bello. Former UN ambassador Ibrahim Gambari is discussed in chapter 5. Other key Nigerian UN ambassadors from an earlier period have included Aminu Kano (from Kano) and Maitama Sule (from Kano). In 2004 Aminu Wali, from a distinguished legal family in Kano, was appointed UN ambassador.

17. Between 1999 and 2003, for example, Nigeria had Muslim ambassadors in Argentina, France, Yugoslavia, Portugal, Poland, and Romania.

18. For full coverage of the tenth session of the OIC in Malaysia, in October 2003, see *Kaduna Weekly Trust*, November 1, 2003. During the previous three years, the OIC had been under the stewardship of the emir of Qatar (Sheikh Hamad Bin Khalifa Al-Thani), and hence in 2003 organizational responsibilities were handed to non-Arab members. The Malaysia meeting was also attended by representatives from India, Russia, and other states with large Muslim minorities.

19. According to official U.S. estimates for 2002, there are 238 million Muslims in forty-eight sub-Saharan African states. In order of magnitude, the countries with the most Muslims are Nigeria, 64 million; Ethiopia, 31 million; Sudan, 25 million; Cameroon, 16 million; Tanzania, 12 million; Mali, 10 million; Côte d'Ivoire, 10 million; Senegal, 9 million; Niger, 8 million; Somalia, 7 million; Guinea, 6 million; Ghana, 6 million; Democratic Republic of Congo, 5 million; Chad, 4 million; and Uganda, 4 million (Cartography Center/MPG 759795AI, B004210 [May 2002]). U.S. estimates for 2003 put the Nigerian population at 133 million, 67 million being Muslim. This distribution of Muslim populations reflects historical realities in the interior of West Africa, the upper Nile and Horn of Africa, and coastal East Africa. For a highly critical analysis of Islam in West Africa, especially the jihadist tradition, see John Alembillah Azumah, *The Legacy of Arab-Islam in Africa* (Oxford, United Kingdom: Oneworld Publications, 2001), p. 100 ff. Azumah states that "Islam is more visible and entrenched in West Africa than East, Central and Southern Africa," and "West Africa felt the impact of military jihad more than any other part of sub-Saharan Africa." For more positive accounts of the jihadist tradition in West Africa, see the papers from the international conference on the Sokoto Caliphate and its legacies between 1804 and 2004 in Abuja, June 14–16, 2004.

20. As the world's seventh largest oil exporter, Nigeria produces close to 3 million barrels a day, 40 percent of which goes to the United States. Oil also accounts for 90 percent of its export revenue. For a discussion of Nigerian oil and its role in OPEC, see "Shell Withheld Reserves Data to Aid Nigeria," *New York Times*, March 19, 2004; and "OPEC Plans Output Cut in April: Support Grows to Raise Range of Prices as Dollar Declines," *New York Times*, March 15, 2004.

21. The most detailed study of the "Qur'an and Sunna" movement in Nigeria is by Ousmane Kane, *Muslim Modernity in Postcolonial Nigeria: A Study of the Society*

for the Removal of Innovation and Reinstatement of Tradition (Leiden: Brill, 2003). I discuss the Nigerian *Izala* movement in chapter 3.

22. See Jibrin Abubakar, "Some Hours with the Hausa Residents of Mecca," *Abuja Daily Trust,* March 8, 2004. Abubakar notes that "when you miss your way in the holy city of Mecca, and ask a passer-by, whether black or white in the Hausa language, and he replies in the same tongue, you will probably conclude that this may be the language of humanity."

23. See, for example, "Facing Death for Adultery, Nigerian Woman Is Acquitted," *New York Times,* September 26, 2003. A number of other capital cases where the penalty is "stoning" are working their way through the court system. The attorney general of Nigeria has tried to introduce a debate as to whether the death penalty should be abolished. See "Let the People Decide on Death Penalty—Attorney-General," *Lagos and Abuja ThisDay News,* November 14, 2003.

24. See, for example, "Sodomy: Sharia Court Sentences Man to Death by Stoning," *Abuja Daily Trust,* September 25, 2003; and "Sodomy: Convict Appeals against Death Sentence," *Abuja Daily Trust,* October, 25, 2003. The conviction was later overturned on appeal.

25. A number of senior Nigerian Anglican church leaders have also condemned homosexuality, making common cause with Nigerian Muslim leaders and arguing that the "breakdown in morals" is a sign of the "end of the age."

26. Six countries in the world—Saudi Arabia, Nigeria, Pakistan, Sudan, Yemen, and Iran—allow for the death penalty by stoning. Yet there are few instances in modern times where such penalties have been implemented. According to *Time* magazine, these six, out of the approximately fifty-six members of the OIC, are referred to as "the stone zone." The practice, *Time* points out, "has spread most recently to sub-Saharan Africa, a region once known for its moderate brand of Islam. Stoning is not actually mentioned in the Koran, but the harsh treatment the holy book prescribes for sex outside of marriage has been invoked to justify what Amnesty International calls, 'the ultimate form of torture.'" See "Casting Stones: The Koran Says Nothing about Stoning. Why Is This Mother Facing Death?" *Time,* September 2, 2002, pp. 36–37.

27. Associated Press, Africa, "US Concerned on Nigeria Stoning," August 20, 2002. For more detailed perceptions of the shari'a issue, see Human Rights Watch, "*Political Shari'a*"? *Human Rights and Islamic Law in Northern Nigeria,* HRW Report, vol. 16 (September 2004).

28. See "Clashes in Nigeria Go Beyond Sectarian Strife: Land and Power Are Crucial Issues, Too," *International Herald Tribune,* May 25, 2004.

29. This disturbance erupted when a Christian female student allegedly blasphemed a Muslim female and was attacked by some Muslims for what was considered a religious slur. When Christians began planning to retaliate, the governor and other prominent persons in the state intervened to avoid a crisis on campus. See "Religious Clashes Averted in ABU," *Abuja Daily Trust,* September 25, 2003.

30. The issue of Christian missionaries trying to convert Muslims and whether

they would "inspire more backlash than belief" was *Time* magazine's cover story for June 30, 2003.

31. USCIRF is located at 800 North Capitol Street, N.W., Suite 790, Washington, D.C., 20002. In August 2003, USCIRF sent a delegation to Nigeria to assess issues of religious freedom, including the patterns of *hudud* punishments in the shari'a states, religious aspects of communal and sectarian violence, and the policy implications.

32. Between September 2001 and May 2004, 53,787 were killed in central Plateau State; the dead numbered 18,931 men, 17,397 women, and 17,459 children. See "Nigeria: 53,000 Killed in 3 Years of Ethnic Conflict," *New York Times,* October 8, 2004.

33. Human Rights Watch, *Revenge in the Name of Religion: The Cycle of Violence in Plateau and Kano States,* HRW Report, vol. 17 (May 2005), available at http://hrw.org/english/docs/2005/05/23/nigeri10993.htm.

34. See, for example, the report of a riot and looting by Muslim radicals sparked by a dispute between twelve-year-old school girls in the northern town of Kazaure: "The group had descended on a local school to protest the principal's alleged reluctance to take action against a Christian girl who, responding to schoolyard taunts from Muslim playmates, had insulted the Prophet Muhammad, an official said. When a policeman shot and injured a 17-year-old protester, the mob took to the streets." See "Nigeria: Girls' Spat Escalates to a Riot," *New York Times,* November 11, 2003.

35. This spread is aided by efforts to make theological training affordable and more widely available in Nigeria, such as the workshop held by Vision International Christian Ministries, a Pentecostal movement. See "Church Holds Talkshop on Evangelism," *Lagos and Abuja ThisDay News,* February 22, 2004. For background on worldwide evangelical and other Christian movements as they affect Nigeria, see Philip Jenkins, *The Next Christendom: The Coming of Global Christianity* (Oxford University Press, 2002).

36. See, for example, Integrated Regional Information Network (IRIN), "Nigeria: Muslim Fundamentalist Uprising Raises Fears of Terrorism" (UN Office for the Coordination of Humanitarian Affairs, January 25, 2004). Referring to an incident in Yobe State at the end of December 2003 (discussed later in this volume), the IRIN writes: "When a student-led Islamic sect launched an armed uprising last month with the aim of setting up a Taliban-style Muslim state in northern Nigeria, the authorities were swift to quell the insurrection. However, political analysts and security officials fear the emergence of the Al Sunna Wal Jamma (Followers of the Prophet) group may be an indication that extremist Islamic groups have found enough foothold in Nigeria to make Africa's most populous country a theatre for worse sectarian violence than it has seen in recent years and actions of terrorism." See also Ariel Cohen and Brett Schaefer, "Addressing Nigeria's Economic Problems and the Islamist Terrorist Threat," Executive Memorandum 933 (Washington: Heritage Foundation, May 19, 2004).

37. See "US Military Arrives in Nigeria This Week," *Lagos Daily Independent,* Feb-

ruary 26, 2004. This contingent consisted of two teams of senior officers, including two generals, whose task was to consolidate American military bases on the continent. This action came "amid a push by some US conservative think tanks urging the Bush administration to do more to secure alternatives from the volatile Middle East." See also "U.S. Training North Africans to Uproot Terrorists," *New York Times,* May 11, 2004. This so-called Pan-Sahel Initiative originally focused on Mali, Mauritania, Niger, and Chad but is being expanded to include Senegal and possibly other countries. The program was begun with $7 million, but the European Command has asked for $125 million for the region over five years. Six groups have been identified to address its principal concerns: a Moroccan Islamic combat group, a Libyan Islamic fighting group, a Tunisian combat group, a Salafist group for preaching and combat, an armed Islamic Group, and defenders of Salafist preaching.

38. See "Muslims Avenge Christians' Attacks in Nigeria: Long-Simmering Ethnic and Religious Tensions Explode," *New York Times,* May 13, 2004.

39. For a discussion of the hypothesis that "market-dominant minorities . . . turn free market democracy into an engine of ethnic conflagration," see Amy Chua, *World on Fire: How Exporting Free Market Democracy Breeds Ethnic Hatred and Global Instability* (New York: Doubleday, 2003), p. 6. Chua specifically argues that the Igbo dominate the market in Nigeria.

40. "Human Rights Watch Accuses Nigeria of Rights Abuses," *Lagos and Abuja ThisDay News,* December 2, 2003. These accusations appeared in a report titled "Renewed Crackdown on Freedom of Expression," which was released as Nigeria prepared to host a meeting of fifty-two Commonwealth heads of government. It blamed the Nigerian government for the killing, torture, and harassment of its critics over the preceding two years. See Human Rights Watch, "Letter to President Obasanjo on Commonwealth Heads of Government Meeting" (HRW.ORG [November 27, 2003]); also, Human Rights Watch, *Nigeria: Renewed Crackdown on Freedom of Expression,* HRW Report, vol. 15 (December 2003); and "Harassment of Witnesses by SSS: ANPP Complains to Tribunal," *Abuja Daily Trust,* December 2, 2003.

41. "Nigeria Still in Political Dilemma—U.S. Envoy," *Abuja Daily Trust,* September 25, 2003.

42. World Bank, *Nigeria: State and Local Government in Nigeria,* Report 24477-UNI (Washington, July 23, 2002).

43. See "US Disburses N16.5m for Civic Education in Nigeria," *Lagos and Abuja ThisDay News,* November 14, 2003. This sum was awarded to eight organizations for civic education under the Education for Development and Democracy Initiative conceived after former president Bill Clinton's visit to Nigeria. American ambassador Roger Meece saw contributions to local civic education programs as a way to help Nigeria build a sustainable democracy and economic growth.

44. Nigeria helped lead the developing countries coalition at the WTO ministerial meeting in Cancun, Mexico, September 2003, in protesting the apparent protectionism of developed countries, especially in areas of agriculture.

45. For Nigerian federalist perspectives, see Kemi Rotimi, *The Police in a Federal State: The Nigerian Experience* (Ibadan: College Press, 2001). Also, Kunle Amuwo and others, eds., *Federalism and Political Restructuring in Nigeria* (Ibadan: Spectrum Books, 1998).

46. The total amount of Nigerian international debt at the beginning of the Fourth Republic was about $30 billion, with the overwhelming portion being owed to European banks and governments, which had formed the Club of Paris.

47. The partition option in Nigeria was attempted during the civil war (1967–70) when Biafra tried to break away from the federation. This experience brought untold misery on all sectors in Nigeria and reinforced the fact that there is no clean way to divide Nigeria, given the patterns of diversity and interdependencies. A north-south split or a six-zone geocultural division is equally problematic. This issue arises at a time when some former eastern European federations have split in ways ranging from the stormy breakup of Yugoslavia to the more peaceful divorce of the Czech Republic and Slovakia. It also enters into the debate about the future of Iraq, where some favor a "three-state" solution consisting of Sunni Kurds, Sunni Arabs, and Shiite Arabs. See, for example, Leslie H. Gelb, "The Three-State Solution," *New York Times,* November 25, 2003.

48. For an assessment of U.S. domestic political dynamics on this issue, see "Evangelicals Sway White House on Human Rights Issues Abroad," *New York Times,* October 26, 2003, which reports: "Administration officials and members of Congress say the religious coalition has had an unusual influence on one of the most religious White Houses in American history."

49. For a fuller discussion of the Bush administration approach, see Ivo H. Daalder and James M. Lindsey, *America Unbound: The Bush Revolution in Foreign Policy* (Brookings, 2003).

50. See Lyman and Morrison, "The Terrorist Threat in Africa," p. 75 ff.

51. For a photograph of President Bush embracing President Obasanjo on July 12, 2003, in Abuja, see Steven Radelet, "Bush and Foreign Aid," *Foreign Affairs,* September/October, 2003, p.105.

52. Despite Nigeria's historic linkages with Iraq (Baghdad holds the tomb of the founder of its widespread Qadiriyya sufi botherhood), the more religiously oriented Nigerian Muslim communities have never felt much sympathy for Saddam Hussein owing to his extreme secularism, his abuse of religious communities, his love of personal statues, and his militarism and belligerence toward his neighbors, including Kuwait. Even Nigerian legalists such as Abubakar Gummi were publicly critical of Saddam Hussein for his attack on Iran in the 1980s, although there was little Nigerian support for Shi'ite Iranian religious politics.

53. President Bush himself has pointed out the "discomfort within his conservative religious base" about the fact that Christians and Muslims worship the same god. See "Bush's Remark about God Assailed," *Washington Post,* November 22, 2003. For a critical Nigerian Muslim perspective that emphasizes economic factors but articulates an attempt to avoid a "clash of civilizations," see Ibrahim Ado-Kurawa, *The*

United States of America and the Muslim World: An Introductory Survey of Relationship (majekarofi@yahoo.com [January 6, 2004]).

54. The foreign policy implications of the Bush reelection victory in November 2004 (with 51 percent of the popular vote) are beyond the scope of this study. Clearly, the issue of religion and "moral values" played an important role in mobilizing key elements of his constituency.

55. Madeleine K. Albright, "Bridges, Bombs, or Bluster?" *Foreign Affairs,* September/October 2003, p. 3.

56. Ibid., p. 9.

57. Chester A. Crocker, "Engaging Failed States," *Foreign Affairs,* September/October 2003, pp. 32–44.

58. Of course, the Middle East is discussed in news items and opinion editorials. See, for example, Abdu-Lateef Adegbite, "Israel-Palestine Conflict: A Threat to World Peace," *Kaduna Weekly Trust,* October 4, 2003. Adegbite, who is secretary general of the Nigerian Supreme Council for Islamic Affairs, argues that "the US and their allies should be persuaded to accept that the prevailing international terror would reduce considerably if justice is entrenched in the Middle East. Give the Palestinians back their land, there will no longer [be] platforms for the Osama bin Ladens of this world to thrive. Without justice there can be no peace."

59. See, for example, Lyman and Morrison, "The Terrorist Threat in Africa."

60. This comes at a time when the U.S. 2002 Patriot Act requires tightened procedures for visas, including medical, security, and background checks as well as an impression of a thumb and index finger from the right and left hands. Eventually, the process is expected to call for eight fingerprints. In addition, student visas require interviews, which have created long delays. Since the U.S. Consul offices are in Lagos rather than Abuja, it is more difficult for northerners to apply, although eventually the facilities will be moved to Abuja. See *Lagos and Abuja ThisDay News,* "Terrorism: US to Take Finger Prints of Visa Applicants," October 31, 2003.

61. See Peter Lewis, "Islam, Protest, and Conflict in Nigeria," *Africa Notes,* 9 (Washington: Center for Strategic and International Studies, 2003).

62. See (Ustaz) Muhammad Nurayn Ashafa and (Evangelist) James Movel Wuye, *The Pastor and the Imam: Responding to Conflict* (Lagos: Ibrash Publications Centre, 1999).

63. Ted Robert Gurr, *Why Men Rebel* (Princeton University Press, 1970).

64. See Sandra Cheldelin, Daniel Druckman, and Larissa Fast, eds., *Conflict: From Analysis to Intervention* (London: Continuum, 2003), esp. chap. 8, "Culture," by Kevin Avruch, pp. 140–53. For background, see Dennis Sandole and Hugo van der Merwe, eds., *Conflict Resolution: Theory and Practice* (New York: St. Martin's Press, 1993). See also John Burton, *Conflict: Resolution and Prevention* (New York: St. Martin's Press, 1990); John Burton, ed., *Conflict: Human Needs Theory* (New York: St. Martin's Press, 1990); John Burton and Frank Dukes, *Conflict: Practices in Management, Settlement and Resolution* (New York: St. Martin's Press, 1990); John Burton

and Frank Dukes, eds., *Conflict: Readings in Management and Resolution* (New York: St. Martin's Press, 1990).

65. See Joseph V. Montville, ed., *Conflict and Peacemaking in Multiethnic Societies* (Lexington, Mass.: Lexington Books, 1991), esp. chapters by Vamik Volkan and Joseph Montville. See also Marc Gopin, *Healing the Heart of Conflict* (Emmau, Pa.: Rodale, 2004).

66. Samuel P. Huntington, *The Clash of Civilizations and the Remaking of World Order* (New York: Simon & Schuster, 1996).

67. Alvin Toffler and Heidi Toffler, *Creating a New Civilization: The Politics of the Third Wave* (Washington: Progress & Freedom Foundation, 1994).

68. Mark Juergensmeyer, *The Next Cold War? Religious Nationalism Confronts the Secular State* (University of California Press, 1993). See also Mark Juergensmeyer, *Terror in the Mind of God: The Global Rise of Religious Violence*, 3d ed. (University of California Press, 2003).

69. Zbigniew Brzezinski, *Out of Control: Global Turmoil on the Eve of the Twenty-First Century* (Oxford University Press, 1993).

70. Daniel Patrick Moynihan, *Pandaemonium: Ethnicity in International Politics* (Oxford University Press, 1993).

71. See James Gleick, *Chaos: Making a New Science* (New York: Viking, 1987).

72. Ted Robert Gurr, Presidential Address to the International Studies Association, 1994. See also Ted Robert Gurr, *Minorities at Risk: A Global View of Ethnopolitical Conflicts* (Washington: U.S. Institute of Peace Press, 1993); and Ted Robert Gurr and Barbara Harff, *Ethnic Conflict in World Politics* (Boulder, Colo.: Westview Press, 1994).

73. See John N. Paden, ed., *Values, Identities, and National Integration: Empirical Research in Africa* (Northwestern University Press, 1980).

74. Ibid., p. 5.

75. See, for example, Robert Levine, *A Geography of Time: The Temporal Misadventures of a Social Psychologist* (New York: Basic Books, 1997).

76. A surprising number of Western popular and policy books still make the mistake of assuming, for example, that the month of Ramadan occurs during a specific month, such as April (or whatever month happens to coincide in that particular year).

77. Paden, *Values, Identities, and National Integration*, p. 5.

78. Ibid.

79. See, for example, John N. Paden, *Religion and Political Culture in Kano* (University of California Press, 1973); John N. Paden, *Ahmadu Bello, Sardauna of Sokoto: Values and Leadership in Nigeria* (London: Hodder and Stoughton, 1986).

80. Huntington, *The Clash of Civilizations*, p. 47.

81. Ibid., p. 42.

82. Ibid., p. 20.

83. Ibid.

84. See Douglas Johnston and Cynthia Sampson, eds., *Religion: The Missing Dimension of Statecraft* (Oxford University Press, 1994), esp. chap. 6 by Cynthia

Sampson, "'To Make Real the Bond between Us All': Quaker Conciliation during the Nigerian Civil War," pp. 88–118.

85. The New York-based Twentieth Century Fund recently commissioned three well-known academics to write a new version of *The Federalist Papers* to respond to the "disenchantment with government" that is "bubbling up to challenge the whole constitutional system." See "Old Concepts, New Challenges in Sequel to 'Federalism Papers,'" *Washington Post*, October 21, 1996, p. A17.

86. See Thomas M. Franck, ed., *Why Federations Fail* (New York University Press, 1968).

87. See, for example, Crawford Young, "The Impossible Necessity of Nigeria: A Struggle for Nationhood," *Foreign Affairs*, November/December 1996, pp. 139–43. According to Young, "The failure of the First Republic pointed out the flaws of a federal structure constructed around the three largest ethnic blocs. The 3 colonial-era regions were progressively divided into 4, then 12, 19, 21, and finally 30 states—perhaps with more to come. Unsustainable as it may seem, this strategy has liberated the smaller ethnic minorities from the oppressive hegemony of the three largest ethnic groups by dispersing those three groups among several states. Carefully ensuring a proportionate distribution of power without creating an explicitly ethnic federation, the Second Republic's constitution and its successors have in many ways been ingenious formulas for national survival." Young concludes: "Nigeria has little cultural logic; its peoples would never have chosen to live together. Over time, though, coexistence became a historical necessity, and citizens came to accept their common nationhood." See also Paul A. Beckett and Crawford Young, eds., *Dilemmas of Democracy in Nigeria* (University of Rochester Press, 1997). For discussion of religious factors, see John Paden, "Islam and Democratic Federalism in Nigeria," *Africa Notes* 8 (Washington: Center for Strategic and International Studies, March 2002); and Robert I. Rotberg, ed., *Crafting the New Nigeria: Confronting the Challenges* (Boulder, Colo.: Lynne Rienner, 2004).

88. Huntington, *The Clash of Civilizations*, pp. 28, 137.

89. Ibid., p. 136.

Chapter Two

1. The dominant party in the First Republic was the Northern People's Congress, which was in a coalition with the National Council of Nigerian Citizens based in the east. The latter had its own alliance with the Northern Elements Progressive Union. The opposition party was the Action Group, mainly in the west, which was in alliance with the United Middle Belt Congress. Following a realignment in 1964, the main northern party re-formed as the Nigerian National Alliance and the major southern parties as the United Progressive Grand Alliance.

2. John Paden, "Sokoto Caliphate," in *The Oxford Encyclopedia of the Modern Islamic World*, vol. 4, edited by John Esposito (Oxford University Press, 1995), p. 89 ff.

3. Niels Kastfelt, *Religion and Politics in Nigeria: A Study in Middle Belt Christianity* (New York: British Academic Press, 1994).

4. For the buildup to the civil war, see John N. Paden, *Ahmadu Bello, Sardauna of Sokoto: Values and Leadership in Nigeria* (London: Hodder and Stoughton, 1986), chap. 19, "Death and Response." There is a vast literature on all aspects of the Nigerian civil war, which includes the memoirs of many of the key military leaders.

5. See "Ineffective Operation, Bane of Nigeria's Constitution—Abubakar," *Abuja Daily Trust*, November 14, 2003. Abubakar reportedly remarked that there was nothing that he violently disagreed with in the constitution, that even the best constitution in the world could go wrong if not operated properly.

6. Muhammadu Buhari, "Alternative Perspectives on Nigeria's Political Evolution" (Washington: Woodrow Wilson International Center for Scholars, April 7, 2004). The argument is that a presidential candidate must receive 25 percent of the votes in two-thirds of the states to avoid a runoff election. If elections in a sufficient number of states are overturned by the Supreme Court, a second election must take place. For Buhari's reaction to the December 2004 appeals court rejection of his legal challenge and his commitment to continue the appeal to the Supreme Court, see "Text of Press Briefing by Major General Muhammadu Buhari, GCFR, Following the Delivery of Judgement by the Court of Appeal December 21, 2004" (http://AmanaOnline.com [December 2004]).

7. Human Rights Watch, "Revenge in the Name of Religion: The Cycle of Violence in Plateau and Kano States," HRW Report, vol. 17 (May 2005), available at http://hrw.org/english/docs/2005/05/23/nigeri10993.htm.

Chapter Three

1. John N. Paden, ed., *Values, Identities, and National Integration: Empirical Research in Africa* (Northwestern University Press, 1980).

2. This distinction between being a "good Muslim" and a "bad Muslim" is obviously an international issue throughout the Islamic world. In its extreme form, it leads to an al Qaeda type of syndrome, where violent means, including terrorism, may be used to attack both democratic and nondemocratic Muslim regimes. Such violent extremism has not been part of the postindependence Nigerian experience. This focus on "bad Muslims" finds its parallel in many contemporary writings of Islamist thinkers in the Middle East.

3. Given the election procedures in a democracy, many such allegations and accusations as to moral character may be aired during the campaign periods. This serves as a safety valve to more violent options of incumbent removal.

4. For background, see "Sufism," in *The Oxford Encyclopedia of the Modern Islamic World*, vol. 4, edited by John Esposito (Oxford University Press, 1995), p. 103 ff. This work broadly describes Sufism as "the interiorization and intensification of Islamic faith and practice. The Arabic term *sufi*, however, has been used in a wide variety of meanings over centuries, both by proponents and opponents. . . . Western observers have not helped to clarify the matter by referring to Sufism as 'Islamic mys-

ticism' or sometimes 'Islamic esotericism.' . . . In general, the Sufis have looked upon themselves as Muslims who take seriously God's call to perceive his presence both in the world and in the self. They tend to stress inwardness over outwardness, contemplation over action, spiritual development over legalism, and cultivation of the soul over social interaction." In West Africa, sufi brotherhoods refer to the organized followers of particular founding "saints."

5. The founding saint of Tijaniyya is Ahmed Tijani and that of Qadiriyya is Abdulkadir Jailani. For details, see John N. Paden, *Religion and Political Culture in Kano* (University of California Press, 1973). In recent years Sokoto affiliation with Qadiriyya has become a controversial issue as the anti-sufi/anti-innovation groups have become more articulate. Yet there is convincing evidence that Usman dan Fodio himself was regarded as a leader of Qadiriyya. See J. M. Kaura, "Relevance of Qadiriyya Sufism in the Jihad and Its Moderating Effect on the Leadership of the Sokoto Caliphate," Conference of Ulama, Sokoto, July 2004.

6. The tomb of Ahmed Tijani is located in Fez, Morocco, and is still a pilgrimage site for Tijaniyya brotherhood followers from West Africa, especially from Senegal.

7. After Emir Sanusi was deposed in 1963 and exiled to Azare, he continued to have influence as the symbolic leader of reformed Tijaniyya in Nigeria, but much of the practical leadership was in the hands of disciples in Kano.

8. See Paden, *Religion and Political Culture in Kano.*

9. A khadi is a court judge, also called *alkali* (singular), or *alkalai* (plural).

10. See Abubakar Gumi, with Ismaila Tsiga, *Where I Stand* (Ibadan: Spectrum Books, 1992). Also, Roman Loimeier, "Islamic Reform and Political Change: The Example of Abubakar Gumi and the Yan Izala Movement in Northern Nigeria," in *African Islam and Islam in Africa,* edited by David Westerlund and Eva Evers Rosander (Ohio University Press, 1997). The Sokoto spelling is actually "Gummi," after the village where Abubakar was born, but it was later shortened to the Kano form, "Gumi." Abubakar Mahmud Gummi passed away on Friday, 14th Rabi'ul Auwal, 1413 (September 11, 1992) in a London hospital. I am grateful for Shaykh Abubakar Gummi's hospitality at his home in Kaduna in June 1990 and for extensive discussions with him.

11. The *Izala* organization refers to itself as *Jama'atul Izalatul Bid'ah Wa'ikhamatul Sunnah* (JIBWIS), that is, "Society against innovation and in favor of Sunnah." Ousmane Kane translates the name as "Society for the removal of innovation and reinstatement of tradition." See Kane, *Muslim Modernity in Postcolonial Nigeria: A Study of the Society for the Removal of Innovation and Reinstatement of Tradition* (Boston: Brill, 2003).

12. Many of Gummi's opinions published in Hausa are widely available. See, for example, Musa Lawal Funtuwa, *Fatawar Abubakar Mahmoud Gummi* (Zaria: Hudahuda Press, 1986; repr., 1990, 2001, and 2003). The book is set up as a series of questions and answers *(fatwas).*

13. In part, this Saudi tolerance was strategic, and due to the historic West African adherence to the Sunni tradition. The Saudis were increasingly in competition with the Shi'ite model of Islam represented by Iran. As custodians of the holy places, the

Saudis made every effort to incorporate African Islam into the mainstream, which meant not imposing their own version of Sunni Islam on others, while at the same time supporting those causes closer to their own interpretations.

14. Babangida's wife, Miriam Babangida, is originally from the Christian Igbo geocultural zone.

15. General Sani Abacha's wife is Shuwa Arab, to be discussed later.

16. See T. G. O. Gbadamosi, *The Growth of Islam among the Yoruba, 1841–1908* (London: Longman, 1978).

17. See, for example, the translation and commentary by A. Yusuf Ali, *The Holy Qur'an* (Amana Corporation, 1992).

18. See, for example, M. K. O. Abiola, "Path to True Democracy," *African Concord,* October 12, 1992. Jakande was a former governor of Lagos.

19. For a positive assessment of this period, see Gabriel Umoden, *The Babangida Years* (Lagos: Gabumo Press, 1992). For a negative assessment, see Joe Igbokwe and Peter Claver Oparah, *2007: The IBB Option* (n.d., ISBN: 978-35037-2-3); see appendix 2.5 for background on Babangida.

20. For one version, see Ibrahim Sulaiman, *The Islamic State and the Challenge of History: Ideals, Policies and Operations of the Sokoto Caliphate* (London: Mansell, 1987); also, *A Revolution in History: The Jihad of Usman dan Fodio* (London: Mansell, 1986).

21. See Ahmad Kani and Kabir Ahmed Gandi, eds., *State and Society in the Sokoto Caliphate* (Sokoto: Usmanu Danfodiyo University Press, 1990). One of the most sophisticated and influential studies was the doctoral dissertation of Mahmud Muhammad Tukur, "Values and Public Affairs: The Relevance of the Sokoto Caliphal Experience to the Transformation of the Nigerian Polity" (Ph.D. dissertation, Ahmadu Bello University, Zaria, 1977). This was revised and published as Tukur, *Leadership and Governance in Nigeria: The Relevance of Values* (Zaria: Hudahuda Press, 1999). See also Usman Bugaji, in *On the Political Future of Nigeria,* edited by Ibrahim Sulaiman and Siraj Abdulkarim (Zaria: Hudahuda Press, 1988). During the Fourth Republic, Bugaji served as political adviser to Vice President Atiku Abubakar. In 2003 Bugaji was elected to the House of Representatives from Katsina, on the People's Democratic Party (PDP) ticket, and became chairman of the House Foreign Affairs Committee.

22. The bicentenary celebration of the establishment of the Sokoto Caliphate in 1804 was held in Abuja on June 14–16, 2004, sponsored by Arewa House, and in Sokoto on June 19–21, 2004, sponsored by the Sokoto state government. President Obasanjo (PDP) was the special guest of honor in Sokoto. This display of bipartisanship by Governor Bafarawa of Sokoto (All Nigeria People's Party) was intended to take the politics out of the celebration. See, "Sokoto Prepares for Caliphate Bicentenary Events," *Abuja Daily Trust,* March 29, 2004. The entire issue of the *Kaduna Weekly Trust* for June 19–25, 2004, was dedicated to "The Caliphate." (The author of this volume was privileged to participate in these events in Abuja and Sokoto and gave the keynote address at the Abuja opening of the conference. This address was serialized in the *Abuja Daily Trust,* June 16 and 17, 2004.)

Chapter Four

1. There is an enormous amount of current research on the Sokoto Caliphate, especially at the northern universities in Sokoto, Kano, and Zaria. See, for example, *Book of Abstracts of Masters and Doctorate Degrees* (Usman Danfodiyo University, Sokoto, May 2003). For a discussion of the intellectual impact of the caliphate, see Hamidu Alkali, *The Chief Arbiter: Wazir Junaidu and His Intellectual Contribution* (Centre for Islamic Studies, Usman Danfodio University, 2002). See also the academic papers presented at the International Conference on the Sokoto Caliphate and Its Legacies, 1804–2004, sponsored by Arewa House, held in Abuja, Nigeria, June 14–16, 2004.

2. For the views of the (late) Waziri of Sokoto, Junaidu, on the idea of "martyr" after the assassination of Ahmadu Bello in 1966, see John N. Paden, *Ahmadu Bello, Sardauna of Sokoto: Values and Leadership in Nigeria* (London: Hodder and Stoughton,1986), chap. 19, "Death and Response." It is unlikely that cultural and religious views on suicide or martyrdom have changed in the subsequent era.

3. No case of coup d'état against a Muslim head of state in Nigeria by a Muslim successor has involved assassination. Shagari, Buhari, and Babangida were all left to the mercies of their individual destinies. By contrast, the Muslim leaders of Nigeria who have been assassinated—Balewa, Bello, Murtala Muhammad—were killed by non-Muslim factions. In some quarters, Sani Abacha's heart attack in 1998 was seen as a "coup from heaven."

4. Distribution figures for those with sufi brotherhood affiliation are not available. For an early survey in one ward in the "Hausa" side of Kano City, see John N. Paden, *Religion and Political Culture in Kano* (University of California Press, 1973), appx. 1, "Bakin Ruwa Ward (Kano City) Religious Survey, 1965." Of the 100 heads of compound interviewed in this survey, 74 percent were members of Tijaniyya, 14 percent were members of Qadiriyya, and 12 percent were unaffiliated with any brotherhood. Since then, the balance has shifted throughout the north, as younger elements have become part of the unaffiliated cohort, including *Izala*.

5. For example, an estimated one-quarter of the population of contemporary Sudan originally came from Nigeria. While this reflects earlier pilgrimage and trade linkages, it also represents "flight" (*hijra*) or emigration patterns. A *hijra* group moving eastward through Yobe State clashed with police and locals at the end of December 2003, with a significant number of deaths on both sides. See "Nigerians Crush Islamic Uprising," *BBC News*, January 5, 2004. This incident attracted international attention because the *hijra* group had called itself *taliban*, with a group leader known as Mullah Omar, and was purportedly flying the flag of Afghanistan. Although Borno State has set up a commission of inquiry to examine the matter, the incident, according to Nigerian sources, does not seem to be related to larger trends in Nigeria, other than the historic pattern of migrating to the east in times of stress.

6. A new Katsina Islamic University is being established by the Katsina Islamic Foundation, based on private funding. The university will be geared toward science

and technology but with instruction in Arabic and English. See *Katsina Islamic University Project,* Information Brochure (Katsina: Government Printer, January 2003). E-mail: uniislam@katislam.com; website: www.katislam.com.

7. In the Hausa language, *mallam* or *malam* (m), *mallama* or *malama* (f), *mallamai* or *malamai* (pl), is comparable to the Arabic *mu'allim,* or Islamic "teacher." The plural, *ulama,* is increasingly used in West Africa as a generic category of learned persons. In English usage in Nigeria, "mallam" has become a general term of respect and greeting. A key function of mallams is to teach basic Qur'anic principles to young children from the neighborhood (or *almajiri* from other areas), or advanced knowledge to students at higher *ilm* levels. For details on northern Nigeria, see M. Ameen Al-Ameen, National Council for the Welfare of the Destitute, *Almajiri and Qur'anic Education* (Kaduna: Rishab Press, 2001).

8. This interdependent relationship of emirs and *ulama* is widespread through the Islamic world. In the state systems of the former Sokoto Caliphate, it became particularly salient in the period after the jihad movement of the early nineteenth century.

9. During the transition to the aborted Third Republic, General Babangida utilized this procedure in what he called "open-secret balloting," also known as Option A4.

10. The rule-of-law issue is important not only to domestic politics but also to the international community, since it is seen as a precondition to many other priorities, such as economic development and the curtailment of corruption.

11. The question of who enforces shari'a also has great bearing on the issue of "the separation of mosque and state," since it shifts major responsibilities for moral behavior directly onto private citizens.

12. It is not clear when the office of *koroma* emerged historically. Possibly it is a carryover from pre-Islamic, or at least pre–Sokoto Caliphate, times.

13. This antihoarding policy was undertaken at the national level in 1984 by General Muhammadu Buhari and his minister of commerce and industry, Mahmud Tukur. The policy tried to break the prevalent patterns of private hoarding and price fixing by encouraging cheap imports of key items, such as canned milk.

14. See Ayuba T. Abubakar, *Maitama Sule, Danmasanin Kano* (Zaria: Ahmadu Bello University Press, 2001), p. 260 ff.

15. For background on Justice Sambo, see Justice Muhammad Bashir Sambo, *Shari'a and Justice: Lectures and Speeches* (Zaria: Sankore Educational Publishers, 2003), and appendix B.

Chapter Five

1. See E. Bolaji Idowu, *Olodumare: God in Yoruba Belief* (London: Longmans, 1962).

2. See David Laitin, *Hegemony and Culture: Politics and Religious Change among the Yoruba* (University of Chicago Press, 1986).

3. The author is grateful for discussions of Islamic patterns in Yorubaland with many scholars from the area, including Abdul Kabeer Thihamiyu Otunuyi, principal programs officer (Arabic), National Commission for Colleges of Education, Abuja, whose research as of June 2004 focused on historical accounts of Arabic culture in Ijebuland and the contributions of its *ulama*. See also "Islam in Southern Nigeria," *Kaduna Weekly Trust,* June 19–25, 2004.

4. An external source of Islamic conversion in Yorubaland came from Pakistan in the early to mid-twentieth century, in the form of Ahmadiyya, which emphasized Western education and technology and was initially very popular. Most other Nigerian Muslims regarded it as a heresy, however. It is based on the belief that Ghulam Ahmad, the nineteenth-century founder of Ahmadiyya in Pakistan, was the "seal of the prophets." In the postindependence era, the Ahmadiyya is no longer recognized by the Saudi and Nigerian pilgrimage boards or the mainstream Muslim umbrella groups in Nigeria. Subsequently, there have been splits within the Ahmadiyya and court cases over the control of property.

5. The author is grateful for discussions with the secretary general of the Nigerian Supreme Council of Islamic Affairs, a Yoruba lawyer from Lagos (Abdu-Lateef Adegbite), in his Lagos offices in January 1997 and on previous occasions; also, for discussions with the Lagos leaders of FOMWAN. (The largest number of mainstream Muslim women's organizations in FOMWAN are to be found in Yorubaland.)

6. The author is grateful to Alhaji Arisekola for his hospitality during a visit to his home in Ibadan on June 11, 1990. The host had prepared a formal welcome speech for the occasion.

7. John N. Paden, *Nigerian Muslim Perspectives on Religion, Society, and Communication with the Western World* (Washington: Office of Research, U.S. Information Agency, November 1990). This study was distributed to senior Nigerian university officials.

8. FOMWAN may be comparable in some ways to Malaysia's "Sisters in Islam" and other national Muslim women's umbrella groups throughout the more moderate Islamic countries.

9. See various issues of the FOMWAN publication, *Muslim Woman.*

10. Paden, *Nigerian Muslim Perspectives.* The "Peace Committees" in the various Nigerian universities usually include key faculty and senior staff members who are ready, on short notice, to intercede at any indication of conflict between Muslim and Christian students or groups. Because such committees have the general respect of all faith-based student groups, they have been quite successful in preventing or mediating conflict.

11. Some scholarships are available to Yoruba university students from Saudi and Gulf states, but in general such resources have been directed to the far northern states. On December 31, 2003, however, postgraduate students who had returned to Nigeria from study in Sudan, and who designated themselves *taliban,* were involved in a confrontation with police in Yobe State. They appeared to be migrating away from the perceived un-Islamic conditions in Nigeria. According to northern per-

ceptions, when it became apparent that some of the students were from well-known Yoruba (although Hausa-speaking) families, the coverage was by and large dropped in the Nigerian press (see chapter 10).

12. Paden, *Nigerian Muslim Perspectives.*

13. The National Secretariat of NACOMYO is located in Ikeja, Lagos. For reactions to the attempted coup of April 1989, see speech made at the press conference held by NACOMYO at the N.U.J. Light House, Victoria Island, Lagos, Monday, May 29, 1990 (4th zhul-Qada, 1410), which was called "to reply to some unfortunate, unguarded and provocative statements that have been made by some Christian leaders since the last abortive coup. . . . Let us state from the onset that our intention for calling this press conference is not out of any confrontational disposition nor is it meant to fuel the already tense and charged political and inter-religious atmosphere of the country. Rather it is to bring to the mental consciousness of all Nigerians the deliberate falsehood and provocative innuendoes being engendered by some so-called religious leaders in order to gain cheap popularity and then cause religious chaos, the end of which may be catastrophic to the political, social and economic stability of this country, God forbid. . . . That is why we regard as unfortunate and condemnable all the provocative statements credited to Dr. Anthony Olubunmi Okogie, President of the Christian Association of Nigeria, in virtually all the newspapers on Wednesday, 23rd of May, 1990." The statement goes on to criticize Okogie for not condemning the attempted coup, with its strong religious overtones.

14. See Sheikh Abdurrasheed Hadiyatulla, director, Sharia College of Nigeria, first national vice president (SCSN), "The Southwest and the State of the Nigerian Nation," Press Conference by the Supreme Council for Sharia in Nigeria, South-West Chapter, May 11, 2005, at the Nacomyo Central Mosque, Osogbo, Osun State, Nigeria (http://AmanaOnline.com [May 31, 2005]). The report details the nominations to the NPRC by state in the southwest, by religious affiliation. With regard to the NPRC's overall composition, the report argues: "The 217 Christian delegates against the 165 Muslims out of 382 was and is corruptly imbalanced, unjust and outright marginalization of Muslims of this country." The report also complains about the "outrageous and obnoxious appointment of 15 directors of the 2005 population census with 12 Christians and 3 Muslims makes one lose confidence in the headcount from the start." It also emphasizes that Yorubas are "more Muslim than tribalistic" and asks why, in view of the large Muslim population in the five Yoruba geopolitical states, "none of the "Pan-Yoruba interest or pressure groups really addresses our Islamic religious faith in their polity," and why Islamic religious leaders were not involved in drafting the 1994 Yoruba agenda (http://AmanaOnline.com/articles/art1129.htm).

15. See John N. Paden, *Ahmadu Bello, Sardauna of Sokoto: Values and Leadership in Nigeria* (London: Hodder and Stoughton, 1986), p. 326 ff.

16. The emir of Ilorin, Alhaji Ibrahim Sulu Gambari, served as chairman of the planning committee for the international conference titled "The Sokoto Caliphate

and Its Legacies, 1804–2004," Abuja, June 14–16, 2004, and has been active in Nigerian national affairs.

17. See appendix B for background on Ambassador Ibrahim Agboola Gambari.

18. An example of Gambari's leadership in a nongovernmental organization can be seen in the Nigeria Development Commission. See also Ibrahim Gambari, "The Role of Religion in National Life: Reflections on Recent Experiences in Nigeria," in *Religion and National Integration in Africa: Islam, Christianity and Politics in the Sudan and Nigeria*, edited by John Hunwick (Northwestern University Press, 1992), pp. 85–99.

19. Ronald Cohen and Abe Goldman, "The Society and Its Environment" in *Nigeria: A Country Study*, edited by Helen Metz (Washington: Library of Congress, Federal Research Division, 1992), p. 120 ff.

20. Wole Soyinka, *Death and the King's Horseman* (New York: Hill and Wang, 1975).

21. Paul E. Lovejoy, "Historical Setting," in *Nigeria: A Country Study*, edited by Metz, p. 22.ff. Lovejoy writes: "Oyo, the great exporter of slaves in the eighteenth century, collapsed in a civil war after 1817, and by the middle of the 1830s the whole of Yorubaland was swept up in these civil wars. New centers of power—Ibadan, Abeokuta, Owo, and Warri—contested control of the trade routes and sought access to fresh supplies of slaves, which were important to repopulate the turbulent countryside. . . . Some of the emerging Yoruba states started as war camps during the period of chaos in which Oyo broke up and the Muslim revolutionaries who were allied to the caliphate conquered northern Yorubaland. Ibadan, which became the largest city in black Africa during the nineteenth century, owed its growth to the role it played in the Oyo civil wars. Ibadan's *omuogun* (war boys) raided far afield for slaves and held off the advance of the Fulani." See also J. D. Y. Peel, *Ijeshas and Nigerians: The Incorporation of a Yoruba Kingdom, 1880s–1970* (Cambridge University Press, 1983).

22. According to Lovejoy: "Although churchmen in Britain had been influential in the drive to abolish the slave trade, significant missionary activity was renewed only in the 1840s and was confined for some time to the area between Lagos and Ibadan. The first missions there were opened by the Church of England's Church Missionary Society (CMS). They were followed by other Protestant denominations from Britain, Canada, and the United States and in the 1860s by Roman Catholic religious orders. Protestant missionaries tended to divide the country into spheres of activity to avoid competition with each other. . . . Catholic missionaries were particularly active among the Igbo, the CMS among the Yoruba." See Lovejoy, "Historical Setting," p. 28.

23. See ibid.: "The CMS initially promoted Africans to responsible positions in the mission field, an outstanding example being the appointment of Samuel Adjai Crowther as the first Anglican bishop of Niger. Crowther, a liberated Yoruba slave, had been educated in Sierra Leone and Britain, where he was ordained before returning to his homeland with the first group of missionaries sent there by the CMS. This was part of a conscious 'native church' policy pursued by the Anglicans and

others to create indigenous ecclesiastical institutions that eventually would be independent of European tutelage. The effort failed, however, in part because church authorities came to think that religious discipline had grown too lax during Crowther's episcopate but especially because of the rise of prejudice. Crowther was succeeded as bishop by a British cleric. Nevertheless, the acceptance of Christianity by large numbers of Nigerians depended finally on the various denominations coming to terms with local conditions and involved the participation of an increasingly high proportion of African clergy in the missions."

24. Rosalind Hackett, "New Religious Movements," in *Religion and Society in Nigeria*, edited by Jacob Olupona and Toyin Falola (Ibadan: Spectrum Books, 1991), p. 282 ff.

25. See ibid., p. 286: "While many movements called for a break with traditional religious allegiances and reliance on traditional charms and medicines, in essence they were seeking a rapprochement with African world-views. An existential recognition of witchcraft and other malevolent forces, counteracted by spiritual or faith healing based on a holistic theory of sickness and misfortune, and communal fellowship and participation, formed the mainstays of what came to be described as the prayer or prophet-healing or spiritual churches. This early wave of religious independence was located chiefly in the Yoruba-speaking areas of south-western Nigeria and was referred to as the *aladura* ('praying-people') movement."

26. Ibid.

27. Jacob Kehinde Olupona, "The Celestial Church of Christ in Ondo: A Phenomenological Perspective," in *New Religious Movements in Nigeria,* edited by Rosalind Hackett (New York: Edwin Mellen Press, 1987), pp. 45–73. This volume also contains other case studies of aladura and new churches in Yorubaland. The classic study of aladura is by J. D. Y. Peel, *Aladura: A Religious Movement among the Yoruba* (Oxford University Press, 1968).

28. Moffat Ekoriko, "Three Years of Abacha: Belt Tightening Squeezes the Poorest," *Africa Today,* November–December 1996, p. 10.

29. The Pentecostal churches have subsequently formed the Pentecostal Fellowship of Nigeria as an umbrella organization.

30. Cohen and Goldman, "The Society and Its Environment."

31. For a detailed discussion of alliance patterns in the First Republic (1960–66), see Paden, *Ahmadu Bello.*

32. See *The Master Plan for Abuja: The New Federal Capital of Nigeria* (Nigeria: Federal Capital Development Authority, February 1979). The author is grateful for the opportunity to participate in the design planning of this project.

33. See Akin Mabogunje, *Urbanization in Nigeria* (New York: Africana, 1969). Also, Akin Magobunje, *Yoruba Towns* (Ibadan University Press, 1962); Peter Lloyd, Akin Mabogunje, and B. Awe, *The City of Ibadan: A Symposium on Its Structure and Development* (Cambridge University Press, 1967).

34. See, for example, Wole Soyinka, "Culture, Memory and Development," in *Proceedings of an International Conference on Culture and Development in Africa* (Washington: World Bank, 1992), p. 215.

35. Paden, *Nigerian Muslim Perspectives.*

36. "Yorubaland: Sharia Implementation Progresses Despite Constraints," *Kaduna Weekly Trust,* July 26, 2003.

37. Ibid.

38. Ibid.

39. Ibid.

40. "If Nigeria Breaks Everyone Will Suffer—Olabode George," *Kaduna Weekly Trust,* August 2, 2003.

41. Ibid.

Chapter Six

1. For further discussion of Aminu Kano, see Alan Feinstein, *African Revolutionary: The Life and Times of Nigeria's Aminu Kano* (Boulder, Colo.: Lynne Rienner, 1987). For my personal comments on Aminu Kano, see the preface to the second edition of this work.

2. For a critical view of a possible Yar'Adua presidency, see Abubakar Rimi, "The Transition Programme has Failed," *African Concord,* October 12, 1992, p. 40. See also Balarabe Musa, "Things Cannot Continue Like This," *African Concord,* October 5, 1992, p. 42. During the Fourth Republic, however, the Yar'Adua organization, that is, the Peoples Democratic Movement (PDM), was revived as a component of the PDP. See "2007: Atiku Begins Exploit in South South," *Ibadan Daily Independent,* October, 27, 2003. For an official biography of Yar'Adua, see Shehu Musa Yar'Adua Foundation, *Shehu Musa Yar'Adua: A Life of Service* (Abuja, Nigeria: Shehu Musa Yar'Adua Foundation, 2004).

3. Centre for Democratic Research and Training, Mambayya House, Bayero University, Kano, January 2001. The center is directed by Attahiru Jega, originally from Kebbi. For a sample of publications, see Attahiru M. Jega and Haruna Wakili, eds., *The Leadership Question and the Quest for Unity in Nigeria: Proceedings of the Symposium in Memory of the Late Malam Aminu Kano* (Kano: Mambaya House, April 17, 2002). On April 17, 2003, a major conference was held at Mambayya House to celebrate the twentieth anniversary of the death of Aminu Kano. By 2004 the facilities for a modern conference center and guest lodgings were complete. Research was being undertaken on important issues such as the training of legislators, the role of the *ulama* in education, and aspects of conflict resolution.

4. See appendix B for a brief biography of the late *Etsu Nupe.* See also "LG Reforms Chairman, Etsu Nupe, Is Dead," *Lagos and Abuja ThisDay News,* September 2, 2003.

5. For further discussion of Balewa, see Trevor Clark, *A Right Honourable Gentleman: The Life and Times of Alhaji Sir Abubakar Tafawa Balewa* (Zaria: Hudahuda Press, 1991).

6. John N. Paden, *Ahmadu Bello, Sardauna of Sokoto: Values and Leadership in Nigeria* (London: Hodder and Stoughton, 1986).

7. See David Williams, *President and Power in Nigeria: The Life of Shehu Shagari* (London: Cass, 1982).

8. See the autobiography of Shehu Shagari, *Shehu Shagari: Beckoned to Serve* (London: Heinemann, 2001). Parts of this book were reproduced (selectively and without permission) by friends of Olu Agunloye for the Obasanjo-Atiku Movement in 2003, under the title *The Buhari I Know,* to try to show that Muhammadu Buhari, who led the coup against Shagari, had treated Shagari badly while the latter was in prison.

9. *African Guardian,* September 7, 1992.

10. Ibid.

11. In addition to Adamu Ciroma, the other leading candidate for the NRC presidential nomination, before the annulment of the 1992 primary elections, was Umaru Shinkafi, who was born in 1937 in Kaura Namoda, Sokoto State. See appendix B for background.

12. Umar Birai, "Islamic Tajdid and the Political Process in Nigeria," in *Fundamentalisms and the State,* edited by Martin Marty and Scott Appleby (University of Chicago Press, 1993), p. 184 ff. In this excellent overview of political-religious patterns in Nigeria prior to the June 12 elections, Birai describes Chief M. K. O. Abiola, "formerly vice-president of ITT and a well-known newspaper editor" as part of the ulama supporting the *tajdid* movement. Birai suggests that "the Islamic revival within Nigeria is best understood as a *tajdid* (renewal) movement. Though the movement has obvious religious and cultural aspects, it has also assumed a political cast and has led to a 'crisis of state and religion'" (p. 184).

13. For a eulogy by a non-Muslim Nigerian, see Ebenezer Babatope, *Murtala Muhammed: A Leader Betrayed* (Nigeria: Roy and Ezete, 1986).

14. Shehu Musa became general staff officer in Lagos (1974) and then commissioner for transport. Following the 1975 coup, he was promoted to brigadier and made chief of staff, supreme headquarters.

15. A full-length biography of Yar'Adua has been published by the Shehu Musa Yar'Adua Foundation; see n. 2.

16. See Moffat Ekoriko, "Three Years of Abacha: Belt-Tightening Squeezes the Poorest," *Africa Today,* November–December 1996, p. 9.

17. See appendix B for background on Buhari. He remains an important symbol of political reform and integrity in the north. But in parts of the south, and perhaps in some parts of the international community, the "religious card" has been played against him, with alarmist labels such as "*Taliban*" or "fundamentalist," or "*Izala*" (in the pejorative sense). According to one Internet account: "General Muhammadu Buhari . . . is a former Head of State, a man perceived by many as too serious and too rigid in his ways to be a President. As a matter of fact, he was dubbed a non-democrat and Islamic fundamentalist by President Obasanjo and his Vice President Atiku during the last elections. The General is very qualified to preside over a democratic Nigeria, but his past antecedents when he was the Head of State keep cropping up. Some pundits say he is neither a democrat nor is he interested in being one. He may

enjoy the support of the Islamic Ulama, especially the Izala sect and their almajiri supporters but, within the elite and Sunni sect he is seen as a very dangerous prospect. Many families in the North have not forgiven him for their loss of income when in 1984 he changed the color of the currency and detained many who had excessive funds in their hands." Max Gbanite, "2007: Problems and Prospects" (maxgbanite@hotmail.com [September 1, 2003]).

18. Ibrahim Badamasi Babangida was born August 17, 1941, in Minna, Niger State. See appendix B for background.

19. Abacha married Maryam Jidah, also from Borno, in 1965. As noted previously, she is associated with the small Shuwa Arab community, which is the only Nigerian ethnic group that speaks Arabic as a first language. They had six sons and three daughters. See appendix B for background.

20. In October 2003, the Swiss authorities announced that $618 million from Abacha bank accounts would be returned to Nigeria, although on the condition that it be used to improve education, health, agriculture and infrastructure. See "Abacha Loot: Swiss Govt Gives Terms for Release," *Daily Champion*, October 3, 2003. The actual amount of Abacha money in Swiss banks was considerably higher, although some of the funds have been returned to the Abacha family.

21. See Mary Smith, *Baba of Karo: A Woman of the Muslim Hausa* (London: Faber & Faber, 1965). See also Catherine Coles and Beverly Mack, eds., *Hausa Women in the Twentieth Century* (University of Wisconsin Press, 1991); and Barbara Callaway and Lucy Creevey, *The Heritage of Islam: Women, Religion and Politics in West Africa* (Boulder, Colo.: Lynne Rienner, 1994). Also, Barbara Callaway, *Muslim Hausa Women in Nigeria: Tradition and Change* (Syracuse University Press, 1987). For a study of a major prototype of a Sokoto *jihadi* woman, see Jean Boyd, *The Caliph's Sister, Nana Asma'u (1793–1865): Teacher, Poet and Islamic Leader* (London: Frank Cass, 1989).

22. See *Women in Nigeria Today* (London: Zed Books, 1985). According to the introduction, "The papers in this book comprise the proceedings of the first seminar on Women in Nigeria, held at Ahmadu Bello University, Zaria, on 27–28 May 1982."

23. See Lateefa Okunnu (*Naibatul-Amirah* of FOMWAN), keynote address delivered at the formal launching of the Lagos State Branch of the Federation of Muslim Women Associations in Nigeria (FOMWAN) on Sunday, February 23, 1986, at the University of Lagos Auditorium, Akoka, Lagos, p. 3: "Before the end of the conference representatives of the various organizations at the meeting discussed the formation of a National Muslim Women Organisation in Nigeria. The need for such a body was unanimously accepted."

24. As of 2004, there were 500 affiliates of FOMWAN in thirty-four of the thirty-six states. They have fifty-three schools in the country for women's adult literacy. FOMWAN has been active in publicizing and protesting the shari'a punishments, which affect women disproportionately. FOMWAN leaders such as Hajiya Bilkisu Yusuf and Zainab Kabir have expressed concern that some of the new penal crimi-

nal codes have been imported from countries such as Sudan, Pakistan, and Iran, and the increased training of Nigerian Muslim scholars in Saudi Arabia has made life more difficult for Nigerian Muslim women. Another nongovernmental organization that provides legal access for women is Women's Rights Advancement and Protection Alternative (WRAPA), founded in 1999. WRAPA has provided legal assistance to Safiya Husseini in Sokoto State and Amina Lawal in Katsina State and has challenged the competence of some shari'a judges who are not properly trained. See also Professional Muslim Sisters Association (PMSA), based in Abuja, which was set up "to render professional and financial assistance to the less privileged members of society, particularly women and children." Long-term projects include setting up health centers for women and children, establishing legal aid clinics, starting a microcredit scheme for women, establishment of a school for disadvantaged children, and assisting existing orphanages, schools and rehabilitation centers for the disabled, and for drug addicts.

25. For details of FOMWAN organization, see FOMWAN, *Constitution: Rules and Regulations,* National Headquarters, Islamic Center, P.O. Box 29, Minna, Niger State, Nigeria, 1985. The constitution came into effect on October 12, 1985. The headquarters of the association rotates, depending on where the *Amirah* (president) is living. Initially, it was in Minna because the *Amirah* was Hajiya B. Aisha Lemu. The deputy *Amirah (Naibatul)* was Alhajia Lateefa M. Okunnu, and the public relations officer was Bilkisu Yusuf, of the Triumph Publishing Company, Kano. See also *An Introduction to the Federation of Muslim Women's Associations in Nigeria,* Islamic Center, P.O. Box 29, Minna, Niger State, Nigeria, 1985.

26. One example of a FOMWAN leader was Lateefa M. Okunnu of Lagos, who served as *Amirah* of FOMWAN in the early 1990s and is a practicing attorney. She has also served as presidential liaison officer in Lagos State. She has been especially interested in marriage law and has written extensively on this subject. Okunnu has taken an active role in coordinating with Muslim women throughout Nigeria. When she became *Amirah* in 1989 to serve her four-year term, her executive committee consisted of *Naibatul,* Hajiya Sa'adiya Omar; secretary general, Alhajia Fatima Oyekan; financial secretary, Alhajia Adiat Fahm; P.R.O, Hajiya Halimat Jibril; *Da'wah* officer, Hajiya B. Aisha Lemu; assistant *Da'wah* officer, Alhajia Muslimat Kamaldeen; legal adviser, Alhaja Ramdat Okunola; ex officio: Hajiya Bilkisu Yusuf, Hajiya Zainab Kabir; Hajiya Fatima Othman; Hajiya Fatima Onanuga. See FOMWAN National Conference on "The Role of Muslim Women in Nation Building," held at Government Girls Secondary School, Kaduna, December 1–4, 1989. I am grateful for extensive discussions with Lateefa Okunnu in 1990, at her home in Lagos.

27. Ibid., p. 1. See also Lateefa Okunnu, "A Focus on Some Aspects of 'Bid'a' in the Conduct of Marriage among Muslims in Lagos," *Muslim Woman,* April 1970, p. 37 ff.

28. The first *Amirah* of FOMWAN (1985–89), Hajiya B. Aisha Lemu, was the British-born wife of Shehu Lemu, grand khadi of Niger State.

29. See Peter Clarke, "The Maitatsine Movement in Northern Nigeria in Historical and Current Perspective," in *New Religious Movements in Nigeria,* edited by Rosalind I. J. Hackett (Lewiston: Edwin Mellon Press, 1987), pp. 93–115. Also, Matthew Hassan Kukah, *Religion, Politics and Power in Northern Nigeria* (Ibadan: Spectrum Books, 1993); and Paul M. Lubeck, *Islam and Urban Labor in Northern Nigeria: The Making of a Muslim Working Class* (Cambridge University Press, 1986), p. 309. For a more theoretical analysis, see Rosalind I. J. Hackett, "Exploring Theories of Religious Violence: Nigeria's 'Maitatsine' Phenomenon," in *Religion as a Human Capacity: A Festschrift in Honor of E. Thomas Lawson,* edited by Timothy Light and Brian C. Wilson (Boston: Brill, 2004), p. 193 ff. The author has interviewed eye-witnesses to the events in Kano City, including those who observed the several weeks it took to remove all the dead bodies by trucks after the heavy-handed police and military confrontation with Maitatsine. Urban legend has it that Maitatsine "edited" the Qur'an in human blood (his own?) to emphasize his role as preordained leader of Muslims. In the midst of the oil boom in Nigeria, he argued that anything having to do with "Western" or "modern" was forbidden (*haram*), even the wearing of wristwatches and bicycle riding. He confronted the traditional emirate and Kano State authorities at every turn. His appeal was to the poor and dispossessed.

30. The NSCIA was actually inaugurated in 1974, on the basis of a meeting in 1973 of Muslim leaders from throughout Nigeria. However, it developed more fully in the 1980s, especially under the leadership of Ibrahim Dasuki and Abdu-Lateef Adegbite. See *Constitution of the Nigerian Supreme Council for Islamic Affairs* (n.d.); also, *The Nigerian Supreme Council for Islamic Affairs (NSCIA): Scope and Structure,* P.O. Box 7741, Lagos, Nigeria (n.d.); and NSCIA, *Islamic Affairs, Prohibitions and Injunctions* (Kaduna: Amdenic Press, n.d.).

31. See *NSCIA: Scope and Structure*: "The Constitution of the Council declares that the body was established to cater for, promote, protect and advance the interests of Islam and the Muslims throughout Nigeria. In this regard, the Council seeks, among other objectives to: (i) promote Islamic solidarity through fostering brotherhood and cooperation among the Muslims in Nigeria and other parts of the World; (ii) serve as a channel of contact with the Governmental Authorities of Nigeria on Islamic Affairs; (iii) coordinate the external contacts, interests and activities of Muslims in Nigeria as individuals or groups. Concerning 2.1 (iii) above, the Council acting directly or through its Agencies undertakes to serve as the channel of contact and communication with external bodies, including Foreign Governments on Islamic matters." (The eleven main standing committees are Elders, *Fatwa,* Finance, *Da'wah,* Research and Policy, Youth and Social Welfare, Media, International Relations, Economic Affairs, Legal Affairs, and Pilgrimage.)

32. The international community has several parallels to the idea of a national umbrella organization of all Muslim identity groups. See, for example, the patterns in Indonesia.

33. Abdu-Lateef Oladimeji Adegbite was born March 20, 1933, in Abeokuta, Ogun State. See appendix B for background.

34. For background, see Jean Boyd, with Manzat M. Maishanu, *Sultan Siddiq Abubakar III, Sarkin Musulmi* (Ibadan: Spectrum Books, 1991).

35. When Dasuki became sultan (and hence president general of NSCIA), the NSCIA consisted of a deputy president general (Alhaji Mustapha Umar El-Kanemi, *Shehu* of Borno), a secretary general (Abdu-Lateef Adegbite, *Seriki* of Egbaland), and a vice president drawn from the thirty states of the federation, including emir of Gwandu, Kebbi State (Alhaji M. H. Al-Rasheed Jokolo); emir of Kano, Kano State (Alhaji Ado Bayero); emir of Bauchi, Bauchi State (Alhaji Sulaiman Adamu); *Alaafin* of Oyo, Oyo State (Alhaji Lamidi Adeyemi III); emir of Katsina, Katsina State (Alhaji M. Kabir Usman); emir of Zazzau, Kaduna State (Alhaji Shehu Idris); *Olukare* of Ikare, Ondo State (Alhaji Akadiri Momoh IV); *Ataoja* of Osogbo, Osun State (Alhaji Iyiola Matanmi III); *Baba Adini* of Yorubaland, Ogun State (Alhaji M.K.O. Abiola); *Mogajingeri* of Epe, Lagos State (Alhaji S.L. Edu); Enugu State (Alhaji Sulaiman Onyeama); *Oba* of Agbede, Edo State (Alhaji M.S. Momodu III); Imo State (*Eze* Abdul Gafar Emetume). The deputy secretary general was D. O. S. Noibi, a professor from Ibadan University.

36. Nigeria joined the OIC in January 1986, under General Babangida. OIC guidelines were interpreted to require that a member country be predominantly Muslim, with a Muslim head of state. When news of Babangida's action became known throughout Nigeria, the reaction was strong on all sides. The NCRA was set up to mediate this issue. Nigeria remained part of the OIC, but in an ambiguous capacity, with diplomats or other notables representing Nigeria at OIC meetings, rather than Nigerian heads of state.

37. Wole Soyinka, in his opposition to the Abacha regime, includes a statement purportedly from Ibrahim Dasuki in support of the Abiola election. See Wole Soyinka, *The Open Sore of a Continent: A Personal Narrative of the Nigerian Crisis* (Oxford University Press, 1996), appx. 1, "Swear in Abiola," by Ibrahim Dasuki, pp. 155–58.

38. The OIC was set up in 1969. See Abdullah al-Ahsan, *OIC: The Organization of the Islamic Conference* (Herndon, Va.: International Institute of Islamic Thought, 1988). See also AbdulHamid A. AbuSulayman, *Towards an Islamic Theory of International Relations: New Directions for Methodology and Thought,* 2d ed. (Herndon, Va.: International Institute of Islamic Thought, 1993).

39. See, for example, Ibrahim Ahmed, "In or Out: Revisiting Nigeria's Membership in the Organisation of the Islamic Conference" (aibrahim54200@yahoo.com [October 26, 2003]): "One would wonder why Nigeria has never had a high level official representation [at the conference]. Could it mean that General Babangida joined the OIC because he is a Muslim and Chief Obasanjo wants to remove Nigeria because he is a Christian? . . . It can be suggested that considering the Christian reaction back then in 1986, which led to the formation of the Christian Association of Nigeria (CAN) . . . Muslim leaders have been cautious about Nigeria's member-

ship, even if it is to show that since 1986, Nigeria has not been turned into an Islamic republic. . . . Past Nigerian Muslim leaders have done more to maintain a balance between Islam and Christianity. . . . In sum, the Obasanjo administration is fighting Islam both openly and secretly. Its attempt to downgrade Nigeria's membership in the OIC to an observer is an oddity and of course a slap in the face of Nigerian Muslims. All well-meaning Nigerians should resist any attempt to pull Nigeria out of such an important organisation. It is time for all of us to mobilize all Muslims and peace and justice loving people in Nigeria to deplore Obasanjo's secret agenda to humiliate Muslims. Never in the history of Nigeria has our membership in any international organisation been downgraded to an observer status and Muslims should not fold their arms to allow this to happen to them."

40. See "NSCIA Dispatches Monitors for LG Polls," *Abuja Daily Trust*, March 26, 2004: "The. . . objective for sending independent monitors to all the 36 states of the country is to ensure a hitch free election in the country." Nationwide, according to international reports, an estimated fifty persons died in the March 2004 LGA elections.

41. It is generally agreed that while General Abacha transferred several billion dollars to Swiss banks, General Babangida "invested in human resources" within the country. (That is, he financed allies and spread the fruits of his off-budget funds to build a political base and protect himself from prosecution.) According to Max Gbanite, "If Babangida accepts to come out (for the presidency in 2007), his supporters within PDP ('sleeper cells' if you like) will surprise the country and probably draft him into the party with the rest joining forces. . . . Mark these words: The same Adedibu with some members of NADECO, OPC, and Agbekoya farmers will throng the streets of Oduduwa land, chanting and rooting for Babangida, once the Azikiwes-500 naira, Ahmadu Bellos-200 naira, and Awolowos-100 naira come to town; Murtalas-20 naira are not accepted during elections!" See Max Gbanite, "Problems and Prospects" (maxgbanite@hotmail.com [September 3, 2003]).

42. For an earlier example, see the cover story of *African Guardian*, "Will Nigeria Survive? Should It?" October 5, 1992. Later, the work of journalist Karl Maier captured some of the national pessimism, in thumbnail sketches in each of the six zones, which conveyed a pattern of widespread disillusionment and despondency. See Karl Maier, *This House Has Fallen: Midnight in Nigeria* (New York: Public Affairs, 2000).

43. See, for example, Mahmud M. Tukur, "Needed: Better Leadership," in *Crafting the New Nigeria: Confronting the Challenges,* edited by Robert I. Rotberg (Boulder, Colo.: Lynne Rienner, 2004), pp. 239–50.

44. "Maccido, in Akure, Canvasses Unity," *African Guardian*, October 22, 1996.

45. Ibid.

46. For further elaboration of orientations to conflict resolution in Nigeria, see John N. Paden, "National System Development and Conflict Resolution in Nigeria," in *Conflict and Peacemaking in Multiethnic Societies,* edited by Joseph Montville (Lexington, Mass.: Lexington Books, 1991), pp. 411–31.

Chapter Seven

1. Olusegun Obasanjo was born March 5, 1937, in Abeokuta, Ogun State. See appendix B for background.

2. For background on federalism, see Rotimi Suberu, *Federalism and Ethnic Conflict in Nigeria* (Washington: U.S. Institute of Peace, 2001).

3. For a northern perspective, see Mahmud Tukur, *Leadership and Governance in Nigeria* (Zaria: Hudahuda Press, 1999).

4. For background, see Herb Howe, "The Nigerian Military," *Association of Concerned Africanist Scholars (ACAS) Bulletin,* no. 65 (Fall 2003).

5. *Constitution of the Federal Republic of Nigeria* (Apapa, Lagos: Government Printer, May 5, 1999).

6. As noted previously, the First Republic (1960–66) opted for strong regionalism and a weak center, with a parliamentary model at regional and national levels. The transition to a "Republican" model in 1963 led to some confusion about the roles of prime minister and president. Traditional leaders still had strong influence, even as power shifted away from them to the regional level, and police powers moved away from local control. The political coalition between the north and southeast began to unravel in 1964, and the southwest was plagued by political crises during the elections. The assassination by a number of junior officers—mainly by non-Muslims from the southeast with grudges against northern (Muslim) politicians—and an unsuccessful coup led to reprisals and to the Biafran (southeast) attempted secession and civil war (1967–70). In the Second Republic (1979–83), a U.S.-style presidential model was initiated, but with strong "state" federalism emerging. Again, there was a national coalition between the north and east, with a weak center. As oil revenues increased, the shift began from Lagos to a new Federal Capital Territory in Abuja. There were messy elections after one term, a breakdown of credibility, and again, political problems in the southwest. A "palace military coup" was undertaken by senior officers. In the "Third" (1993, aborted) Republic, the constitutional design was again based on a U.S. presidential federal model with two parties (left-center and right-center). The June 1993 elections were canceled in part, but with clear evidence for a southwest-northeast dominant coalition, even though the results were annulled. Again, there was sustained turmoil in the southwest. See appendix A for electoral patterns during these periods.

7. The local government elections of March 27, 2004, saw a poor turnout and increasing tensions. Ongoing electoral challenges are beyond the scope of this study.

8. The Land Use Decree, stating that all subsoil minerals, including oil, belong to all the people of Nigeria and not just those from the area, was incorporated into the 1999 constitution. This would be difficult to change without going through the arduous task of amending the constitution.

9. In the summer of 2002, the national legislature filed articles of impeachment against President Obasanjo for alleged abuses of power, much of the support coming from the president's own political party (PDP). By the fall, however, political

accommodations began to emerge, and with the impending elections of 2003, the focus shifted to party conventions and the upcoming campaigns.

10. A major legal challenge by the ANPP against the "swearing in" of President Obasanjo on May 29, 2003, was dismissed by a panel of the Supreme Court on November 19, 2003. Throughout 2004 and into 2005, challenges were in the court system until July 1, 2005, when the Supreme Court ruled against the ANPP.

11. Governor Dariye was replaced by a military general, Chris Alli, who was a Christian but whose father was a Muslim imam (his mother was a Christian). Alli was well regarded in the north for being impartial on Muslim-Christian relations. In January 2004, preexisting tensions erupted, and Muslims burned a Christian church. In April, a commission was established to look into the matter, headed by the emir of Zaria. Then in May 2004, Christian retribution occurred, with a large number of killings. A state of emergency, as spelled out in Section 305 of the constitution, was approved by the federal government. This was protested by many leaders in the Christian Association of Nigeria, as well as by evangelical leaders in Plateau State. The state of emergency was supported widely by the northern Muslim community. A government report on the crises in Plateau State published in October 2004 revealed that between 1999 and 2004 nearly 54,000 people had been killed. For results of the Plateau State Peace Committee recommendations, see chapter 10. See also Human Rights Watch, *Revenge in the Name of Religion.*

12. *Constitution of the Federal Republic of Nigeria,* sec. 133. Although the constitution was not promulgated until May 5, 1999, the provision for "federal character" voting requirement was used throughout the transition to civilian rule.

13. Ibid., 3d schedule, pt. 1, sec. C, 7–8.

14. The Independent National Electoral Commission organized the 1999 elections in record time. Despite the haste, some international observers found them relatively free and fair. However, former U.S. president Jimmy Carter, who monitored the elections as leader of the Carter Center/NDI delegation, felt that the elections were flawed and that it was impossible to determine, categorically, who had won. The team report labeled the election a transition to civilian rule, not a transition to democracy.

15. See *Abuja Daily Trust,* May 13, 2003.

16. Muhammadu Buhari was born December 17, 1942, in Daura, Katsina State. See appendix B for background.

17. See, for example, Max Gbanite, "2007: Problems and Prospects" (maxgbanite@hotmail.com [September 1, 2003]). Muhammad Buba Marwa finalized his declaration for the PDP in late April 2005, having registered earlier in Michika, his hometown. In Yola, he was supported for a presidential bid in 2007 by notables such as Bamanga Tukur. See "Bamanga Tukur Backs Marwa's Presidential Ambition," *Ibadan Daily Independent,* May 2, 2005. Marwa was popular as Lagos state administrator and in general is acceptable in the southwest.

18. See Atiku Abubakar, "Progress Building Democracy in Nigeria," speech delivered at Woodrow Wilson International Center for Scholars, Washington, May 2,

2005. Abubakar described his mother's determination to see him through second-ary school despite extreme poverty and his own efforts, through odd jobs, to support her dream and his own desire for self-improvement through education. He grew up to have a successful career in public service and business and eventually joined the movement to help return Nigeria to democratic civilian rule, though it nearly cost him his life and forced him into "exile" in the United States when a "murderous dic-tatorship" came to power. After its fall, he returned to successfully run for a state governorship and then became President Obasanjo's running mate, winning election in 1999 and 2003. In his speech, Abubakar noted: "Surviving the extent of the poverty I grew up in and coming this far greatly informed my belief that we live in a country of good people, a country of immense opportunities, just like the United States. We only need to work harder in Nigeria, with vision, focus and determina-tion to build a country of endless possibilities for its citizens. That is what our government has been trying to do since 1999. And that is what we plan to continue to do in the years ahead."

19. The Saudi system follows the Hanbali rather than the Maliki school of jurisprudence.

20. Zamfara State of Nigeria, *Shari'ah Penal Code Law* (Zamfara, January 2000).

21. Kano had been a center for sufi learning, Borno for non-sufi learning, and Sokoto a mixture of the sufi and legal legacies. Kano and Sokoto have been historic rivals, although Sokoto always has pride of place as the capital established in the early nineteenth century by the founders of the Sokoto Caliphate, which included all twelve shari'a states except Borno and Yobe.

22. Kaduna State was a major center for *Izala* thinking, with its emphasis on going back to the Qur'an for guidance on legal and other matters.

23. For a discussion of conflict resolution efforts in the northern states, see *Peace-Works News*, the official newsletter of Academic Associates/PeaceWorks, esp. vol. 4, no. 2 (August 2003) and subsequent editions.

24. Thus, the APP states were Jigawa, Sokoto, Yobe, and Zamfara. The PDP states were Bauchi, Niger, Kaduna, Kano, and Katsina. The states that were about equally divided were Borno, Gombe, and Kebbi.

25. For a sample of opinion, see Mustafa Ibrahim, director of information man-agement, National Development Project, "The Shariah Project in Nigeria: Achievement, Problems and Prospects," paper presented at a training program organized by the Centre for Democratic Research and Training, Bayero University Kano, in Gusau, October 2004.

26. See John N. Paden, *Ahmadu Bello, Sardauna of Sokoto: Values and Leadership in Nigeria* (London: Hodder and Stoughton, 1986), chap. 6, "Judicial Reforms of 1959."

27. See Peter Lewis, "Nigeria: Elections in a Fragile Regime," *Journal of Democracy* 14 (July 2003). Also, A. Carl LeVan, Titi Petso, and Bodunrin Adebo, "Elections in Nigeria: Is the Third Time the Charm?" *Journal of African Elections* 2, no. 2 (2004); Darren Kew, "The 2003 Elections: Hardly Credible, but Acceptable," in *Crafting the*

New Nigeria: Confronting the Challenges, edited by Robert I. Rotberg (Boulder, Colo.: Lynne Rienner, 2004), pp. 139–73. The U.S. monitors included teams from the National Democratic Institute and the International Republican Institute. The European Union delegation wrote one of the toughest reports. In addition, the Commonwealth and the African Union teams sent observer delegations. These reports are available on the respective delegation web sites. The domestic monitors, who numbered about 40,000, included civil rights and religious nongovernmental organizations (some of them Catholic, Muslim women's groups, and Muslim men's groups), plus organized labor groups.

28. For an assessment of economic issues, see Ahmed I. Shekarau, "The Nigeria Economic Summit: A Post-Mortem," *Kaduna Weekly Trust,* October 4, 2003.

29. Chief Chukwuemeka Odumegwu Ojukwu was born November 4, 1933, in Zungeru, Niger State. See appendix B for background.

30. Okadigbo died in September 2003, after the apparent use of tear gas by police to break up a political rally in Kano, which he was addressing. It was well known that he had asthma, which was aggravated by the tear gas. See "Hold FG Responsible for Okadigbo's Death—NCP," *Lagos and Abuja ThisDay News,* October 3, 2003. Also, Obadiah Oghoerore Alegbe, "The Death of Senator Okadigbo Should Call Us to Reflection" (Oghoerore@oviri.com.ar [October 3, 2002]). Chuba Okadigbo was born December 17, 1941, in Ogwashi-Uku, Bendel State. See appendix B for background.

31. "We will never lose heart in struggle for democracy—Buhari," *Kano Triumph,* September 25, 2003.

32. In mid-November 2003, President Obasanjo failed to persuade the Supreme Court to have the Buhari legal challenge quashed. See "Obasanjo Loses to Buhari at Supreme Court," *Vanguard,* November 15, 2003: "Piqued by the Tribunal's decision, Obasanjo stormed the Supreme Court, seeking to upturn the decision and consequently terminate the Buhari challenge to his election victory." On November 19, 2003, a seven-member panel of Supreme Court justices, led by Justice Modibbo Alfa Belgore, declined to nullify the swearing in of President Obasanjo and claimed that the matter was not one for constitutional interpretation. See "Supreme Court Upholds Obasanjo's Swearing In," *Ibadan Daily Independent,* November 20, 2003.

33. See Mohammed Haruna, "Obasanjo, NTA and the Politics of Religious Broadcast" (kudugana@yahoo.com [October 3, 2003]).

34. Governor Shekarau had been involved in education throughout his career, as teacher, principal, and permanent secretary of education. He secured the ANPP nomination for governor against several wealthy businessmen, in large part because he had a real plan for linking education with economic development.

35. "Sultan Launches Scholarship Scheme," *Abuja Daily Trust,* September 25, 2003: "Awards were disbursed . . . in Sokoto, at an international seminar on the contributions of the Sokoto Jihadists to the development of science and technical education. Speaking at the occasion, the Sultan said the annual scholarship is being supported by the Islamic Foundation for Science (IFS). He announced that he also

plans to establish a College of Science and Islamic Studies, bearing his name. On the seminar, the Sultan said it was organised by the IFS at a time when the Muslim world was being challenged 'to come out with more scientific and technical research, because Muslims are the inheritors of science and technology.'"

36. "Katsina Islamic University to Open July, 2004," *Abuja Daily Trust,* October 7, 2003 (see discussion in chapter 3). See also "Wazirin Katsina Bags Doctorate Degree," *Abuja Daily Trust,* October 28, 2003. Alhaji Sani Abubakar Lugga received a doctorate in management from the St. Clements University in British West Indies. His dissertation was titled "Conflict Management in Hausaland: The Role of Traditional Rulers." He also has degrees in management, manufacturing, and agriculture. He is serving as the secretary general of Katsina Islamic University.

37. See Abdulrahman Muhammad Dan-Asabe, "Almajiri Syndrome in Arewa: An Open Letter to General Ibrahim Babangida (Rtd)" (muhdan@yahoo.com [November 2003]). The author criticizes Babangida for doing nothing about this issue during his eight years in power, and then, in 2003, coming out with proposals for dealing with the issue.

38. See "Welcoming the National Peace Forum," an editorial in the *Kano Triumph,* September 25, 2003, which welcomed the peace committee as a means to "assist the federal government in soothing 'frayed nerves' across the country's social and political groups."

39. For background on Shehu Malami, see Shehu Malami, *Nigerian Memories: An Insight into Some Aspects of Nigerian Public Life* (London: Frank Cass, 1985). Also, Shehu Malami, *Sir Siddiq Abubakar III, 17th Sultan of Sokoto* (Nigeria: Evans Brothers, 1989). A direct descendant of Usman dan Fodio, Shehu Malami was born in Sokoto in November 1937. He read law at the Middle Temple, London, and served as private secretary to the sultan of Sokoto. He holds the title Sarkin Sudan of Wurno. He was a close ally of Muhammad Maccido in the succession dispute after the death of Sultan Abubakar III.

40. The author is grateful for discussions with Shehu Malami, at his home in Sokoto, in June 2004.

41. See Aliyu Tilde, "Memo to Liman Ciroma Committee" (aliyutilde@yahoo.com [October 3, 2003]).

42. After states were created in 1966, key functions of local government—such as maintaining the police, prisons, and judiciary—were taken over by the states and federal government. In 1976 there was an attempt to harmonize such reforms throughout the country. The 1979 constitution established local governments but was unclear as to whether state governors could dissolve them, although the courts declared this unconstitutional. More local councils were created in 1984. The 1999 constitution created more local government authorities, although their relationship to states is far from clear, especially since governors were regarded as having the power to supervise local elections and in many ways control the block grants that fund local authorities.

43. See "Local Government Review Committee Wants 774 Councils Retained,"

Abuja Daily Trust, November 14, 2003.

44. See "Committee Seeks Parliamentary System for LGs," *Lagos and Abuja This-Day News,* November 14, 2003. The councilors were to follow a parliamentary system and select one of their own as chairman, thereby doing away with executive chairmen. Liman Ciroma passed away in May 2004.

45. See Ibrahm Ado-Kurawa, "Recommendations of the Kano Emirate Council," AmanaOnline.com, May 24, 2005 (ibrahimado@yahoo.com [May 12, 2005]). Of special interest are recommendations for decentralizing the police.

46. The chief justice of the Supreme Court, Muhammadu Lawal Uwais, was born in 1936, in Zaria. See appendix B for background.

47. The PDP has decided to zone the presidency to the north for eight years, starting in 2007. See "Presidency Zoned to North for 8yrs—Ogbeh," *Lagos and Abuja ThisDay News,* November 30, 2003. In late 2004, Audu Ogbeh resigned under presidential pressure as chair of the PDP.

48. For insights into the Babangida followers, see Tukur Othman, "That Gathering in Minna," *Kaduna Weekly Trust,* October 4, 2003, who argues that Babangida is someone who can resolve conflicts, and "is a man of the people—always with them in office and out of office. He is versed in international relations. He is a very patriotic Nigerian and can do anything for his country. Surprisingly, he is also a good Malam, versed in Koran, Hadith and Fiqhu. He sometimes leads even Friday prayers. In Islam this is a good leadership quality. He is exceedingly generous, witty and intelligent. He hardly says No to any request. He does what he can to please you. He is a good family man, and highly religious." In November 2003, Babangida confirmed that he was a member of the PDP. See "IBB Confirms Membership of PDP," *Abuja Daily Trust,* November 14, 2003. He also confirmed his support for an "open-secret system of voting called Option A4.... He said that the open-secret balloting was the best thing that had happened in Nigeria's electoral system because it was transparent and free of sharp electoral practices." For an assessment of potential candidates, see "Presidential Election 2007: Prognosis," *Kaduna Weekly Trust,* September 27, 2003.

Chapter Eight

1. The British relied heavily on standard Maliki law texts, which they arranged to have translated. See, for example, F. H. Ruxton, *Maliki Law* (being a summary from French translations of the Mukhtasar of Sidi Khalil, with notes and bibliography), published by order of Sir F. D. Lugard, Governor-General of Nigeria (London: Luzac, 1916). For subsequent translations of other key Maliki texts, see, for example, Imam Malik, *Al-Muwatta* (Norwich, England: Diwan Press, 1982).

2. The ANPP governor of Zamfara State (Ahmed Sani) was quick to point out that since 2000, Zamfara has had the lowest crime rate of any Nigerian state, and that more than 90 percent of its Muslim population was overwhelmingly supportive of shari'a. The governor and his supporters also stressed that the initial Christian fears

in the state have calmed down, and that there have been no significant religious clashes in Zamfara. The PDP proponents in Zamfara (who were also overwhelmingly Muslim) countered that the implementation of shari'a was politically based, with obvious cases of corruption by ANPP supporters not handled by the shari'a courts. For the flavor of this debate, see "Shari'a in Zamfara Has Failed—PDP Scribe," *Kaduna Weekly Trust,* September 6, 2002. Also, "Inside Zamfara Politics: Shari'a Defines 2003 Guber Race," *Kaduna Weekly Trust,* September 6, 2002.

3. There have been periods, during the nineteenth and twentieth centuries, when these three northern city-states have competed with each other. Only in recent years have they been divided up into smaller states, in large part by the military regimes as a means of control, via divide and rule.

4. It should be noted that Zamfara did not have "a separate traditional ruler" but was part of the Sokoto system and hence directly under the sultan of Sokoto. However, title holders from Zamfara have emerged, including the governor (Ahmed Sani) who holds the title of *Yerima* of Bakura.

5. Atiku Abubakar chose to leave his governorship of Adamawa State in 1999 to run for the PDP vice presidency. He is not from a notable or royal family but because of close ties to the military served as head of customs in Nigeria. At present, he holds the title of *Turaki*. Other political heavyweights from Adamawa include Bamanga Tukur, former managing director of Nigeria's Ports Authority and former civilian governor of the defunct Gongola State (later, Adamawa), and Jubril Aminu, former minister of education, minister of petroleum, Nigerian ambassador to the United States, and PDP senator from Adamawa in 2003. According to one favorable account of Atiku Abubakar: "The go-getter spirit in Atiku Abubakar largely accounts for his meteoric rise politically," despite his "plebian background." However, some accused him of denouncing the introduction of shari'a, and they questioned "the hypocrisy of our leaders in the name of Sharia. Ordinary Muslims, who are victims of the corruption and greed of our leaders are today the human guinea pigs of Sharia implementation, while the political leaders who continue to steal, fornicate and indulge in unspeakable debauchery, are treated with kid gloves." Kasimu Bala Tondi, "Atiku's 2007 Bid: Why Are the Croakers Unnerved?" (ibrahim@webstar.co.uk [September 3, 2003]). For a critical perspective on Atiku Abubakar, see Hannatu Mohammed, "Atiku: Thou Shall Not Speak Ill of the Dead" (hkanomohammed@ yahoo.com [September 3, 2003]), in which the author claims Abubakar has fabricated part of his family history and distorted his personal relationship with General Abacha to gain more distance from the negative symbolism of General Abacha.

6. The APP evolved into the ANPP, led at the national level by former head of state General Muhammadu Buhari, originally from Daura in Katsina State.

7. See, for example, Sanusi Lamido Sanusi, "The Hudood Punishments in Northern Nigeria: A Muslim Criticism" (Leiden, Holland: Institute for the Study of Islam in Modernity, October 1, 2002). Also, Sanusi Lamido Sanusi, "The Shari'a Debate and the Construction of a 'Muslim' Identity in Northern Nigeria: A Critical Perspective," paper prepared for seminar "Shari'a Debate and the Construction of

Muslim and Christian Identities in Northern Nigeria," University of Bayreuth, Bayreuth, Germany, July 11–12, 2003. See also Center for the Study of Islam and Democracy, *The Implementation of Shari'ah in a Democracy: The Nigerian Experience*," Conference Report (Abuja, July 2004). For an external view, arguing that shari'a has only been applied to poor people, see "Islamic Law in Nigeria: Shilly-Shallying with Sharia," *Economist*, September 27, 2003, p. 46.

8. For a pessimistic assessment of implementation of shari'a in Nigeria, see Lawal Karmanje, "2003 Events: Is Political Shari'a Prematurely Dead?" (LawalKarmanje@aol.com [July 14, 2003]).

9. For a discussion of "political shari'a," see "'Political Shari'a'? Human Rights and Islamic Law in Northern Nigeria," *Human Rights Watch*, vol. 16 (September 2004).

10. The *Kaduna Weekly Trust* did a special investigative reporting project on the implementation of shari'a. This newspaper is perhaps the most insightful of the northern journals with regard to the shari'a issue and tries to make a point of interviewing senior people from a variety of perspectives. The newspaper is a major barometer of thought in Muslim northern Nigeria.

11. "Poor Shari'a Monitoring in Sokoto," *Kaduna Weekly Trust*, July 26, 2003.

12. Ibid.

13. "Shari'a: Yarima vs. the Mallams," *Kaduna Weekly Trust*, July 26, 2003.

14. "No Misunderstanding between Government and Ulama," *Kaduna Weekly Trust*, July 26, 2003. As of November 2003, the screening of judges was still under way. See "Zamfara Assembly Screens Shari'a Judges Tomorrow," *Abuja Daily Trust*, November, 3, 2003. The reason given for the delay was "some perceived anomalies," specifically, the "appointments were not done according to laid down rules [and] had no blessing of the judicial service commission, the chief judge, Ulama consultative forum, the attorney-general, and the Grand Khadi."

15. See Global Network for Islamic Justice, "Almajiranci: The Menace of Child-Begging: Control and Solution," "Being a proposal submitted to Zamfara State Government with special consideration to shari'ah practising in Northern States of Nigeria" (P.O.Box 55, Gusau, Zamfara State) (glonij@justice.com [December 2003]). The seventeen-page report compares the current situation to the traditional or classic tradition of Qur'anic study, blaming the change on "multiple problems in the society in the form of harsh economic conditions, technological age, insecurity of lives and lack of concern from the general public and governments. Coupled with their numbers, which have skyrocketed, the institution is now being abused and the Almajiri gets less and less charity and support. Suddenly, the 'almajirai' are seen as constituting social menace and the almajiri child is seen and identified with some unique features of destitution." The GNIJ called on the state to regulate such child begging.

16. "Shari'a Implementation in Katsina, the Journey So Far," *Kaduna Weekly Trust*, July 26, 2003.

17. "Katsina Deputy Governor Heads Shari'a Committee," *Abuja Daily Trust*, October 28, 2003.

18. See, for example, "An Open Letter to Kano State Governor, by Aminu Muhammad" (ambabazaria@yahoo.co.uk [September 28, 2002), indicating that the Qadiriyya and Tijaniyya sects had reportedly warned "that they will unleash violence" if the state "did not stop the Azalea [*sic*] movements from establishing schools and mosques in Kano, citing Al-Montana al-Islamic Mosque and school at Dray as one of the targets of their hatred. . . . Going back in history, these are the same set of people who tried to stop imam Malik, imam Abu Hanifa and imam Ahmad ibn Hanbal from spreading knowledge."

19. "Kano Govt Failed to Support Shari'a—Ustaz Rabo," *Kaduna Weekly Trust,* July 26, 2003. For interviews with the Waziri of Kano, see "Shari'a Not Active in Kano—Isa Waziri," and "'I Have Never Been Detained for Preaching,'—Sheikh Isa Waziri," *Kaduna Weekly Trust,* August 2, 2003.

20. "Two years of Shari'a in Kano: Shekarau's Humanistic Approach," *Kaduna Weekly Trust,* July 26, 2003.

21. "Jigawa: Effective Zakkat System, Poor Shari'a Implementation," *Kaduna Weekly Trust,* July 26, 2003.

22. " 'Ours Is a Step-by-Step Approach'—Deputy Chief Imam," *Kaduna Weekly Trust,* July 26, 2003.

23. "Shari'a: Politics of Implementation in States," *Kaduna Weekly Trust,* July 26, 2003.

24. "Ulamas Hail Muazu over Shari'a," *Lagos and Abuja ThisDay News,* July 14, 2003.

25. See, "Shari'a Won't Affect Games in Bauchi Centre," *Lagos and Abuja ThisDay News,* October 4, 2003: "The management of Zaranda Hotel, Bauchi, has assured the organisers of the 8th All Africa Games that the Islamic legal code, shari'a, would not affect the games in the city. . . . Reminded that the shari'a legal system was being fully practised in the state, the hotelier said 'though we have been given some concessions because the hotel is an international one, but we will not do anything that will be offensive to people's religious sensibilities.' According to him, 'this is an international hotel and that does not make it a shari'a-free zone as reported by a section of the media.' He explained that the hotel management respects the people's culture and religion . . . morality and ways of life."

26. "Shari'a: Politics of Implementation in States," *Kaduna Weekly Trust,* July 26, 2003.

27. For background on the Kaduna riots, see "Nigeria: The 'Miss World Riots': Continued Impunity for Killings in Kaduna," *Human Rights Watch Report,* July 21, 2003.

28. "Kaduna: Beyond the Three-Legged Judicial System," *Kaduna Weekly Trust,* July 26, 2003.

29. Ibid.

30. "Islamic Bank Promoters Shop for N 2.5b," *Vanguard,* October 23, 2003.

Chapter Nine

1. Human Rights Watch, "Nigeria: The 'Miss World Riots': Continued Impunity for Killings in Kaduna," *Human Rights Watch Report* (July 21, 2003). The figure of 2,000–5,000 deaths in Kaduna within a relatively short time frame is extremely high by world standards of ethnoreligious conflict. Interpretation of the riots and culpability continue to be controversial. See, for example, "Troublemakers Get Quit Notice in Kaduna," *Lagos and Abuja ThisDay News,* November 25, 2003. According to this account, the Kaduna state government blamed the ethnoreligious strife on non-indigenes and called on them to leave the area as soon as possible.

2. Although I have interviewed eyewitnesses to the 2002 Kaduna riots, it is impossible to draw any firm conclusions until the government reports are available, except to say that the Christian protest march in February 2000 against the possible introduction of shari'a was a major triggering factor. The march deteriorated into violence, and elements of *Izala* youth groups became involved.

3. The leading NGO training effort in conflict resolution in Kaduna has been headed by the team of Pastor James Movel Wuye and Imam Mohammed N. Ashafa at the Inter-Faith Mediation Centre (Muslim/Christian Dialogue Forum). Wuye and Ashafa are the coexecutive national coordinators of the Inter-Faith Mediation Centre. See Ashafa and Wuye, *The Pastor and the Imam: Responding to Conflict* (Lagos: Ibrash Publications Centre, 1999). Also, personal discussions with Wuye and Ashafa, in Washington, March 2004, and in Kaduna, June 2004. The center has extensive training in conflict prevention and mediation sessions for youth groups and others and has developed a "paramilitary" cadre of youth groups who are trained in intervening to prevent violence. The center also cooperates with police training exercises directed at conflict management.

4. Human Rights Watch, "Nigeria," p. 4.

5. Ibid., p. 5.

6. Ibid., p. 6.

7. Ibid., p. 7.

8. Signed August 22, 2002, by the following Christian leaders: Archbishop B. A. Achigili, Elder Saidu Dogo, Bishop Joseph Bogobiri, Bishop A. B Lamido, Rev. Y. B. Sidi, Rev. Habu Mari, Pastor J. Ajayi, Rev. Peter Ahmed, Rev. Jessy Adam, Evangelist James M. Wuye, Mr. E. B. Yero. The declaration was also signed by the following Muslim leaders: Alhaji Ja'afaru Makarfi, Sheikh Zubairu Sirajo, Sheikh Yusuf S. Rigachikun, Sheikh Umaru Suleiman, Mallam Muhammad A. Sa'id, Mallam Ibrahim Nakaka, Imam Muhammad S. Isah, Mallam Hamza A. Ibrahim, Imam Muhammad N. Ashafa, Alhaji Ibrahim Kufena, and Alhaji Balarabe Jigo.

9. Human Rights Watch, "Nigeria," p. 8.

10. A quasi-governmental organization, the National Interfaith Religious Council (NIREC), had been set up by the government in Abuja in September 1999, with twenty-five Muslim and twenty-five Christian leaders. These included such notables in Abuja as Roman Catholic Archbishop John Onaiykan (vice president of CAN) and

Hon. Justice Muhammad Bashir Sambo (chairman, Code of Conduct Tribunal), who have been key to interfaith relations in the federal capital. However, NIREC appears to have had little influence or impact at the northern state level, including Kaduna.

11. An example of the power of Islamic symbols is evident in the disturbances in Makarfi town, in Kaduna State, in April 2004: a Christian youth had allegedly desecrated the Qur'an, and in response an angry mob of Muslim youth set the police station and eight Christian churches on fire. See United Nations, "Nigeria: Tension in Kaduna as Irate Muslims Burn Churches and Police Station," IRIN Report, April 6, 2004.

12. For a discussion of gateways in northern Nigeria, see John N. Paden, *Ahmadu Bello, Sardauna of Sokoto: Values and Leadership in Nigeria* (London: Hodder and Stoughton, 1986).

13. At the end of Ramadan in November 2003, many of the emirate leaders in the north called for peace and tolerance. The emir of Ilorin, Alhaji Ibrahim Sulu Gambari, said "no meaningful development could be achieved in an atmosphere devoid of peace.... Also, governors, other political and religious leaders across the country used the occasion of the Eid-el-Fitr celebration to urge Nigerians to embrace peace [and] to embrace values which will be beneficial to national development." See "Reforms: Obasanjo Pleads for Patience," *Lagos and Abuja ThisDay News*, November 25, 2003.

14. "Two Years of Shari'a in Kano: Shekarau's Humanistic Approach," *Kaduna Weekly Trust*, July 26, 2003.

15. Personal discussions with Governor Shekarau, Washington, April 2004.

16. See "Maccido Tasks FG [federal government] on Security," *Lagos and Abuja ThisDay News*, November 25, 2003. Maccido reportedly cautioned against "the new innovations being introduced into Islam which are against Sharia. He said Muslims should at all times ensure that whatever they do was in agreement with the teachings of the Holy Quran and Hadith of the Holy Prophet. His words: 'You should shun those things that are capable of dividing you and try to unite with one another as one family as the religion of Islam cannot be practised with ignorance.' Maccido appealed to Muslims to intensify efforts in propagating the religion of Islam and work towards enhancing Sharia so as to get maximum blessings from Allah."

17. *Arewa* in Hausa means "northern."

18. The director of Arewa House, Hamid Bobboyi, originally from Adamawa, has taken a key role in providing a "neutral" history of the Tiv-Jukun conflicts in an effort to reduce violence.

19. Personal discussions with Imam Ashafa, Washington, March 2004, and in Kaduna, June 2004.

20. For a sense of northern Christian perspectives on interfaith relations in the First Republic, see Chief Sunday B. Awoniyi, *Sir Ahmadu Bello's Style of Leadership* (Kaduna: Arewa House, Centre for Historical Documentation and Research, Ahmadu Bello University, November 2000).

21. See, for example, "ANPP Protests Obasanjo Interference with Judiciary," *Abuja Daily Trust,* August 8, 2003.

22. Thus three days before the April 19, 2003, elections, the main opposition political parties, chaired by Muhammadu Buhari, called a press conference in Abuja to protest excessive intimidation by the police and military, who were seen to have a clear pro-incumbent (that is, PDP) bias. A key document in the appeals process has been an apparent intercept of a central police directive to support the incumbent national party. See Muhammadu Buhari, "Alternative Perspectives on Nigeria's Political Evolution" (Washington: Woodrow Wilson International Center for Scholars, April 7, 2004).

23. See, for example, "Jihad! Terrorists Invade Nigeria 'Terrorists Were Invited to Kill People in Plateau'—Rev. Yusuf Pam," cover story in *Insider* magazine, no. 24, June 14, 2004. Also, "Emergency Fallout: Ethnic Militias Threaten More Killings; Tension Rises in 5 States; Plot to Cause Chaos in Lagos," cover story, *Week* magazine, June 14, 2004. The inflammatory nature of Nigerian press coverage of violence is also matched by the press's lack of intercultural sensitivity regarding religious symbols, as should be clear from the Miss World incident. The destruction of the *ThisDay* offices in Kaduna was not the first time Muslim youth have attacked northern media houses accused of insulting Islam.

24. As mentioned previously, the *Kaduna Weekly Trust* may provide the best insight (in English) into the crosscurrents within the northern Muslim community.

25. See, for example, "Journalists Cautioned on Reporting the Sultanate," *Lagos and Abuja ThisDay News,* August, 16, 2003.

26. See, for example, Usman Bugaje, "The Caliphate in Modern Nigeria: Ending It, Mending It, or Reinventing It?" *Kaduna Weekly Trust,* August, 8, 2003. Also, Sanusi Lamido Sanusi, "Democracy, Rights and Islam: Theory, Epistemology and the Quest for Synthesis," text presented at an international conference, "Shari'ah Penal and Family Law in Nigeria and in the Muslim World: A Rights-Based Approach," organized by the International Human Rights Law Group, held at Rockview Hotel, Abuja, August 5–7, 2003; and Abdullahi Doki, "Muslim North, the Caliphate, and Sharia States: Reislamization Uncompleted," *Kaduna Weekly Trust,* August 9, 2003.

27. See, for example, "Why Cultists Shun BUK VC," *Abuja Daily Trust,* November 14, 2003. In this article, the Muslim Students Society and other religious bodies in Bayero University, Kano, are credited with helping to curb "the menace of cultism in the institution." The prohibition on alcohol was cited as another factor helping to keep student unrest at bay for at least five years. In addition, "students themselves report any signs of cult activities on the campus to the university authority. . . . [N]on-interference in the union activities of the students also creates understanding and trust between the school authority and the students."

28. In May 2004, when mobs of Muslim youth from urban Kano invaded Bayero University, Kano (BUK), intent on killing Christian staff and students in retribution for the massacres of Muslims in Plateau State, the BUK Muslim Student Society formed a human wall to protect their Christian classmates from harm. This averted a tragedy of even greater proportions.

29. For much of the year before the elections of 2003, the entire university system in Nigeria was shut down over staff wage disputes.

30. The director of Academic Associates/PeaceWorks is Judith Asuni, based in Abuja.

31. The executive director of BAOBAB for Women's Human Rights is Ayesha Imam, originally from Kano. BAOBAB is based on Victoria Island, Lagos.

32. In addition, some Abuja-based law firms have provided free legal counsel to shari'a women defendants. Thus Hauwa Ibrahim has successfully defended Amina Lawal and many others on a pro bono basis.

33. For example, the JNI has complained that there are only sixteen Muslim federal ministers, and none from the southwest.

34. The need for security clearly requires cooperation with traditional rulers. See "Maccido Tasks FG on Security," which notes that Sultan Maccido called on traditional rulers to work hand in hand with security agents because "the royal fathers know their areas of administration better than any other persons."

35. See "Islamic Law in Nigeria: Shilly-Shallying with Sharia," *Economist*, September 27, 2003: "Northerners were tired of rising crime and rampant corruption in public office. Many Muslims believed that the implementation of religious law would bring greedy officials to book, curb violent crime and clean up what they saw as a morally decadent society. It also created thousands of jobs: Islamic vigilantes, and *sharia* preachers and judges are on state payrolls."

Chapter Ten

1. John N. Paden, *Ahmadu Bello, Sardauna of Sokoto: Values and Leadership in Nigeria* (London: Hodder and Stoughton, 1986).

2. According to one account, "On October 13, 2001, days after the commencement of the U.S. military campaign in Afghanistan, several hundred demonstrators gathered in Kano—the largest city in Nigeria's predominantly Muslim northern region—to protest the American action. The protesters carried banners criticizing the United States, and many reportedly displayed images of Osama bin Laden. The peaceful demonstration was immediately followed by rioting and street battles between Christians and Muslims, in which more than 100 people died. The international media reported these events as the most militant anti-American protest around the world since the beginning of hostilities in Afghanistan, and the violence was described as part of a rising tide of Islamic militancy and religious conflict in Nigeria." See Peter Lewis, "Islam, Protest, and Conflict in Nigeria," *Africa Notes*, no. 9 (Washington: Center for Strategic and International Studies, December 2003).

3. The theme of migrant youth and the Islamic schools in Kano in relation to security concerns was addressed in a paper presented at the National Conference on Chieftaincy and Security, to mark the fortieth anniversary of the emir of Kano (Ado Bayero) on the throne, in October 2003. See Ibrahim Ado-Kurawa, "*Ci rani, alma-*

jirance and Security in Kano" (www.kanoonline.com/ibrahimadomajekarofi@ yahoo.com). This sixteen-page report addresses the historical and contemporary practices of voluntary migration during the hot season (*ci rani*) of the *almajirai*, which refers to those who leave home for another place in search of knowledge. The report provides insight into the patterns of Islamic education in Kano, the relationship of the *almajirai* to the state, issues of security, and strategies of socioeconomic development and security.

4. See Moffat Ekoriko, "Three Years of Abacha: Belt Tightening Squeezes the Poorest," *Africa Today*, November–December, 1996, p. 10: "In Owerri, capital of Imo State, irate crowds burned down the homes and business premises of those whom they suspected—including top businessmen and traditional rulers—of taking part in money-making rituals after the discovery of the head of a missing child, two tongues, skulls and other human remains on the premises of the Overcomers Church, one of the so-called 'new breed' Pentecostal churches."

5. See Cynthia Sampson, "'To Make Real the Bond between Us All': Quaker Conciliation during the Nigerian Civil War," in *Religion: The Missing Dimension of Statecraft*, edited by Douglas Johnson and Cynthia Sampson (Oxford University Press, 1994).

6. Anthony Olubunmi Okogie was born June 16, 1936, in Lagos. See appendix B for background.

7. The archbishop of Lagos, Anthony Olubunmi Okogie, has always been regarded as a "political" actor in Nigerian affairs. See, for example, "Okogie Decries Fresh Fuel Price Hike," *Lagos and Abuja ThisDay News*, October 3, 2003. In September 2003 Okogie was elevated to the position of cardinal by Pope John Paul II. After his return from the installation ceremonies in Rome (October 2003), Cardinal Okogie criticized the Nigerian federal government for lack of due respect but praised General Babangida for his congratulatory messages and thanked Babangida "for the leadership he provided the country during his tenure as president." See "Okogie Chides FG: Says Greeting Is Belated; Lauds IBB for Good Leadership," *Daily Independent of Lagos*, October 28, 2003.

8. Sunday Coffie Mbang was born August 26, 1936, in Idua, Eket, Akwa Ibom State. See appendix B for background.

9. See Matthew Hassan Kukah, *Religion, Politics and Power in Northern Nigeria* (Ibadan: Spectrum Books, 1993).

10. Paden, *Ahmadu Bello*.

11. John N. Paden, *Religion and Political Culture in Kano* (University of California Press, 1973).

12. There are many perceptions of what happened in Plateau State in 2004. For a Muslim view, see Audu Zongo, "The Federal Government Should Extend the State of Emergency in Plateau State to Consolidate Peace Gains" (auduzango@yahoo.com [October 31, 2004]): "The State of Emergency in Plateau state has saved the lives, honour, and property of innocent citizens from a murderous ethnic militia supported by cruel politicians and some diabolical 'men of God'. The fact that the State

of Emergency has worked is manifested by sudden cessation of incitements and violence in Plateau state. The secondary effect is felt in neighbouring states where ethnic/religious tension has suddenly waned. . . . The task of the current care taker government is to fish out those who have incited, abated or given material support (arms, ammunition & vehicles) to the murderers that committed the ethnic cleansing (bandits that murdered people in Shendam and the retired soldiers/thugs that murdered people in Yelwa). . . . The social problem of ethnic/religious discrimination and persecution, especially against Muslim tribes must be halted. Their exclusion in civil service as well as recruitment in the military and police must be addressed as a matter of urgency." See also the press reports in *ThisDay News,* October 3, 2004, which note that under the state of emergency "the state has been divided into pro and anti-return of the suspended governor."

13. *Daily Independent of Lagos,* October 26, 2004.

Chapter Eleven

1. See Mazi Njaka, *Igbo Political Culture* (Northwestern University Press, 1974).

2. See ibid. This volume was part of a series on African political cultures and national integration, edited by John Paden and Ronald Cohen.

3. Moffat Ekoriko, "Three Years of Abacha: Belt Tightening Squeezes the Poorest," *Africa Today,* November–December 1996, p. 11.

Chapter Twelve

1. As noted previously, the deadly clash in late December 2003 between the *"hijra"* group in Yobe State and local authorities and police has caused alarm in government circles. (Local hunters reportedly killed many of the group, after they killed the leader of the hunters.) The fact that the group had been migrating east, and for whatever reason attacked the local police station on New Year's eve, raises questions about the role of local authorities and police in monitoring such movements. According to *BBC News,* "Tracking Down Nigeria's Taliban Sect," January 14, 2004, the group was located about 2 kilometers outside Kannama village, Yobe State, in makeshift tents, and "all but seven of an estimated 60 known members have been killed or captured." The group was known locally as *Ahlul Sunna Wal Jama* and, some feared, was part of a worldwide movement. If the group had continued east, they would have come to Borno State, and then on to Chad Republic. Hence Borno State has set up a commission of inquiry. See "Borno Govt. Sets Up Panel on 'Taliban,'" *Abuja Daily Trust,* January 13, 2004. The *Kaduna Weekly Trust* undertook a series of investigative reports on the group in early 2004, but it was not clear in the immediate aftermath who the members of the group were, except that they appeared to be young, educated, and possibly related to well-known families in the southwest.

2. See *The Nigeria Democracy Act,* H. Rept. 2697 (Government Printing Office, 1995).

3. Matthew Hassan Kukah, *Religion, Politics and Power in Northern Nigeria* (Ibadan: Spectrum Books, 1993), p. 204.

4. Ibid., p. 221.

5. The outmigration of professionals from predominantly Muslim countries has been a common phenomenon, especially in the Arab world. Diaspora members returning to countries such as Iraq or Afghanistan in the aftermath of regime change may well be able to influence conflict resolution efforts both before and after the advent of political crises.

6. The standard estimate for the extent of HIV infections in Nigeria is about 5 percent of the population. In a country of 130 million or more, this is a high number. Nigeria's media often quote a figure, as of 2004, of 8 million such HIV infections. For more detailed analysis, see Daniel J. Smith, "HIV/AIDS in Nigeria: The Challenges of a National Epidemic," in *Crafting the New Nigeria: Confronting the Challenges,* edited by Robert I. Rotberg (Boulder, Colo.: Lynne Rienner, 2004), pp. 199–217.

7. Muhammadu Buhari has cautioned the United States and the world that ignoring Nigeria will have far-reaching negative consequences for the region and beyond: "An unstable Nigeria driven by internal wars, insurrections, or other manifestations of a failed state has the potential to destabilize the whole continent of Africa. The common symptomatic phenomena of internal disarray by way of civil wars and refugees and internally displaced persons have been dealt with by the world with varying successes in the past. . . . But the break-up of Nigeria with a population of 130 million will produce a refugee crisis of unimaginable proportions. African countries will be overwhelmed and both Europe and Asia will be under severe strain. The highest number of refugees the world has had to deal with has never exceeded 25 million, with another 30 million or so displaced persons. This is about one-third of the refugee potential of a war-torn Nigeria. The international community, especially the U.S. will see it in their interest to forestall this major tragedy for Africa and for the world." See Muhammadu Buhari, "Alternative Perspectives on Nigeria's Political Evolution" (Washington: Woodrow Wilson International Center for Scholars, April 7, 2004).

8. See Donald G. Morrison, Robert C. Mitchell, and John N. Paden, *Black Africa: A Comparative Handbook,* 2d ed. (New York: Paragon House, 1989).

9. The emirate combination is more in the British tradition, where there is no independent judicial review, rather than in the U.S. separation-of-powers tradition. The emir in northern Nigeria was essentially a chief justice, responsible for administering "justice," and was encouraged to be impartial by the protection of lifetime appointment.

Appendix A

1. For full names of political parties, see the list of abbreviations.

2. The death of Aminu Kano in April 1983 prior to the election and the succession of Hassan Yusuf to leadership in the PRP clearly affected the election results in Kano.

3. Regarding the 1983 elections in Hausaland, see William Miles, *Elections in Nigeria: A Grassroots Perspective* (Boulder, Colo.: Lynne Rienner, 1988).

4. According to some "fresh facts," twenty "leaders of thought" in Yorubaland (including the chief of general staff, Lieutenant-General Oladipo Diya) came out in support of Abiola's continued incarceration at a secret meeting in Hamdala Hotel (in Kaduna) in June 1994, in return for plum contracts and political appointments. See "Secret Document Exposes Yoruba Betrayal of MKO," *Ibadan Daily Independent,* October 3, 2003. At the time, Diya (Yoruba/Christian) was second in command to Abacha. (Diya was born in 1944 in Ogun State and attended Yaba Methodist primary school in Lagos, before going on to his military career. He was promoted to major-general in 1988.)

Index

Aare Musulumi, 65, 100–01, 102. *See also* Alao, Abdul Azeez Arisekola

Abacha, Sani: background and biography of, 63, 123, 240; death of, 157; deposition of the sultan of Sokoto, 88, 128, 129; as military ruler, 43, 50, 123, 124; six-zone system, 209, 227

Abacha (Sani) regime: Abubakar, Atiku, and, 146; characteristics of, 28; emigration of professionals, 132, 211; hanging of Ken Sara Wiwo and others in *1995*, 25; international community and, 24; plots against, 110, 123; religious and political issues, 101, 195, 196–97, 207, 208–09; response to conflict, 213; Zakzaki, Mallam Ibrahim, and, 187

Abdul-Kareem, Ustaz Abubakar Rabo, 167

Abdulsalami, Abubakar, 209

Abeokuta (Ogun, Nigeria), 49, 100, 108

Abiola, M. K. O.: arrest of, 231; Dasuki, Ibrahim, and, 129; election of *1993* and, 49, 106, 121, 195, 196, 231; political leanings of, 65, 121, 195; religious leanings of, 113–14, 196

Abortion, 103

Abubakar III (Sultan), 127, 186, 197

Abubakar, Abdulsalami, 63

Abubakar, Atiku: background of, 158–59, 269n18, 274n5; dropping of title of "Alhaji," 192; elections of *2007* and, 146,

155; as a political leader, 63; political leanings of, 121; views of shari'a, 156, 187

Abubakar Rimi faction, 116, 117. *See also* Rimi, Abubakar

Abuja (Federal Capital Territory, Nigeria): Christian facility in, 190; courts in, 51; Miss World riots and, 174; mosque in, 126; Muslims in, 63, 59; as federal capital, 19, 25, 50, 66, 110–12, 140–41, 181, 193, 218; petroleum revenues and, 23; Western diplomats in, 22, 24, 28

AD. *See* Alliance for Democracy

Adamawa state (Nigeria), 45, 63, 142, 144, 149, 207

Adegbite, Abdu-Lateef Oladimeji, 65, 127, 170, 185–86, 236

Adesanoye, Festus Ibidapo (Oba), 135

Adesida, Adeboboye (Oba), 135

Academic Associates/Peace Works, 180, 280n30

ACF. *See* Arewa Consultative Forum

Afghanistan, 187, 280n2

Africa: identities and values in, 34, 83; Muslim communities and populations in, 45–46, 244n19; religious issues in, 18; violent conflict in, 217; United States and, 223–24; Western views of, 28. *See also individual countries, states, and cities*

African syncretist churches, 189

African Union (AU), 15, 223

Agricultural issues, 97, 193, 195, 214–15

Ahmadiyya, 257n4

Ahmadu Bello University (Zaria, Nigeria), 22, 60, 68, 98, 180, 191. *See also* Nigerian College of Arts and Science

Aku Uku of Wukari (Jukun), 46

Aladura (praying people) movement, 189, 191, 260n25. *See also* Christians and Christian communities; Religious issues

Alao, Abdul Azeez Arisekola, 65, 100–01, 170. *See also Aare Musulumi*

Albright, Madeleine, 15, 26–27

Alhaji (someone who has made the pilgrimage), 192

Alkur'ani Maigirma Zuwa Harshen Hausa (Gummi; Holy Qur'an in Hausa), 61

Alliance for Democracy (AD). *See* Political parties—specific

Alli, Chris, 196

All Nigeria People's Party (ANPP): democratic federalism and, 51; elections of *2003*, 123, 145–46, 149, 153, 159–61; elections of *2007*, 155; judicial process and, 155; military officers and, 124; National Political Reform Dialogue and, 212; north-east alliance and, 205; progressive-conservatives and, 118–19; shari'a and, 161–62, 182

All Peoples Party (APP). *See* All Nigeria People's Party; Political parties—specific

All Progressive Grand Alliance. *See* Political parties—specific

Al Qaeda, 2, 214, 241n2, 252n2

Amana (trust), 69

Aminci, Abdullahi Garba, 167

Aminu Kano movement, 115–17. *See also* Kano, Aminu

Anglican Church, 189, 190, 191, 204. *See also* Christians and Christian communities; Religious issues

Anglican Church Missionary Society (CMS), 108, 259n22, 259n23

Animists and pagans. *See Maguzawa*

Annual pilgrimage. *See* Mecca; Muslims and Muslim communities

ANPP. *See* All Nigeria People's Party

APP. *See* All Peoples Party

Arewa Consultative Forum (ACF), 178

Arewa House (Kaduna, Nigeria), 153, 177, 278n17

Arinze, Francis (Cardinal), 18

Arna (pagans), 69

Asia, 82

Atta (of Igala and of Igbirra), 46, 65

Attah, Mahmud, 65–66

AU. *See* African Union

Awoniyi, Sunday, 178

Babangida, Ibrahim Badamasi: attempted assassination of, 128, 194; attempted coup of *1989* against, 105; background and biography of, 63, 65, 123, 236; coup of *1985* and, 50, 193; Dasuki, Ibrahim, and, 127; democratic federalism and, 50; elections of *2003* and, 154, 216; elections of *2007* and, 123; leadership qualities of, 273n48; as presidential candidate, 146, 155, 156; primary elections of *1992* and, 229–30; religious leanings of, 124; reorganization of *1991*, 206; transition to civilian rule, 87; Yar'Adua, Musa, and, 122

Babangida (Ibrahim) regime, 194, 208, 229

Babangida, Mariam, 66

Bachama, 46–47

Bafarawa, Attahiru, 146, 163

Balewa, Abubakar Tafawa, 63, 119

Bangladesh, 2

BAOBAB, 181, 187

Baptist Church, 191, 204. *See also* Christians and Christian communities; Religious issues

Barewa College (Zaria, Nigeria), 119

Ba sarki sai Allah (no king but God), 204

Bauchi, Dahiru, 61

Bauchi city (Nigeria), 169

Bauchi emirate state (Nigeria), 63, 78, 149, 158, 160, 169, 194

Bayero University (Kano, Nigeria), 68, 98, 117, 180, 279n28

Begging, 166, 275n15

Bello, Ahmadu, 59, 60, 63, 119, 158, 177, 186

Bello, Mohammed Attahiru, 166

Bello, Muhammad, 68

Bendel state (Nigeria), 228

Benedict XVI (Pope), 18. *See also* Christians and Christian communities; Religious issues; Roman Catholic church

Benue province (Nigeria), 192

Benue state (Nigeria), 63, 142, 149, 228

Beriberi, 46, 64

Bhutto, Benazir, 103

Biafra, 42, 189, 192, 205, 248n47. *See also* Civil war

Bible, 101, 102, 190

Bin Laden, Osama, 26, 34, 36, 187

Birnin Kebbi (Nigeria), 206

Bornawa, 46

Borno city-state (Nigeria): authority in, 66; civic culture of, 219; Dasuki, Ibrahim, and, 185–86; emirate states and, 80; ethnic and community issues, 67; as an Islamic community, 45–46, 57, 62, 63–64; location of, 149; partitioning of, 194–95, 206; political parties in, 143–44, 227, 228; shari'a in, 148, 158, 168, 170; *shehu* of, 63; in the six geocultural zones, 45; women in, 124

Borno empire, 37, 58

Bosnia, 36

Britain. *See* United Kingdom

British Commonwealth. *See* United Kingdom

Brzezinski, Zbigniew, 33

Buhari, Muhammadu: background and biography of, 123, 132–33, 237–38; coup of *1983* and, 50; elections of *2003* and, 132–33, 153–54, 171; as military head of state, 114, 193; political leadership and, 63; as presidential candidate, 146, 155–56, 159, 160, 197, 216; progressive-conservatives and, 118–19, 124; role of, 209; views of, 262n17, 283n7; Yar'Adua, Musa and, 122

Buhari (Muhammadu) regime, 208

Buhari Organization, The (TBO), 153, 154, 159, 212

Bush, George H. W., 27

Bush, George W., 15, 26, 27

Bush (George W.) administration, 26–27

Calendars. *See* Culture and cultural issues

CAN. *See* Christian Association of Nigeria

Carter, Jimmy, 269n14

Catholic church. *See* Roman Catholic church

Center for Strategic and International Studies, 18

Central Bank of Nigeria, 119, 120

Centre for Democratic Research and Training (Bayero University), 117

Chad, 23

China, 20, 35, 222

Chirac, Jacques, 26

Christian Association of Nigeria (CAN): background of, 191; divisions in, 197; FOMWAN and, 103; head of, 190, 194; membership of, 178; NSCIA and, 128–29, 178; power sharing and, 194; shari'a and, 191–92; violence in Kaduna and, 174

Christians and Christian communities, 18, 75. *See also* Benedict XVI; John Paul II; Religious issues; *individual denominations and churches*

Christians and Christian communities—Nigeria: branches of, 188–89; in the caliphal system, 77–78; churches on public space, 190; conflict resolution, 175; education and, 104, 105; evangelization and proselytizing by, 78; history of, 108–09; in Kaduna, 172, 174; killing of Muslims in *2004*, 23; missionary work by, 22–23, 108–09, 149, 189, 190, 259n22; Muslim community and, 9, 22, 23, 100, 101–02, 104, 105; Muslim views of, 77–78, 120; National Council for Religious Affairs and, 127; propaganda, 105; religious pluralism, 214; tolerance and conflict, 188–97, 204; at the University of Ibadan, 104; in Yoruba-speaking areas, 107–09

Christian Religious Knowledge (CRK), 102

Church of England. *See* Anglican Church

Ciroma, Adamu ("*Dallatun Fika*"), 64, 119–21, 229

Ciroma, Liman, 64, 154

Civic society. *See* Culture and cultural issues

Civil and human rights issues, 2, 21–22, 25. *See also* Culture and cultural issues

Civil/civic culture and society. *See* Culture and cultural issues

Civil war (*1967–70*): assassinations preceding the war, 192; civic culture and, 221; coalition during, 213; First Republic and, 50; lives lost in, 3, 192; participants, 42; partition option and, 55, 248n47; postwar period, 184, 193; religious factors, 189–90; Yar'Adua, Musa, and, 122

Civil war (*1890s*), 45

Clinton, Bill, 15

CMS. *See* Anglican Church Missionary Society

Cold war, 17, 32–33

Commission on International Religious Freedom, U.S. (USCIRF), 23

Conflict and disputes: calendar and seasonal effects on, 71; conflict and tolerance in the Muslim community, 183–88; constitutional federal character provision, 160, 194; economic factors of, 32; evaluation of conceptual models, 213–19; flight and, 210; Muslim civic cultures and, 219–22; religious conflicts in Nigeria, 30–32; role of a "free press" in, 174–75; symbolism and, 184; tolerance and conflict between Muslims and Christians, 192–97; types, patterns, and study of, 32–33; values, identities, and civic cultures, 33–34. *See also* Christians and Christian communities—Nigeria; Muslims and Muslim communities—Nigeria; Peace committees; Religious issues; Shari'a; Theories and models; *individual cities and states*

Conflict resolution: civil/civic society and, 4, 29, 32–35; churches and, 191; communications and crisis management networks, 197–99; cultural issues of,

205, 210–12; due process and, 22; effect of civil values on conflict and its resolution, 203–06; exile, 210; expectations and realities and, 32; jailing, 211; mechanisms of, 171, 210–13; National Commission on Peace and, 154; nongovernmental organizations and, 174, 180–81; NSCIA and, 130; political factors, 3, 8, 194–95

Conflict resolution—Nigeria: challenges of, 222, 225–26; central role of law, 97–98; civil/civic values and, 203–06, 219–22; civil war and, 193; culture of, 210–12; democratic federalism and, 206–08; evaluation of conceptual models, 213–19; federal government policy, 181–82; in the Fourth Republic, 176; mechanisms of, 5, 15, 21–22, 29, 32, 52, 212–13; nongovernmental organizations and, 181; orientation toward, 92–97, 135–36; power sharing, symbolism, and leadership, 55, 208–09; in shari'a states, 174–82; traditional rulers and, 158; United States and, 223–24; Yoruba rulers and, 100. *See also* Emirs; National Council for Religious Affairs; Peace committees; Shari'a; *individual cities and states*

Constitutions and constitutional issues: bans on cults and secret societies, 189, 216; conflict mediation and, 182; economic issues, 207; decolonization and, 40; federal character provision, 9, 141, 142–43, 157–58, 160–62, 181, 194, 208, 218; judicial and legal issues, 142, 147, 152–53; individual and fundamental rights and, 81, 152; national constitutional councils, 212; National Political Reform Dialogue and, 140; police and military security, 176, 179; presidential issues, 142–43, 155; press and free speech issues, 212–13; religious freedom, 152, 216; shari'a, 146–53, 199; six-zone system, 141, 227; state and religion, 199; three-tier vertical federalism, 44, 207. *See also* Shari'a

Constitutions and constitutional issues—
specific constitutions: *1979*, 140, 160,
272n42; *1989/1993*, 140; *1999*, 44, 50,
140, 160, 179, 182, 227, 269n12, 272n42
Constitutional Conference (Nigeria; *1957*),
40–41
Council of Ulama (Zaria, Nigeria), 212
Council on Foreign Relations, 18
Country Reports on Human Rights Practices
(U.S. Department of State), 19
Coups, 255n3; *1966*; 59, 220–21, 268n6;
1983, 50, 193; *1985*, 193; *1990*
(attempted), 105–06; 128, 214, 258n13
Crime. *See* Culture and cultural issues; Emi-
rates and emirate states; Republics,
Nigerian—Fourth Republic
Criminal Code of Northern Nigeria, 96
CRK. *See* Christian Religious Knowledge
Crocker, Chester, 27–28
Cross River state (Nigeria), 228
Crowther, Samuel Adjai, 259n23
Culture and cultural issues: calendars, 34,
71–73, 129; civic cultures, 3, 4, 8, 33–34,
29, 55, 70–77, 203–09, 219–22, 223; conflict and conflict resolution, 17, 29, 36,
52, 203–09, 219–22; crime and punishment, 245nn23–26; of emirates, 83;
ethnic affiliation and identity, 80, 203;
family and customary laws, 102; geocultural divisions, 227, 231, 248n47;
instructors of, 72; lineage, 205, 211;
marriage and divorce, 63, 79, 80, 83, 101,
102, 103, 112, 125; of Muslims, 2, 17, 64,
183, 190, 219; orientations to time,
70–77, 205; overlapping dimensions of,
3–4; religion and, 82; variations in identities and values, 55–69; Western culture,
134

Da'awah committees (Islamic promotion
groups), 167
Danforth, John, 24
Dantata, Aminu, 170
Darfur. *See* Sudan
Dariye, Joshua, 142
Dass area people, 46–47

Dasuki, Ibrahim (Sultan), 62, 88, 127–28,
129, 185–86, 194, 196
Dasuki, Sambo, 128
Death and the King's Horseman (Soyinka),
107–08
De Gaulle, Charles, 17, 141
Democracy, 26, 27
Democratic federalism: alternatives to, 35;
civil/civic society in, 3, 4, 29, 52; conflict
resolution and, 35, 206–08; forms of, 17;
local and national government in, 25,
29; Nigerian attempts at, 3, 5, 8–9, 15,
17, 28, 29, 49–51, 52, 206–08, 223; political evolution and, 222; postcolonial
states, 35; shari'a-based policy and, 68;
shift from military rule to, 8. *See also*
Nigeria—Fourth Republic
Diya, Oladipo, 209

Economic Community of West African
States (ECOWAS), 15, 55, 135, 223
Economic issues: conflict, 32; criminal fac-
tors, 27–28; ethnic market dominance,
23; in the Nigerian emirates, 90–91;
shari'a, 170; sociopolitical stability, 24;
technological development, 32; trade
and trading networks, 64, 88. *See also*
Globalization and global issues
ECOWAS. *See* Economic Community of
West African States
ECWA. *See* Evangelical Church of West
Africa
EDDI. *See* Education for Democracy and
Democracy Initiative
Edo of Benin, 49
Educational issues: begging, 166, 275n15;
FOMWAN, 103; government takeover of
schools, 190; in Ibadan, 102; intergenerational tensions and, 132; Islamic
beliefs, 69; Izalatul group schools, 169;
leadership training, 225; *madrasas*, 154;
Muslim students, 104–06, 245n29,
246n34, 246n36, 257n11, 279n27,
279n28; peace committees, 198, 212,
225–26, 257n10; progressive and
progressive-conservative values, 115,

116, 119; school closings, 105; science
and technology courses, 154; secular-
nonsecular friction, 216; security
regulations, 224; sufi and non-sufi
learning, 270n21; of traditional rulers,
118; universities and educated elites,
180; U.S. aid to, 243n14, 247n43;
women's education, 103, 104, 125; Western education, 184, 190–91; in
Yorubaland, 102. *See also* Universities;
individual universities
Education for Democracy and Democracy
Initiative (EDDI), 24
Efik, 49
Egba state (Nigeria), 48
Egypt, 2, 18, 82–83, 211
Ekiti Parapo state (Nigeria), 48
Elections: aftermath of the *2003* elections,
153–56; appeals, 178–79; Buhari,
Muhammadu, and, 123; candidates, 49;
federal character provision and, 142–43;
federal elections, 141; Fourth Republic
and, 51, 139, 140; political parties in,
143–46, 160–62; runoffs and appeals,
252n6; three-tier elections, 142–43. *See
also* Political issues; Political parties
Elections—specific: *1951–52*, 40; *1959*, 41,
205, 231; *1964*, 231; *1979*, 193, 227, 228,
229t, 231; *1983*, 193, 227, 228, 229, 230t,
231; *1992*, 229–31; *1993*, 66, 106–07,
113–14, 119, 120, 121, 129, 195, 196,
205, 231, 232, 268n6; *1998–99*, 49, 140,
142–44, 195, 269n14; *2003*, 9, 49, 51,
123, 144–45, 153–56, 160–61, 171,
181–82, 195, 197, 216, 269n10, 270n27,
279n22; *2004*, 267n40, 268n7; *2007*, 181,
267n41
Emirates and emirate states: administration
and administrative appointments in,
78–79, 82, 84, 87–88, 91–92; authority
patterns and legal systems in, 70, 80–81,
84, 86–88, 91, 92–98, 204; during the
colonial period, 70, 78, 80; conflict and
conflict resolution in, 89, 92–98, 106,
183, 205, 210, 213–14; cultural and ethnic factors, 57, 83, 110, 205, 206, 219;
economic issues, 90–91; geocultural
zones and, 45, 48f; international relationships, 82–83; leadership in, 63,
86–87; lingua franca of, 70, 80; mallams
of, 85–86, 87, 88, 90, 94, 97, 98; military
and defense in, 89–90; mystical traditions in, 72, 74, 75, 76; orientations to
authority, community, and time, 70–88,
185; personal and historical destiny,
75–77, 81; political systems and communities, 78, 79–81, 82, 86–87, 143–44;
private and public sectors in, 89–92;
religious issues in, 75, 78–79, 81, 83–84,
213–14; role of law in, 97–98, 147; scope
of the state and civic space, 88–92;
shari'a in, 89, 92–93, 95, 147; women's
issues in, 124–25. *See also* Sokoto
Caliphate; *individual emirate states*
Emirs ("royal fathers"; *sarki*): body guard
of, 93–94; conflict mediation and,
135–36, 175, 176, 191, 198, 205, 210,
220, 283n9; elections of *1999* and, 141;
elections of *2003* and, 154; exile and
flight of, 210; NSCIA and JNI members,
177; palace guard of, 89–90; political
issues and, 70, 156; role and powers of,
79, 84, 85, 88, 91, 94–95, 97, 118
England. *See* United Kingdom
English (language). *See* Languages
Etsu Nupe. *See* Ndayako, Umaru Sanda
European Union (EU), 21–22. *See also individual countries*
Evangelical churches, 23, 175, 190, 214, 223.
See also Christians and Christian communities; Religious issues
Evangelical Church of West Africa (ECWA),
190–91

Fasinro, Hassan, 113
Fatwas (legal opinion decrees), 171, 174
Federal Capital Territory (Nigeria). *See*
Abuja
Federal character. *See* Constitution and con-
stitutional issues
Federal Character Commission, 143
Federal Decree *30*, 191

Federalism, 204, 206, 219. *See also* Democratic federalism

Federation of Muslim Women's Associations in Nigeria (FOMWAN), 102–04, 125–26, 130, 178, 181, 186, 263n24

Fez (Morocco), 82

Fika (Borno, Nigeria), 64

Fika, Adamu, 64

First Bank Plc, 170

Fodio, Abdullahi, 68

Fodio, Usman dan: death of, 58; *Izala* and, 59; jihad of, 101, 183; Muslim purification movement of, 57; reforms of, 63; Sokoto caliphal system and, 76–77

Fodio, Uthman Dan (Shaykh). *See* Fodio, Usman dan

FOMWAN. *See* Federation of Muslim Women's Associations in Nigeria

France, 17, 140, 141, 222

Fulani empire and emirs, 37, 49, 62, 82, 206

Fulani invasion (nineteenth century), 64

Fulbright program (U.S.), 19

Fundamentalism, 2, 32–33, 215

Futi, Umar, 58

Gambari, Ibrahim Agboola, 106, 233–34

Gambari, Sule, 106

Gambari, Sulu, 176

Ganduje, Abdullahi Umar, 168

Gbagyi (Gwari), 46–47, 66, 73

George, Olabode, 113

Gidado, Ibrahim, 163

Globalization and global issues: complexities of, 1; effects of, 2; federalism and, 139; political issues of, 27; stability, 3; of technologies and communications, 29; U.S.-Saudi alliance and, 20. *See also* International community

Global Network for Islamic Justice (GNIJ), 166

GNIJ. *See* Global Network for Islamic Justice

Gombe state (Nigeria), 63, 148, 149, 158, 160, 169

Gongola emirate state (Nigeria), 63, 78. *See also* Taraba state

Government. *See* Nigeria; States and governments

Gowon, Yakubu, 193, 209

Great Britain. *See* United Kingdom

Great Nigeria People's Party (GNPP). *See* Political parties—specific

Gulf War (*1990–91*), 132. *See also* Iraq War

Gummi, Abubakar (grand khadi; Northern Nigeria), 59, 60–61, 131, 147, 184–85

Gurr, Ted, 3, 33

Gusau (Zamfara, Nigeria), 166

Gwari. *See* Gbagyi

Habe rulers, 57

Hadith, 59, 60, 97, 185, 221

Haruna, Boni, 142

Hassan, Yakubu Musa, 167

Hausa (language). *See* Languages

Hausa communities: *bori* traditions, 72; decisionmaking culture in, 204; in the emirates, 206; establishment authorities, 183; Hausa Christians, 172; migrants, 23; nineteenth-century rulers, 57; trading system of, 58; youth movement of, 59. *See also* Languages—specific

Hijra (flight), 170, 188, 255n5

Hisba (enforcers), 163, 166, 167, 168, 169

History and historical destiny, 75–77

Human rights issues. *See* Civil and human rights issues

Human Rights Watch, 23–24

Huntington, Samuel, 32, 34–35, 36, 213–14, 218

Hussein, Saddam, 26, 248n52. *See also* Gulf War; Iraq; Iraq War

Ibadan (Oyo, Nigeria): assassination of government leaders in, 192; capital city issues, 111; centers of power in, 108; creation of, 48; customary law in, 104; Hausa migrants to, 23; mosque in; Muslim community in, 99–101, 102; national conference in *1950*, 40; scholars from, 65; shari'a law in, 112; Tijaniyya brotherhood in, 58. *See also* Tijaniyya brotherhood; University of Ibadan

Ibibio, 49

IDB. *See* Islamic Development Bank

Identities, 2, 34, 35

Idiagbon, Tunde, 114

Ife (Nigeria), 48, 100

Igbirra (Nigeria), 65

Igboland and Igbo communities: construction in Abuja by, 193; geocultural zoning and, 45; political issues in, 48f, 49, 228; religious issues in, 107, 189; as a segmental society, 110, 204; violence in Kano and, 192; Yoruba and, 205

Igbo language. *See* Languages

Ihiyaus Sunnah wa Ikhmadul Bidi'ah (*Izala;* "In favor of Sunna and against innovation"), 59. *See also* Izala

Ijaw, 49

Ijebu city state (Yoruba, Nigera), 48

Ijebu-Ode (Nigeria), 113

Ijo Orunmila (Church of Orunmila), 109

Ikhwan, 69

Ile Ife town (Osun, Nigeria), 47–48

Ilesha state (Nigeria), 48

Ilorin emirate state (Nigeria): as bridge or flashpoint, 100, 106; as city and emirate, 100, 106; culture of, 45, 49, 106; emirs of, 106; religion in, 72, 106; scholars from, 65; Sokoto conquest of, 48

Ilorin (Kwara State, Nigeria), 49, 64

India, 2, 36, 222

Indonesia, 2, 26

Institute of Peace (U.S.), 19

Inter-Faith Mediation Center (Kaduna, Nigeria), 29, 171, 178, 180–81, 277n3

International community, 13, 17, 21–29. *See also* Globalization and global issues

Iran, 2, 68–69, 76, 83, 129, 187

Iraq, 82, 248n52

Iraq War (*2003–*), 26–27, 132, 133. *See also* Gulf War; Hussein, Saddam

Ireland, 189

IRK. *See* Islamic Religious Knowledge

Islam. *See* Muslims and Muslim communities

Islamic Development Bank (IDB), 170

Islamic Religious Knowledge (IRK), 102, 105, 188, 256n7

Islamic Science Institute (Sokoto, Nigeria), 163

Islamic way. *See* Shari'a

Itsekiri, 49

Izala (anti-innovation legalists), 177, 184, 253n11, 270n22

JAIZ International, 170

Jakande, Lateef, 65

Jama'atu Nasril Islam (JNI; Society for the Victory of Islam), 174, 177, 178, 185–86, 212

Jesus (*Isa*), 81. *See also* Christians and Christian communities

Jigawa state (Nigeria), 63, 148–49, 168, 206

Jihad: definition of Hausa rulers, 57; of Fodio, Usman dan, 101, 183; intentional suicide during, 75; of the nineteenth century, 78; patterns of Muslim identity, 63; political axis from Ibadan to Lagos and, 64; Sokoto jihadists, 46

Jinns (spirits). *See* Mysticism

JNI. *See Jama'atu Nasril Islam*

John Paul II (Pope), 17–18. *See also* Christians and Christian communities; Religious issues; Roman Catholic church

Joint Services Command and Staff College (Shrivenham, UK), 122

Jokolo, Mustapha, 156

Jos town (Plateau, Nigeria), 60–61, 149, 184, 190, 196

Judaism, 75

Juergensmeyer, Mark, 32–33, 34, 213, 215–16, 218

Jukun people, 149

Jurisprudential systems. *See* Conflict and dispute resolution; Nigeria

Justice, 2, 22, 23, 25. *See also* Conflict and dispute resolution; Nigeria; Shari'a

Kabara, Nasiru (Shaykh; Kano), 58, 61

Kaduna city (Kaduna, Nigeria), 60–61, 147, 153, 158, 171–75, 184

Kaduna Peace Declaration of Religious Leaders, 173

Kaduna state (Nigeria): assassination of government leaders in, 192; caliphal system and, 63; Christians in, 172; colonial period and, 37; elections of *2003*, 159, 161; ethnoreligious conflict in, 23, 78, 169, 170, 171, 172–75, 182, 192; government of, 158; *Izala* in, 60–61; Kano and, 184; leadership in, 176; location of, 149; political issues, 96, 148; religious issues in, 158; shari'a in, 163, 169–70, 172–73, 277n2; sufi brotherhoods and, 59; violence in, 23, 172–75, 277n1, 277n2

Kaduna Weekly Trust, 177, 275n10

Kafanchan (Kaduna, Nigeria), 172

Kafirai (non-Muslims), 57

Kano, Aminu, 59, 115, 116, 117, 119. *See also* Aminu Kano movement

Kano city (Nigeria), 121–23, 126

Kano emirate and state (Nigeria): Buhari, Muhammadu, rally in, 153; as a caliphal area, 63; civil war in, 45, 184; conflict resolution in, 175, 177, 178; elections of *2003*, 159, 160, 161; emirate council, 155, 188; ethnoreligious conflict, 78, 171; location of, 148–49; market in, 88, 90; partitioning of, 194–95, 206; political parties in, 143, 146, 188, 227, 228; political points of view in, 117, 159; rivalries with, 184; shari'a in, 148, 158, 161–62, 167–68, 188; students and study in, 58; sufism in, 59, 61, 167, 184, 188; violence in, 23–24, 185, 187–88, 192, 196, 265n29, 279n28, 280n2

Kano School for Arabic Studies (KSAS), 98

Kanuri peoples, 37, 64

Kanuri (language). *See* Languages

Kataf community, 172

Katsina Islamic University, 154, 255n6

Katsina state (Nigeria): as a caliphal area, 63; elections of *2003*, 159, 160, 161; political parties in, 143; religious issues in, 78; shari'a in, 148–49, 166–67; violence in, 187, 194

Kebbi state (Nigeria), 63, 148

Kerry, John, 27

Khartoum, 24

Khomeini, Ruhollah (Ayatollah), 187

Kingibe, Baba Gana, 64, 121, 195, 231

Kofa (gateway), 175

Kogi state (Nigeria), 63, 149, 190

Koran. *See* Qur'an

Koroma (person in charge of grains), 90–91

KSAS. *See* Kano School for Arabic Studies

Kuwait, 61

Kwankwaso, Rabiu, 161

Kwara state (Nigeria): as a caliphal area, 63, 64, 100, 149; ethnoreligious conflict in, 78; as a non-shari'a state, 149; political parties in, 144, 228. *See also* Ilorin; Kogi state

Lagos city (Nigeria), 110–12

Lagos state (Nigeria): assassination of government leaders in, 192; Christianity in, 108, 189; during the colonial period, 37; coup of *1990* and, 194; ethnoreligious conflict in, 23; House of Representatives in, 40; jihad and, 64; move of diplomats from, 28; Muslim identity in, 63, 99–100; political parties in, 145; shari'a courts in, 113. *See also* University of Lagos

Languages: geocultural and ethnolinguistic issues, 17, 19–20, 36, 37–39, 45–49, 50, 63, 221; lingua francas, 20, 70, 80, 224; in Nigeria, 45, 46, 47, 49, 134; sufi brotherhoods and, 131

Languages—specific: Arabic, 64, 69, 79, 101, 105, 126, 130, 131, 185, 211, 221; English, 69, 125, 126, 130, 131, 211, 221; Fulfulde, 79, 131; Hausa, 20, 46, 47, 61, 65, 70, 71–78, 79, 84–85, 89–91, 93, 94, 100, 131, 147, 185, 221, 224, 256n7; Kanuri, 46, 64; Igbo, 45, 49, 66; Yoruba, 49, 64, 65, 72, 100–01, 221. *See also* Hausa communities; Yorubaland and Yoruba communities

Libya, 129

Liquefied natural gas (LNG), 13. *See also* Petroleum and petroleum industry

LNG. *See* Liquefied natural gas

Lokoja (Nigeria), 37

Lugard, Frederick, 37
Lukman, Rilwan, 19
Lyman, Princeton, 18, 28

Mabogunje, Akin, 111
Maccido, Muhammad (Sultan), 127, 128, 135, 186, 197
Madina, 64, 210
Madrasas, 154
Maguzawa (animists, pagans), 77–78, 107, 204
Mahdi and *Mahdi* movement, 76, 129, 216
Maitatsine cult, 185. *See also* Marwa, Muhammad
Makarfi, Ahmed Mohammed, 146, 169, 173, 177
Makarfi town (Kaduna, Nigeria), 278n11
Malami, Shehu, 128, 154, 176
Malaysia, 15
Mali, 23
Maliki law and tradition, 97, 147, 183, 273n1
Mallam, 256n7. *See also* Emirates and emirate states
Mambayya House, 117. *See also* Kano, Aminu
Mande, Bala, 161, 162
Maps: African long distance trade routes, 16; ethnic distribution in Nigeria, 43; Islam in Africa, 14; Muslim population in Nigeria, *1952*, 44; Nigeria and its states today, 6–7; Nigerian states with shari'a law, 51; political coalitions by zones, 48; Sokoto Caliphate, 41; state systems, 45, 46, 47; unification of Nigeria, *1914*, 40; Yorubaland, 41, 42, 43
Marriage. *See* Culture and cultural issues
Martyrs, 75, 122
Marwa, Buba, 113, 146
Marwa, Muhammad (Maitatsine), 74, 126, 129, 185, 265n29
Mass media: coverage of Muslims, 105; coverage of violence, 279n23, 280n2; freedom of the press and, 174–75; language and, 134–35; Miss World contest and, 173–74; Nigerian use of the media, 179–80; the Shi'ite conspiracy, 187

Mauritania, 23
Mbang, Sunday Coffie, 190, 240
Mecca (Saudi Arabia), 14, 20, 64, 105, 210
Meece, Roger, 24
Messiah, 216
Methodist Church, 189, 190, 204. *See also* Christians and Christian communities; Protestant churches; Religious issues
Methods, 33–34, 55. *See also* Theories and models
Middle Belt zone (Nigeria): calendrical issues, 72–73; civic culture in, 219; education in, 191; geocultural zones and, 45; identity and value patterns in, 57, 62, 63, 65–66, 67; missionary work in, 190; political parties in, 145; religious issues in, 80, 109, 193; women in, 124. *See also* Benue state; Kogi state; Kwara state; Nasarawa state; Plateau state; Taraba state
Middle East, 17, 19–20, 223, 249n58. *See also individual countries*
Middle-tier states. *See* Bauchi state; Gombe state; Kaduna state
Migration, 81–82
Military issues. *See* Emirates and emirate states
Military rule: bans on political activities, 187; chaos theory and, 217; coup of *1983* and, 193; ethnoreligious balance in, 208–09; interim government of *1993*, 231; local government and, 141, 207; migration of professionals from Nigeria and, 215; periods of, 140; primary elections of *1992*, 229; religious issues of, 193, 216; shari'a and, 147–48, 182; views of universities, 180
Miss World riots (*2002*), 171, 173, 277n1
Models. *See* Theories and models
Morocco, 26
Morrison, Stephen, 18
MSO. *See* Muslim Sisters Organization
MSS. *See* Muslim Students Society
Mu'azu, Ahmed, 146
Mufti (interpreter of shari'a law), 101
Muhammad (prophet), 67

Muhammad, Murtala Ramat, 63, 110, 117, 121, 124, 132, 193

Musa, Bunu Sheriff, 170

Muslim League for Accountability, 130

Muslims and Muslim communities: African, Arab, and Asian Muslims, 14, 24, 62; calendars of, 71–73; civic culture and conflict resolution, 52; countries and communities of, 33; criteria for being a good or bad Muslim, 183, 184, 252n2; day of judgment, 76, 81, 205; five pillars of Islam, 105; historical time and destiny, 75–76; legalists, 72; links with international Muslim community, 62, 72, 82, 83; nature of ideal and "real" Islam, 52, 67–69; orientations to community, 77–79; populations of, 2, 244n19; prayers of, 72, 184; return of the *Mahdi*, 129; Roman Catholic relations with, 17–18; shari'a system, 62; social networks of, 58–59; state power and, 82–83; U.S. policies and, 13, 19. *See also* Mecca; Reforms

Muslims and Muslim communities— Nigeria: anti-innovation legalists, 60–62, 131; caliphal/Madina model identities, 67–69; change and transformation in, 132–35; Christians and Christianity, 9, 22, 23, 100, 104, 105, 134, 192–97; civic culture and conflict resolution, 175, 219–22; crime, 94–96; elections of *1993*, 231; links with international Muslim community, 14–15; Muslim identity in Nigeria, 52, 62, 63, 126–30; National Council for Religious Affairs and, 127; in Nigerian states, 45–46, 48–49, 56, 57; orientations to authority, community, and conflict, 130–36, 204, 217; political issues of, 19, 20, 28, 59–60, 67, 78, 220; Qur'an in, 61, 62; role of women, 103; rulers in, 57; Saudi Arabia and, 61–62; shari'a in, 9, 22, 50–51, 60, 62, 69; tolerance and conflict, 35, 78, 183–88, 191–97, 204; traditional ethnic and locational identities, 62–67; transregional identities and links, 57–58; youth vio-

lence, 186–88, 245n29, 246n34. *See also* Emirates and emirate states; Sufism; Yoruba Muslim community

Muslim Sisters Organization (MSO), 125

Muslim Students Society (MSS), 60, 185, 279n27, 279n28

Muslim Woman, The (magazine), 125

Mutallab, Umaru, 170

Mysticism, 72, 74, 224, 252n4. *See also* Sufism

NACOMYO. *See* National Council of Muslim Youth Organisations of Nigeria

Nasarawa state (Nigeria), 63, 149

National Commission on Peace, 154–55, 176

National Council for Religious Affairs (NCRA), 102, 104, 127, 191, 194, 197, 212

National Council of Muslim Youth Organisations of Nigeria (NACOMYO), 101, 105–06

National Council of Nigeria Women, 103

National Interfaith Religious Council (NIREC), 197, 277n10

National Joint Muslim Organization, 100

National Peace Commission. *See* National Commission on Peace

National Party of Nigeria (NPN), 119, 227, 228

National Political Reform Conference (NPRC), 155, 258n14

National Political Reform Dialogue (NPRD), 155, 178, 182, 212

National Republican Congress, 195

National Republican Convention (NRC). *See* Political parties— specific

National Youth Service Corps, 181

Nationhood, 55

Native Baptist Church, 108. *See also* Christians and Christian communities; Religious issues

NCRA. *See* National Council for Religious Affairs

Ndayako, Umaru Sanda (*Etsu Nupe*), 118, 154, 176, 234–35

NEPU. *See* Northern Elements Progressive Union

NGOs. *See* Nongovernmental organizations

Niass, Ibrahim (Shaykh; Senegal), 20, 58, 82, 184

Niger Delta, 13, 23

Nigeria: administration of, 227; census of *2005*, 155, 181; colonial period of, 78, 80, 147, 158, 204, 205, 220; decolonization period (*1946–60*), 40–41, 220; diplomats and ambassadors, 18, 19, 20, 21t, 106, 135. 154, 158, 160; economic issues, 15, 16, 19, 22, 36, 50, 111, 132–33, 186–87, 207, 214–15, 217–18, 242n3, 248n46; geocultural and ethnolinguistic issues, 17, 19–20, 36, 37–39, 45–49, 50, 63; government in, 3, 5, 40–44, 94, 220, 221, 222, 228t, 272n42; governorships, 145–46, 158–60, 176, 177, 207; leadership in, 55, 133, 176–77, 208–09, 225, 226; legal and judicial issues, 147–48, 157, 220; migration of businessmen and professionals, 106, 211, 215–16, 283n5; population of, 2, 5, 18, 244n19; post-colonial federalism in, 35–36, 80–81; states of, 6–7, 56, 63, 80, 146–53, 206–07, 228t, 272n42; Western public opinion and policy perspectives in, 21–29. *See also* Christians and Christian communities—Nigeria; Constitutions and constitutional issues; Democratic federalism; Emirates and emirate states; Muslims and Muslim communities—Nigeria; Petroleum and petroleum industry; Political issues—Nigeria; Political parties; Shari'a; *individual cities, states, and areas*

Nigerian Central Bank, 170

Nigerian College of Arts and Science (Zaria, Nigeria), 119. *See also* Ahmadu Bello University

Nigerian Military School (Zaria, Nigeria), 122

Nigerian Muslim Council (NMC), 113

Nigerian Muslim Society, 125

Nigerian People's Party (NPP). *See* Political parties—specific

Nigerian Students in Defense of Democracy, 153

Nigerian Supreme Council for Islamic Affairs (NSCIA): Adegbite, Abdu-Lateef, and, 65; Christian Association of Nigeria and, 178; Dasuki, Ibrahim, and, 128–30, 186; early ecumenical movement and, 185; FOMWAN and, 125; *Jama'atu Nasril Islam* and, 127, 185–86; leaders and leadership of, 102, 135, 197, 266n35; members of, 177; reformation and, 131; role of, 212, 265n31

Niger Republic, 81–82

Niger emirate state (Nigeria), 23, 45, 63, 72, 149, 158, 170

9/11. See September *11, 2001*

Ningi (Bauchi, Nigeria), 46–47, 169

NIREC. *See* National Interfaith Religious Council

NMC. *See* Nigerian Muslim Council

Nongovernmental organizations (NGOs), 24, 174, 180–81

North-Eastern State. *See* Borno

Northern Elders' Committee, 212

Northern Elements Progressive Union (NEPU). *See* Political parties—specific

Northern People's Congress (NPC). *See* Political parties—specific

NPC (Northern People's Congress). *See* Political parties—specific

NPN (National Party of Nigeria). *See* Political parties—specific

NPP (Nigerian People's Party). *See* Political parties—specific

NPRC. *See* National Political Reform Conference

NPRD. *See* National Political Reform Dialogue

NRC (National Republican Convention). *See* Political parties— specific

NSCIA. *See* Nigerian Supreme Council of Islamic Affairs

Nuclear power and weapons, 76

Nupe religion, 72, 206

Nwachuku, Ike, 216

Obas (chiefs, kings, leaders), 47–48, 100, 107, 110, 135

Obasanjo, Olusegun (*"Baba"*): Abacha regime and, 196–97; alliance with Yar'Adua, Musa, 110, 117, 122; brief biography of, 237; as a born-again Christian, 192, 237; elections of *1999* and *2003* and, 154; ethnoreligious violence and, 29; family religious mixing, 113; home of, 49; impeachment efforts against, 141, 268n9; Iraq War and, 26; jailing of, 123, 237; as president of the Fourth Republic, 139, 153, 155, 181, 193; as a presidential candidate, 216; priorities of, 24; shari'a and, 197; as successor to Muhammad, Murtala Ramat, 122

Obasanjo (Olusegun) government, 22, 142, 156, 266n39

Och'Idoma (Idoma), 46

Ogbeh, Audu, 181

Ogoni, 49

Ogun state (Nigeria), 63, 64, 100, 112

OIC. *See* Organization of the Islamic Conference

Oil and oil industry. *See* Petroleum and petroleum industry

Oja-Oba mosque (Ibadan, Oyo, Nigeria), 112

Ojukwu, Chukwuemeka Odumegwu, 216, 238

Okadigbo, Chuba, 153, 239, 271n30

Okogie, Anthony Olubunmi, 190, 194, 239

Old Oyo (eighteenth century), 48

Olodumare (the supreme deity), 109

1004 Estate Central Mosque, Victoria Island (Lagos), 112

Organization of Petroleum Exporting Countries (OPEC), 13, 217–18, 223

Organization of the Islamic Conference (OIC): condemnation of terrorism, 187; controversy of *1987*, 127; Nigeria and, 14–15, 20, 129, 186, 191, 194, 266n36, 266n39; role of, 62, 223

Orunmila (deity of divination), 109

Osun state (Nigeria), 63, 64

Owerri (Imo, Nigeria), 281n4

Oyo state (Nigeria): creation of, 48; cults in, 107; Muslims in, 63, 64, 65, 100; shari'a in, 112, 113; wars of the nineteenth century and, 108

Pagans. *See Maguzawa*

Pakistan, 2, 96, 257n4

Pan-Sahel Initiative, 246n37

PDP. *See* People's Democratic Party

Peace committees, 180, 212, 225–26, 257n10

Penal Reform Laws, 153

Pentecostal churches, 109, 175. *See also* Christians and Christian communities; Religious issues

People of the Book (*ahl kitab*), 69, 77–78, 177, 204, 205

People's Democratic Party (PDP): ANPP and, 188; chairman of, 181; elections of *1999*, 140; elections of *2003*, 160–61; elections of *2007*, 155; governorships and, 146; under the Fourth Republic, 118–19, 120, 121; military officers and, 124; National Political Reform Dialogue and, 212; north-east alliance and, 205; Obasanjo, Olusegun, and, 110; party strength by states and zones, 144–45, 145t; PDP states, 270n24; shari'a and, 149, 156, 157, 158–60, 161–62, 182; state party patterns and, 143–44; Yar'Adua, Musa and, 110

Peoples' Redemption Party (PRP). *See* Political parties—specific

Petroleum and petroleum industry, 13–14, 131, 132, 133

Petroleum and petroleum industry— Nigeria: building of Abuja and, 23; civic cultures and, 221; coup of *1983* and, 50; effects of, 61, 116, 122, 185, 193, 214, 224; Land Use Decree and, 268n8; Niger Delta and, 13; oil prices and earnings, 133, 141, 186, 207, 214, 242n2, 242n3, 244n20; political issues, 141, 220–21; production of, 244n20; U.S. petroleum needs and, 18; violence and, 23

Petroleum Trust Fund (PTF), 123

Pilgrimage, 71. *See also* Mecca; Saudi Arabia

Plateau state (Nigeria): governors in, 142; missionary work in, 190; as a non-shari'a state, 149; peace conference of *2004*, 196; political parties in, 228; violence in, 24, 149, 171, 175, 195–96, 217, 246n32, 269n11, 281n12

Political issues: conflict mediation, 175; dialogue approaches, 2; Iraq War, 27; leadership, 209; management of symbols, 209; nation states, 131; partition, 35; power politics, 2; power sharing, 208, 209; religious factors, 192–97; role of women, 103. *See also* Democratic federalism

Political issues—Nigeria: assassinations, 255n3; benchmark events, 38–39, 55; civilian rule, 140, 147–48; crime and corruption, 142; democratic federalism, 3, 15, 17, 206–08, 218, 219, 225–26, 227; ECOWAS, 15; education, 154; emirate versus cultural states, 5; gateways, 175; global and African stability, 3, 36; governorships, 159t; leaders and leadership, 208; military factors, 121–24, 131, 134, 139, 140, 219; national political leadership, 63; national umbrella organizations, identities, and values, 126–30, 221; north-east alliance, 205; north-south regionalism, 37–44; partition, 35, 49, 52, 55, 133, 139, 141, 194, 221, 222, 225, 226, 248n47; party politics in the shari'a states, 158–60; political coalitions by zone, 48f; political spectrum, 118; progressive-conservative identities and values, 118–21, 125, 131, 134; progressive identities and values, 115–17, 125, 131; religious politics, 214; shari'a, 157; six-zone horizontal federalism, 207–08, 227; Tijaniyya brotherhood, 59; women's organizational identities and values, 124–26. *See also individual cities and states*

Political parties: coalitions, 143, 227, 228, 231; First Republic and, 120–21, 227; Fourth Republic and, 118–19; gateways (*kofa*), 175; party congresses, 155; party patterns by zones, 143–45; religious-based and ethnic parties, 115; Second Republic and, 227

Political parties—specific parties: Alliance for Democracy (AD), 143, 144, 145; All Peoples Party (APP), 143, 144, 148, 149, 158, 270n24; All Progressive Grand Alliance, 153; Great Nigeria People's Party (GNPP), 227, 228; National Party of Nigeria (NPN), 227, 228; National Republican Convention (NRC), 119, 121, 229–31; Nigerian People's Party (NPP), 227, 228; Northern Elements Progressive Union (NEPU), 59, 116; Northern People's Congress (NPC), 120–21; Peoples' Redemption Party (PRP), 116–17, 122, 227, 228; Social Democratic Party (SDP), 116, 117, 121, 122, 195, 229–31; Unity Party of Nigeria (UPN), 228. *See also* All Nigeria People's Party; People's Democratic Party

Potiskum (Borno, Nigeria), 64

Powell, Colin, 15, 24

Presbyterian Church, 204. *See also* Christians and Christian communities; Protestant churches; Religious issues

Protestant churches, 107, 108, 109, 175, 189, 190, 204. *See also* Christians and Christian communities; Religious issues; *individual churches and denominations*

PRP (Peoples' Redemption Party). *See* Political parties—specific

PTF. *See* Petroleum Trust Fund

Public Complaints Commission, 96

Qadiriyya brotherhood: founding saint of, 253n5; Iraq and, 82; Kabara, Nasiru, and, 58; Kano and, 167, 188; member survey, 255n4; reformed Tijaniyya and, 59; Sokoto and, 63–64, 184. *See also* Sufism

Qur'an: concept of humanity, 83; crime and punishment, 245n26; family planning and, 103; Ibadan Muslim leaders and, 102; interest in and access to, 59, 221; interpretation of, 62, 69, 71, 83, 84, 147,

185; Kano, Aminu, and, 117; knowledge of the future and, 74; marriage in, 103; Muslim behavior and, 185; Muslim Students Society and, 185; religious tolerance and, 104–05; return to, 60; teaching of, 105; translation of, 61, 65, 97, 147, 185; symbolism of, 174–75, 278n11, 279n23

Ramadan (month of fasting), 61, 71, 83
Ramatism, 121
Ratzinger, Joseph (Cardinal), 18. *See also* Benedict XVI; Christians and Christian communities; Religious issues; Roman Catholic church
Reformed Tijaniyya (Nigeria), 20, 116, 184. *See also* Sufism; Tijaniyya brotherhood
Religious Affairs Councils, 105
Religious issues: authority patterns, 204; calls for dialogue, 18; civil war of *1970–80*, 193; coming of a mahdi or messiah, 216; conflict and conflict resolution, 32–33, 35, 197–99; cultural identity, 35; day of judgment, 76, 81, 205; federalism, 35; FOMWAN and, 103, 125; fundamentalism, 215–16; interfaith councils, 212, 225–26; monotheism and polytheism, 204; North American missionary work, 22–23; political factors, 192–97; religious knowledge and education, 102, 125; religious identity, 2, 77; secularization, 34; students and, 104–06; in Sudan, 36; survey of religious beliefs, 241n3; symbols of leadership, 208; time, 205; tolerance, 102, 104–05; as a value system, 203; violence, 149, 167, 169–70, 207; Western emphasis on, 4. *See also* Christians and Christian communities; Muslims and Muslim communities; Pentecostal churches; Protestant churches; Roman Catholic church; University of Ibadan; University of Lagos
Religious issues—Nigeria: ethnicity, identity, and values, 203–04; religious conflicts, *1979–97*, 30–31; religious identity patterns by state, 56, 57; religious

leadership, 64, 108; successor to Pope John Paul II, 18; violence and conflict, 4, 214; Western public opinion and, 21–22; Yoruba patterns of religious identification, 64–65; Yoruba wars and, 108. *See also* Christians and Christian communities—Nigeria; Muslims and Muslim communities—Nigeria
Republics, Nigerian: First Republic (*1960–66*), 41, 50, 59, 94, 96, 116, 118, 119, 120–21, 130, 147, 155, 177, 206, 209, 227, 251n87, 251n1, 268n6; Second Republic (*1979–83*), 42, 50, 118, 119, 122, 130, 141, 147–48, 208, 209, 220, 227, 251n87, 268n6; Third Republic (*1993*), 42–43, 50, 66, 119, 130, 194, 227, 256n9, 268n6;
Republics, Nigerian—Fourth Republic (*1999–*): centralization in, 17; civilian and economic transformations in, 24–25; conflict and crisis in, 32, 49, 142, 175–82, 187, 192, 195, 206–08, 219; crime and corruption in, 142, 146–47, 148, 151–52, 163–70, 179; democratic federalism in, 139–42, 180, 206–08, 223, 225–26; economic issues, 141, 153, 166; establishment and model of, 8, 15, 17, 43–44, 50–51, 141; ethnic and religious issues of, 209; federal structure and states of, 45, 130, 141, 143, 147, 150–51, 157–58, 181, 218; foreign affairs and the international community, 19, 25, 160, 222–26; free speech in, 213; geocultural zones of, 45–49, 141, 143; Iraq War and, 26; legal and judicial factors, 142, 146–47, 151–52, 155, 174, 178–79, 181–82, 225, 245n23, 256n10; military issues, 139, 141, 142, 152, 161, 176, 178, 179, 181, 196, 216, 225; ministers and ministries of, 160, 161, 162t, 197; polarization in, 3, 142, 195; political parties, 118–19; police and law enforcement, 25, 141, 142, 152, 174, 176, 179, 225; presidents of, 110, 141, 142–43, 146, 155, 208, 218; security and terror concerns, 26, 139, 141, 142; shari'a in, 9, 112, 140,

146–53, 155–56, 157–82, 187, 195, 216; states and states rights in, 146–53, 157–58, 160, 161t; sufism and, 59; umbrella organizations in, 130, 131, 177–78, 221; U.S. and, 15, 18–20, 24, 26, 28; violence in, 29, 195–96, 217. *See also* Constitutions and constitutional issues; Obasanjo, Olusegun

Rhodesia, 37

Rimi, Abubakar, 121, 146, 185. *See also* Abubakar Rimi faction

Rivers state (Nigeria), 228

Roman Catholic church: civil war of *1967–70* and, 189–90; as a gateway for conflict resolution, 175; in Igboland, 204; missionaries of, 108, 189; NCRA and, 191; relations with the Muslim world, 17–18; in Yorubaland, 107. *See also* Benedict XVI; Christians and Christian communities; John Paul II; Religious issues

"Royal fathers." *See* Emirs

Royal Military Academy (Sandhurst, UK), 122

Russia, 140, 222

Saleh, Ibrahim, 61

Sambo, Muhammad Bashir, 235

Sani, Ahmed, 146–47, 148, 157, 161, 170

Sanusi, Muhammad (Emir), 58, 253n7

Sarki (emir). *See* Emirates and emirate states

Saudi Arabia: flight to, 211; Gummi, Abubakar and, 147; links with Nigeria, 14, 19–20, 60, 61; pilgrimage to, 61–62, 82; settlers from emirate states, 82; strategic tolerance in, 253n13; sufism in, 62; Sunni Arabs and *Wahhabiyya*, 82; terrorism in, 26; U.S. and, 20. *See also* Mecca; Organization of the Islamic Conference; *Wahhabiyya* and *Wahhabi* tradition

Savanna zones, 64, 67, 190

Scottish Presbyterian Church, 189. *See also* Christians and Christian communities; Religious issues

SDP (Social Democratic Party). *See* Political parties—specific

September *11, 2001* (*9/11*): conflict and, 32; effects of, 4–5, 13, 17, 33, 51, 187; Western policy perspectives following, 24, 25. *See also* Terrorism; War on terrorism

Shagari, Shehu, 63, 119, 193, 209

Shango (god of thunder), 107

Shari'a: All Africa Games and, 276n25; apostasy cases, 152, 165; British acknowledgment of, 101; challenges of, 157–70, 182; Christian groups and, 191–92, 195; conflict mediation and, 175–82; courts, 101, 112, 148; crime and, 21–22, 163; death penalty decisions, 21–22; debates over, 221; definition and interpretation of, 5, 89, 149, 151–53, 169–70, 220; in the emirates of Nigeria, 89, 92–93, 95, 96; financial and economic issues of, 170; FOMWAN and, 125; implementation and enforcement of, 22, 162–70, 256n11, 280n35; in Iran, 83; Maliki law and, 147; military rule and, 147–48, 182; in Nigeria, 9, 22, 50–51, 60, 62, 69, 98, 112, 146–53; non-shari'a northern states, 151; politics of, 158–60, 161–63, 170, 182; shari'a states, 150, 163–70, 175; in Shi'ite communities, 83; sociopolitical conflict, 9, 171–82; Supreme Council for, 112; as the ultimate definer of the community, 62; United States policies toward, 225; in the Yoruba language, 101; in Yorubaland, 103, 112–13. *See also* Nigeria—Fourth Republic; *individual states and cities*

Sharia *1* and *2* riots (Kaduna city, Kaduna, Nigeria), 171, 172–75

Shata, Mamman, 73

Shehu (of Borno), 66

Shekarau, Ibrahim, 153, 154, 160, 177

Shendam (Nigeria), 196

Shi'ites, 68–69, 83, 187

Shinkafi, Umaru, 158, 235

Shittu, Suleiman, 112

Shuwa Arabs, 64

SIM. *See* Sudan Interior Mission

Slaves and slavery, 108, 259n21, 259n22, 259n23

Social Democratic Party (SDP). *See* Political parties—specific

Social sciences, 3–4

Society for the Victory of Islam. *See Jama'atu Nasril Islam*

Sokoto Caliphate: Abacha regime and, 101; bicentenary celebration, 254n22; emirate states and, 38, 45, 70, 100; end-of-century markers, 75–76; federal structure of, 204; founding of, 68, 76–77; Muslim community and, 62–63, 65; role of, 84; Kano and, 184; sardauna of, 158; shari'a and, 98, 163, 166, 168; sufi brotherhoods in, 58, 184; wars of the nineteenth century and, 108. *See also* Emirates and emirate states; Emirs

Sokoto Caliphate—sultans: *Aare Musulumi* and, 101; appeals to, 88; appointment of emirs by, 106; attempted coup of *1990* and, 194; conflict resolution and, 135; as head of NSCIA, 127, 128, 177; modern sultans, 127–28, 130; scholarships for Muslim students, 154; sultanship succession, 127–28, 186. *See also* Abubakar III; Dasuki, Ibrahim; Maccido, Muhammad

Sokoto empire, 37

South Africa, 15, 20, 154

Soviet Union, 35, 36, 82

Soyinka, Wole, 107–08, 111

Spirits (Jinns). *See* Mysticism

Sri Lanka, 36

State, Department of (U.S.), 19, 22

States and governments, 27–28

Stoning, 22, 172

Sudan: civil war in, 24; criminal code, 96; culture in, 64; Darfur region of, 24; flight and migration to, 210, 211, 255n5; Mahdist movement in, 76; Nigerian students in, 188; strains of, 36

Sudan Interior Mission (SIM), 190

Sudan United Mission, 190

Sufism: authority patterns of, 204; during the colonial period, 78; definition of,

252n4; in the emirates, 72, 74; in Kano, 167; legacy of, 185; in Nigeria, 20, 62; political issues, 59; rivalries in, 126; sufi brotherhoods, 58–60, 62, 76, 78, 131, 167, 177, 184, 185, 213–14, 255n4; women in, 124. *See also* Qadiriyya brotherhood; Tijaniyya brotherhood

Suicide, 75

Sule, Maitama, 96, 119, 209

Sultans, 66, 88, 101. *See also* Sokoto Caliphate—sultans

Sunna, 59, 105

Sunni tradition, 68–69, 83, 187

Supreme Council for Shari'a, 112, 167, 177

Supreme Court (Nigeria), 155, 225

Switzerland, 222–23

Symbols and symbolism: Abuja, 50, 111, 199; civil war, 192; elders and leaders, 45, 47, 66, 88, 100, 102, 106, 110, 191, 209, 211; political use of, 195, 197; power sharing, symbolism, and leadership, 208–09; prayer, 184; reformist and revolutionary symbols, 187; religious symbols, 55, 133, 175, 176; shari'a, 170; Shi'ites, 68–69; sultans, 128

Syncretism, 72, 189

Taliban, 170, 187, 188, 255n5, 257n11

Tanzania, 217

Taraba state (Nigeria), 63, 142, 149, 190

TBO. *See* Buhari Organization, The

Technology: conflict and, 32; global communications, 223, 224; Internet, 57, 180; mass media, 131; telecommunications, 83; transportation and travel, 58, 83

Terrorism: approaches to, 27, 187; detection and prevention of, 29, 249n60; international approaches to, 3, 27; models of, 213–19; Nigeria and, 142, 223, 241n2; provocation to fear and hysteria, 226; state failure and, 27–28; suicide and, 75. *See also* September *11, 2001*; War on terrorism

Theories and models: catastrophe theory, 216; chaos theory or model, 33, 34, 213, 216–17, 218–19; civilization-clash model, 213–14, 218; complexity theory, 216; of conflict analysis and resolution, 32–33; global economy model, 218; Nigerian model, 217–18, 219; pandae-monium, 33; religious-secular model, 213, 215–16, 218; statist model, 219–20; three-wave socioeconomic clash model, 213, 214–15, 218

Three-M (Muslim, Middle Belt, and Minor-ity) groups, 63, 65

Tijaniyya brotherhood: Fez, Morocco, and, 82; founding saint of, 253n5; in Kano, 63–64, 167, 184; Kano, Aminu, and, 59; member survey, 255n4; reformers of, 76; spread of, 58. *See also* Reformed Tijaniyya; Sufism

Tijjani, Ahmed, 82

Tilden Fulani (Bauchi, Nigeria), 169

Tivs and Tiv communities, 46–47, 149, 192

TMG. *See* Transition Monitoring Group

Tofa, Bashir, 121, 231

Toffler, Alvin, 32, 34, 213, 214

Toffler, Heidi, 32, 34

Tor Tiv, 47

Transition Monitoring Group (TMG), 181

Turkey, 2, 26

Ugoh, Sylvester, 121, 231

UK. *See* United Kingdom

Ukraine, 36

Ummah (worldwide Muslim community): concepts of, 77; Dusaki, Ibrahim, and, 127–28; future of, 17; global trends and, 52; locational and ethnic identities and, 65, 69; national Muslim groups and, 129; need for tolerance within, 131; Nigeria and, 81. *See also* Muslims and Muslim communities

UN. *See* United Nations

United African Methodist Church, 108

United Kingdom (UK): flight or migration to, 82–83, 211, 215; Nigeria and, 19, 21, 37, 40, 80, 189, 220, 223; policy of indi-rect rule, 70

United Nations (UN), 15, 19, 24, 106, 223, 244n16

United Native African Church, 108

United States (U.S.): ambassadors of, 24; federalism in, 17, 35; flight or migration to, 211, 215; Nigeria and, 15, 18–19, 28, 223–25, 246n37; nonpreferentialism, 199; post-*9/11* policies, 13, 25; stoning issue, 22. *See also* Bush, George W.; Iraq War; War on terrorism

Unity Party of Nigeria (UPN). *See* Political parties—specific

Universities, 180, 185, 186, 189, 212, 257n10, 279n27. *See also* Educational issues

University College, Ibadan, 119

University of Ibadan, 104, 180

University of Lagos, 104–05, 180

University of Maiduguri, 180

U.S. *See* United States

USCIRF. *See* Commission on International Religious Freedom, U.S.

Usman, Muhammadu Kabir, 167

Usman, Tijjani, 58

Usmanu Danfodiyo University (Sokoto, Nigeria) (Usman Danfodio University), 68

Uwais, Muhammadu Lawal, 155, 239

Values, 34. *See also* Culture and cultural issues

Wahhabiyya and *Wahhabi* tradition, 20, 62, 82

War on terrorism, 1–2, 13, 23, 26. *See also* Bush (George W.) administration; Sep-tember *11, 2001*; Terrorism

West Africa: administration of borders, 82; demographic patterns in, 15; Islam in, 62, 83; Maliki law, 183; Muslim culture in, 224; role of Nigeria in, 3; Saudi Ara-bia and, 20; Tijaniyya brotherhood in, 58; United States and, 223–24

West African Sudanic zone, 210

Western world: approach to Muslim world, 1; calendars of, 72; conflicts with other civilizations, 35; effects of Western cul-ture, 134; inclusion in the Muslim community, 65, 67, 72; interests in Nigeria, 3; mass media in, 105; public opinion and policy perspectives of Nigeria, 21–28; study of social sciences in, 3–4; views of Africa, 28

WIN. *See* Women in Nigeria

Wiwo, Ken Sara, 25

Women in Nigeria (WIN), 103, 125

Women's issues: *Aare Musulumi* and, 101; in Ibadan, 102; organizational identities and values, 124–26, 181; political participation of, 115; progressive thought regarding, 117; seclusion, 103–04, 124, 125; Yoruba Muslim women, 102–04. *See also* Federation of Muslim Women's Associations in Nigeria

World Bank, 24, 223

World Trade Organization (WTO), 24, 223

Wusasa (Zaria, Nigeria), 172

Yar'Adua, Shehu Musa (*Shehu; Tafidan Katsina*), 63, 110, 117, 122–23, 124, 196, 229

Yar'Adua, Umaru, 159

Yelwa town (Nigeria), 23, 196

Yobe state (Nigeria): creation of, 206; patterns of Muslim identity in, 63; political parties in, 143–44; as a shari'a state, 148–49, 168; *taliban* in, 170, 188; violence in, 246n36, 282n1

Yoruba (language). *See* Languages

Yoruba city-states (Nigeria): ethnic and locational identities in, 66–67; geocultural zones and, 45; heritage and culture of, 47–48; leaders in, 100; religious factors, 48–49, 57, 64–65; rivalries between, 110

Yorubaland and Yoruba communities (Nigeria): *Aare Musulumi* and, 65; *Alikali* families in, 101; authority patterns in, 204, 211; capital city issue, 111; Christians and Muslims in, 101–02, 106, 189; civic culture in, 107, 110, 219; conflict and conflict resolution in, 106–07, 205, 211, 213; culture of, 66, 100, 204; election of *1993*, 195; emirates and, 205, 206; family values and shari'a, 112–13; history of Islam in, 100, 101, 257n4; leaders of, 110; maps, 41, 42, 43; metaphysics of, 107–08; nineteenth-century wars and, 108; political issues of, 110, 213, 228; religious issues of, 109, 110, 113–14, 204, 213; Sokoto caliphal domination of, 64; women in, 102–04, 124, 125, 224; violence in, 192, 212. *See also* Lagos; Languages—specific

Yoruba Muslim community: Christians and traditionalists and, 107–09; conflict and conflict resolution in, 106–07; Dasuki, Ibrahim and, 185–86; family values and shari'a, 112–13; migrants to, 23; religious mixing in, 113–14; traditional and religious leaders, 65, 100–02; women of, 101, 102–04

Yugoslavia, 36

Young Turks, 115

Zakzaki, Mallam Ibrahim, 187

Zamfara state (Nigeria): breaking away from Sokoto, 77; as a caliphal area, 63; creation of, 148, 206; governor of, 146; political issues of, 143, 148, 160, 161; shari'a in, 146–47, 148, 152, 157, 159–60, 161–62, 163, 166, 176–77, 187, 273n2

Zangon-Kataf (Kaduna, Nigeria), 172

Zaria emirate (Nigeria), 148, 158, 176, 180, 269n11

Zaria state (Nigeria), 63

Zawiya (Sufi social networks), 58–59